※ **Cassius Marcellus Clay** ※

CIVIL WAR AMERICA

*Caroline E. Janney, Aaron Sheehan-Dean,
and Gary Gallagher, editors*

This landmark series interprets broadly the
history and culture of the Civil War era through
the long nineteenth century and beyond.
Drawing on diverse approaches and methods,
the series publishes historical works that explore
all aspects of the war, biographies of leading commanders,
and tactical and campaign studies, along with select editions
of primary sources. Together, these books shed
new light on an era that remains central to our
understanding of American
and world history.

A complete list of books published
in Civil War America is available at
https://uncpress.org/series/civil-war-america.

Cassius Marcellus Clay
The Life of an Antislavery Slaveholder and the Paradox of American Reform

ANNE E. MARSHALL

THE UNIVERSITY OF NORTH CAROLINA PRESS Chapel Hill

This book was published with the assistance of the Fred W.
Morrison Fund of the University of North Carolina Press.

© 2025 Anne E. Marshall
All rights reserved

Manufactured in the United States of America
Set in Miller and HTF Didot by codeMantra

Cover art courtesy of Library of Congress.

Library of Congress Cataloging-in-Publication Data
Names: Marshall, Anne E. (Anne Elizabeth), 1975- author
Title: Cassius Marcellus Clay : the life of an antislavery slaveholder
and the paradox of American reform / Anne E. Marshall.
Other titles: Civil War America (Series)
Description: Chapel Hill : The University of North Carolina Press, 2025. |
Series: Civil War America | Includes bibliographical references and index.
Identifiers: LCCN 2025013917 | ISBN 9781469690995 cloth alk. paper |
ISBN 9781469684734 epub | ISBN 9781469691008 pdf
Subjects: LCSH: Clay, Cassius Marcellus, 1810-1903 | Slaveholders—Kentucky—
Biography | Politicians—Kentucky—Biography | Antislavery movements—
United States—History—19th century | BISAC: HISTORY / United States / Civil
War Period (1850-1877) | SOCIAL SCIENCE / Slavery | LCGFT: Biographies
Classification: LCC E415.9.C55 M37 2025 |
DDC 973.7/114092 $aB—dc23/eng/20250424
LC record available at https://lccn.loc.gov/2025013917

For product safety concerns under the European Union's General Product
Safety Regulation (EU GPSR), please contact gpsr@mare-nostrum
.co.uk or write to the University of North Carolina Press and Mare Nostrum
Group B.V., Mauritskade 21D, 1091 GC Amsterdam, The Netherlands.

To Jim, Walt, and Eleanor Giesen

Contents

List of Illustrations / viii

Introduction / 1

Chapter 1. INHERITANCES / 7

Chapter 2. UNERADICABLE DISEASE / 25

Chapter 3. LAMENTABLE INCONSISTENCIES / 40

Chapter 4. THE *True American* / 59

Chapter 5. FIGHT LIKE A MAN / 74

Chapter 6. THE NAME OF REPUBLICAN / 96

Chapter 7. SHOT AND SHELL / 121

Chapter 8. UNREWARDED SACRIFICE / 144

Chapter 9. UNDIPLOMATIC DIPLOMATIST / 159

Chapter 10. THE CONSTITUTION AND THE UNION / 181

Chapter 11. RESTORING THE AUTONOMY OF THE STATES / 199

Chapter 12. LION OF WHITEHALL / 215

Coda: THE LEGEND OF CASSIUS CLAY / 235

Acknowledgments / 243

Notes / 247

Bibliography / 277

Index / 295

Illustrations

Mary Jane Warfield Clay, ca. 1845 / 18

Cassius M. Clay as a college student / 19

Bond for Clay's enslaved laborers / 52

Cassius M. Clay, 1844 / 57

Building that once served as the *True American* newspaper office / 62

Currier and Ives lithograph of Clay / 75

Prominent presidential candidates, 1860 / 141

Mary Jane Clay, ca. 1862 / 161

Cassius M. Clay in *Vanity Fair* / 175

"Proclamation of Emancipation" / 179

White Hall under siege, 1897 / 224

William H. Townsend, ca. 1959 / 229

Introduction

Those who have taken part in the struggle of the liberties of men, have voluntarily chosen this position; it remains for impartial history to award the deserts of each.
—C. M. Clay, April 1, 1848

"Peaceful," began the headline, cascading down the front page of the Louisville *Courier-Journal*.

> End To the Life of Gen. Cassius M. Clay.—
> The Veteran Sinks In Death.—
> As Quietly As If Falling Into a Gentle Sleep.—
> In His Ninety-Third Year—
> Children At His Bedside In Hour of Dissolution—
> Long and Eventful Career—
> A Statesman, Soldier, Diplomat, Editor and Orator—
> An Ishmaelite In Last Days.

The soaring epitaph was but a prelude to the lengthy obituary that followed. Nearly all who read it on July 23, 1903, would have noted the irony of the nonagenarian's quiet death because few people in Clay's time were more famous for having an unquiet existence.[1]

Nearly sixty years before, Clay had risen to fame as a young politician from Kentucky. Slaveholding was not only legal but widely practiced in the Kentucky of Clay's youth. His own family was privileged and influential, with a long history of enslaving people. Indeed, Clay himself owned dozens of men, women, and children. But he came to believe that the institution of slavery hindered white Americans' opportunities for advancement, and his political rise featured outspoken calls for the elimination of slavery. While his views outraged many of his fellow white Kentuckians, they intrigued and inspired people around the nation. The idea that a man of Clay's station and influence would turn his back on the very system of labor that supported his lifestyle seemed remarkable. That he dared challenge the system of slavery from within a slave state was extraordinary, and the lengths to which Clay went to defend his beliefs became the stuff of legend.

In the 1840s, Clay defended both his reputation and his life in multiple Bowie knife fights, once killing his assailant. When Clay decided to publish an antislavery newspaper in 1845 in Lexington, the heart of the slave-owning Bluegrass region, he fortified his printing office with lead panels and two four-pounder cannons. After only two months of the *True American*'s publication, a mob of proslavery citizens still managed to dismantle its office. The Northern antislavery community, outraged by this affront to free speech, lavished him with praise and sympathy. Their goodwill soon dissipated, however, when only months later, Clay enlisted in the Mexican-American War, a conflict he had previously denounced as a proslavery fight.

As the sectional crisis deepened, Clay turned his attention to national antislavery politics. He first joined the Free-Soil Party and then helped to found the Republican Party in 1854. His name appeared on the vice presidential ballot in 1860; though he was not elected, Abraham Lincoln rewarded his service to the party by appointing him minister to Russia, a post he held intermittently until 1869.

When he returned to the Unites States, Clay changed course yet again, spurning the party he helped launch. With slavery abolished, he criticized Republicans for their purported corruption and their Reconstruction policies. He first joined the ranks of the breakaway Liberal Republicans, in 1872, and then the Democratic Party. As a Democrat, he advocated for the removal of US military troops from Southern states and a return to "home rule."

As thrilling and unpredictable as Cassius Clay's antislavery career was, by the end of his long life he had grown more infamous for his personal foibles, which included a divorce, an adopted son of suspicious paternity, and a second marriage at age eighty-four to a fifteen-year-old girl. After a long life of dodging enemies, nursing grudges, and alienating loved ones, Clay's "stirring life," as his obituarist Henry Watterson put it, "began to tell on him in late years."[2] For all his exploits as an editor, politician, duelist, author, and statesman, at the end, Watterson assessed, Clay was "an old man, deserted by his children, declared insane by the courts, bereft of his child wife around whom his heart was wrapped, alone and barricaded in his grim hall."[3] The soaringly poetic life of the obituary's beginning came to a far more humbling end.

Watterson also erred in dubbing Clay a "Pioneer Abolitionist," invoking a term Americans had used in pre–Civil War America to describe people who believed slavery to be morally wrong and who demanded its immediate end. Clay, however, had not been an abolitionist. Rather, his primary opposition to the "peculiar institution" was economic and political, not moral or humanitarian. He advocated that slavery be phased out gradually over time by individual states and that owners should be compensated for the enslaved individuals they manumitted. This vision of ending slavery reflected his belief that enslaved people were a valid, if unfortunate, form of property protected by the US Constitution.

Watterson misrepresented yet another facet of Clay's career: the manumission of his enslaved laborers at great personal expense, for which he was lauded during and after his lifetime. Few people realized that as he was freeing nine individuals in 1845, he simultaneously pressed charges against another of his enslaved laborers—a woman named Emily—on the grounds that she had murdered his infant son. When a jury acquitted her, Clay sold Emily as well as her mother, brother, and daughter to a slave trader. Most people remained unaware then (or now) that he never freed all of his enslaved laborers. He retained dozens of bondspeople (who were entailed to his estate through his father's will) even after the issuance of the Emancipation Proclamation and kept them toiling away at his home and farm through the end of the Civil War.[4]

In short, Clay was a man often misunderstood by both his contemporaries and by future generations. Some of the confusion was due to his own obfuscation. In autobiographical writing Clay portrayed his antislavery efforts as simpler and more self-sacrificing than they actually were. Many Americans took their cue from his self-aggrandizing accounts of his motivations and deeds, which cast him as the epitome of noble manliness, a person who faced down danger in the name of a cause that he recognized as right even when others did not.

During his long life and after, it became difficult for the American public to sort the real Cassius Clay from the fictional one. Both the tales that accumulated around him and his genuine complexity have made him a character of interest to writers and raconteurs over the years, and myriad published accounts of his life appeared in popular periodicals and books during his lifetime and after. Interest in Clay only intensified in the 1960s with the emergence of another fighter named in his honor: Cassius Marcellus Clay Jr., who would later renounce his "slave name" and become Muhammad Ali. In the transition from the last century to the present one, however, much of the notoriety and historical significance accrued to Clay has faded, leaving behind little more than caricature to accompany his recognizable family name and familiarity to those who know Kentucky history. As esteemed Kentucky historian Thomas D. Clark once wrote: "Clay's life story, like his reforms, is a badly disjointed one. Many prospective biographers have backed away, shaking their heads, and muttering, 'He lived too long.'"[5]

Since David Smiley's biography of 1962 remembered Clay as the *Lion of White Hall*, a few academic historians have written about Clay's antislavery career in piecemeal fashion, focusing on his status as an antislavery Southerner and, in this vein, casting him as an outlier. This is understandable, given that Clay operated in the border South, where citizens accommodated the sort of discussion of emancipation that, while limited, was unthinkable in states farther south. As such, they have, by and large, considered Clay as an example of the promise but ultimate failure of the antislavery movement in the South. The focus on Clay's gambit to end slavery in Kentucky, however, has implicitly discouraged historians from seeing him as representative of the broader national antislavery movement.[6]

I write this book with an new premise: that despite the extreme manner in which he defended his views, Cassius Clay's brand of antislavery thinking was typical rather than exceptional. Viewing Clay in the context of state, region, and nation from the 1840s through the Civil War, we see him as one of a growing number of moderate white Americans who demanded the eventual, rather than immediate, end of slavery because as a system of labor and a property regime it limited their political and economic opportunities for advancement. Despite his reputation as an outrageous character, by the mid-1850s, Clay's politics were quite mainstream, and as such, his career can tell twenty-first-century Americans much about the most important political reform movement of the nineteenth century.

By emphasizing the entirety of Clay's antebellum political career and situating him within a growing antislavery political coalition that emerged during the 1840s and 1850s, this book shows him operating not simply as a lone figure, raging against a flawed labor system in Kentucky, but as part of a larger coterie of collaborators and correspondents on the national stage. Many of Clay's compatriots were journalists who shaped public opinion and politicians who crafted legislation and political party platforms, which, in turn, drew thousands of average American voters to the polls to vote for antislavery politicians in their own states, eventually culminating in the formation of the Republican Party and its presidential victory in 1860.

Examining Clay's role in the antislavery coalition building of the 1850s reveals a number of important and frequently forgotten features of political antislavery. It underscores the idealistic determination with which a growing number of white Americans sought to eradicate a form of unfree labor that had been entrenched in their country for more than two centuries in favor of a free labor society that promised opportunity for property, employment, education, and upward mobility for white Americans. But

Clay and his antislavery collaborators, including such men as Salmon P. Chase, Horace Greeley, and William H. Seward, also remained committed to property rights and state sovereignty, two concepts enshrined within the Constitution. Their understanding that slavery was a constitutionally protected form of property that could be done away with only by individual states informed the parameters of their thinking and limited the acceptable range of actions. Furthermore, a closer look at the reality of Clay's personally conflicted and entangled relationship with the peculiar institution can help modern readers better understand the apparent legal challenges of ending the slave property regime within the United States and why it took a war to do so.

Through Clay's legendary deeds as well as their often forgotten or misunderstood motivations, this book offers a more nuanced portrayal of the political ascendancy of antislavery thought in America. Studying the convictions of Clay as well as his collaborators helps to reorient our understanding of antebellum antislavery sentiment. While abolitionists exerted an outsized influence on the moral conscience of American society, they did not represent the vast majority of white Americans who opposed slavery before the Civil War. Such white Americans worried that enslaved labor not only drove down wages for white workers but symbolically degraded all labor by associating it with African Americans, and they believed that slavery's extension would close off entire areas of the United States to the settlement of free labor. Unlike abolitionist beliefs, which usually assumed some level of basic human equality, this antislavery rationale often evoked a disturbing racial prejudice that, thanks to the way most Americans study and remember the antislavery movement today, seems unrecognizable.[7]

Clay's own thinking shows, however, that there was seldom a neat distinction between moral and pragmatic antislavery views. In his writings and speeches, Clay consistently argued that slavery's worst feature was that it restricted economic and social opportunities for common white laborers, yet he often adopted rhetoric declaring it a moral liability for the country. Similarly, he regularly issued racist pronunciations regarding the inferiority of African Americans but also asserted that they were capable of advancement and entitled to some level of political equality. Then there was Clay's own incongruous relationship with slavery: he forged a twenty-five-year-long career fighting the institution yet continued to claim ownership over enslaved people himself until the ratification of the Thirteenth Amendment in 1865.

The purpose of this study of Clay's life is not to disentangle and somehow reconcile these contradictory views. Rather, it is to recognize that they existed and that Clay was not alone in holding them. Indeed, I argue that it is precisely *because* Clay's views are impossible to delineate neatly or fix within familiar categories that his life provides important insight into the politics of slavery and emancipation. In a time when we routinely categorize citizens as conservative, liberal, or occasionally as moderate and when those labels are often read backward onto earlier eras, Clay reveals the contingency and complexity of a mainstream antislavery politician's thinking, action, and legacy.[8]

Cassius Clay's story also encourages us to reappraise the successes and failures of antislavery politics beyond the Civil War. In following Cassius Clay's trajectory on issues of freedom and racial equality from the antebellum era through Reconstruction, this book attempts to help us better understand why the Civil War led to emancipation but did not translate into enduring equality and justice for African Americans. In Clay and his moderate colleagues we see that adherence to constitutional principles not only limited the scope of political antislavery reform before the war but also restricted the lengths to which most American leaders and voters would go to ensure Black freedom after it. Tracing the thinking of Clay and his fellow political antislavery reformers from the antebellum through the postwar periods reveals that the seeds of Reconstruction's demise and the ensuing century-long delay in legislating legal equality lay firmly in the philosophical underpinnings of mainstream antislavery.[9]

Above all, this book offers a complicated and measured portrait of Cassius Marcellus Clay and posits that in all his manifestations—as the brave, fiery, scandal-ridden giant, as well as the moderate, orderly purveyor of constitutional logic—he has much to tell us about one of the most pivotal eras of American history.

⇥ Chapter 1 ⇤
Inheritances

When Sally Clay birthed her sixth child on October 19, 1810, she and her husband, Green, christened him Cassius Marcellus. It was a big name for a tiny infant and one that revealed his parents' sense of possibility both for him and for their young nation. The two-story brick house in which Cassius Clay was born, though grand by early Kentucky standards, lay only a few miles west of Boonesborough, Kentucky's iconic pioneer settlement, and sat in what had been wilderness just two decades before. Cassius's next eldest brother, Brutus Junius, had been born two years earlier, separated from their four older siblings by both years and their parents' choice of name. Eliza, Sally Ann, Paulina, and Sidney, all born before 1804, bore traditional family names, but by the time his last two sons were born, Green looked instead to Roman history (as family lore had it, by way of a Latin textbook) as his inspiration. He found it in two conspiratorial politicians who had assassinated the tyrannical Julius Caesar in order to save the Roman republic—for many the very paradigm for American government—from corruption and ruin.[1]

Anyone who knew Green Clay would have understood his thinking. At the time of his second son's birth, the United States was still a new experiment in republicanism, and Green Clay seemed to epitomize the opportunity it held for white men. In 1780, at the age of twenty-three, he had joined a growing number of settlers who struck out for the Kentucky territory during the American Revolution. Under British dominion, the Kentucky territory lay beyond Proclamation Line of 1763 and was officially off-limits to settlement, but a growing number of American colonists disregarded legalities and moved west of the Cumberland Mountains anyway. In the midst of the struggle for independence, the "buzzel about Kaintuck"—stories of a verdant paradise, a fertile farmland teeming with game—swirled through the Virginia air as thickly as musket smoke, beckoning the brave across the Appalachian Mountains toward new opportunities.[2]

Where once the lush lands of central Kentucky had attracted long hunters such as Daniel Boone, ready to violently oppose any resistance from the region's Indigenous people, by the end of the eighteenth century, it drew young men who yearned to acquire property and an independent future.

The state of Virginia became an obliging ally, issuing military land warrants to Revolutionary War veterans in payment for their service and selling land to others through treasury warrants, with 100 acres priced at forty dollars, cash or credit. Penniless farmers, well-heeled scions of Virginia's first families, and opportunistic speculators all rushed to grab their share of the territory.[3]

Though Green Clay hailed from a well-connected landowning family in Powhatan, Virginia, as the youngest of eleven children, he was unlikely to inherit any of it. His service as a lieutenant in the Virginia militia entitled him to several thousand acres of Kentucky land, but he had bigger plans. When he arrived at Estill Station in central Kentucky in 1780, he became a surveyor, a profession that was crucial to the process of land acquisition for warrant holders. Both poor settlers and wealthy Virginians paid surveyors on the western side of the mountains to locate, measure, and enter land as a deed into public record, thereby claiming their piece of Kentucky. Surveyors ventured into densely wooded forests, alluvial valleys, and thickly tangled cane breaks. Armed with compass, chain, and long rifles, they carved up the landscape one acre (or sixty-six chains) at a time. In the cash-scarce eighteenth century, payment for their services came in the form of a portion of the land they recorded, making this the quickest way to amass some of the best land available on the continent.

Green Clay slept inside the walls of Estill Station for protection from the Indians by night, commandeering their hunting grounds by day. With his Gunter's chain slung over his shoulder and a compass in hand, he crisscrossed what would become the Bluegrass State, measuring, marking, and recording it metes and bounds at a time. As his own payment he entered "lands on the shares," claiming a portion (sometimes up to a half) of every plat he recorded.[4]

Within a short time, he laid claim to thousands of acres of rich Kentucky farmland stretching across what would become several Bluegrass counties. He settled in what became Madison County, in the inner Bluegrass region, where he owned 40,000 acres, compounding his wealth by leasing much of his vast holdings to the unfortunate settlers who found themselves unable to buy their own land as prices soared in the 1780s and 1790s. While men like Clay monopolized land possession, tenants, who had little hope of owning land themselves, did the work of improvement and provided the landowners a steady source of income.[5]

When Clay began to develop and farm a portion of his Madison County holdings, his most valuable crop was tobacco, which, in the cash-scarce eighteenth century, served not only as a commodity but as a medium of exchange, with magistrates often using the golden weed to pay salaries of local officials. He also grew corn and rye and bred cattle and merino sheep. Like other farmers, he built and operated mills to grind his corn into feed for cattle and distilleries to turn excess corn into potable and portable whiskey.[6]

He soon emerged as the largest landowner and most influential leader in Madison County. Clay served as local tax commissioner, county militia captain, and magistrate, a position that proved particularly powerful. Magistrates collected taxes, issued liquor licenses, commissioned the construction of roads, ferries, and turnpikes, and approved the building of warehouses, mills, and taverns. They also appointed local officials such as surveyors, attorneys, clerks, and constables. Becoming a magistrate was both a confirmation of prestige and a conduit to the accumulation of even more power and wealth, and Clay used his position to full advantage. He approved the construction of three roads across his property and charged tolls to farmers who traveled these roads to take their crops to market. He established a tobacco warehouse in which he and neighboring farmers stored their crops, and he also licensed his own distilleries and taverns. In short, Green Clay was a canny entrepreneur who built a fortune from highly diversified economic interests, by producing, selling, and transporting a variety of goods and crops and charging others to do the same.

In the coming decades, his distant cousin, Henry Clay, who also emigrated from Virginia to Kentucky, became famous for advocating the "Bluegrass system" (which he later nationalized to the American System), an economic ideology that embraced the idea of interdependent agricultural and manufacturing economies, supported by government-funded infrastructure. But Green deployed that strategy at least a decade before Henry canonized the concept. With his combination of ambition, tenacity, and shrewd handling of legal matters, he became an early American success story.[7]

Clay's marriage in March 1795 to Sally Anne Lewis, nineteen years his junior, cemented his social position. Sally was the daughter of Thomas Lewis, magistrate in Fayette County, a delegate to the inaugural Kentucky constitutional convention in 1792, and the official who administered the oath of office to Isaac Shelby, the state's first governor. Green and Sally married in the parlor of Kilmore, the Lewises' fashionable Lexington residence, before making their marital home in Green's rudimentary dirt-floored log dwelling in Madison County. Within three years of their wedding, however, Green had commissioned and completed a residence befitting his station and his bride, the handsome brick house where their children were born. Clermont, as the Clays later christened it, sat near the steep banks of the Kentucky River, a fitting perch for a powerful man.[8]

Inheritances

As land rich as Green Clay became, it was another form of capital wealth that made his diversified assets so profitable. By 1810, the year of Cassius's birth, Clay's household included seventy-six bondsmen and women. This number made him one of the state's largest slaveholders in a time when the number of unfree African Americans in Kentucky increased from 11,830 to 41,038 — a higher growth rate than the white population.

Among Kentuckians, however, there was some ambivalence regarding the place of slavery in the new republic. Some questioned the right of one human to own another, while others feared the threat of slave insurrection. The most common concern among white Kentuckians, however, was that a slave-owning oligarchy seemed at odds with white yeoman equality. The delegates to Kentucky's constitutional convention in 1792 roundly debated the future of slavery in their new state. With the slaveholding class well represented, most delegates followed the lead of the convention's dominant figure, George Nicholas, in deciding that the constitutional protection of slave property was crucial to attracting wealthier emigrants to Kentucky. In the vein of philosopher John Locke, Nicholas argued against constitutional emancipation measures, insisting that they ran counter to the essential purpose of government, which was to protect the private property of its citizens. Delegates enshrined the protection of slave property in the ninth article of Kentucky's first constitution, explicitly forbidding the state to emancipate enslaved people without consent or payment of their owners.[9]

In 1799, Madison County voters elected Green Clay a delegate to Kentucky's second state constitutional convention. There he was among the majority of the delegates voting to reaffirm the same slaveholding protections outlined in the version of 1792. While Clay favored slavery, he was not averse to granting free African Americans some rights. At the convention, he headed a committee that supported a provision that allowed free African Americans to vote if they owned property. For Green Clay, the republican ideal of landownership as a qualification for full citizenship prevailed. He was in the minority, however, and while the revision to the constitution in 1799 instituted policies that made the electoral process more democratic for white men, it also introduced a new provision that explicitly disenfranchised "blacks, mulattoes, and Indians."[10]

Few white Kentuckians owned as many bondspeople as Green Clay, but by 1800, one quarter of Kentucky heads of households claimed enslaved people, with the average holding four. No matter how many men and women they enslaved, many white Kentuckians relied on these enslaved laborers for clearing, plowing, planting, and tending land, as well as building fences to enclose it. In Kentucky fields, they harvested corn, hemp, and tobacco and also fed cattle, sheep, and horses. Inside Kentucky houses, they cooked and cared for children.[11]

There is little to suggest that Green or Sally Clay were ever ambivalent about the moral or economic rectitude of claiming ownership over other humans. Sally hailed from a Baptist family who in her youth broke away from their antislavery church to create a separatist proslavery congregation. For his part, Green Clay considered the people he enslaved his most valuable assets, and he worked to increase their numbers throughout his life. At his death, his will listed his ownership of 105 individuals. He was, by Cassius's later account, a very pragmatic manager of his human chattel. "No man understood better how to manage his dependents," Cassius would later insist, claiming that his father "provided first class food and shelter for his slaves; but always was rigid and exacting in his discipline." Green allowed enslaved people to raise chickens and tend garden plots to supplement their rations, and he raised a surplus of sheep in order clothe them in warm woolens. "Better to lose the value of the coat than the workman," he thought.[12]

The Clay children enjoyed an upbringing that was equal parts privilege and obligation. At Clermont they had free run of the thick forests and rolling pastures of Madison County. They could fish out of streams that, as Cassius later recalled, "bubbled up with never-ceasing music" and enjoyed long days riding horses and hunting. He developed his sense of physicality and pugnacity at an early age, wrestling whoever would take him on—the son of an overseer, a young enslaved boy, and once even a sheep tied to a tree. It was Sally Clay, along with the family's enslaved nursemaids, who quite literally had more of a hand in raising the Clay children. As a strict Baptist, Sally countenanced no disobedience or dishonesty from her children and was quick to take the switch to them when they fell out of line. "She was not a woman to be trifled with," Cassius later wrote admiringly.[13]

But if the advantages of being Green Clay's children were great, so, too, were the expectations. A sense of order and discipline undergirded the freedom and privilege they enjoyed, grounded by the expectation that his sons would become educated and upstanding citizens of the young republic. Green had definite ideas about how his progeny should be shaped into young adults. "He spent little time with the children," recalled his youngest son, "and did not assume control. Yet he directed in the main what was to be done." What Green thought was to be done was a combination of applied and formal learning. He took charge of his sons' practical education himself, imparting both his business acumen and his love of animal husbandry and agriculture to his children. Green also imbued them with a sense of self-sufficiency at an early age. He taught his two eldest sons how to survey land and sent them on trips to western Kentucky to secure tenants on his lands there. Green dispatched Cassius to Cincinnati, some 100 miles away, on a solo errand when he was only twelve or thirteen years old.[14]

Decades later, Cassius could readily recall the "homely but terse apothegms" his father imparted, including: "Never say to anybody what you would not have proclaimed in a court-house yard" and "Keep out of the hands of the doctor and the sheriff"—all words of an eminently practical man who rose in life through much hard work and guile. He also demonstrated the importance of military service. In May 1813, boasting the rank of brigadier general, the elder Clay led 1,200 Kentucky militia men into Ohio to successfully reinforce William Henry Harrison's besieged garrison at Fort Meigs. Martial honor was perennially valued in the Bluegrass State but became the stuff of legend during the War of 1812, when as the song "The Hunters of Kentucky" put it, the state's men fought as though "half horse and half alligator."

Like many upwardly mobile Americans in the early republic, Green and Sally hoped that future generations of Clays would do successively better for themselves. By the 1820s, their hopes seemed to be fulfilled. All three of their daughters succeeded in making propitious marital matches. Eliza married local Madison County attorney and politician J. Speed Smith, while Paulina wed William Rodes, son of a Madison County businessman and owner of a hemp factory. Sally Ann married Edmund Irvine, a member of one of Kentucky's founding families. Tragically, she became a widow soon after when Edmund died while dueling a Richmond newspaper editor. Soon thereafter, she married attorney Madison Johnson, brother of future vice president Richard Mentor Johnson.[15]

Green had little formal schooling himself, and even though his practical skills and entrepreneurial spirit had taken him far in life, he wanted more for his children. When they were young, Brutus and Cassius walked over a mile to the local common school, housed in a log cabin, taking turns carrying a single lunch basket. Once they advanced through the rudimentary local options, the brothers boarded with Joshua Fry, a prominent landowner who established a small academy in his Garrard County home. There he educated the sons (and occasionally daughters) of the Kentucky elite. In Fry's household, the Clay brothers studied Latin and literature, as well as dancing and the social graces.[16]

The greatest symbol of the Clay family's rising status came when Sidney enrolled in Princeton University, joining the ranks of hundreds of other wealthy Southerners who traveled north each year seeking an Ivy League education. While there, Sidney maintained an active correspondence with distant cousin Henry Clay, who offered to help him get into diplomatic service. Brutus, whose love of agriculture and animal husbandry most resembled his father's, seemed content to remain closer to home and attended Centre College in Danville, Kentucky. After his time in Joshua Fry's academy, in 1827, Cassius enrolled in Saint Joseph's, a Jesuit college in Bardstown, Kentucky. The school attracted Catholic students from as far away as Louisiana and was well known for teaching French, then the primary language of diplomacy and elite learning. Cassius boarded with the school president and begrudgingly honed his skills by writing long letters to Brutus in the Gallic language.[17]

In the spring of 1828, Cassius was in his final term at Saint Joseph's when a family crisis distracted him from his studies. At Clermont, Green was in the final throes of his excruciating struggle with oral cancer. Throughout the preceding months, Brutus had kept him apprised of his father's losing battle. When the school term ended in April, Cassius made his way home, riding east on the rutted roads that cut through the lush, undulating terrain of the Bluegrass region to Madison County.[18]

At Clermont, Cassius found his father pragmatic to the last. In contrast to his deeply religious wife, Green was a deist, and in his final months, rather than contemplating what awaited him in the afterlife, he concerned himself with earthly matters. As Cassius later recalled, he "looked death steadily in the face without the tremor of a nerve" and used his dwindling days to get his affairs in order. As he lay on his deathbed, the seventy-one-year-old had a considerable fortune in the form of thousands of acres of land spread across several states, as well as 105 enslaved people within his distributable patrimony. There were also the ferries, mills, and distilleries he had amassed during the previous half century. Considering that he had come to the Bluegrass country in 1780 with nothing to his name, the process of inventorying and apportioning his wealth among his children must have given him a good deal of satisfaction at the assets he had accrued over his lifetime.[19]

Green Clay inventoried his life's very estimable achievements, a testament to his faith in the future republic and a legal apparatus to protect against anything that might derail it. Green's instructions filled eight pages of tight script in a county probate book. He divided several thousand acres of land in Bourbon, Madison, and Estill Counties, as well as 40,000 to 50,000 acres of land along the Tennessee River, among his sons, Sidney, Brutus, and Cassius. He also bequeathed each of them some land in Illinois. With Sidney and Brutus already settled in Bourbon County, Green gave Cassius most of his Madison County land, including Clermont and its grounds.[20]

In keeping with the English legal tradition of retaining property in the paternal bloodline, Green stipulated that his daughters had the full use of houses, land, and enslaved laborers he had given them on their marriages but granted the legal ownership of this property to his sons. He bequeathed his daughter Paulina Rodes the use of land in Richmond, the seat of Madison County, as well as eleven enslaved individuals, but under Cassius's trust. Cassius also held legal title to the land and nine enslaved men and women willed to his sister Eliza Smith. Such specifications reflected a widespread testamentary custom before most states allowed married women to own property, protecting family assets from being sold to pay debts incurred by less-than-dependable husbands. Such worries were not abstract. Before his death, Green Clay had watched Eliza's husband, J. Speed Smith, run up gambling debts. Smith eventually resorted to selling the house Green had built for the couple on their marriage to repay his debts. William Rodes, Paulina's husband, would also face financial difficulties a few years later.[21]

Green employed a similar legal strategy to secure his terrestrial and human property from the whims or financial exigencies of his own sons. He bestowed them outright ownership of some enslaved laborers but stipulated that others were to be held in trust for future generations. Sidney received six slaves outright, but also ten that Green instructed him to let Brutus use. Brutus received another eight slaves outright. Green willed Rachel, Frank, Jim, Emily, Solomon, Milly, Alsey, Lucy, Jackson, and Hannah Jr. to his son Sidney but specified that Cassius would have use of their labor. For all but legal intents and purposes, Cassius claimed mastery over them, but he would not count them as assets that could be paid to creditors in the case of debt or bankruptcy. Green also willed Cassius another fourteen enslaved individuals to be held in his own name: Mingo, Scott, Riley, Joe, Esther, John, Ursley, John Jr., Huldy, Nancy Jr., David, Matt, Adam, and Ned.[22]

In addition to shielding human assets from loss in the event that his sons incurred debt, Green may have also been hedging against the possibility that they might develop some ambivalence about owning slave property. While he was at Princeton, Sidney had become an emancipationist, joining the ranks of Americans who recognized slavery as a legally legitimate but unfortunate institution. This idea prevailed in many Northern states by the time of the American Revolution, and they began implementing gradual emancipation provisions in their constitutions. Upper South states such as Maryland and Virginia began to follow suit. A significant number of Bluegrass State residents acknowledged the present legality and usefulness of slavery but simultaneously considered it an "evil necessity." Some religious sects believed slavery to be immoral. Other critics charged that the institution was undemocratic, unrepublican, and bad for the work ethic of whites. Still others worried about racial unrest and slave rebellion. Though Kentucky constitutional delegates had failed to do so in both 1792 and 1799, many opponents looked for means of gradually ridding their state of the peculiar institution.[23]

In the first decade of the nineteenth century, a few fledgling antislavery groups formed, including the Kentucky Abolition Society, but their ranks never exceeded a couple of hundred members. Their primary goal was to convince individual owners to manumit their enslaved laborers, an effort hindered by the belief of most white Kentuckians that African Americans were inferior developmentally and intellectually and would require a great deal of education and character formation to become productive members of society. Many whites did not think that such improvement was even possible and could not envision white and free Black Kentuckians living safely and peaceably side by side.[24]

Instead, most emancipationists turned to the idea of colonization, which entailed the voluntary and compensated manumission of enslaved men and women who would resettle in the African colony of Liberia. Colonizationists worked to relocate previously manumitted slaves and to raise funds to purchase currently enslaved people from their owners. Henry Clay, who was perhaps the most famous early opponent of slavery in Kentucky, was at the forefront of this movement and cofounded the American Colonization Society in 1816. He would serve a long term as its president, during which he explained the colonizationist impulse in a speech in 1827: "Our object has been to point out the way, to show that colonization is practicable, and to leave it to those States or individuals who may be pleased to engage in the object, to prosecute it." Colonization, according to Clay, would decrease the number of African Americans (free or enslaved) in the United States and engender "domestic tranquility, and render [Americans] one homogenous people." Implicit in this strategy was an assumption that African Americans could not coexist with whites and a fundamental recognition that slaves were a constitutionally protected form of property. By the end of Green Clay's life, colonization was gaining popularity in Kentucky, and Sidney had become a proponent. Knowing this, Green likely constructed labyrinthine trust arrangements in part to preclude any future sale based on his sons' moral or political qualms.[25]

Green's passing carried serious and tragic implications for Clermont's enslaved laborers. While some already lived dispersed across three Bluegrass counties within the households of the Clay children, for others, his death spelled the separation of family and kin groups they had forged over decades.

Green Clay also did something unexpected for a man who was so committed to the institution of slavery and so aware of the financial value of his bondsmen and women: he freed ten of them. His will stipulated that Henry and his wife, Hannah, Comfort, Fanny, and Kitty, as well as Nancy Jr. and her four children, received their freedom along with twenty dollars each and fifty of the many acres of land he owned south of the Tennessee River. Although he offered no explanation for manumitting them, it may have been a reward for faithful service. And although the land he offered them lay hundreds of miles from the place they considered home, his willingness to relocate them within the state illustrated that Clay did not share the conviction of many white Kentuckians that unbound African Americans must leave the state.[26]

He offered an alternate, if callous, pathway to freedom for his other female laborers. "As an encouragement to the raising of children," he stipulated, "I direct that in all time to come such female [*sic*] as shall raise 10 children all living at the same time, she shall be thenceforth emancipated and free for all intents and purposes." In other words, as a reward for increasing the property of his heirs through their own reproductive labor, and by consigning their resulting progeny to a life of unfreedom, enslaved women could secure their own. Such a prescription was in keeping with Green Clay's "shrewd" management of enslaved property.[27]

Clay's will dictated a very different fate for eight other enslaved people. He directed that Peter, Squire, Sarah, Daniel and his wife, Winney, Grace, Isabella, and Mary Jr. be sold by his executors. The reasons for the sale of seven of these men and women listed are unknown. Mary Jr.'s fate, however, came as a result of a murder she had committed several years earlier. One day in 1820, she had come running through the yard of Clermont, a butcher knife clutched in her hands and covered in the blood of the Clay family's overseer, John Payne. Mary cooked and cleaned in Payne's household, where she endured his hot temper and verbal abuse daily. On this day, it had proved too much for Mary, and she unleashed invectives back at him. Afterward, Payne sent her off to work, but suspecting some sort of retribution, she grabbed a butcher knife as she went. When she returned, as she expected, Payne physically attacked her. Mary attempted to escape but found that he had locked all the exits of the house. Trapped, she used her hidden knife to defend herself, killing him in the process.[28]

This incident shook the whole Clay family. Cassius, who was working alongside his sister Eliza in the garden when the blood-soaked and screaming Mary came running up to Clermont, never forgot the incident.

At the time, Kentucky slave codes entitled bondsmen and women accused of capital crimes to jury trials. Mary was to stand trial in Madison

County, but Green petitioned to move the proceedings to a more impartial locale. In October 1820, the state general assembly transferred her trial to Jessamine County, where a jury decided her guilty. Mary was sentenced to execution by hanging, but Green Clay successfully petitioned Governor John Adair to pardon her, sparing her life. Under Kentucky's slave codes, Green would have been reimbursed by the state had Mary had been executed, so he seemed to have some motive beyond protecting his monetary investment. Perhaps he felt some responsibility for having placed her in the presence of such an abusive man. Kentucky's slave codes also mandated, however, that enslaved individuals convicted of capital crimes eventually leave the state. Mary could remain in Kentucky so long as Green Clay was alive, but his death meant banishment by sale.[29]

Cassius described the tragic situation: "As was the custom in border slave States, Mary was, by his will, ordered to be sent South, I suppose to make murder odious." As executor, his emancipationist brother Sidney was forced to sell the slaves designated for removal in Green's will. Cassius recalled, "Never shall I forget—and through all these years it rests upon the memory as the stamp upon a bright coin—the scene when Mary was tied by the wrists and sent from home and friends . . . into Southern banishment forever."[30]

Whatever the contours of their individual views on slavery, there was no question that Green's children benefited immensely from the labor of the enslaved people he willed them. Though they were listed in his will as legal chattel, it was their very human labor that made the rest of the Clay children's inheritance—the land, the livestock, the houses—functional and profitable. Indeed, Green took painstaking care in allocating his enslaved individuals, not because they were human, but because he understood that they were by far the most valuable assets he was leaving to his children, and their children after. The Clay brothers' legal entailment to land and slave property made them heirs not only to their father but to the promise of upward mobility that the early American republic seemed to offer for free white males. Green Clay could slip his earthly bonds content in the knowledge that he had set his children up as best he could to carry on his lineage, his assets, and his success. On October 31, 1828, he summoned Cassius to his bedside, pointed in the direction of the family graveyard, and muttered, "I have just seen death come in at that door," before quietly expiring.[31]

In ways both real and symbolic, his father's death ushered in Cassius Clay's coming of age. At eighteen, he found himself the owner of a considerable fortune in the form of land, a large home, and enslaved men and women. In addition to these assets, Green had also provided for Cassius's education. Soon after his father's passing, he enrolled in Lexington's

Mary Jane Warfield Clay. *Oil portrait by George Healy (ca. 1845). Though painted more than a decade after she met Cassius, this likeness captures her beauty and vivacious personality, which he found so alluring. (Eastern Kentucky University Libraries, Special Collections and Archives, Richmond)*

Transylvania University, with his enslaved manservant in tow. The first college west of the Appalachian Mountains, Transylvania enjoyed an excellent reputation for its classical curriculum, as well as its legal and medical schools. Lexingtonians were duly proud of the college, whose academic reputation contributed to the town's cosmopolitan character and helped it lay claim to the title Athens of the West. Cassius excelled in his studies at Transylvania, earning a position near the top of his class.[32]

Cassius had grown into a man in other ways, too. At twenty, he was over six feet tall, with a robust, but trim, physique. His abundant light brown hair crested dramatically across his broad forehead. He bore a wide, handsome face and full lips that could curl into a teasing grin or recede into a firmly set expression.

While he was in Lexington, he grew smitten with a similarly attractive young woman. Five years his junior, Mary Jane Warfield was a vivacious and flirtatious beauty who beguiled Cassius from their first introduction.

College-aged Cassius Clay. (Schomburg Center for Research in Black Culture, Jean Blackwell Hutson Research and Reference Division, New York Public Library)

Years later, Cassius rhapsodized in his memoirs about Mary Jane's younger self. She "had the complexion of her Irish ancestor—a fair smooth skin at times touched with rose color; a face and head not classical, with rather broad jaws, large mouth, flexible lips, rather thin and determined, but with outline well cut, and an irregular nose." "Her hair was a light auburn color or nut-color, long and luxuriant," he recalled. "Her eyes were a light greyish-blue, large and far apart, with that flexibility of the iris which gives always great variety and intensity of expression."[33]

Her vivacious personality and arresting looks were not all Mary Jane had to recommend her. Her parents, Elisha and Maria Barr Warfield, both from prominent Maryland families, had moved to Kentucky in the 1790s and were well connected socially. Elisha was a physician who specialized in obstetrics and taught at the Transylvania University medical school. His real passion, however, was horse breeding, and he eventually left medicine to devote himself to his bloodstock operation. Warfield helped to construct Lexington's first racetrack and founded the Kentucky Association, which established the rules and culture of horseracing in the city. His greatest achievement would come several decades later when he bred Lexington, the most highly regarded thoroughbred of the nineteenth century. Already in 1830, when Cassius and Mary Jane met, Elisha Warfield was well on the way to earning his title, Father of the Kentucky Turf.[34]

At the tender age of sixteen, however, Mary Jane was too young to marry, and Cassius was too young to settle down. After a year at Transylvania, Cassius followed the lead of his eldest brother, Sidney, and set his sights on an Ivy League education. Armed with a sheath full of letters of introduction, he headed for New England, stopping along the way in Washington, Baltimore, Philadelphia, and New York. His familial connections brought him meetings and dinners with political luminaries including Andrew Jackson and Martin Van Buren. In Boston he met abolitionist poet John Greenleaf Whittier and politicians Daniel Webster and Edward Everett. He soaked in the art and architecture. "Every thing here is new and interesting," he wrote to Brutus. "I could find myself quite employed here, even without going to College." He eventually yielded to responsibility, however, enrolling in Yale College as a member of the junior class. There he applied himself to a curriculum of classical languages and history. His favorite subject, however, was rhetoric, and he began to develop the speaking and debating skills that would define much of his later career.[35]

One issue that Cassius found of particular interest in the Northeast was the public discussion surrounding slavery. He arrived in the region as an increasing number of whites, inspired in part by the moral fervor of the religious revival known as the Second Great Awakening, began to organize around the principle of abolitionism. Unlike other emancipationists, abolitionists believed that holding humans in bondage constituted a moral sin and that slavery needed to be eradicated immediately, with no provisions for compensating owners. One of the leading voices of this movement belonged to the young Boston-based William Lloyd Garrison, a fervent Christian who began his newspaper, the *Liberator*, in January 1831, just before Cassius Clay's arrival in Connecticut. In the *Liberator*'s inaugural issue, Garrison called for the immediate end of slavery and for Black enfranchisement, pledging to eschew any moderation in his discussion. "I will be harsh as truth, and as uncompromising as justice," he promised.[36]

Only months after the *Liberator*'s launch, Clay attended a speech that Garrison gave at New Haven's South Church in which the editor was no more equivocal. Garrison's moral certitude and fervor struck Clay immediately, and he later remembered how "in plain, logical, and sententious language he treated the 'Divine Institution' so as to burn like a branding-iron." The idea that slaves should and could be emancipated sooner rather than later shocked Clay. "This was a new revelation to me," he remembered. "I felt the horrors of slavery; but my parents were slaveholders; all my kindred were slaveholders; and I regarded it as I did other evils of humanity, as the fixed law of nature, or of God, and submitted as best I might. But Garrison dragged out the monster from all his citadels, and left him stabbed to the vitals, and dying at the feet of every logical and honest mind."

The following night a speaker appeared at the South Church to offer a proslavery rejoinder to Garrison's remarks, and Clay returned to hear him. The oration, he recalled, was full of "sophism after sophism, and false conclusion from more false assumption." Aroused and angered, he resolved there and then to "give slavery a death struggle." Chroniclers of Cassius Clay's life often point to this passage from his memoirs, written more than fifty years after Garrison's appearance at South Church, as an indication of a conversion moment for the young college student.[37]

Yet it was another influence from Cassius's time in the Northeast that provided the continuous tinder to stoke the fire Garrison kindled: the free labor economy. By the time Clay arrived in New England, America's industrial revolution was in full swing. Factories turned Southern cotton into cloth and forged iron into armaments, carriage parts, and cookware. Cassius noticed that the region's nascent manufacturing sector intersected efficiently with its subsistence farming base to form a thriving, diversified economy. As he recalled of New England in one of his early political speeches, he was astounded to see "a people *there* living luxuriously on a soil which [in Kentucky] would have been deemed on the high road to famine and the alms-house."[38]

Furthermore, he came to admire the region's culture, which, at least in theory, respected white working-class labor and the upward mobility it produced. Cassius had been raised in a society that often claimed the slave-based system of labor as a culturally superior one that allowed the natural elite to pursue the finer things: learning, recreation, and political matters. White Southerners often looked down on the self-conscious striving inherent in Yankee personal and commercial industry alike. "I had been taught to regard Connecticut as the land of woolen nutmegs and leather pumpkin seed," he remarked, "—yet there was a land of sterility without paupers, and a people where no man was found who could not write his name, and read his laws and his Bible." "These were strange things" to him, but he became a convert to the Northern free labor system and, during his time in New Haven, came to see "liberty, religion, and education" as the "true foundation for individual happiness and national glory." As Clay would assert in writings and speeches throughout his career, it was the inefficiency rather than the inhumanity of slavery that was the most important lesson he took away from his time in the North.[39]

Inheritances

Clay seriously contemplated the future of slavery during his time at Yale. In a letter to Brutus in December 1831, he predicted: "The time is coming when you as well as myself will have to put into requisition all the real power of understanding and firmness, which either of us have to boast. The slave question is now assuming an importance in the opinions of the enlightened and human, which prejudice and interest can not long withstand." Slaves, he asserted, "must soon be free!"

Writing just months after Nat Turner and his compatriots revolted and killed dozens of whites in the Virginia countryside, Clay conjectured that "the greater part of the United States is against slavery, not speculatively, but actively, and in the event of insurrection we are to expect to engage not only the blacks but the whites of the Free States. These are surmises of mine, but we may live to see the event." Anticipating the sectional strife caused by divergent views of slavery, he added: "I think moreover there will be a dissolution of the general government before 50 years—however much it may be deprecated and laughed at now."[40]

Whether Brutus, already a very committed slave owner, took his brother's premonitions seriously or simply attributed them to the follies of youth is another matter. In the same letter, Cassius bragged about his freewheeling college lifestyle, telling his brother: "I've been to Boston, West Point, and 'the fine points'—and have been on the point of going to gaol." Perhaps Brutus hoped that such half-baked views on slavery would dissipate once his brother returned to Kentucky and his adult responsibilities.

But while Cassius talked about the fate of slavery with some certainty, he was less sure what might be in store for his own future. Sally Clay had remarried to a Baptist minister, Jeptha Dudley, and relocated to Frankfort, Kentucky, clearing the way for his return to his birthright at Clermont. He was not sure that this was what he wanted, though. His letters to Brutus were full of ambivalence. He admired his brother's chosen agrarian path. "I look upon your situation as the most select in life," he wrote him, "—you have the objects of ambition in view, without the probability of failure."[41] Yet he feared that his brother's path might not satisfy his restless temperament. It was clear that Clay had abundant personal ambition and longed to be more than an "empty name." He wrote Brutus that he hoped to come back to Kentucky and continue the family livestock business but that it was "with dread" that he thought "of the plough and the hoe." "I fear that when I return home," he told his brother, "it will only be to prepare for a more lengthy and dangerous journey." Several months later, however, to assuage Brutus's concerns about his future, he reassured him that once he graduated, he would "return home and enter on that course of life which prudence and necessity impel me to lead."[42]

When Cassius graduated from Yale in spring 1832, despite what he had told Brutus, he decided to reenroll in Transylvania University to study law in preparation for a career in politics. He was also drawn back to Lexington by Mary Jane Warfield. Now Clay pursued her in earnest. After a fall day of hickory nut hunting, he recalled, Mary Jane tumbled into Cassius's lap and pledged herself to be his, an act that "attacked nearly all [of his] senses at once!" By this time, Mary Jane had accumulated several suitors, but she seemed to have her heart set on Cassius, and he on hers.

The Warfield parents, however, seemed reluctant to accept Cassius as a potential son-in-law. And several days before their wedding, scheduled for February 26, 1833, Maria Warfield made the fateful decision to show Clay a letter Mary Jane had received from John Declarey, a Louisville physician and competitor for Mary Jane's affections. The missive, Clay later claimed, was "depreciatory of [his] character" but contained no serious claims. "It should have been thrown into the fire and nothing shown to me," he judged. But once Cassius had seen this affront to his reputation, the code of honor that prevailed among the upper-class citizens of nineteenth-century Kentucky compelled him to act.[43]

Acting with the impetuousness that would become his hallmark, the thin-skinned Cassius set off to confront his slanderer. He and his best man, James Rollins, hightailed it to Louisville, where they tracked down Declarey and presented him with the offending missive. When the physician offered no explanation or apology, Cassius whipped out a hickory stick and began caning him in the middle of a busy street. After a sufficient bludgeoning, Clay backed off and retired to a room in a hotel to await Declarey's challenge to a duel—something sure to follow. Within a few hours, the two men arranged to meet the next morning, just across the Ohio River, in Indiana. By the time the two arrived, a large crowd, estimated to consist of 500 onlookers, greeted them. The men agreed to reconvene at another, less populated spot. But Declarey never showed.

In danger of missing his own wedding, Clay returned to Lexington the next morning. That evening, with the groom rumpled and travel-weary, Cassius and Mary Jane exchanged vows in the parlor of the Warfields' stately home. The wedding was the talk of the town and, according to one contemporary, "produced several large and splendid parties."[44]

The near-duel was also the subject of much public discussion. Clay's confrontation with Declarey unfolded according to accepted protocol of honor in early nineteenth-century Kentucky. Yet, if resorted to injudiciously, dueling might be frowned upon and the participants deemed incautious and irresponsible. In the aftermath of such affairs, it was traditional for the public to parse the circumstances to determine if conflict could have been avoided. On this account, Cassius appeared to have acted appropriately. As one contemporary Kentuckian noted, following his encounter with Declarey, Clay "received great credit here for his perseverance and firmness and his conduct is highly approved by those best acquainted with the circumstances." Still, the whole affair was concerning to Cassius's family, who were no strangers to the high costs of defending personal honor, given that a duel had cost Sally Clay Irvine her first husband. Then there was also Cassius's personal reputation. But in the days that followed, an acquaintance of Sidney Clay's wrote to reassure him that there was "no particular censure cast on either" party and that the affair had mostly blown over.[45]

Declarey felt differently, however. Embarrassed by his public bludgeoning, he painted Clay's departure from Louisville as an act of cowardice. Though Clay knew that marriage vows had sealed his triumph over the doctor, he could not withstand such insult and returned to Louisville to give Declarey "a full test of [his] manhood." On seeing his adversary, Declarey turned pale and fled again. Clay lingered in Louisville another few days, ready for, but not provoking, a confrontation. When none came, he returned to Lexington. Days later, however, came the shocking news that on seeing Clay, Declarey had retreated to his room, locked the door, slit his wrists with a razor, and bled to death. Such were the costs of dishonor in nineteenth-century Kentucky.

Chapter 2
Uneradicable Disease

At the age of twenty-two and newly married, Cassius Clay knew that he could no longer hold his inheritance—with both its gifts and its burdens—at arm's length. But having a new bride on his arm made the prospect of returning to Clermont more palatable, if no less daunting. By 1833, no member of the Clay family had lived in the house for several years. On her remarriage and relocation to Frankfort, Sally Clay Dudley had left Clermont in the care of the family's enslaved laborers, with Nancy overseeing the house. "A trifling overseer is worse than none," she had explained to Cassius while he was still at Yale. "The negroes manages [*sic*] as good as I could expect."

On his return, Cassius found a laborious task to revive Clermont as a working farm. One challenge was that Clay was land and slave rich but cash poor. He had resorted to borrowing money from his mother, who also offered support in the form of her "negroes," suggesting that if their labor was not needed, he could hire them out for cash.[1]

Cassius organized his business and farming ventures in Madison County along the same lines his father had drawn. He continued to run the sawmill as well as the Kentucky River ferry and added a grist mill to his operations. As he had promised Brutus, Cassius resumed and even expanded Clermont's livestock breeding operation, adding to the number of hogs, mules, and merino and Southdown sheep. His true agricultural passion, though, became shorthorn beef cattle. The same limestone-enriched water and bluegrass pasturage that produced strong, fast racehorses also nurtured fleshy, sturdy beef cattle interbred from shorthorn, longhorn, and Hereford cows imported from England. Farmers kept meticulous records of the breedings of these highly prized specimens, developing pedigrees as extensive as those belonging to their equine counterparts. When Brutus settled into his inherited homestead after Green's death, he began a bovine breeding operation and happily aided Cassius's effort several years later, forming a collaborative business venture and a shared passion that would transcend their differences on other matters in coming years.[2]

Cassius's preoccupation with business and agricultural pursuits did nothing to extinguish the flame of his personal ambitions or his political inclinations, however. In 1834, he ran as a Whig candidate for election to the state general assembly, even though, at age twenty-four, he was one year shy of the age for office eligibility. One of his opponents quickly pointed out this breach, forcing Clay to withdraw. Instead, in move that would have made his father proud, he accepted a position as secretary for a turnpike construction project set to run between Lexington and Richmond, which, if completed, would traverse through some of his Madison County land and intersect the Kentucky River at his ferry operation.[3]

The following year, the newly eligible Clay once again stood for election, and Madison voters elected him to one of the county's two seats in the Kentucky General Assembly. Clay threw himself into the world of state politics with gusto. In his inaugural term in Frankfort, he focused his attention on promoting traditionally Whiggish issues, supporting protective tariffs and state subsidies for internal improvements such as turnpikes and railroads. He promoted the same expanded infrastructure and sound credit systems on which he was reliant in his business life to market his crops and to make the most from his mills and ferry operation.

Early in the session, however, Clay and his fellow legislators had to contend with questions regarding the future of slavery in Kentucky.[4] Despite its firmly protected status in the state constitution and its economic importance to the state, white Kentuckians could not seem to agree among themselves whether the peculiar institution was a virtue or a burden. Decades-long disagreements over slavery grew more heated in the late 1820s and early 1830s, especially after Nat Turner's rebellion in Virginia in 1831. The stealth and ease with which Turner and his followers had killed dozens of unsuspecting white men, women, and children as they slept in their beds made many Kentuckians uneasy about the significant presence of rebellious slaves in their own state. The census of 1830 revealed 24 percent of Kentucky's population to be enslaved, marking what would be the highest proportion ever, while free African Americans made up less than 1 percent. Concerned for racial order and security, many whites felt that these numbers were too large. Like Virginians, who engaged in a robust debate over the safety and economics of slavery in 1831–32, white Kentuckians began to look for solutions.[5]

Some doubled down on colonization as the answer to this demographic danger. Advocates had founded the Kentucky Colonization Society (KCS) in 1829 as an auxiliary to the American Colonization Society. In the wake of Turner's rebellion, local chapters proliferated, and by 1832, Kentucky boasted at least thirty-one societies scattered around the state. Joshua Fry, Brutus and Cassius Clay's former tutor, served as president of the Danville branch. Members of the KCS worked to relocate previously manumitted slaves to Liberia and to raise funds to purchase currently enslaved people from their owners.

Colonization initially proved popular in Kentucky in part because its aims appealed to a people along a broad spectrum of views on slavery, attracting both proslavery and antislavery moderates who wished to whiten the state's population. Over time, however, proslavery members of the KCS began to suspect that their antislavery compatriots harbored a hidden agenda to slowly kill the institution. They need not have worried. Between 1829 and 1859, the KCS sent fewer than 700 free African Americans to Liberia. The spirit of colonization was no match for slaveholders' reticence to relinquish their Black labor, even with the promise of compensation. Free African Americans, many of whose families had been living in the United States for generations, were also loathe to leave their native land for uncertain prospects in Africa.[6]

Both within and outside of the rubric of colonization, antislavery moderates increased their activism in Kentucky in the early 1830s. Presbyterian clergyman John C. Breckinridge and Centre College president John C. Young dominated the antislavery movement, advocating a slow and patient end to slavery, which would respect the property rights of slaveholders and prevent the social upheaval and public endangerment that whites believed immediate and wholesale abolition would surely bring. Along with colonization, they favored postnati (born after) schemes similar to those used by northeastern states after the American Revolution, which stipulated that enslaved persons born after a given date would be considered free at some point decades later.[7]

In 1833, doubts about the merits and safety of slavery prompted the general assembly to pass a nonimportation law, which prohibited out-of-state whites from moving into Kentucky with enslaved laborers intended for sale. Many antislavery advocates supported the law, believing that ending the sale of imported slaves in the state would eventually cause the institution to atrophy and die. The measure also appealed to a significant number of slaveholders who reasoned that halting the import of slaves would force Kentucky slave buyers to purchase human chattel from within the state, keeping the value of their own bondsmen and women high.[8]

But if the nonimportation law of 1833 marked a victory for antislavery reformers, they also faced increased pressure to distinguish themselves from the increasingly vocal Northern abolitionists. In 1832, the year after Clay had been so inspired by his New Haven rhetoric, William Lloyd Garrison and his compatriots founded the New England Anti-Slavery Society, which, in turn, spawned the national American Anti-Slavery Society in 1833. Unwilling to contain their views safely in free states, they launched an aggressive campaign to convince white Southerners of slavery's evils. In the following years, Garrison and New York abolitionist Elizur Wright began mailing hundreds of thousands of antislavery pamphlets to white Southerners, who in turn became not only angered by the moral criticism in this literature but fearful that it might fall into the hands of enslaved African Americans and prompt them to insurrection. Thus, although voices of moderate opposition to slavery grew stronger in the state in the early 1830s, so did the intolerance of any antislavery sentiment deemed immoderate.[9]

One person who discovered this firsthand was James G. Birney. A native of Danville, Kentucky, he had joined the thousands of Upper South farmers who relocated to Dixie with their slaves in coffles and dollar signs in their eyes. Within a decade of establishing a cotton plantation in Huntsville, Alabama, in 1818, however, Birney became disenchanted with slavery for both moral and economic reasons. In 1833, he returned to Danville, where he founded the cumbersomely named Kentucky Society for the Gradual Relief of the State from Slavery. Promoting the voluntary, gradual, and total manumission of the state's enslaved people, the society attracted some sixty to seventy members. Birney freed his slaves the following year and paid them wages to continue working for him. In 1835, he founded the Kentucky Anti-Slavery Society, an affiliate of the abolitionist American Anti-Slavery Society, and made plans to launch an antislavery newspaper he called the *Philanthropist*. On the eve of publication, however, proslavery locals chased Birney's would-be printer out of town and threatened the editor himself. He lost hope in the prospect of enacting change in Kentucky and relocated his family and his newspaper to Cincinnati. Dejected, he wrote abolitionist Gerrit Smith that "Christians" may as well leave slaveholding states, as "there would be no cessation of the strife, until Slavery shall be exterminated, or liberty destroyed."[10]

Shortly after Birney moved across the Ohio River, Cassius Clay took his seat in the Kentucky General Assembly and found himself confronted with the question of slavery's future. A small but committed faction of moderate white Kentuckians pushed the legislature to call a convention during which they hoped to modify the state constitution to allow for the gradual phasing out of slavery in the state. Despite the opposition to slavery he developed as a college student at Yale, the freshman legislator flatly opposed calling such a meeting. Channeling the same fear that many slaveholders expressed in the aftermath of Nat Turner's rebellion, Clay spoke to his colleagues from the assembly floor, referring to the twin threats posed by rebellious slaves and zealous abolitionists. "Is this a time [to consider such a measure]," he asked, "when the arm of the law is averted, and deeds of violence go unredressed throughout the land, when a horde of radical incendiaries are springing up in the North, threatening to spread fire and blood through our once secure and happy homes?" He denounced abolitionists for demanding that the US Congress address issues of slavery, decrying the "spirit of dictation and interference arising in the North" and the "genius of discord speaking in threatening accents in the federal legislature."[11]

Clay also expressed frustration at what he saw as the ineffectual and futile efforts of colonizationists, describing their efforts as "lame and feeble." He did, however, admit his ambivalence about slavery into the public record for the first time, equivocating: "I am bound to confess that there was a time when I favored gradual emancipation." Referring to his time in New England, he explained, "Having had some experience of society in the state of slaveholding and non-slaveholding communities, to say nothing of the moral and social condition, in a political point of view, I am candid in saying that the free states have largely the advantage." The prospect of possible emancipation would, however, at least at that moment, present a danger to social and governmental stability. Unsure of how slavery could be ended orderly and safely, he opined: "I almost cease to hope—I almost give way to the belief that slavery must continue to exist, till, like some uneradicable disease, it disappears with the body that gave it being."[12]

This public disavowal revealed that whatever his previous and future views on Garrison and the abolitionists, in the mid-1830s, Clay shared the feeling of most white Americans that radical antislavery was a dangerous nuisance. In this opinion, Clay was right in step with his fellow lawmakers. That spring, the legislature passed a resolution, which Clay supported, denouncing abolitionists as fanatics, condemning them for creating "a spirit of discontent, insubordination, and perhaps insurrection within the slave population of the country." Unsurprisingly, the motion for a constitutional convention also failed.[13]

In a time when state general assembly elections occurred yearly, running for office was an arduous and fickle business. Cassius lost his bid for reelection in 1836 when Democratic candidates swept Madison County. He reluctantly returned home to his farming and commercial interests. Happily, when he ran for election again in 1837, voters returned him to Frankfort. Not all was well, however, as Clay's preoccupation with his political career caused his businesses to suffer. He slipped into debt as his sawmill and ferry failed. The situation grew worse when he assumed some of the debts of his bankrupt brother-in-law, William Rodes, the husband of his sister Paulina. Clay also faced difficulties with his labor force. The number of enslaved people at Clermont had expanded when Sidney Clay died suddenly in 1834 and Cassius took several of his brother's enslaved laborers into his own household. One of them—a man named Luke—broke into a Madison

County residence and stole twenty dollars, a felony that could have garnered him a whipping and possibly even hanging. As Green Clay's will stipulated should be done with errant slaves, Cassius sold him "to the South" several months later for $850, because, as he explained to his brother, "he was too outrageous to keep." He also had trouble controlling those bondsmen whom Sally had loaned to him. "Ma's negroes mostly drink to excess and I don't want them," he complained to Brutus, "so if you can let me have four hands who don't drink, send them over [to the mill]." Members of the Clay family considered their slaves as a common labor pool that they could shuffle among their households as needed.[14]

In 1838, Cassius and Mary Jane decided to relocate from rural Madison County to the more cosmopolitan city of Lexington. With the birth of baby Green in 1837, the young couple had started their family. After several years of country life, Mary Jane longed to be closer to her family. Much to Cassius's consternation, she "commanded" that they move back to her hometown, "assuming to herself authority not granted by the constitution or the laws of marriage," as he wrote irritably in his ledger book. The upside of the move, though, and one that Cassius may himself have calculated, was that the consistently Whig leanings of a commercial center like Lexington might provide a more stable base for his political aspirations.

Clay purchased one of the city's handsomest residences, a house known as Morton Place, situated on North Limestone Street, just outside of downtown. The couple's entrance into Lexington society, however, belied the sorry state of their finances. Unbeknownst to most locals, Cassius could buy the home only because Brutus cosigned the note. By this time, he was borrowing money from his financially stable brother with steady frequency. Despite the change of address, his financial troubles followed him. In 1840, George Weddle, his partner in the Madison mill, went bankrupt. Clay had provided the security for over $8,000 of Weddle's loans, and the mill failure plunged him even deeper in debt. Several creditors sued Clay, forcing him to borrow yet more money from Brutus.[15]

His money problems did nothing to quell Clay's political ambitions, however. In 1840, with Lexington now his legal residence, he decided to run for one of three Fayette County seats in the state legislature. But the move to a new political district brought Cassius into the orbit of the formidable Wickliffe family. Robert Wickliffe, dubbed the Old Duke, was the wealthiest and one of the most powerful men in the state. With his sons following closely behind, Wickliffe cast a powerful presence within politics in Kentucky. In the legislative race of 1840, two of the county's three seats were considered to be locked up by incumbents, which left as Cassius's main opponent for the third the Harvard-educated Robert Wickliffe Jr.

As his popular moniker implied, the "young Duke" often held the same political positions as his father.[16]

As the campaign of 1840 commenced, thirty-year-old Cassius differentiated himself from the younger Wickliffe by arguing against the possible repeal of the nonimportation law of 1833, an issue the legislature was reconsidering. He hoped this stance would be a winning one in Lexington, where many slave owners believed that the law kept the value of their slave property high. Robert Wickliffe Sr. did not concur. Though he was the largest slaveholder in the state, Wickliffe had once served as the first president of the Kentucky Colonization Society, renouncing the organization once slavery opponents began to dominate the group. By 1840, he considered colonization as nothing but a ruse to slowly end slavery and had grown suspicious of any means that might limit the institution's growth. He declared the nonimportation law to be an "abolition tinder-box." For his part, Robert Wickliffe Jr. remained silent on the issue, but this strategy only led voters to believe that he shared his father's stance, thereby setting this matter as the primary point of policy difference between himself and Clay.[17]

The campaign of 1840 prompted the debut of the antislavery stance that would define Cassius Clay's political career. Going far beyond the issue of slave importation, he built his platform on the far more expansive contention that the institution of slavery was economically deleterious for the state of Kentucky. This position marked a distinct turning point in his public views on the issue. Only a few years earlier, Clay had declared antislavery too dangerous a sentiment to be entered into political debate. During his second term, he had revealed some hint of opposition to slavery when he complained that proslavery lawmakers tended to be the least likely to support internal improvements and sound currency, the two key Whig issues. By the campaign of 1840, however, he adopted the argument that slavery should end because it was an economic blight on Kentucky, a position that would characterize his views through the Civil War.[18]

During the campaign of 1840, Clay oriented the issue of the law of 1833 away from questions of whether the policy would whiten the state or how it would affect slaveholders, instead focusing on the impact slavery had on white workers. Slave labor, he began to argue, both undercut and demoralized the labor of working-class whites. It reduced their wages because they were competing with laborers who had no leverage to set their rate of pay, allowing employers to maintain the upper hand. Furthermore, because in a slave economy work was associated with Blackness and unfreedom, it undercut the very dignity of white labor. By the late 1830s, the idea that slavery demeaned white labor and, in turn, retarded broader economic and social development of the slave states had become a common trope. Such logic was a prime feature in the economic antislavery critique, and Cassius Clay was not the first person to find the economy and values of Kentucky wanting in comparison to those of the North.[19]

Alexis de Tocqueville singled out the Bluegrass State to illustrate slavery's adverse effects in the second volume of *Democracy in America*, published in 1836. In 1831, the same year Clay arrived in New Haven, the noted French political observer journeyed west on the Ohio River by steamboat, chronicling the pronounced differences between the states on either side. "The traveler who, positioned at the center of the Ohio River, drifts downstream to its junction with the Mississippi is," he asserted, "steering a path between freedom and slavery, so to speak, and has only to look about him to judge immediately which is the more beneficial for mankind." "On the left bank of the river the population is sparse; occasionally a troop of slaves can be seen loitering in half-deserted fields," the Frenchman observed. "Society seems to be asleep; man looks idle while nature looks active and alive." In Ohio, "by contrast, a confused hum announces from a long way off the presence of industrial activity; the fields are covered by abundant harvests; elegant dwellings proclaim the taste and industry of the workers; in every direction there is evidence of comfort; men appear wealthy and content; they are at work."[20]

According to Tocqueville, it was not just that Kentucky lacked overall economic development but that the condition of slavery, as a marker of inferiority and servitude, debased any labor performed by anyone in a slave society. "On the left bank of the Ohio," he insisted, "work is connected with the idea of slavery, on the right bank, with the idea of prosperity and progress; on the one side, it is a source of humiliation, on the other, of honor; on the left bank of the river no white laborers are to be found as they would dread to look like slaves; they have to look to Negroes for such work." "On the right bank," alternately, "the whites extend their energy and intelligence to every sort of work." According to such logic, middle- and upper-class Kentucky whites' disdain for labor stifled the spirit of enterprise throughout the state.[21]

Cassius Clay understood that Tocqueville's generalizations reflected real labor competition between white and Black workers in slave states. Kentucky's white workers competed with enslaved laborers for both manufacturing jobs and agricultural work. Factory owners throughout the state relied on enslaved laborers to work in ironworks, at textile shops that made the rough "Kentucky jeans" worn by many Deep South slaves, and on the rope walks that turned hemp into ship cordage rigging and bagging for Southern cotton. Enslaved laborers also performed backbreaking work in the state's coal and salt mines. Factory and mine owners often leased enslaved workers from slave owners, usually on a yearly basis, but sometimes by the month, the week, or even the day. Whatever the rental term, the cost to the factory owners was significantly less than the wages they paid to white workers. These bondsmen routinely worked alongside white workers in factories, furnaces, and mills. Because white workers were seen as replaceable (or at least interchangeable) with enslaved laborers, they had little leverage to demand higher wages or better working conditions. This hybrid white and Black labor system thrived in the Bluegrass State and ensured that the owners and employers reaped the benefit of early industrial capitalism within Kentucky's antebellum economy.[22]

Clay and other critics argued that the damage wrought by slavery went far beyond individual white laborers, to impede the development of the larger economy and civic society. The specter of competition with slaves or from farmers who owned them drove thousands of Kentuckians to move to newer states such as Ohio, Indiana, and Illinois during the first decades of the nineteenth century, leaving the Bluegrass State with fewer citizens, a smaller tax base, and less congressional representation, along with fewer public resources and less incentive to create schools and other civic institutions.[23]

The state's public education system, in particular, suffered because of the inequality produced by slavery. New England states and those created from the Northwest Ordinance of 1787 boasted permanently funded public school systems maintained through substantial taxation by townships and localities. Kentucky, by contrast, followed Virginia's example of setting up a piecemeal system of academies. Funding was based on tuition, which cost an average of ten to twenty dollars annually, more than many poor and middling Kentucky families could afford. In 1838, the state created a system of common schools, but these were chronically underfunded by public tax dollars and plagued by state government mismanagement and misappropriated funds. The census of 1840 showed that Ohio, with double the population of Kentucky, had nearly nine times as many students enrolled its common schools. According to historian William Ellis, "The prevailing belief of the elites was that the commonwealth needed trained ministers, businessmen, lawyers, and other public servants and not an educated general population."[24]

Most pronounced in the counties with the highest rate of slave ownership, this phenomenon produced a hybrid system in which schools relied on both tuition and funding from the general public school tax. Tuition was high enough to put schooling out of reach for all but the wealthy, so relatively few students were subsidized by taxpayers who by and large reaped no benefits. Cassius Clay knew that the tendency of the state's slaveholding

Uneradicable Disease { 33

elite to protect their exclusive access to education protected their political dominance at the expense of broader civic and economic development. In New England and midwestern states, government officials acknowledged that education was key for the upward mobility of white farmers and workers, as well as for the establishment of a robust middle class and the development of well-informed citizens. The slave owners of Kentucky, however, formed a contented oligarchy, ruling the state without the opposition of a strong middle-class voting bloc.[25]

Cassius marshaled all of these themes as he tried to win the confidence of Fayette County voters. In contrast, Robert Wickliffe Jr. refused to take a position on the nonimportation law. Soon the contest escalated into a heated and more expansive discussion over the fate of slavery in the Bluegrass State. Despite the limited nature of Clay's critiques of the institution, the Wickliffes denounced him an "abolitionist at heart." Should Clay win the election, Robert Wickliffe Sr. promised, it would prompt the "abolitionists to get up a war between the slave holders and the non-slave holders," a result that would, he insisted, "accomplish the emancipation of every slave in the state." Such rhetoric produced what one Lexington man described as an "exceedingly animated & personal contest."[26]

After the first two days of voting, Cassius led the contest by thirty-two votes. Victory was in his sight. Rumors that the political fight might turn physical swirled around the state, reaching the ears of Sally Clay Dudley in Frankfort. No doubt remembering how her son's altercation with John Declarey had ended years before, she wrote: "I heard a report in town that you and Rob. Wickliffe were expected to fight; altho' I can't believe it; still I feel unhappy knowing your disposition & sense of honour." Sally need not have worried this time. In the end, Cassius eked out a narrow victory. With this he gained entrance, once again, into the state government as well as into the Wickliffes' eternal bad graces.[27]

Though he had initiated it out of political expediency, Cassius quickly expanded the antislavery platform he had launched during the campaign and began to develop it in ways that would provide the ideological basis for his career. Shedding any trace of tentativeness, Clay issued a protracted public statement a month after the election in which he declared: "I believe *slavery* to be an *evil*—an evil morally, economically, physically, intellectually, socially, religiously, politically—evil in its inception, in its duration, and in its catastrophe—an unmixed evil, without palliation or defense, save in *necessity*."[28]

He continued to advocate for slavery's gradual end on the basis of its negative effect on the economy and the prospects of white workers in Kentucky. The law of 1833, which was still under debate, had been crucial, he claimed, in "roll[ing] back the tide of black population, which like a lava flood, threatened to ruin our Kentucky." "Every slave imported drives out a free and independent Kentuckian," he warned. Realizing that white Kentuckians had no patience for antislavery radicalism, however, he took pains to make clear that he was opposed to any extreme measures. "Still I am no emancipationist, far less an 'abolitionist,'" he insisted, "but like nine-tenths of the slave-holders in all the world, rest now where I was in the beginning." Linking himself to reformers who wanted some safe, slow, if undefined, end to the institution and also making clear that he was no racial egalitarian, he insisted: "My sympathies are for the white man—bone of my bone and flesh of my flesh—his industry, independence and comfort are the strength, the wealth, and the glory of the State."[29]

In classifying himself as an antislavery enslaver, Cassius embraced an identity that to twenty-first-century Americans seems both perplexing and duplicitous. But here Clay was representative rather than an exception. Many of the state's most outspoken critics of the peculiar institution, including John C. Breckinridge, John C. Young, and, most famously, Henry Clay, continued to hold slaves themselves. The seeming hypocrisy of this situation was to early nineteenth-century white Kentuckians simply a seemingly intractable reality. Human chattel composed much of their family assets on which they relied as a form of invested generational wealth as well as for all of their household and agricultural labor. In yet another paradox, slaves also conferred upon their owners a social and political status that they felt enabled them to engage in their war against slavery. As prominent Kentucky antislavery advocate Joseph Underwood explained, emancipators "cannot associate upon terms of equality, with their former slave-holding associates, who retain their slaves." Because most antislavery Kentuckians viewed the institution as a social rather than a humanitarian problem, they tended to see its evil as something inflicted on society at large, rather than on slaves themselves. Furthermore, they regarded it as a problem that could only be solved wholesale, rather than through individual acts of manumission. Although a few antislavery enslavers had embraced colonization, most believed that for the present, the safe and prudent course mandated that enslaved people be held in bondage until slavery ended for all.[30]

As his term began, Clay professed the superiority of a free labor society with even greater ferocity. In a speech during his first month in office in 1841, he spoke passionately and specifically about slavery's opportunity costs. "How many more years shall our hearts fail with the sickness of 'hope deferred' before we shall share in [the manufactured] creations of 'Yankee' genius?" he implored his fellow lawmakers. In the meantime, poor and middling whites were suffering because of slavery. "The white Kentuckian has been driven out by slaves, by the unequal competition of unpaid labor," he charged. "The mass of our people are uneducated . . . , the children of white Kentuckians [are] crying for bread, whilst the children of the African [are] clothed, fed, and laugh!"[31]

Clay aimed to tear the scales from the eyes of complacent Kentucky whites, but he did not intend to alarm them. He stressed his belief in the constitutional legality of slavery, eschewed any trace of sympathy for slaves themselves, and disclaimed radical intentions. "I am no reformer of governments," he insisted. "I leave slavery where I found it. It is not a matter of conscience with me; I press it not on the consciences of others." Clay, like most white Americans of his day, regarded African Americans—enslaved or free—as inferior and undesirable members of society. Unlike many white Americans, he did not, however, question their basic humanity. "Slaves, then, are not mere things," he asserted, "but persons; the foundation of representation: possessing all the feelings of humanity, and some of the privileges of free white citizens," though what these privileges were he did not say.[32]

In one sense, it seemed a propitious time to try threading the needle between antislavery radicals and proslavery conservatives. By 1841, most white Kentuckians recognized that the enslaved population of their state was in relative decline, not because of internal policies, but as a result of market forces. As the cotton kingdom boomed in the Deep South, demand for slaves to work the cotton and sugarcane fields exploded. Slaveholders from Upper South states such as Kentucky, who engaged in less intensive agriculture that required fewer laborers, now had the opportunity to sell their human chattel at great profit. Between 1830 and 1840, Kentucky enslavers sold nearly 20,000 slaves (about 12 percent of the enslaved population in 1830) to markets in the Deep South, and the census of 1840 revealed that the growth of the state's white population was outpacing that of African Americans for the first time since statehood.[33]

But Clay's efforts at nuance failed as, either out of anger at his outspokenness or fear of radicalism, proponents of slavery turned against him with ferocity. He later wrote that with his speech in 1841, he was "drawn into open war with the slave-power." "They knew their strength," he contended, "and wisely determined to crush all liberal thought in word, or progression in action, in the bud." In some ways, Clay presented his fellow elite white Kentuckians with a specter much more alarming than Northern agitators. As much as they might have feared rebellious slaves, they were more frightened by Clay's class-based appeal to their fellow white Kentuckians. As in the rest of the South, Kentucky slave owners were a numerical minority and maintained political control within the state politics and local judicial systems because of their wealth and social clout. They saw great danger in Clay's blatant appeal to the laboring class and the potential common ground he drew between free and enslaved laborers. In his speech of 1841, he pointed out that "nine-tenths of the free whites in Kentucky [were] non-slaveholders and *working men*." "Will they ever be so blind and infatuated as to lower the price of labor, and starve their own families," he demanded?[34]

This apparent attempt to sow class divisions immediately put many Kentucky slave owners on guard and made Clay politically vulnerable. Robert Wickliffe Sr. and Jr. wasted no time in antagonizing him out of both spite and principle. Sore and angry from losing to Clay in 1840, Robert Jr. again tarred his old opponent as an abolitionist. "Wickliffe has commenced war upon my course in the legislature," Cassius wrote angrily to Brutus in April 1841.

Later that month, at a proslavery gathering in Lexington, Clay and Wickliffe sparred face-to-face. On the podium, the "young Duke" once again accused Clay of being a puppet of Northern abolitionists. For his part, Cassius continued his attack on both Robert Wickliffe Jr. and his father. Wickliffe fought back, alleging that Cassius's in-laws disapproved greatly of their son-in-law's antislavery politics. Though this charge was true, Clay felt its sting. Wickliffe had not only struck at a personal level but had broken a taboo by introducing Mary Jane's name into his public speech. In an age when Americans considered the rough-and-tumble world of politics to be the exclusive province of men, virtuous women were not to be invoked, even rhetorically. Clay considered Robert Wickliffe Jr.'s rhetorical choice positively "inadmissible." Both men had ventured beyond the political and delved into the personal. Each believed that the other had egregiously offended their honor, a situation that among Kentucky gentlemen had only one logical end. In short order, Clay challenged Wickliffe to a duel.[35]

Rumors of the impending contest spread quickly. Eight years after Clay's first dueling challenge to John Declarey, Elisha Warfield harbored no doubts as to whether his hot-headed son-in-law would follow through with this engagement. Alarmed, he wrote to Brutus, asking him to "take such move in the matter as your judgment may direct." Whatever he felt about his son-in-law's evolving politics, he worried more about the stability of his family and his daughter's peace of mind: "Mary Jane knows nothing of our fears, nor will she, if we can prevent her from such disturbing intelligence," he wrote. Concerned that this duel might make his daughter a widow and leave her to parent the couple's two young children, Green and Mary Barr (who had been born in 1839), as well as the unborn child Mary

Jane was then carrying, Warfield begged Brutus to intervene. A few days later, J. Speed Smith, husband of Cassius's sister Eliza, also wrote Brutus to report that Cassius had sent a messenger to Wickliffe, presumably carrying a written challenge. Given Wickliffe's conduct, conceded Smith, "Cassius could do nothing less." Even if Clay's slavery politics were at odds with those of nearly everyone in his immediate and extended kin network, his relatives understood that the challenge to Cassius's honor undermined their integrity as well, and they banded together to support him. "Wickliffe must back out or there must be a fight . . . we must attend," demanded his brother-in-law, "[Cassius] is *right* and we must be there."[36]

Anticipation of a duel filled the correspondence and the parlor talk of Kentucky's elite denizens. "Great apprehensions are to be had as to the result," wrote Louisa Bullitt of Louisville. "Both are excellent shots and it must be fatal to one or both of the parties. . . . The Wickliffes are in great distress." This was no wonder, given their familiarity with the potential for tragedy such affairs of honor held. In 1829, Robert Wickliffe Sr.'s oldest son, Charles, had been tried for killing Thomas Benning, the editor of the *Kentucky Gazette*, in a duel. Swayed by a robust courtroom defense presented by Henry Clay, the jury acquitted him. Several months later, however, Charles challenged another editor to a duel on the grounds that he had insulted Robert Wickliffe Sr. in the pages of his newspaper. This time Charles did not live to see the inside of the courtroom.[37]

While duels were born of hastily made and ill-considered slights, their execution took careful planning. It was mid-May before both men could assemble a team of seconds and agree on terms. Wickliffe had as his second Albert Sidney Johnston, the future Confederate general who was then serving as the secretary of war for the Republic of Texas. Cassius's second was William McKee, a member of another prominent Bluegrass family who had attended Transylvania University with Clay. A two-page memorandum outlined the precise conditions for the meeting. It stipulated that the duel would take place on May 13 and that the duelists would use "smooth-bored pistols, with barrels not exceeding ten inches in length, nor carrying less than thirty balls to the pound, with flint or percussion locks." Clay and Wickliffe were to stand exactly twenty-nine feet apart and to speak and act according to a very specific choreography and script. Last, in order to avoid a public spectacle, the agreement dictated that only select friends chosen ahead of time would be allowed to observe the affair.[38]

On the appointed day, Clay and Wickliffe met on the grounds of Locust Grove, the pastoral Louisville estate belonging to John Croghan. Adhering to their carefully delineated protocol, the men squared off and exchanged shots. Fortunately, both missed their mark. The duel might have ended here, but Cassius insisted that his honor had yet to be satisfied. Wickliffe's transgression of bringing Mary Jane and her family into public political debate was, he insisted, too great, and Cassius demanded another round. Thankfully, however, Johnston and McKee negotiated an end to the conflict, and both Clay and Wickliffe lived to walk away from the dueling ground. "No apology was made on either side, and no reconciliation was proposed; and we left the ground enemies as we came," Cassius later wrote. In the aftermath of the duel, Robert Wickliffe Jr., feeling that the affair had diminished Clay, wrote to his brother-in-law: "His reputation for talent and being dangerous is not so great this year as it was the last. His friends do not crow quite so loud and even the bullies and the blacklegs no longer speak of him as the 'Little Black Bull with hair on his back three inches long.'" But in this, Wickliffe was wrong. As news of the incident spread, outsiders accorded both men credit for bravery and honor in the defense of their personal reputations. The *Louisville Journal*'s assessment that they had "displayed great coolness" was reprinted in newspapers as far away as Richmond, Virginia, and New Orleans. The duel had served its purpose, and each man considered it a success, believing that he had gotten the better of the other.[39]

Soon, however, Wickliffe Jr. would get the better of Cassius. In the election of 1841, Clay wanted victory as never before, writing Brutus, "I must not be beaten in this race. . . . [It] is the crisis in my life and I must meet it or fall." But fall he did. Whatever ambivalence toward slavery might have existed in Kentucky, there was not enough outright opposition to make it a winning issue. If Clay was to harness antislavery politics to electoral victory, he would have to seek a different constituency.[40]

The conflict with Wickliffe provided a lesson for Cassius. His antislavery theory, which rested on census figures, crop yields, and real estate values, may have emerged from cold, hard logic, but the process of advocating for abolition would inevitably become personal and emotional. As a slaveholder within a larger kin network of slaveholders, his antislavery crusade was bound to put him into conflict with the most powerful people in Kentucky. The experience also taught him that defending his views would take all of his seemingly preternatural courage and that his antislavery fight would have to be conducted within the honor-driven framework that defined his slaveholding society.[41]

Chapter 3
Lamentable Inconsistencies

Cassius Clay's electoral defeat in 1841 left him a broken man in more ways than one. His political career seemed stalled, perhaps even dead. Even more worrying, his personal finances remained in shambles as his obligations had grown. With the birth of baby Sallie earlier that year, he now supported a wife and three young children, as well as households in two counties. He owed a $6,000 payment on a banknote, cosigned by his brother, that was due January 1, 1842. Filled with shame as he sat in his handsome Lexington residence—the same house financed by Brutus three years earlier—Cassius wrote to him on Christmas Eve: "You have been so much to me that I am mortified that I am unable to meet this debt and that your credit will suffer by me."[1]

Desperate, he suggested selling his most liquid assets: the enslaved African American men and women considered his personal chattel property. Clay found himself in the ranks of the thousands of slaveholders in American history whose financial mismanagement made the fate of their human assets all the more precarious. At the time, he claimed ownership of thirty-two enslaved people, most of whom, by the terms laid out in his father's will, he held in trust for his heirs. He did own nearly a third of these men and women outright, however, and was free to sell them. He also owned thousands of acres of valuable central Kentucky land, but in the early 1840s, human chattel was eminently easier to divest. Lexington, fast becoming one of the South's most important slave markets, was a prime destination for interstate traders who both bought and sold slaves for use in the cotton and sugar fields of the Deep South. Indeed, in the 1840s, white Kentuckians sold an average of 2,000 slaves a year, a number that jumped to 3,400 in the 1850s. The city's auction block, located in an area known as Cheapside adjacent to the Fayette County courthouse, lay several blocks south of Cassius's home. A few weeks later, he informed Brutus that he had "not yet sold any one negro" but advised him: "If you know of a buyer send him down." He hoped he might fetch as much as $300 per sale. There is no evidence to suggest that Cassius ultimately followed through on this suggestion, however; it is likely that Brutus covered his younger brother's debts yet again.[2]

Amid his financial woes, however, a bright spot appeared in March 1842 with the arrival of a letter from Salmon P. Chase, expressing his admiration for Clay's outspoken opposition to slavery. Chase, a New Hampshire native who moved to Ohio in his youth, was then a Cincinnati attorney on his way to becoming one of the nation's leading political antislavery reformers. From his vantage in a major Ohio River port city, he could see daily the realities and legalities of slavery and freedom bump up against each other. Though Ohio was a free state, Cincinnati was a way station for steamships carrying enslaved people and their owners from one destination to another. The city had a dual personality regarding slavery. In the 1830s, it had been home to Lane Theological Seminary, a cradle of abolitionist theology and thought. The city was also a major hub of the Underground Railroad and provided a temporary haven for many of the hundreds of Kentucky slaves who attempted escape each year. But Cincinnati was also home to thousands of racially conservative whites who held more sympathy for the slaveholders across the river than for the white abolitionists or free African Americans in their midst.

James Birney discovered this less generous side of the city when he had attempted to print his newspaper, the *Philanthropist*, there in 1835. In 1836, a mob raided his printing office and destroyed his press, dumping its parts into the Ohio River as law enforcement and Cincinnati's mayor looked on in silent approval. When another mob headed toward Birney's home, Chase sprang to action, meeting the crowd in Birney's doorway and barring their entry. Chase was motivated by what he saw as popular infringement on the civil and property rights of its proponents even more than the cause of abolition. After the destruction of the *Philanthropist*, Chase represented Birney in his lawsuit seeking damages against the members of the mob.[3]

Chase drew closer to both Birney and the abolitionist cause when, in 1837, the editor asked for his assistance in defending a Black woman named Matilda who was then working in his household. Unbeknownst to Birney when he hired her, Matilda was an escaped slave living in Cincinnati in violation of the Fugitive Slave Act of 1793. Chase agreed to represent Matilda and her right to freedom in court. In doing so, he presented an argument he would reuse in subsequent cases that would eventually become known as his "positive law" theory. The basis of his reasoning was that the US Constitution left control of all domestic institutions, including slavery, to the states. Because Ohio was, by the terms of the Northwest Ordinance, a free state, its authorities had no duty to enforce laws pertaining to slavery. "Slavery is admitted, on all hands to be contrary to natural right," Chase claimed, and "wherever it exists at all, it exists only in virtue of positive law."

Lamentable Inconsistencies

It was, he argued, "a right, which in its own value, can have no existence beyond the territorial limits of the state that sanctions it." While this argument proved ineffective in Matilda's case, he would use his "positive law" theory again in coming years to defend other fugitives and their abettors.[4]

Chase eventually broadened this rationale to argue not only that the privilege and purview of matters pertaining to slavery policy belonged exclusively to states but also that it was unconstitutional for the federal government to sanction, protect, or extend the institution to existing areas (such as Washington, DC) and new territories under its jurisdiction. This philosophy would later become the legal basis for the Free-Soil movement and later Republican thought when their political platforms claimed that federal efforts to defend slavery by returning slaves (fugitive or not) violated states' rights.

In his brilliant, if often unsuccessful, arguments, Chase was a Kentucky slaveholder's worst nightmare, doing his best to make the Fugitive Slave Act of 1793 unenforceable. Accepting several fugitives' cases between 1837 and 1845, Chase became known as the Attorney General for Runaway Negroes.

It's no wonder, then, that in the early 1840s, Chase became intrigued by Clay, who was so brazenly denouncing and frightening his fellow slaveholders using much the same logic.[5] In the spring of 1842, the two initiated a correspondence that grew to friendship and political collaboration spanning several decades.

Exchanging letters with Chase alleviated the increasing sense of isolation Cassius felt as an antislavery man in a proslavery society. He told Chase gratefully in March 1842: "You have aroused the depths of my spirit. . . . I find little sympathy here and with you I may speak as not to a man in the dark having neither eyes or ears." Chase proved to be a sympathetic confidant, but Cassius still felt the need to justify his decision to remain in Kentucky rather than departing for the free states and abandoning his slaveholding, as James Birney had done. "I shall stand by the land of my birth and rise or fall with her," he told Chase. "Many noble Kentuckians have fallen as I have—and left the state: That is all wrong—here is the place for me."

While some of his fealty for his state was genuine, based on attachment to family and place, it was also a matter of finances and logistics. Cassius told his new friend: "If I leave the state I lose my caste—if I carry my doctrines into execution, I am branded as an abolitionist and lose my power to do good. Such are the difficulties which surround me." Clay also understood that as a member of the social elite he derived status from participating in the very practice he was trying to end. Perhaps most importantly, his wealth was bound up in both the enslaved men and women and the land he owned in Kentucky, most of which, by the terms laid out in his father's will, was entrusted to future generations of Clays. These people served as collateral for his current debts and future loans. Lacking the ability to pay off his debts, and without other liquid assets or the inclination to work toward rebuilding his business interests, Cassius could not have left Kentucky even if he had wanted to.[6]

Chase and Clay were men of contrasting personalities. Chase was staid, stolid, and calculating, while Cassius was spontaneous and passionate. But in addition to their common disdain for slavery, both men had a keen sense of political ambition. They also shared a similar reading of the US Constitution. Hewing to the Constitution as a framework also meant that both Clay and Chase shared a vision for ending slavery carefully, legally, and with as little disruption to the social and economic order as possible. "I wish to do nothing hasty or inconsiderate—revolutions should be slow—and in pace with the wills of the people," Cassius told Chase.[7]

Clay also captured the attention of another antislavery reformer, Horace Greeley. In 1841, Greeley had launched the *Tribune*, a daily newspaper that quickly grew in political and social influence, both locally and nationally. In its pages, he touted the benefits of an activist Whig government, land reform measures including a homestead act that would make western lands readily and cheaply available to settlers from overcrowded northeastern cities, and various other social reforms. Greeley was particularly preoccupied with the upheaval that the transition from skilled to wage labor presented for northeastern workers. Within this framework, he developed a critique of slavery both as a moral wrong and as a source of unfair labor competition for whites. That Clay was denouncing slavery along similar lines from within a slave state intrigued and excited Greeley; he hastened to publish the Kentuckian's speeches and letters in his fledgling newspaper. The *New-York Tribune*, with its rapidly rising circulation, helped bring Clay to the attention of the Northern reading public.[8]

This national exposure convinced Clay to continue beating his antislavery drum. In 1843, the state general assembly once again considered repealing the ban on importing slaves of 1833. No longer able to fight from within the legislature, he took up his pen and wrote a series of three letters for publication in the *Lexington Intelligencer*, a small Whig-leaning newspaper, in which he urged legislators to uphold the ban. These missives bore a seemingly incongruous combination of racist fearmongering and genuine compassion for African American slaves. Clay's first letter reiterated his past argument that the nonimportation law was critical to maintaining a majority white population in Kentucky and presented a specter of an alternative scenario in which white Kentuckians would, like Southerners in places with higher slave densities such as South Carolina, need to be prepared to "crush domestic insurrections." He also warned, "Our morals are to be still more corrupted" by the prospect of miscegenation, thanks to the debauchery of white men, producing "more mulattoes to stand as eternal curses, before the lovely eyes of our wives, our daughters, our mothers—most damning monuments of our self-abasement and crime, diluting the boasted purity of our Saxon blood."[9]

While his admonitions about racial amalgamation matched the most racist thinking of the time, Clay also managed to express sympathy for the plight of enslaved individuals. Much of his second letter to the *Lexington Intelligencer* laid out comparisons between slavery in ancient civilizations and that which existed in the present-day South, castigating the US slave laws as oppressive in comparison for the utter lack of human rights they accorded the enslaved. By the time he penned his third letter for the newspaper, the general assembly had voted once again to maintain the ban on slave importation; Cassius used his platform to defend himself from the charges leveled by his enemies that his was a "*factious* and *dangerous* man." In closing, he announced, with great self-importance: "I retire to that privacy, where the public ban has placed me, where baring too boldly my breasts to the shafts, which, piercing me, a common soldier, perhaps yet saved my country."[10]

But angry Kentucky slavery proponents, incensed by Clay's visceral warnings and accusations, would not let him "retire" in peace. Rumors spread about a group of men calling themselves the Black Indians who threatened him with violence and "summary punishment." News of both Clay's letters and the public anger against him garnered the attention of antislavery newspapers in the North, including William Lloyd Garrison's *Liberator*, which reported that both Clay and the editor of the *Intelligencer* faced threats to their property and were "told that they would be lynched." In response, Clay began carrying a set of pistols and a Bowie knife with him wherever he went. It was not long before he found occasion to use them.[11]

In the summer of 1843, Clay offered to campaign for Garrett Davis, a Whig incumbent candidate for Kentucky's Eighth district congressional seat. Davis's opponent was Clay erstwhile nemesis, Robert Wickliffe Jr. Tensions heightened once again between the old enemies when Wickliffe charged Davis and his fellow Whigs with gerrymandering the district to increase their odds of winning. Clay attended a number of political debates between Davis and Wickliffe throughout the summer, each time loudly refuting Wickliffe's claims. Finally, hostilities erupted in August when, at a political rally north of Lexington at a location known as Russell's Cave,

Wickliffe once again repeated these charges. As was his routine, Clay interrupted him to deny them.[12]

This time, however, Clay's protests were answered by a hulking figure who charged through the crowd, shouting, "Sir, it is not true." Clay turned to the man, whom he did not recognize, and accused him of lying. The stranger responded by repeating his insult and lunging at him with his umbrella. Clay tried to fend him off with his horsewhip, but the attacker wrested the whip away from him. Then Clay reached beneath his shirt, unsheathing the Bowie knife strapped to his chest, and told his assailant to back away.

When his warning went unheeded, Cassius landed a blow to the man's head before several members of the crowd managed to pull them apart. Then a bystander handed Clay's attacker a revolver, while another member of the crowd yelled for him to "shoot the damned scoundrel." Clay's assailant complied, firing a shot that miraculously hit the silver-lined scabbard of Clay's Bowie knife strapped to his chest. Knowing that his assailant likely had several more bullets at his disposal, Cassius charged at him again with his knife and began hacking away. By the time he had finished, Clay had, according to one newspaper's cataloging of his gruesome handiwork, "cut his left eye out, his left ear entirely off, and inflicted a severe wound in his shoulder near the corner of his collar bone."[13]

It was a ghastly scene, even by the standards of rural Kentuckians, who were accustomed to violent altercations. One bystander later told his brother that it was "the most desperate personal encounter I have ever witnessed." Clay's foe had been "about the head, face, and shoulders . . . literally cut to pieces, the blood running from every direction from every wound down his body." The mutilated man, now unable to shoot, stood stunned while several members of the crowd grabbed Clay and beat him with fallen hickory limbs, a chair, and whatever other nearby objects they could find. The affray finally ended when several men threw Clay's attacker over a steep embankment to keep him out of harm's way. Only later did Clay learn the man's identity. His name was Samuel Brown, and he was a New Orleans–based postal agent serving under the leadership of Postmaster General Charles A. Wickliffe, Robert Wickliffe Jr.'s uncle. The news led Clay to believe that the Wickliffes had hired Brown to provoke and kill him.[14]

The fallout from the episode was swift. Although Brown had somehow survived his maiming, the Wickliffes convinced the Commonwealth of Kentucky to try Cassius for "inciting mayhem." Worse than the legal charges, however, was the public disapprobation for use of a knife that was considered a particularly disreputable weapon The Bowie knife, named for Rezin Bowie, the Louisiana settler who designed the original prototype, featured a single blade, 9¼ inches long and 1½ inches wide, to be used as a hunting tool. It gained greater notoriety when Rezin's more famous brother, Alamo hero James Bowie, used one to kill a man on a Mississippi River sandbar in 1827. The "Arkansas toothpick," as the knife was widely called, quickly became the defensive weapon of choice for men on the American frontier. But the knife's use in fights became so notorious and widespread that several states banned its use for all purposes except hunting; some prohibited the Bowie knife's sale altogether and mandated a lengthy prison sentence for its use in fighting. In precincts away from the western frontier, the weapon became associated with savagery and a weak civil society, in that the knife, as one London newspaper put it, enabled any wielder to act as "judge, jury, and executioner of his own law."[15]

The duel between Wickliffe and Clay a year earlier, while controversial, had at least adhered to a gentlemanly code of conduct. Cassius's savage use of a Bowie knife, however, cast a pall of over the Russell's Cave incident. As the news spread to national outlets, the press was quick to convey its disgust, variously dubbing it a "Monstrous Affray" and "a bloody recontre." "Both parties are probably to blame, as usually happens in such cases," assessed a New York newspaper, "but no *civilized* man would cut and hack an opponent with his knife. The instinct of a brute would condemn such conduct." Both Clay and Brown contended that they had only acted in self-defense. A number of witnesses, however, reported that Clay had attacked Brown with the Bowie knife before the postal agent fired his first shot, while Clay published a letter outlining his version of events, asserting that Brown was the initial aggressor. "Knowing that he could shoot me five times in quick succession," Clay explained, "I closed in on him and cut away in good earnest until we were parted."[16]

The damage to Clay's reputation came just as his fame was growing in the North. He knew that antislavery sentiment was strongest in the urban centers of the Northeast and Northwest, areas where the culture of honor was becoming more associated with personal restraint and where his actions would cause people to doubt his character and his judgment. As he wrote to Salmon Chase a month after the altercation: "I think the public now agree that I saved my life by action, when nonresistance would have been fatal." "I know the sentiment which prevails in your country against the duel and affray and have long since acknowledged the miserable mockery of honor and valour which the duel would affect," he added, "but I must confess that I have not as yet disciplined my feelings and self-control as to be insensible to the mortifications which result in a community like ours from taking the high ground which reason and humanity dictate—yet I trust that I am fast attaining that point and that ere long I shall give the force of my example against this relic of barbarous times."[17]

It is somewhat of an irony then, that Cassius Clay came to rely on the methods and the culture of the slaveholder in his crusade against the peculiar institution. Historians have long connected Southern violence to slaveholding and mastery, noting that the threat of force was not only the mechanism by which Southern enslavers coerced their bondspeople to work and prevented them from revolting but also characterized their "personal insecurity in the absence of law and order" in the rural South. By contrast, middle-class Northerners and westerners for various reasons, including evangelical religion, market capitalism, and even intellectual movements such as transcendentalism, had begun to embody a different set of values that focused on individual rather than community standards. But in the early republic, what continued to matter most to Southerners and westerners was the esteem in which their neighbors held them. More than political agreement or religious accord, what counted was respect for a person's character, integrity, and, for men, manhood. As Clay wrote later in his memoirs: "I knew full well that the least show of the 'white feather' was not only political but physical death. So it was with me here policy rather than impulse. I wanted to show those who lived by force that it would be met at all times, and in all places, with force." He understood that he lived in a world where a man's honor remained the primary currency of social acceptance, and his ability to defend himself physically was what guaranteed his very survival.[18]

Fortunately for Clay, the Northern horror at his knife-wielding was offset by confusion over the nature of the dispute with Brown. "Mr. Clay has been denouncing slavery in its strong hold, and probably the assault grew out of his freedom of speech on an interdicted topic in slave holding communities," speculated the *Cleveland Herald*. And though the immediate topic of controversy had been about political mechanics, as Cassius himself maintained to Chase, Brown's attack on him would not "have been countenanced by the public for a moment had it not been for the deep seated enmity cherished towards me on account of my views upon slavery." That preaching the antislavery gospel in a slave state was dangerous business became even clearer when, two months after the Russell's Cave incident, a would-be assassin shot at Clay as he was traveling, throwing him from his horse.[19]

When the Commonwealth of Kentucky charged him with "mayhem" and "intent to kill" by assault with a deadly weapon, Cassius had reason to worry about his fate before a jury of his peers. Fortunately, however, he was able to retain the legal counsel of his illustrious distant cousin Henry Clay. The more famous Clay had resigned his US Senate seat in 1842 in preparation for his all-but-certain nomination to the presidency in 1844. At home in Lexington, he tended his farming and business interests, and in the fall of 1843, he offered his legal services to Cassius. He might have done so out of loyalty to his distant kinsman, but the more likely reason was that he, too, bore a political grudge against the Wickliffe family. Whatever the case, Henry Clay formed an association with Cassius that he would come to regret within the next year.[20]

The participation of the great "Harry of the West" ensured that newspapers across the nation granted Cassius's trial good coverage. Henry's defense of Cassius marked the first time the elder statesman had appeared in the Fayette County courtroom in over a dozen years, but he quickly proved that he had lost none of his flair before the bar. His eloquent closing defense lasted a full hour and a half, through which the audience and jury sat "with breathless interest, save when admiration and delight were too highly excited to be constrained by a court of justice," as Henry bade the jury members to disregard their feelings regarding Cassius's political views and to consider only whether he, like any other proper Kentucky man, ought to have the right to defend his own life with honor. "Standing, as he did, without aiders or abettors, and without popular sympathy; would you have had him meanly and cowardly fly? Or would you have had him to do just what he did do—stand in defense or there fall?" he demanded. Jury members recessed only briefly before acquitting Cassius Clay on all charges.[21]

The trial and his new connection with his illustrious cousin only elevated Cassius's national profile, and newspapers across the country seemed as ready as the Lexington jury to forgive his bloody deeds. In December, Horace Greeley offered Cassius the opportunity to write a letter for the *New-York Tribune*, an invitation he gladly accepted. In addition to the national exposure he would gain, Clay hoped that Southern newspapers would take notice of his arguments and reprint them, thereby reaching nonslaveholding whites who would then, in theory, turn against the institution. In his letter, Clay reiterated many of his earlier points to his imagined Southern audience. Slavery was bad for the enslaved, "depriving nearly three millions of men of the best gift of God to man—liberty," and bad for the whites, corrupting them "by necessary association with an abandoned and degraded race." He repeated his claims that slavery degraded labor and retarded public education, literacy, and skilled labor in the South and doubled down on his class-based condemnation of slavery, stating: "It is evil to the free laborer, by forcing him by the laws of competition—supply and demand—to work for the wages of the slave, food and shelter. The poor, in the Slave States, are the most destitute native population in the United States."[22]

Along with these familiar refrains, Cassius also offered a novel premise for his time. Emancipation, he argued, was safe for the white population of the South—much safer, in fact, than the current system of slavery. The region's Black population was increasing in proportion to that of whites, he explained, and this was bad for society. "The dullest eye can also see that the African, by association with the white race has improved in intellect, and by being transferred to a temperate clime, and forced to labor and to throw off the indolence of his native land, he is increasing in physical power," he contended. Meanwhile, he insisted, that "the white, by the same reversed laws, is retrograding in the same respects." The social stability that slaveholders so badly craved was impossible, Clay reasoned, and the end result would be the uprising of slaves they so badly feared.[23]

Emancipation, according to Clay, offered the only security for the slaveholding class. It need not be a frightening specter. "*Emancipation is entirely safe*," he intoned, as long as the freed men and women had the promise of some upward mobility. To this end, he cited examples of ancient civilizations—Athens, Sparta, Sicily—where slaves were freed and incorporated safely into society. He also pointed to British West India as a more recent successful example of emancipation, where the British employed "regiments of black men who make fine soldiers—protectors, not enemies of the empire." White Southerners had to look no further than the Northern states in their own country to see this as true. "One-sixth of the whole black race in America are already free! No danger or evil consequence has ensued form the residence of these 386,265 free blacks," he noted. "Who then will be so absurd as to contend that the liberation of the other five-sixths will endanger the safety or happiness of whites?" he asked.[24]

In the scheme of contemporary antislavery thought, Clay's arguments were extraordinary. At a time when many Northern states continued to pass laws prohibiting free African Americans from settling within their borders and when the colonizationist impulse was still strong among Southern antislavery moderates, it was highly unusual for a Southern slave owner to advocate for the safety of emancipation as well as the possible coexistence of whites and free African Americans. Yet however radical his vision of racial coexistence might have seemed, he also used the *Tribune* letter to underscore his conservative stance on the mechanisms by which emancipation could be enacted. "Congress having no power over slavery in the States, the States, each one for itself, where its Constitution does not forbid, certainly has and should exercise the power of purchase and emancipation," he stated. "In Kentucky the Constitution forbids the Legislature to act upon the subject. We must therefore look to a Convention, or that which I most hope, to voluntary emancipation."[25]

Alongside the published letter, Horace Greeley encouraged his readers to spread the Kentuckian's message: "We do hope Mr. Clay's burning appeal will be copied and read through the Slave States. He is himself a Southern man, who has grown up amid Slavery, and has a clear right to speak of its evils and suggest remedies. Will the South hear and heed him?" Despite his initial hopes, Clay seemed to think not, as the next month he wrote in dejected tones to Salmon Chase: "My letter to the *Tribune* has not been published in the slave states and I have not been able to force it into the press by any means; it has however been very generally read among the higher class of slave-holders meeting with both high appreciation and also bitter denunciation some have told me that they heard other say that I deserve the halter, and other said I would get it. But I will let them know that they may hurt the body but not suppress the aspirations of the soul." Nonetheless, the *Tribune* was an invaluable outlet for his ideas and brought Clay's Kentucky-focused campaign to end slavery to the attention of a national audience.[26]

Despite his respect for property rights and gradual emancipation, Clay also captured the imagination of abolitionists who espoused immediate emancipation. In 1843, William Lloyd Garrison began regularly covering Clay's activities in the pages of the *Liberator*. Garrison praised Cassius's outspoken condemnation of slavery, which he did "nobly and bravely." Clay reveled in the attention from the Northern abolitionist community, which, as historian Stanley Harrold has written, saw Southern emancipationists, even those more conservative than themselves, "as symbols of progress, as anti-slavery heroes, as proof of the effectiveness of the Northern abolitionist tactics, and as illustrations of the oppressiveness of slaveholders." Yet the support of Northern immediatists did not cause Clay to grow any more radical in his ideas on the basic constitutionality of slavery or in his general racial attitudes.[27]

Soon Clay's growing fame in the North began to underscore the uncomfortable duality of his thoughts and practice. In 1843, Marenda B. Randall of Woodstock, Vermont, wrote him a letter after reading his *New-York Tribune* article, in which she told him: "At the same time I am gratified and instructed by the fruit of your pen I am also pained by the report that you are a Slave-holder.... Can it be possible that Cassius M. Clay is a Slaveholder! Can a man be surrounded by such influences as shall induce him to write like an angel of mercy and at the same time be *acting* like an inhuman demon!!" Garrison also tempered his own praise, chastising Clay for continuing to hold his own slaves: "Let him emancipate his own slaves," he wrote in May 1843, "then will his rebukes come with redoubled force." In the *Liberator* in December 1843, he reprinted Clay's *Tribune* letter, praising him for his eloquent "thunder-tones" and his "rare courage and talent," but would not let hypocrisy stand unrecognized. "Mr. Clay," he penned, "not withstanding his vivid perceptions of the crime of slaveholding, is himself a slaveholder. Lamentable inconsistency!" Garrison proved unrelenting, pushing Clay to manumit his bondspeople, noting that "others [would] be induced by his example to 'go and do likewise.'"[28]

Garrison's reproach of Cassius Clay reflected a larger geographic and generational split emerging among opponents of slavery in the 1830s and 1840s. In the Kentucky in which Clay grew to adulthood, almost all of the leading antislavery voices were conservative, and many were slaveholders themselves. To the preceding generation, to be antislavery and a slaveholder was no measure of "lamentable inconsistency," as Garrison had put it, but rather a personal bind in which they found themselves, unable to free their slaves without serious risk to both their own financial security and, as they saw it, the larger social order. Theirs was an unfortunate situation from which they hoped future generations of Southerners would be spared when slavery would supposedly die a natural death.[29]

By the time Cassius joined the national antislavery conversation, however, it was clear that slavery was not dying. With the moral strains of Northern abolitionists growing ever louder, the logic of antislavery slave owning began to erode and became politically unsustainable in much of the United States. Even before the abolitionist criticism against him swelled at the end of 1843, Cassius initiated plans to manumit the nonentrusted slaves Green had willed him as well as four others whom he had inherited from his aunt. In a twist of fate dictated by trust law and Cassius's political aspirations, the same enslaved people who nearly went to the auction block only two years earlier now gained their freedom.

Cassius's actions certainly constituted an economic sacrifice. His financial situation was still tenuous, necessitating the recent sale of his Madison County mill. Indeed, he was so short of money that he could not afford to post the manumission bonds that the Commonwealth of Kentucky required to ensure that the freed slaves would not become wards of the state. He wrote his brother Brutus in January 1844: "I propose getting free papers from the county court for the slaves I have already liberated. . . . I wish you to be here to go my security which is in reality truly nominal." Cassius could not afford the loss of labor either. Several lines later, he asked Brutus, who regularly hired out a dozen or so enslaved individuals each year, to lend him "all [his] force" to help him clean his pasture for a couple of months over the summer.[30]

KNOW ALL MEN BY THESE PRESENTS, That we, *C. M. Clay and M. C. Johnson* are held and firmly bound unto the Justices of the Fayette County Court, in the penal sum of *$2400 ($400 for each slave).* Dollars, current money of Kentucky, the payment of which well and truly to be made, we bind ourselves, our heirs, &c. jointly and severally, firmly by these presents. Sealed and dated this *13* day of *January* 18*45*.

The Condition of the above obligation is such, that whereas, the County Court of Fayette, have this day permitted said *C. M. Clay* to Emancipate his slave,s *Scott, Riley, Dave Crews, David, Lotty & Zilla* Now, if said *Slaves* shall not, at any time hereafter, become a County charge, then this obligation to be void, else to be and remain in full force and virtue.

C. M. Clay ✱SEAL✱

M C Johnson ✱SEAL✱

The manumission bond for six of the nine individuals Clay manumitted in 1845. (Schomburg Center for Research in Black Culture, Jean Blackwell Hutson Research and Reference Division, New York Public Library)

Accounts of the number of enslaved people Cassius Clay manumitted in early 1844 vary, but the only known deed of emancipation, dated a year later, in January 1845, indicates that he freed nine individuals: Adam, Joe, Matt, Scott, Riley, "Henry's Dave," Dave Crews, Lotty, and Zilla. Years later, in his autobiography, he professed to have freed "all the slaves I inherited from my father," meaning only those not held in trust for his heirs or specified for the use of his two sisters. He also claimed to have emancipated thirteen others, which he purchased "to bring families together." "The buying and liberating of these slaves," he later wrote in his memoirs, "half of whom never entered my service cost me about ten thousand dollars." His decision to free his slaves at a time when he could ill afford to lose their labor or the collateral they represented, along with his threat to sell them just a few years earlier, seems to indicate that emancipating them was as much a political decision as a humanitarian one.[31]

Whatever his motives, Cassius's gambit to shore up his antislavery credentials worked. Newspapers around the country soon picked up the news and spread an abundance of misinformation regarding the scope of his act of manumission. The Washington *Whig Standard* announced Clay's intentions to "emancipate all his slaves in the present year." The same account appeared in newspapers in Vermont, New York, Ohio, and Mississippi. Other exaggerated accounts of Clay's actions held that he was on the verge of emancipating "some sixty of his slaves." In the *New-York Tribune*, Horace Greeley rejoiced that Clay had "just given new proof of the sincerity and depth of his conviction by *emancipating all his own slaves*—thus divesting himself of legally entrenched Rights of Property worth some $40,000."[32]

At home in Kentucky, Cassius's political enemies sought to reveal the more modest nature of his manumission. Members of the Wickliffe family scurried to the Fayette County courthouse, where they found records—presumably the bond of emancipation—which indicated that he had applied to free only nine slaves. "Cheap Philanthropy," a Lexington newspaper called it. "Shameful deception," cried the *Ohio Statesman*, dubbing Clay a "miserable humbugger." As criticism grew, Clay defended himself, saying, "It is true that I never emancipated but NINE slaves, but they were all I owned, and I have incurred as much responsibility here by emancipating at all, as if I had set free a thousand. I have about 25 more slaves which are entailed on my children by my late father in which I have a life estate only, and this is the cause why my emancipation has been magnified."[33]

The American political party system had also begun to reflect the receding middle ground of compromise on slavery. Whereas such abolitionists as William Lloyd Garrison rejected the idea of sullying the moral character of the antislavery movement in the dirty waters of politics, a critical number of reformers, ranging in their views from immediate abolitionists to those who were content with halting the institution's future spread, believed that their cause would be furthered most expediently through political legislation. A small group of these people found themselves increasingly unwilling to countenance the prevarication of both major parties on the issues of slavery. Many Whigs, especially, found themselves dismayed by the equivocation of their perennial leaders, including Henry Clay and Daniel Webster. They founded the Liberty Party in 1840 and in the same year nominated James Birney as their presidential candidate. Though Birney garnered fewer than 7,000 votes out of more than 2 million cast, some voters saw in the Liberty Party the possibility to eventually build a much broader antislavery political coalition by pulling antislavery politicians and voters away from both regular parties. Salmon Chase, who broke with the Whig Party in 1841, after the death of William Henry Harrison thrust slaveholder John Tyler into the White House, was a very enthusiastic supporter of the third-party strategy.[34]

From his first association with the Liberty Party, Chase worked to reorient the organization away from its more radical members, including Birney. At a party convention in Buffalo, New York, in 1843, Chase drafted a platform that included a general appeal for equal rights of African Americans but a moderate call for a gradual end to slavery. The platform reasserted the opinions Chase had spelled out in his legal cases that slavery was strictly a state rather than a federal matter. He aspired to recruit more Southerners like Clay for what he hoped would be a massive political project that would lead to slavery's demise. For his part, Clay applauded Chase's moderation. After the convention in Buffalo in 1843, he wrote to Chase approvingly: "It seems to me also that a strict adherence to the constitution is not only the only *just* mode of procedure—but the only *safe* one—the power of action lies in the *ballot box* and should be used. . . . If any other course is pursued you unite the south against and divide the north. For the great mass of mankind are united in affection merely to *security of property* and will oppose all obstructions or real reforms which jeopardize it by seeming or real revolution."[35]

Nonetheless, in early 1844, Clay rebuffed Chase's invitation to join the Liberty Party as it prepared to again run James Birney for president. His allegiance to the Whig Party ran deep, in part because he shared its economic agenda, but also because the party and its longtime leader, Henry Clay, had so defined his political and economic principles. Though the Whigs counted among their numbers both vehemently pro- and antislavery men, there were enough of the latter that Clay, like many members, believed their party to be the ideal political vehicle to extinguish the institution. It was, as he told Chase, "the party of liberty." "I believe that the great mass of the true lovers of liberty and conservative government belong to that class," he wrote him.[36]

As he redoubled his commitment to the Whigs, Clay took to the public stage again in Kentucky, this time to speak against the annexation of Texas. The Lone Star Republic had existed as a self-declared separate entity since its settlers had announced their independence from Mexico in 1836. Since then, Texans had lobbied the United States to annex the republic. Many American politicians and citizens alike bore reservations about doing so, however, not only because Mexico had never actually acknowledged the sovereignty of the Texas Republic but also because it would enter the Union as a slave state. After President John Tyler moved toward annexation in semisecret in April 1844, it became the central issue in that year's presidential contest. With Congress poised to consider the treaty, citizens throughout the country argued among themselves about the moral and political prudence of incorporating a slave territory that Mexico still claimed. In

April, the *New-York Tribune* published a letter in which Cassius argued that annexation of Texas was yet another symptom of "the devouring appetite of slavery." He denied "the constitutional possibility of Annexation of new Slave States to the Union" and advocated letting "slavery subside into its Constitutional limits."37

In May, Clay agreed to take the anti-Texas position in a debate in Lexington against Thomas F. Marshall, a Whig-turned-Democrat who had represented Kentucky's tenth district in Congress. During his short time in Washington, Marshall had distinguished himself through both his profligate drinking and his notable oratorical prowess. The two traits often coincided on the congressional floor in what his fellow congressman John Quincy Adams described in his diary as "alcohol evaporating in elegant language." Like Cassius, Marshall had carried his politics and honor outside of legislative halls when, in 1842, he wounded New York congressman and editor James Watson Webb in a duel. With two such notorious and effective speakers at the podium, the Lexington debate drew a large crowd. Marshall extolled the virtues of annexation for three hours, after which Cassius offered his rebuttal. Arguing that annexation was simply a destructive attempt to expand slavery, Cassius also added that it would be diplomatically reckless and cause intraparty strife, calling it "a revolutionary movement, despotic in its character, and fatal in its results."38

Though such sentiment did little to boost Clay's approval in Kentucky, where popular sentiment for annexation was strong, it did endear him to Northern Whig Party organizers. Citing his fame as a proponent of emancipation, opponent of annexation, and entertaining orator, a number of them, led by New York political operative Thurlow Weed, invited him to campaign for his cousin. Their hope was that Cassius Clay's endorsement would burnish Henry Clay's credibility among Northerners and prevent them from voting for Liberty Party candidate James G. Birney.39

Clay leapt happily into the turbulent world of presidential politics, and the Whigs' reliance on his growing fame played to his sense of self-importance and ambition. For several months in the summer and fall of 1844, with Mary Jane by his side, Clay stumped for his cousin throughout Ohio, Michigan, Massachusetts, and then New York, a Liberty Party stronghold where Weed especially desired his help. The trip also provided Mary Jane a brief respite from a household that was feeling emptier after the death of their infant (named Cassius) a year earlier. The first month of the campaign took the Clays through Ohio, where they traveled by locomotive and horse and buggy across the state. He made several stops in the Western Reserve region of the state, including Jefferson, the hometown of Whig congressman Joshua Giddings, before heading to Michigan.40

Enthusiastic crowds thronged him at each stop. Decked out in a dark blue suit double columned with gleaming brass buttons, Cassius, who had not often experienced friendly audiences, gloried in the torchlight parades and cavernous assembly halls filled to capacity. He reveled in the attention, glorying in the gasps the crowds emitted as he regaled them in his stentorian voice with his tales of the persecution and assassination attempts he faced back home in Kentucky and in their laughter at his humorous anecdotes. Throughout his stumping, Cassius garbed his antislavery policies in distinctly Whig clothing. When he attacked Southern slaveholders, it was not because of their inhumanity but because they had sabotaged the party initiatives of internal improvements and protective tariffs. He spoke more often against the Southern slave power than against slavery itself. When he opposed Texas annexation, it was on the grounds that Texas should be annexed only on the condition that it would be "without dishonor, without war, with the common consent of the Union, and upon just in fair terms."[41]

Such moderate reasoning proved popular with the rank-and-file Whigs but alienated Liberty Party sympathizers, who took him to task for supporting his slaveholding cousin. Such accusations put Cassius on the defensive but also gave him the opportunity to flaunt his recent decision to manumit some of his slaves. "Mr. Clay is indeed a Slave-holder—I wish he were not. Yet it does not become *me*, who have so lately ceased to be a Slaveholder myself, to condemn *him*," Cassius explained virtuously in a letter to W. I. McKinney, the mayor of Dayton, Ohio. The letter first appeared in the *New-York Tribune*, after which newspapers around the country reprinted it, further circulating the idea that Clay had freed his slaves and obscuring the fact that he remained a slaveholder.[42]

Whig leaders soon began to regret their decision to retain Cassius's services as his claims to live consistently with his antislavery conviction seemed only to call attention to Henry Clay's own line-straddling on the issues of slavery and Texas annexation. The candidate himself questioned the wisdom of employing his cousin as a spokesman when Cassius began to depict him as being definitively antislavery. In a letter published in the *New-York Tribune*, Cassius declared of Henry, "I believe his feelings are with the [antislavery] cause," and asserted that "the great mass of Whigs are, or ought to be, antislavery." Understanding that this perception could cost him the support of Southern Whigs, Henry rushed to repair the damage, explaining, "Mr. C.M.C.'s letter was written without my knowledge, without any consultation of me, and without any authority from me," adding, "He has entirely misconceived of my feelings."[43]

In an effort to clarify his position and to chasten Cassius for his disclosure, Henry wrote him in September, exhorting, "I am perfectly persuaded

Daguerreotype of Cassius M. Clay by Matthew Brady, taken in 1844 while Clay campaigned for his cousin Henry Clay. (Library of Congress)

of your friendly intentions, and feel grateful for them. But you can have no conception, unless you had been here, of the injury your letter to the *Tribune* was doing." Henry contended that Cassius's sharing of his "private feelings" regarding slavery were endangering Whig chances in Southern states and even in his home state of Kentucky. He articulated his precarious position: "At the North I am represented as an ultra supporter of the institution of slavery, whilst at the South I am described as an Abolitionist; when I am neither one or the other. As we have the same sirname [*sic*], and are, moreover, related, great use is made against me of whatever falls from you." "After all," he added, "I am afraid you are too sanguine in supposing that any number of the Liberty men can be induced to support me."[44]

Unfortunately for the Great Compromiser, this private missive to his cousin became public. He had sent it through a common acquaintance, Willis Greene, who was to hand it off to Horace Greeley, who was then to deliver it to Cassius on the campaign trail. Instead, the letter somehow ended up in the hands of a Democratic newspaper, which printed it. Other papers around the country followed suit, laying out Henry Clay's political machinations for the country to see. Even though voters might well have imagined these political calculations in play, it was another thing to see them put so baldly in Clay's own words. Both Democratic and antislavery papers spared him no mercy. The *New York Morning News* commented that it presented a "miserable picture of the shuffling and dissembling of a politician."[45]

Even without this embarrassing exposure, Cassius's consistent appeals to the economic, rather than the moral, detriment of slavery fell flat with Liberty Party partisans. The *Anti-Slavery Bugle* was representative in denouncing him for "regard[ing] law as paramount to the rights of man" and believing "'that is property which the law makes property.' A more pro-slavery doctrine than this never fell from the lips of a man. It virtually exalts legislative enactment above the government of God."[46]

As many had anticipated, the election did come down to the electoral votes of New York, where James Birney took just over 2 percent of the electorate but deprived Clay of enough support to grant all of the state's electoral votes to Democrat James K. Polk. Although blame for Henry Clay's loss in what would be his final attempt at the presidency did not rest solely on Cassius's shoulders, his involvement in the campaign certainly contributed to the defeat. But if Cassius felt at all culpable or chastened, he did not show it. He and Mary Jane returned from their three-month-long excursion energized by the crowds, the adulation, and a vision of the broader political horizons that lay beyond Kentucky.

Chapter 4
The *True American*

The energy Cassius Clay had felt on the campaign trail prompted him to double down on his efforts to effect change at home. In a letter titled "An Address to the People of Kentucky," which he distributed to the state's newspapers, he explained that he intended to rid Kentucky of the peculiar institution by modifying Kentucky's constitution. Clay's remedy, which was in line with his understanding that only individual states had the right to allow or prohibit slavery within their borders, called for a convention to determine if and how a mechanism for phasing out slavery might be added to the current state constitution. "*Let candidates be started in all the counties in favor of a convention, and run again and again,*" he demanded, "*till victory shall perch on the standard of the free.*" Yet he knew that even if such a meeting were convened, the method would be conservative and the results distant. Clay's was a patient, moderate, and constitutional strategy. "*Whether emancipation be remote or immediate,*" he declared, "*regard must be had to the rights of owners, the habits of the old, and the common good of the people.*"[1]

Clay sought to foment what he envisioned as the state's nascent antislavery voting bloc consisting of what he repeatedly referred to as Kentucky's "600,000 white laborers." To convert and mobilize them, he decided to launch a newspaper. He understood that Kentucky slaveholders monopolized the presses in the state. As he once remarked to Salmon P. Chase, "The people receive no light and are filled with prejudices carefully instilled into them." Only by establishing his own news organ could he hope to change local minds.[2]

By 1845, dozens of antislavery newspapers existed in the North, but Clay knew that starting one in the heart of slave country presented a challenge. He had only to remember how Danville, Kentucky, citizens had shut down James G. Birney's newspaper and sent him into exile across the Ohio River in 1835. More tragic was the fate of antislavery editor Elijah Lovejoy, who died at the hands of a mob while defending his Alton, Illinois, paper in 1837. Indeed, Clay was realistic about the reception such a publication would have in Kentucky, telling Chase that "the slavery-men are united and can move in mass the others not knowing their friends could hardly concentrate in time to save a friend," he assessed. Nor, he told him, would a mob be prosecuted, as "the monopoly of all the offices by the slave-holders would insure impunity to violence as yet I fear." Yet he bore a sense of optimism, telling Chase he thought the tides could turn.[3]

Cassius intended for his newspaper, the *True American*, to be distinct from other antislavery papers, such as Garrison's *Liberator*, and other abolitionist papers, such as the Ohio-based *Anti-Slavery Bugle*. Clay would focus on political rather than moral suasion, with the goal of achieving slavery's end by moderate means. He explained in his prospectus, printed in February 1845 in the *Lexington Observer and Reporter*, that he proposed to publish a newspaper "devoted to gradual and constitutional emancipation, so as to some definite time to place our state on the firm, safe, and just basis of liberty."

"Our press will appeal *temperately* but *firmly* to the interests and the reason, not the passions, of our people," he assured the people of Lexington. "We should take care rigidly to respect the legal rights of others, because we intend to *maintain our own*. We shall attempt to sustain in good faith the '*freedom of the press.*'" Common white workers were his target audience, he insisted, and his paper would "regard the high place which labor holds in the economy of nature, and insist upon its enjoyment of a fair distribution of the products of capital."[4]

Clay's venture, however, came as white Lexingtonians saw slavery as an increasingly charged issue. Their hometown political hero had lost the recent presidential election over the issue of slavery's expansion into Texas, and many slave owners worried about threats to their enslaved property.

A sensational incident had also occurred in Lexington the previous fall when a young teacher named Delia Webster conspired with a visiting abolitionist named Calvin Fairbank to transport an enslaved family to freedom. A native of Vermont, Webster was a proper, well-educated woman who directed a female academy, where she educated pupils from the city's most esteemed families. At the time he showed up in Lexington, Webster and Fairbank were relative strangers. But both attended Oberlin College, a bastion of antislavery thought, and had mutual contacts within the abolitionist movement.[5]

In September, the two abolitionists rented a carriage and under the cover of night collected an enslaved man named Lewis Hayden, as well as his wife, Harriet, and their young son. The group of five fled Lexington in the dark of night, headed for Ohio. After escorting the Hayden family safely to the Buckeye State, Webster and Fairbank returned to Lexington, where authorities promptly arrested them. The state tried Webster in December 1844. She assembled a strong defense team, which included Cassius's brother-in-law and personal attorney, Madison C. Johnson. Meanwhile, Lexington roiled with public outrage at the "negro-theft." In January 1845, just as Cassius Clay was unleashing his "Address to the People of Kentucky," a judge sentenced Delia Webster to two years' confinement and hard labor in the state penitentiary. Calvin Fairbank's trial and conviction followed the next month. So when Clay released his prospectus, the editorial staff of the *Lexington Observer and Reporter* remarked that while they did not doubt Clay's constitutional right to start such a paper, he had picked "the very worst time" to "begin the agitation over this great and delicate subject," and they surmised that the paper would be "a very hopeless undertaking."[6]

Although Clay claimed that the paper would be the effort of "numbers of Kentuckians," he had trouble attracting staff to manage the press. Cassius hired T. B. Stevenson, the editor of the *Frankfort Commonwealth* and a devout antislavery Methodist, to serve as the paper's editor. But before printing began, locals threatened Stevenson and he bowed out of the project. Clay eventually hired William L. Neale, a local man, to manage the printing.[7]

Next, he rented a nondescript two-story brick building near the center of town at 3 North Mill Street to serve as his office and set about transforming it into a veritable fortress. With the help of architect Thomas Lewinski, he fitted the building with folding doors, which he could unchain just far enough to reveal the mouths of two brass four-pounder cannons loaded with shot and nails. He also stocked the office with a collection of guns and Mexican lances, which he imagined a half-dozen or so sympathetic compatriots might wield in his defense. Clay and Lewinski lined the outside doors of the building with sheet metal in case a mob tried to set fire to it. Finally, they installed a trapdoor in the roof through which Cassius and his defenders could escape should other measures fail. The emergency plan stipulated that the last man through would light a prepared powder keg, which would, as he later wrote, "set off, and blow up the office and all my invaders." To Lexingtonians, Clay's extensive fortifications seemed at odds with his reassurances that he would be legal and temperate in his message and approach, and coming less than a year after his bloody knife work on Samuel Brown, they wondered whether there was a madman in their midst.[8]

In April, with preparations for the *True American* underway, Cassius did another puzzling thing when he pursued charges of murder against his enslaved woman Emily for allegedly poisoning his infant son two years earlier. He and Mary Jane decided to do so after they began to suspect that Emily was trying to poison their newborn son (also named Cassius) born in the wake of his brother's death. The Clays believed that Emily's mother,

The building, located on Lexington's Mill Street, which once housed the well-fortified offices of the True American. *(Schomburg Center for Research in Black Culture, Jean Blackwell Hutson Research and Reference Division, New York Public Library)*

Rachel, her brother Solomon, and her daughter had been aware of the enslaved woman's treachery and had possibly aided and abetted it. Perhaps realizing that evidence of such collusion was shaky and would not hold up at trial, Cassius sold Emily's family members to a trader who transported them to New Orleans for sale. This course of actions complied with Green Clay's will, which specified that in "all cases where slaves behave amiss . . . they should be sold, and the money settled in land for the benefit of those for whom the trust was created."[9]

It is unclear why, aside from some compulsion for legal justice, Clay decided to charge Emily with murder on the eve of the launch of his antislavery paper. He must have realized that this action would attract attention to the fact that he was still an owner (and now a seller) of human property and that it would elicit cries of hypocrisy from both pro- and antislavery quarters. Nonetheless, he pushed the Commonwealth of Kentucky to prosecute Emily and sent her to stay in a local slave pen known as Megowan's, which, incidentally was attached to the jail where abolitionist Delia Webster had awaited her day in court only months earlier. There Emily would have resided among slaves marked for sale, pondering what might happen next.[10]

In 1811, Kentucky had passed a statute addressing the legal consequences for the crime of poisoning "with evil intent that death may thereupon ensue." Any slave "duly convicted of voluntary manslaughter" would "suffer death." Another Kentucky statute dictated that if Emily were to be executed for murder, the state would be obliged to reimburse Cassius Clay for her assessed value, perhaps providing another motivation for him to try her for murder rather than to sell her. She bided her time, no doubt fretting over the whereabouts of her mother, brother, and own child. News of the case against Emily drew attention and, not surprisingly, criticism from some quarters. "Cassius here acknowledges that he has sold three of his slaves, and into the bondage of the southern cotton region . . . he attempts to escape of hypocrisy by pleading the requisition of his father's will," pronounced the *Cincinnati Enquirer*. "We have no faith whatever in the man. He stands before the people of the north and south a self-branded hypocrite unworthy of the confidence of slavery or anti-slavery communities."[11]

So it was that when Cassius assembled the inaugural issue of the *True American*, published on June 3, 1845, he felt compelled to devote an entire column to defending his actions regarding Emily. He reprinted a *Cincinnati Gazette* editorial in which the sympathetic author argued that any person in Cassius and Mary Jane's situation might have pursued the same course. "The responsibility certainly, in the case supposed, is a fearful one," asserted the writer, "and it is hard to say what any of us would do; nay, to determine what is right; for it will be borne in mind, first, that these abettor-slaves could not be set free—second, if retained in Kentucky, that their lives were forfeited; and, third, that they were sold to avoid this sad alternative, to a purchaser who knew the history of the whole matter." The editorialist further surmised that the case "may lead us to doubt [Clay's] self-control and wisdom as a leader, or legislator; but if we understand it aright, it would make us love him more as a man."[12]

The other contents of the *True American's* first issue, laid out in four six-columned pages, were unsurprising to anyone familiar with Clay's work. As he had proposed from the beginning, the paper served as a venue for various moderate antislavery writings. He reprinted an article from the *New-York Tribune* on class and labor relations, a snippet from the *Washington Patriot* on the prevalence of kidnapping of free African Americans within the slave trade, and a piece about the deleterious effects of slavery on the "poor, degraded, ignorant" whites of South Carolina. Though he featured coverage of national affairs, he engaged extensively and directly in local politics in his efforts to coalesce the votes of antislavery forces in the state, a strategy that would prove risky.[13]

The *True American* launched just two months before a congressional election that pitted Cassius's old acquaintance, Whig candidate Garrett Davis, against his recent debate opponent, Democrat Thomas Marshall. In the context of this contest, the pages of the *True American* became the new battlefield of the old war between Cassius Clay and the Wickliffe family. The Old Duke, Robert Wickliffe Sr., now elderly and in ill-health, had written a letter to the voters of Fayette County warning them of the collaboration between the Kentucky Whigs—Garrett Davis in particular—and abolitionists in the halls of Washington and had advocated that only the Democratic Party could save the country from such abuses. Referring to the *True American*, Wickliffe warned: "An abolition paper is to be started, when the cause of abolitionism will be openly advocated; and if the people bear that, then the slaveholders of Fayette may expect every living whig organ in the State to openly demand the emancipation of their slaves."[14]

Feeling visceral enmity toward Wickliffe and realizing the risk of having his paper turning into a political wedge, Clay fired back with full (and perhaps ill-considered) force. He reminded his readers that despite Wickliffe's warning that antislavery politics would incite African Americans to violence, the Old Duke himself had once accused a young white woman raped by a Black man of being a prostitute and that, in another instance, he had "covertly and insidiously procured a pardon" for an enslaved woman who stood accused of poisoning a Lexington citizen. Referring to his attack on Sam Brown, Clay seethed, "Old man, remember Russell's cave—and if you still thirst for blood shed and violence, the same blade that repelled the assault of assassin-sons, once more in self-defense, is ready to drink of the blood of the hireling horde of sycophants and outlaws of the assassin-sire of assassins."[15]

Clay's antislavery logic may have been moderate, but his temperament was not. The *Lexington Observer and Reporter* responded with tongue-in-cheek understatement that the inaugural issue of the *True American* had signaled "at the outset to relieve the somewhat and monotonous and dull tone of the Press" but dubbed "Mr. Clay's enterprize [sic] utterly impractical, if not quixotic." The editorial staff stated that if they could give him one suggestion in his "new career," they would advise that "we have seldom known the public taste to be pleased so long with so much severity of tone as that which characterizes his first number."[16]

The *True American*'s appearance quickly attracted much excitement from antislavery reformers throughout the nation. In the *New-York Tribune*, Horace Greeley rejoiced at Clay's "wholesome moral agitation," since it was "only in an atmosphere of silence and stagnation that the friends of Slavery [could] hope to perpetuate its existence." William Lloyd Garrison also lauded Clay efforts in pages of the *Liberator*, while a Vermont paper pronounced: "No man in this country occupies a prouder position than Cassius M. Clay, of Kentucky. Freedom never had a bolder champion, nor truth a sterner vindicator, than this lion-hearted son of the West."[17]

Defenders of the peculiar institution also took notice. In a letter to John C. Calhoun, South Carolina politician and slavery apologist James Henry Hammond complained of "the most powerful appeal" that Clay was making. He accused him of "preaching insurrection to both black & white" and fretted that Clay was "growing up a powerful abolition excitement." Hammond found the newspaper's existence vexing and a worrisome sign of slavery's weakness in the Upper South. Clay "could not be tolerated a moment, if Kentucky was sound or his friends less powerful," he assessed. In his reply, Calhoun agreed, calling Clay "one of the most rabid of the fanaticks," who was going "to all lengths against the South and its institutions."[18]

At home in Kentucky, Clay's provocative editorializing incensed many locals. As the election for the US Senate and for Lexington's congressional district seat neared, Democrats began using accusations of antislavery as a political weapon against even the most conservative Whigs. Clay's endorsement of Whig senate candidate Robert Todd (father-in-law of Abraham Lincoln) and congressional candidate Garrett Davis in the *True American* became a liability for the party. In his debates with Thomas Marshall, Davis denounced the newspaper and any association with Cassius. Even so, Clay tried to help Davis by editorializing that Marshall had only recently adopted his avowed proslavery position and that in a speech only several years before he had called slavery "a cancer" and "A Dark Plague Spot." As even moderate Whigs became vulnerable to accusations of being soft on slavery, the once even-tempered *Observer and Reporter* lost patience with Clay and his meddling. "Whenever an impudent political schemer in politics wishes to make a breeze, he begins at once to bawl out about slavery, abolition, emancipation," claimed the editor. "It is time, full time, that the slaveholders of Fayette should have peace."[19]

Though the *True American*'s target audience was white laboring Kentuckians, locals began to accuse Clay of trying to agitate enslaved African Americans. He responded with reassurances that he had put measures in place to prevent the newspaper from being distributed to slaves and asserted that even if a copy should fall into their hands, the paper contained no content that might incite them to rebellion. Still, he received hate mail, including a red-lettered missive (penned in either blood or turnip juice, he surmised) that was signed by a group calling themselves "The Revengers." "You are meaner than the autocrats of hell," they charged him. "You may think you can awe and curse the people of Kentucky to your infamous course. You will find when it is too late for life, the people are no cowards." "The hemp is ready for your neck," they warned. "Your life cannot be spared. Plenty thirst for your blood—are determined to have it." As if to spite them, Clay reprinted the letter for his readers to see. He was fearless and reckless in the face of such threats, bombastically promising to defend his rights to free speech with force if needed. The right to do so, he wrote, "loses none of its force by being backed with 'cold steel and the flashing blade,' 'the pistol and the Bowie knife!'"[20]

Such visceral opposition to the *True American* troubled Clay's family. In mid-July, his brother-in-law J. Speed Smith informed Brutus that Mary Jane's uncle had called on him to say that he was "fully impressed with the belief that Cassius [would] be killed if he remains here & continues his paper." Another family member had informed Smith that Sally Clay Dudley's own brother had suggested organizing a group of people to "to wait on Cassius & urge him to discontinue this paper, & if he refuses, to tear down his office and destroy his press." "This is the course proposed by his uncle," fretted Smith. "What are we to expect then from strangers? He is now looked upon here as an open abolitionist."[21]

But it was a pathogen that felled Clay before any of his human enemies did. Only five weeks into the publication of the *True American*, he suffered a bout of typhoid fever. Typhoid was a common menace in nineteenth-century America, when poor sanitation helped spread the bacteria, which plagued its victims with high fever, headache, dysentery, and malaise. Clay himself hinted at origins of the outbreak in a graphic editorial about the city's insalubrity in the July 15 edition of the *True American* when he complained about Lexington's revolting streets full of animal carcasses "and such a salmagundi from the kitchen tubs as would make a dog go fasting for a month." Presciently, he joked that the threat of stench and disease might be more dangerous than his human antagonists. "In vain have we escaped a mob if we are to fail thus!" "We shall scatter our types, burn our office, and be off!" he declared in a threat on which many white Lexingtonians wished he would make good.[22]

And "fail thus" he did. Clay contracted typhus only days after writing this article. He continued to put the paper to press, directing operations from his bed while at times packed in blocks of ice to reduce his fever. Increasingly, however, he wrote shorter editorials, relying on the submissions of others to fill its pages. Amid the typhoid outbreak, Lexington residents endured the stress of the election, which took place over three days between August 3 and 5, and when the ballots were tallied, both Todd and Davis had eked out narrow victories over their Democratic opponents.[23]

Many Lexingtonians also blamed Clay for stoking racial tension in the city. Some residents told a visiting reporter that "the conduct of the slaves in Fayette" had "changed since the publication of the *True American*." They had become "idle and insolent, and, in some instances had refused to labor." There were other reports that enslaved workers "were singing daily to the praise of Cassius M. Clay, boasting that he was about to break the chains of their bondage, and would, by the force of his character and influence elevate them to an equality with their masters," causing Lexington's white citizens to become "alarmed for their security."[24]

By late summer, the election, the specter of slave insolence, and the menace of abolitionists and typhus had combined to produce a public anxiety as hot and heavy as the late summer air. Amid it all, on August 12, Clay printed an editorial that finally gave his opponents the premise they needed to close in on him. The piece, submitted by an anonymous slaveholder, appeared on the third page of the paper in the spot where his own editorials usually sat. In a lengthy discourse on the ultimate futility of slavery, the author reminded Kentucky slaveholders that they were geographically surrounded by states in which people disdained slavery on both moral and economic grounds and asserted that they were threatened from within by slaves, susceptible to the "light of information." Clay himself followed up this already provocative opinion with his own aggressive, apocalyptic warning: "But remember you who dwell in marble palaces—that there are strong arms and fiery hearts and iron pikes in the streets, and panes of glass only between them and the silver plate on the board and the smooth skinned women on the ottoman." "When you have mocked at virtue, denied the agency of God in the affairs of men, and made rapine your honied faith," he snarled, "tremble! for the day of retribution is at hand—and the masses will be avenged."[25]

This promise of moral retribution and slave insurrection provided the pretext proslavery Lexingtonians needed to justify shuttering Clay's press. On August 14, a group of elite men, including Henry Clay's son James and the recently defeated Thomas F. Marshall, coauthored a letter to Cassius requesting that he discontinue the publication of the *True American*, deeming it "dangerous to the peace of our community, and to the safety of our homes and families." Clay replied, defending his right to free speech and denying that the *True American* had encouraged a spirit of rebellion among the city's enslaved population. True to his nature, he ended his letter with an indignant threat: "Go tell your secret conclave of cowardly assassins that C. M. Clay knows his rights and how to defend them."[26]

With Clay's refusal to yield, the coterie of proslavery elites convened a meeting at the Fayette County courthouse on August 15. Against Mary Jane's wishes, Cassius heaved himself from his sickbed to attend. During the proceedings he lay collapsed on a bench, able to sit up only intermittently, as he listened to some of Lexington's most influential citizens berate the *True American* as a public menace. Clay, faint and feeble, tried to respond, but his foes gave him no chance. He returned home and immediately began dictating a series of handbills, which he sent to his office for printing. In the first, he appealed to his fellow Kentuckians, whether they agreed with his antislavery sentiments or not, to aid him in defending his right to free speech. Capitulating to its suppression, he contended, would make *them* slaves. "If you stand by me like me, our country shall yet be free," he told them, "but if you falter now, I perish with less regret when I remember that the people of my native State, of whom I have been so proud, and whom I have loved so much, are already slaves."[27]

While he attempted to sway locals with his words, he prepared to defend his press physically with his weapons and his life. He rallied his handful of supporters, wrote his will, and moved a cot into his office, prepared to occupy it. "Every relative believed I would be murdered," he later recalled, "and all, but my wife and my mother, advised me to yield up the liberty of the press; but I preferred rather to die." Sally Clay Dudley's sense of honor was almost as great as her son's but was tempered by both her pragmatism and her Calvinist fatalism. She wrote her youngest child: "Cassius, my son, once more I beg to impress on your mind your real situation. You have acted imprudently, and I can not deny my conviction of the truth, although my great and ardent affection for you would make me bury all your wrongs in everlasting forgetfulness. However pure your motives may have been, you have acted in a way to give your enemies plausible means to take advantage of you." "Be still until you can see your way clear," she entreated him. "If you act hastily, your life is lost." Yet, proving that her sense of honor was as fervent as her son's, she told him: "If you prefer death to dishonor, so do I." Like Sally Dudley, George Prentice also understood Cassius's fortitude. The *Louisville Journal* editor predicted that Clay's opponents would try to "demolish" the *True American*'s office but added that they had their work cut out for them. "Everybody understands that the editor will have to be killed first, and that he is somewhat difficult to kill." "This is the most lamentable state of affairs," Prentice told his readers. "What effect the killing of C. M. Clay will have in the free states, in exasperating the Abolitionists and swelling their numbers, you can judge as well as I."[28]

Meanwhile, Clay seemed to heed his mother's plea. On August 16, as Mary Jane wiped his fevered brow, he wrote another handbill exclaiming his moderation. He spelled out his plan of gradual emancipation for slaves over the age of twenty-one, for whom owners would be compensated by payments from the state of Kentucky. "By this plan," Clay explained, "the payment habits of our people would not be suddenly broken in upon, while, at the same time, we believe that it would bring slavery to almost utter extinction in our State within the next thirty years." He did not advocate "forcible expulsion" of the manumitted slaves, believing that Kentucky could aid in their voluntary emigration.[29]

With public anger unabated, Clay penned yet another handbill the next day. Clearly on the defensive at this point, he once again emphasized his moderation, stating that he hated slavery, not slaveholders. He reminded Lexingtonians that he was one of their own and to "remember that every blood relation I have in the world that I know of, and every connexion, are slaveholders," and that though they differed in their views over slavery, he was "upon terms of the most harmonious" with them. To underscore his sincerity, Clay removed the weapons from his office and promised to suspend any more discussion of emancipation until he was fully recovered and had regained his full faculties.[30]

But the so-called Committee of Sixty would wait no longer. On the morning of August 18, a Lexington judge issued an injunction on Clay's property and seized the keys to his office. Outside the Fayette County courthouse, Thomas Marshall told the crowd of 1,200 incensed citizens that they were acting in "consideration the safety of the community" because the *True American*'s existence, though legal, had become dangerous. Marshall proceeded to skillfully, if deceptively, connect Clay to Northern abolitionists and their dangerous ideas, insisting that the editor encouraged a "war of colors." Shutting down the *True American*, Marshall argued, was an issue, not of free speech, but of public safety. "With his speculative opinions we presume not to interfere," he declared. "With his practical exertions, in our midst, to disturb the settled order of our domestic life, to inflame to discontent and rebellion our household slaves, we have the most direct and incontestable connection."[31]

As evidence of Clay's true menace, Marshall pointed to his fortress of a printing office, proof that Cassius had "acted as though he were in an enemy's country." "He has employed scientific engineers in fortifying against attack," he exclaimed, "and prepared the means for destroying the lives of his fellow citizens, it is said, in mines of gunpowder, stands of muskets, and pieces of cannon." "Why should a peaceful citizen engaged in a lawful calling, make preparation suited to repel an invading army?" Marshall demanded. In rebuffing their "wonderfully mild" request to stop the paper Clay had proven that he was "a madman" or had "prepared himself for a civil war, in which he expected the non-slaveholding laborers along with the slaves, to flock to his standard, and the war of abolition to begin in Kentucky." As such, Marshall explained, the "committee of sixty" could "no longer to endure the presence of an armed Abolitionist, hurling his firebrands of murder and of lust into the bosom of a peaceful and polished city."[32]

At Marshall's urging, a group of citizens marched two blocks to the unoccupied *True American* office, where the city marshal handed them the key. Mayor James Logue met them at the door and notified them that entering the premises was illegal but that city authorities would not prevent them from doing so. Once inside, they dismantled the press piece by piece, painstakingly cataloging and packing equipment into crates for shipment to Cincinnati. The committee and its supporters were self-satisfied by what they considered the organized and restrained removal of the press. The *Observer and Reporter* reported smugly that "no act of violence was committed, but everything was done in a quiet, orderly, peaceable manner." Many Kentuckians, however, even some who opposed the antislavery cause, were outraged at what they viewed as a violation of the First Amendment right to free speech. George Prentice wrote in the *Louisville Journal* that although Clay had acted indiscreetly, his opponents had "set a precedent that we hope we may not live to see imitated here or elsewhere." "While, therefore, we heartily disprove [sic] of the sentiments and doctrines avowed by Cassius M. Clay in his paper," Prentice continued, "we must at the same time enter our solemn protest against the measures which were resorted to for the purpose of shutting up his mouth." Indeed, the *True American*'s fate influenced Prentice to announce a moratorium on all discussion of slavery in his own paper, in the belief that the people of Kentucky were too alarmed to properly distinguish moderate antislavery theory from radical abolitionism.[33]

One fortunate outcome of Clay's otherwise bleak situation in Kentucky was that the destruction of the *True American* only increased his standing with antislavery advocates throughout the North and West. The editors of the *Anti-Slavery Bugle* wrote: "Although it is pretty well clear that we do not regard Cassius M. Clay as an abolitionist occupying the true position, but [as] one who opposed the institution of slavery in a manner and by means which we utterly disapprove." They praised him still as "an honest foe to that accursed system" and "as one who knows his rights and knowing dare maintain them—as a brave man who fears not to beard a lion in his den, and who is determined to uphold what he believes to be right 'come life or death.'" In the pages of the *Liberator*, William Lloyd Garrison struck a similar tone, remarking: "It is not that Cassius M. Clay occupies true antislavery ground, or makes an uncompromising application of the principles of our glorious cause . . . but because we have faith in his sincerity of mind and purpose, his desire for the early extinction of slavery from the American soil, and his steady progress towards the only right position that can be occupied by the champions of human rights, that feel an interest in his cause." In Pittsburgh, a group calling themselves the "friends of C. M. Clay" gathered to voice their support for him. The news of the *True American*'s suppression reached Frederick Douglass, who was then visiting Ireland. He wrote to William Lloyd Garrison deploring the "sad intelligence of the fate of Cassius M. Clay's press." Douglass declared: "I can now remember no occurrence of mobocratic violence against the anti-slavery cause which sent such a chill over my hopes, for the moment, as the one in question." "I regarded the establishment of his press in Lexington, Kentucky as one of the most hopeful and soul-cheering signs of the times—a star shining in the darkness beaming hope to the almost despairing bondsman, and bidding him to suffer on, as the day of his deliverance is certain. But, alas! The mob has triumphed and the star apparently gone out."[34]

In the following weeks, both Clay's friends and foes waited anxiously to see whether he would recover from typhoid and live to resuscitate the *True American*. They need not have fretted. Even in his weakened state, Clay lost little of his angry bluster. He filed a lawsuit against the Committee of Sixty for committing "riot." They went to trial in September, and much to Clay's dismay, the jury acquitted them. Clay did, however, punish his attackers by failing to quickly repossess his press, forcing his enemies to continue paying for its storage. In early October, after only a few weeks' hiatus, Clay began to publish the *True American* once more. His printing office and equipment remained in Cincinnati, and he hired John Vaughn, a former South Carolina slaveholder turned abolitionist, to serve as associate editor while Clay remained in Lexington. Along with business agent Paul Seymour, Vaughn oversaw the daily operations in Cincinnati, and the *True American* reappeared again on October 7.[35]

Given the public sentiment against Clay, many Kentuckians thought that resuming the paper's publication was threatening and foolish. "There is no man, we believed, but C. M. Clay who would again attempt this rash procedure," the *Lexington Observer and Reporter* exhorted, chastising him for "exhibit[ing] a trait of character for which none can feel any possible respect." Suggesting that the stalwart editor might not survive the second run of his paper, in Virginia the *Richmond Times* announced: "Cassius Clay has revived the *True American* at Lexington, and seems ambitious of making a martyr of himself." Other news outlets, however, celebrated his recovery, with a Michigan editor exclaiming, "This distinguished patriot and defender of human rights is again under full sail. He has arisen from his supposed bed of death—buckled on the armor of truth—seized the helmet of defiance, and is again sounding the war-cry of freedom through the caverns and on the Mountain tops of Old Kentucky."[36]

On October 14, few weeks after the Committee of Sixty went before the bar, Emily's murder trial finally commenced in the very same courthouse. The Fayette County sheriff summoned Cassius and Mary Jane Clay, along with the other witnesses to the alleged poisoning. They included two physicians—Mary Jane's father, Dr. Elisha Warfield, and her uncle, Dr. Lloyd Warfield—as well as three enslaved women from the Clays' household: Caroline, Hannah, and Nancy. The final witness was another enslaved woman, identified as "Geo. Brand's nurse." The only extant court document reveals little about the case except for the accusation of Cassius and his wife, Mary Jane, that Emily, "feloniously and willfully intending to kill and murder one Cassius Clay," mixed arsenic and water, which she fed to the child. No record of the proceedings inside the courthouse exists on which to assess the evidence against Emily, the probability of her guilt, or the strength of the Clays' case against her. Still, we can wonder at her culpability or innocence or the possible motivations she may have had for harming the infant Cassius. The alleged poisoning would have occurred on the eve of Clay's manumission of Adam, Joe, Matt, Scott, Riley, Dave, Lotty, Dave, and Zilla. Perhaps she was resentful after watching her enslaver prepare to manumit several of her fellow enslaved men and women, with whom she had lived and toiled for years. Or maybe she resented his growing fame for his antislavery politics while he maintained ownership over her body. Was Emily bitter enough about her continued enslavement to retaliate against her master? Did she attempt to fight unfairness with unfairness? The jury decided there was not enough evidence to prove that she did. Their verdict stated: "We the jury find the prisoner Emily not guilty of the charge laid in the indictment." Distraught and angry, Cassius blamed the results on a proslavery jury made up of his "grateful enemies."[37]

Although the jury may have spared Emily's life, they did not save her from further misery. Indeed, she was to share the same fate as her mother, brother, and daughter. After her acquittal, Cassius sold her to a slave trader who, according to a later account, "took her to the torrid cotton fields of Mississippi." Amid the news of the *True American*'s revival, short notices of Emily's fate appeared in newspapers around the country. "The negro girl, Emily, belonging to Cassius M. Clay, indicted for attempting to take the life of his child by poison, was tried in the Fayette Circuit Court week before last and acquitted," read one. "The testimony was by no means sufficient to establish her guilt, though quite sufficient to have created suspicion." But the news that he sold her never appeared at all. The persecution of Clay and the *True American* made him a hero in some quarters and a dangerous scoundrel in others. His subsequent lionization by the Northern antislavery press seems to have subsumed the news of Emily's acquittal. Notice of her fate and Clay's apparent hypocrisy in owning her and selling her family members quickly faded from public conscience.[38]

In its brief tenure in Kentucky, the *True American* exerted an influence well beyond its small subscription base. In the fall of 1846, Clay claimed 700 subscribers in Kentucky and 2,700 in other states. He estimated that copies of the paper passed through the hands and before the eyes of multiple readers, and he professed, as a result, to see some progress in his efforts to create a political movement dedicated to emancipation. A handful of small papers scattered around the state endorsed Clay's writings, and at least one candidate for the state legislature that year ran as a representative of the Emancipation Party. By far the biggest impact of the newspaper, however, was its propulsion of Cassius Clay to a new level of national notoriety. In his brave refusal to capitulate to the demands of his angry enemies, he had become an inspirational hero to Americans who opposed slavery and a formidable foe to those who supported it. People in both camps looked anxiously to see what he might make of his newfound prominence.[39]

⫷ Chapter 5 ⫸
Fight Like a Man

On a gray and rainy day in April 1846, William Henry Seward knocked on the door of Morton Place, hoping to meet its famous resident. The New York politician had initially ventured to Lexington to visit Henry Clay, but when his carriage driver pointed out Cassius Clay's home on the way into town, Seward decided to pay an unannounced call. Like many Northerners, Seward had followed the *True American* drama and wondered with great interest what Clay would be like in person. He knocked on the door and found himself greeted, as he later wrote, by a "gentleman of thirty-five, fine, straight, and respectable in his look.... We were soon 'well acquent.'" Seward found the embattled Clay "sensitive, and not a little grieved by the alienation of friends, neighbors, and virtually the whole community," and very grateful for Seward's visit.[1]

At the time of Seward's visit, Clay had recovered from his illness and was overseeing the resuscitated *True American* from Lexington while John Vaughn and Paul Seymour managed its production in Cincinnati. He found the work tedious, however. As he told Salmon Chase that year, "I never intended from the beginning to edit the paper and it is a [sore] task to me; I could do much more 'on the stump' and shall be glad to be relieved at some near future time of the painful *duty*." In January, he jumped at the chance to tour the Northeast as adoring crowds in Philadelphia and New York flocked to see this newly minted martyr. While there, Clay met Horace Greeley. The ever-doting *New-York Tribune* editor described Clay's appearance at the Broadway Tabernacle as attended by "sympathetic thousands" and compared his visit to the Marquis de Lafayette's tour of the United States in 1824, during which throngs of admirers materialized everywhere the French general appeared.[2]

Northern audiences and commenters celebrated Clay not only for his antislavery stance but also for his vigorous defense of the freedom of the press. Cassius had daguerreotypes of his likeness made in both New York and Philadelphia. In them, he looked improbably young but resolute, clad in his black suit and waistcoat, his thick brown hair cresting upon his forehead. One of these images was reproduced in lithographic form by Currier and Ives, who titled it *Cassius Marcellus Clay: Champion of Liberty*

{ 74 }

This mass-marketed lithograph by Currier and Ives (ca. 1846) confirmed Clay's rising fame. (Library of Congress)

and depicted him holding a copy of the Declaration of Independence. Interested Americans could now see and even purchase Clay's imposing countenance.[3]

With neighbors who hated him and a newspaper to manage, Clay's everyday life on return to Lexington was quite an unfortunate contrast. The visit from Seward, who was by then a rising political star, was a welcome surprise. By 1846, with the help of New York newspaper editor and political mastermind Thurlow Weed, the gregarious forty-five-year-old New Yorker had achieved the kind of professional success that had eluded Clay. Empire State voters had elected Seward governor in 1838 when he was just thirty-seven, and he served two terms pursuing a characteristically Whig agenda of social reform, public school expansion, and internal improvements. Seward shared with Clay a fervid opposition to slavery, which came to national attention during the so-called Virginia Controversy in 1839. In September of that year, a ship from Norfolk, Virginia, docked in the port of New York carrying a fugitive enslaved man. Article 4, section 2 of the US Constitution compelled the State of New York to return the man to his owner, but Virginia officials went a step further and demanded the arrest and return of three African American seamen who stood accused of hiding the runaway aboard the ship. Seward refused to comply and in 1840 pushed the New York state legislature to pass laws guaranteeing jury trials to accused fugitives and aiding free people illegally captured and enslaved. While Seward's antislavery stance featured a hearty strain of moralism, his rhetoric often rested on the same economic and civic arguments issued by Clay and the two recognized each other as kindred spirits. Seward gratefully accepted Clay's offer to show him around Lexington. As they walked, Seward noticed a pervasive hostility toward his guide, who suffered, as he later wrote, from "the alienation of friends, neighbors, and virtually the whole community."[4]

Only a few months after Seward's visit, Clay decided he could withstand the alienation and hostility of his neighbors no more. In June 1846, he caught both his admirers and enemies off guard when he decided to enlist in the US war against Mexico. The war materialized out of the US annexation in 1845 of the Texas territory, which Mexico still claimed. Americans were divided in their opinions of this action and more broadly over the issue of continental expansion. Some wholeheartedly embraced the idea of America's Manifest Destiny to spread its Anglo-Saxon superiority and democratic government over the entire continent. Others questioned the rectitude of seizing land from another republic, as well as the inevitable consequences of incorporating more Southern territory into the United

States since it was clear that President James K. Polk and other supporters of expansion intended for Texas and any additional Mexican territory to add to the number of slave states in the Union.

Cassius Clay's opposition to Texas annexation had been central to his antislavery position and to his rising fame since 1843, and it featured prominently in his campaigning for Henry Clay in 1844 as well as within the pages of the *True American*. After Congress declared war on Mexico in May 1846, Clay charged Polk with "marching a hostile army" into Mexican territory with "the sole purpose of enlarging the slave-market, and strengthening the despotism of the South." He urged his readers to stand up to the "infamous tyrants" and demand that they "withdraw [the] army from another's soil . . . and let slavery, the cause of all our woes, cease on the whole continent."[5]

Yet less than a month later, the June 17, 1846, issue of the *True American* bore a different message. "We have volunteered for the war," it announced. Writing from Louisville, where he was waiting to muster into service, Clay recapitulated his opposition to the conflict's proslavery premise but added that war had been declared by a duly elected government and that it was his duty as a loyal citizen to support it: "Our opinion is that the war, so unjustly begun, should be pursued with vigor." Furthermore, he insisted that he could continue to oppose slavery even as he fought a war whose purpose was to extend it. "Not a jot of principle do we give up!" he told readers. "Not a hair's breadth of sentiment, of opinion, or of opposition, shall we yield to the curse which, vampire-like, is sucking away the life blood of the nation," Clay assured them.[6]

Predictably, many of Clay's admirers were at first disbelieving of and then disappointed by his course of action. "We scarcely know how to express our surprise and regret at this intelligence," wrote his friend Horace Greeley in the *New-York Tribune*. "We are persuaded that this involvement on his part will greatly impair that moral influence on which depends, in a great degree, the success of his labor against slavery." The editor of the *Cincinnati Herald*, who was no supporter of Clay's, sneered sarcastically: "Doubtless Captain Clay will inform his readers of the *True American* of his intention to occupy a new field of labor, and explain to them how it is that, after having denounced the war, one week, as a bloody war to extend and perpetuate slavery, the next week he enlists as a volunteer in it."[7]

Abolitionists also expressed frustration at Clay's decision. Lucretia Mott wrote fellow reformer Maria Weston Chapman that his enlistment made him "lamentably fallen & degraded." "[My] cringing soul is continually saying 'deal justly with the young man,'" she wrote, adding that she would end her subscription to the *True American*, a fact she bemoaned, since the paper "reache[d] many minds in our South land, who would think nothing of his present course."[8]

What both his disappointed admirers and his smug detractors missed was that Clay's enlistment had less to do with patriotism than with his very social and economic survival. The backlash from the *True American* controversy had carried severe legal as well as social repercussions. Though Clay had aimed his editorial voice at white nonslaveholders, Kentucky lawmakers cited the broader danger that his writings posed. The slave insurrection they had so feared in the summer of 1845 had not materialized, but many white Kentuckians continued to blame Clay both for destabilizing the system of slavery and for endangering public safety. As a measure of this, in January 1846, members of the Kentucky legislature moved once again to strike the Non-Importation Act of 1833. They also put forward legislation that would prohibit "seditious publications" on the topic of slavery. The latter measure was clearly a direct reaction to the *True American*. In a statement of support for the legislation, the *Lexington Observer and Reporter* credited Clay's "ill-advised and dangerous movement" as its inspiration.[9]

When the bill passed in February, it stipulated that "any persons who shall wickedly and maliciously attempt to excite to insurrection, rebellion or insubordination, any slave or slaves within this Commonwealth, oral discourse with such slave or slaves, or by delivering to or dissemination directly or indirectly amongst the slaves and newspaper, pamphlet, or other document, wither written or printed, calculated to produce insurrection, rebellion, or insubordination, shall be deemed guilty of high misdemeanor." Anyone convicted of this crime could be punished by fines and imprisonment. As the inspiration for this legislation, Cassius Clay represented a grave social menace.[10]

While his Northern speaking tour in the winter of 1846 had offered a temporary respite from the pervasive local hostility, Clay remained bound to his home state by his kin and all of his entailed assets, both human and terrestrial. Clay justified his decision to Salmon Chase, telling him that the publication of the *True American* had led to the accusation that he was "the enemy of the *whites*." Marching off to war, by contrast, showed that he was "the foe of slavery not of the people." Neither his feelings on Texas nor his sentiments on antislavery had changed, he assured Chase. "The cause of emancipation has lost none of my affections, on the contrary this war ought to aid by its murdered people to arraign the whole moral sense of the republic against the slavery monster that rips the foundations of the social system and stains our constitution with blood and crime." Though he remained disappointed by Clay's enlistment, Chase understood this rationale and even defended his friend's actions to abolitionist Gerrit Smith, explaining that Clay hoped to "effectually silence the clamor of his adversaries that he would, on his return to Kentucky, be enabled to wield a far more influence than ever in behalf of Liberty." Simply put, in order not only to succeed as an antislavery spokesman but to regain even a shred of respect among his neighbors in Lexington, Clay needed to prove himself a patriot.[11]

For Clay, going to Mexico offered both an escape from his hateful neighbors and an opportunity to raise his esteem among them. The war was enormously popular in Kentucky, where many citizens had personal connections to Texans and had supported the cause of annexation for years. When President James K. Polk finagled congressional approval for his war in May 1846, thousands of young Kentuckians clamored to enlist. Kentucky had no problem filling its portion of the troops called for by the president, with three regiments mustering into service in early June. Many young Kentuckians, including those from prominent families, volunteered for an opportunity to prove their manly prowess and their national loyalty. Just as the War of 1812 had for their fathers and grandfathers, the conflict with Mexico provided a testing ground for patriotism, citizenship, and martial bravery.[12]

Cassius Clay had served as colonel in the state militia, and he believed he could convince Governor William Owsley to parlay this into a commission of the same rank. Multiple slaveholders protested this appointment, however, so Clay joined the Lexington "Old Infantry," the same regiment his father had commanded during the War of 1812. He was able, however, to convince the captain of the regiment to resign and hold an election for a replacement. After Clay offered to contribute several thousand dollars to equip the unit, the men quickly elected him to the position. With his new captaincy secured, Clay and his regiment marched out of town to great fanfare, mounted on some of Kentucky's finest horseflesh, to join the First Kentucky Cavalry under the command of Col. Humphrey Marshall. His rank also entitled Cassius to bring his enslaved manservant, Jack, along with him on his military adventure. Newspaper accounts made no mention of Jack's presence or the irony that it presented: a man marching off to war to extend the slave system he opposed with an enslaved manservant by his side.[13]

Clay's was one of ten companies mustered into service at Louisville in June. Mary Jane, who was early in her pregnancy with the couple's sixth child, traveled with him and bid him goodbye. The troops remained in the city for nearly a month awaiting supplies, orders, and transportation from the army, during which time Clay marched and conditioned his men.

According to one local observer, who had heard about the small fortune Cassius had spent outfitting his troops, he boasted "the finest looking and best mounted company" in the city.[14]

Finally, in early July, Clay and his regiment boarded a steamboat that would take them to Memphis. The *Memphis Enquirer* reported on the regiment's arrival there by noting their well-clothed gallantry, but they also noted a curious fact: Clay's regiment included Mason Brown, the son of Samuel Brown, whom Clay had maimed with his Bowie knife five years before, as well as Thomas Marshall, his primary antagonist during the *True American* controversy. Owing to their "recent political prominency," noted the reporter, Marshall and Clay "attracted much attention and curiosity."[15]

From Memphis, the regiment planned to travel overland through Arkansas and east Texas south to San Antonio. Shortly after crossing the Texas border, Clay and another soldier named Kendall obtained permission to embark on a buffalo hunt through Comanche territory. Years later, Cassius would remember this excursion in vivid detail and devote nearly fifteen pages of his memoir to describing it. "The blood flowed merrily through our veins," he recalled, "making existence himself a pleasure." In the barren plains he could, at last, find the adventure and the freedom from his troubles he so craved. What was supposed to be a brief excursion turned into weeks. When Clay and Kendall had been gone for twenty-one days, reports emerged that two dead bodies fitting their description had been found in the area. Both their regiment and Clay's family back in Kentucky assumed the worst.[16]

Clay and Kendall finally emerged from the chaparral unscathed and rejoined their unit, finding the men much worse for the long overland journey. The volunteers were unused to such arduous marching, and supply problems meant that they sometimes went days without food and water. Many of them had traded layers of their once smart-looking uniforms for basic provisions. The *Lexington Observer and Reporter* relayed to readers that "a large number" of their noble young men were ill from the exhaustion and exposure, with four hundred on the sick list.[17]

Partway through their march, the Kentucky troops rerouted to Port Lavaca on the Gulf of Mexico. By the time they arrived, they had diminished to half of their original numbers and still had yet to see any action. Now under the command of Brig. Gen. John Ellis Wool, the commander of the US Army's Central Division, they waited impatiently for military engagement of any kind. Unimpressed by his situation, Clay described Lavaca in a letter to his brother as "the most unhealthy part of Texas" and deemed half of his command "unfit for service" owing to illness. He anticipated an imminent march to Camargo, a town on the Rio Grande, the disputed boundary between Texas and Mexico. Though the route would take them through desert conditions, it would, he said, be preferable to the "inglorious inaction" they were currently enduring. Along with many in his regiment, he was smarting after Humphrey Marshall's failure to move the troops inland toward the action, a reticence that the troops felt had caused them to miss the Battle of Monterrey the month before.[18]

Clay also echoed the disillusionment and racist judgments of many American troops when he assessed that "Texas is a miserable country ... the whole state is not worth six cents an acre, as the climate is warm and sickly and innervating and ... inhabited by a semi-civilized and degenerate people." Still, he took pride in that his company had "maintained its ascendency for good deportment and military bearing"—no easy feat as bored American troops were becoming notorious for their intemperance as well as the depredations they inflicted on the civilian populace. The whole Second Kentucky Infantry was "incompetent from inebriation," Henry Clay Jr. had written home to his father in February 1847. Cassius could at least take comfort that his erstwhile nemesis, Thomas Marshall, had been arrested for fighting a duel and was "as usual drunk and unpopular."[19]

Even thousands of miles from home, Cassius continued to wrestle with the issue of slavery. His experience in Texas had only reinforced his antipathy to the practice. "The more I see of slavery in the South the less I like it," he told Brutus. "I am sorry you have so much invested in slaves as troublesome times are ahead," he told his brother with more chastisement than pity. Such sanctimonious musings surely fell flat with Brutus, whom Cassius had saddled with the responsibility for managing the *True American*. Despite his fatigue with the newspaper business, he instructed Brutus to continue its publication until he returned. Unbeknownst to him, however, it was too late. Just a week before Clay penned the letter to his brother, Paul Seymour, the *True American*'s business manager, had informed Brutus that an estimated 1,200 readers had canceled their subscriptions, likely out of anger at Clay's decision to enlist in a war for slavery expansion. The paper now had a mere 4,150 subscribers and brought in only enough money to pay a fourth of its printing and distribution expenses. Seymour and editor John Vaughn hoped Brutus and Mary Jane would continue to back the paper financially until they could find new funding. Given Cassius's desperate personal finances, however, Brutus decided to withdraw support, and he and Seymour made plans to terminate publication.[20]

While his antislavery front collapsed at home, Clay was proving successful in the primary objective of his army enlistment. Even in the absence of military engagement, reports of his admirable behavior found their way to American readers. In October, a newspaper correspondent who happened upon Clay's regiment reported that he was the most popular man in it: "When off duty he was but one of the company, faring as the rest. He conversed freely, joked with all." The reporter also noted that a staff member at the US commissary in Fulton, Arkansas, had judged Cassius's company to be the "best disciplined of any he had supplied." A Milwaukee newspaper reported that "despite the prejudice against him for his peculiar notions touching slavery," Clay was winning "golden opinions" from his men. "A braver or more patriotic heart beats in no man's bosom," the paper assessed. Clay's fellow Kentuckians read similar estimations when the *Lexington Observer and Reporter* printed the remarks of a correspondent who professed: "I find that this gentleman, who had gained an unenviable notoriety by his mad and selfish course on the slavery course on the question, is acquiring, by his strict discharge of duty, more standing as an officer than probably any other individual in the regiment."[21]

As Clay had anticipated, in mid-October, Wool's army decamped from Port Lavaca and marched through Corpus Christi to Camargo. There they waited again for action until finally Marshall's cavalry, now better provisioned, was ordered to march 150 miles into the interior toward Monterrey. But with President Polk demanding that Gen. Zachary Taylor remain on the defensive, no combat materialized.[22]

One reason that Clay's men held him in such high regard was his continual effort to alleviate the boredom of their inaction by volunteering them for patrol operations. It was such an expedition that ended his fighting career in Mexico. In mid-January, Wool's column moved toward Saltillo, Mexico, to await Gen. Antonio López de Santa Anna's army, which was rumored to be marching toward them. On January 19, 1847, Clay and a group of thirty men under the command of Maj. John Gaines journeyed south on a mission to assess enemy strength. They rode past Saltillo for three days without locating the enemy, finding only a detachment of Arkansas cavalry under Maj. Solon Borland. When a storm came upon them, Clay's men and the Arkansas troops sought shelter for the night in a hacienda known as Encarnación. As morning dawned, the men awoke to discover themselves surrounded by an estimated 3,000 Mexican cavalrymen. After briefly contemplating what would have been a futile defense, they gave themselves over to the Mexicans as prisoners of war.[23]

During their surrender, however, one of Borland's men managed to escape the group. The Mexican commander, fearing that others would follow, ordered his troops to kill their captives with their lances. What happened next would become the cornerstone of Clay's popular redemption. He ordered all of the American troops to lie on the ground in utter submission while he remained standing. Then, parting the top buttons of his uniform as the Mexicans rushed them, he yelled out, "Don't kill the men: they are innocent. I only am responsible." This spectacle was enough to halt the charge and gave Cassius time to convince his captors that the remaining men would make no attempt to escape. Once again, Clay made a brave, if foolhardy decision in a critical moment. This time it paid off, and the Mexican commander called off the charge and took Clay and the other men as prisoners.[24]

As Clay's feckless detachment endured a long and grueling march toward Mexico City, their regimental comrades finally found the action for which they so longed on February 23 and 24 at Buena Vista. Although the battle would be remembered as an American victory, it came at a great cost, paid disproportionately by Kentucky troops. Sixty-one of Humphrey Marshall's 288 men were killed, wounded, or missing. The Second Kentucky Volunteers fared even worse. Especially devastating to their ranks were the deaths of Lt. Henry Clay Jr. and Col. William R. McKee, who had served as Cassius's second in the duel with Robert Wickliffe Jr. five years before.[25]

Once in Mexico City, Mexican forces kept Clay and his fellow prisoners in a vermin-infested monastery where they slept on the floor with only buffalo rugs and their horse blankets for bedding. As Winfield Scott's forces approached the city in the summer of 1847, their captors moved them southwest to the city of Toluca, a location Cassius found to be a welcome contrast to the capital. He described the lush and verdant area as "an elysium" and found its physically attractive inhabitants to be "a new race of natives, unlike any others in America." He was particularly impressed by the women, whom he found to be "beautiful, with large brains," and whose wardrobes featured "the chemise low cut, and the arms well exposed." He found one young woman named Lolu, whom he assumed to be around sixteen years old, particularly bewitching. Clay enjoyed his tenure in Toluca, finding it a rejuvenating antidote to the strain and anxiety of the *True American* experiment. There, he later remembered, he enjoyed "not only a needed rest, but the greatest luxury."[26]

At home in Kentucky, Mary Jane enjoyed no such respite. During her husband's absence she directed her Lexington household and oversaw the agricultural and livestock operations in Madison County. She also handled most of the family's financial affairs, including shuttering the *True American*. With Brutus's constant counsel, she arranged for the repayment of Cassius's creditors. "Debt oppresses me," she confided to her brother-in-law. Mary Jane's most pressing concern, however, was her growing family, which swelled to include six with the birth of a new son. In March, she begged Brutus to come visit her, saying, "I am quite anxious to introduce a little stranger to you, by the name of Brutus Clay, born the 20th of

February." It was not surprising that when she gave birth to her baby boy, she would name him after the brother-in-law, who had, despite their philosophical differences on slavery, stood loyally by her family throughout the tumult of recent years.[27]

Mary Jane's anxieties heightened that spring when, despite rumors that Cassius and his men were to be exchanged for Mexican prisoners, he failed to come home. Unaware of her husband's secure and luxurious situation, she grew sick with worry. "I cannot think, think for me!" she fretted to Brutus. Cassius and his men, however, were unable to convince their captors to exchange them until after Gen. Winfield Scott captured Mexico City in mid-September and American emissaries negotiated a peace. Once freed, they joined Scott's forces in October. Clay and his troops then marched to Veracruz, where they boarded a steamship for New Orleans.[28]

In the waning days of his captivity, Clay continued the project of rehabilitating his reputation. In July, he penned a letter meant for public consumption in which he defended his troops' surrender at Encarnación and suggested that the reconnaissance obtained from the mission contributed to the American victory at Buena Vista. Clay also commissioned several men in his company to write a letter to a Lexington newspaper in which they elaborated on the story of their capture and Cassius's intervention, in which his quick thinking and self-sacrifice, they claimed, had spared them from mass execution. The men testified that on the long march to Mexico City, Clay had let struggling soldiers ride his mule and, once they were imprisoned, had sold the mule, his watch, and clothing to buy them necessities. Painting Clay as a hero, the story of his rash bravery had the benefit of seeming completely in character. "Who but C. M. Clay with a loaded pistol to his head and in the hand of an enraged enemy, would have shown such magnanimous self-devotion?" asked the editor of a newspaper that reprinted the testimony.[29]

On his way home, Clay continued to win fans, especially in New Orleans, where newspaper reporters seemed downright smitten with him. The *New Orleans National* noted that "there are some sentiments entertained by this gentleman in conflict with those we advocated, but this should not prevent us from expressing our high estimate of a true-hearted American—a gallant spirit." On his return through the Crescent City, a reporter from the *New Orleans Delta* interviewed the "gallant young Kentuckian" and found him to be "no more like the man we took him to be, than a dove is like a hawk. His manner and appearance indicate a quiet reserve approaching nearly to diffidence, which but little accord with the fiery courage, fervid eloquence, and strong feelings, which mark his character as developed in this political and military history. He has the manners of an amiable gentleman and warm-hearted Kentuckian, and leaves upon every person with whom he converses a very pleasing impression."[30]

The only opinions that really mattered to Cassius's ability to survive in his home state, however, were those of his neighbors. On this account, he was gratified. A throng of friends and family greeted his boat when it finally steamed into Louisville on December 8, 1847. "Among the gallant band that Kentucky sent to the field, no one has sustained her reputation better than Cassius M. Clay," reported the *Louisville Daily Courier*. "It was not his fortune to shine of the battle field, but he has proved himself preeminent in all that makes the soldier, in many trying situations." No one was more thrilled at Cassius's return than his family. Mary Jane and four of their children reunited with him in Frankfort the following day. When he returned to Lexington to a public welcome and a procession featuring three military companies and thirteen rounds of cannon, his redemption seemed complete. "My reception everywhere has been triumphant," he wrote to Salmon Chase.[31]

The question now, however was what direction Clay's career might take next. With a redeemed reputation and newfound respect from his neighbors, Clay might have found this an ideal time to pursue a quiet life of agriculture and attend to his finances, which were no more stable than they had been before he left for Mexico. His household coffers and farming and livestock ventures all needed attention. He was also still in debt from the *True American* and feared that some of his Cincinnati creditors might sue him. Cassius and Mary Jane moved back to their Madison County home, which they now called White Hall, to economize. Although "much embarrassed by [his] circumstances," he told Salmon Chase, he had no intention of ceasing his crusade against slavery, explaining that his "present purposes" were "as ever to work for the same cause" through public talks and writing. He achieved success at the latter when Harper and Brothers published a collection of his writings, speeches, and editorials in 1848.[32]

Chase, however, urged his old friend back into the political arena and continued to urge him to shed his Whig affiliation and join the Liberty Party. Chase had done so himself in 1841, and over the next several years, he worked patiently and deliberately to piece together an antislavery political coalition, both in Ohio and nationally. The Liberty Party made impressive gains in the presidential election of 1844, garnering over 62,000 votes as opposed to under 3,000 in 1840, and significant inroads in such states as Ohio, Massachusetts, and New York.[33]

Yet convincing Whigs and Democrats, who had fundamental differences in their philosophical and policy outlooks, to abandon their affiliations to vote for an upstart political party devoted to a single issue presented an uphill battle. Cassius Clay was a case in point. "I have lost none of my interest in the Liberty party, they have my sympathies and my confidence not as a party but as men good and true and impelled by noble resolves," he told Chase in 1845, but he maintained that his "usefulness [would] best be preserved by maintaining an isolated position." "Perhaps I flatter myself," he continued, "but I think I have had some little influence in bringing the Whigs to higher anti-slavery ground than they ever before venture to occupy... indeed I look forward to the time not distant when the Whigs and liberty party will occupy the same ground."[34]

In the aftermath of the war, however, Chase had new reason to be hopeful for the future of an antislavery party. Indeed, the national political landscape had shifted thanks to questions about the place of slavery in the territory gained from Mexico, in which the limitations of the Missouri Compromise of 1820 would not automatically apply. The specter of millions of acres of land opening to slavery alarmed many Northern whites, who increasingly saw the institution's expansion as a Southern conspiracy that would shut them out of vast swaths of an expanding United States. This concern found its way into congressional debate early in August 1846, as Clay and his fellow Kentucky troops were making their way to war, when a group of anti-Polk congressmen led by Pennsylvania Democrat David Wilmot attached a rider to an appropriations bill meant to fund negotiations with Mexico. Understanding that the appropriations would allow Polk to purchase territory beyond his stated purpose of buying Texas, the authors of the amendment, which became known as the Wilmot Proviso, stipulated that slavery be prohibited from all of it. The nature of their opposition to the peculiar institution was clear. Wilmot, who referred to the amendment as the "White Man's Proviso," stated that it would "preserve for free white labor a fair country, a rich inheritance, where the sons of toil, of my own race and own color, can live without the disgrace which association with Negro slavery brings upon free labor." The bill with the amendment passed the House of Representatives, where nearly every Northern Democrat and Northern Whig voted for it. Congress adjourned before the Senate could vote on it, but the legislation reemerged during the following congressional session as a subject of constant debate.[35]

Though it never became policy, the Wilmot Proviso reflected the fluctuating national conversation about the future of slavery in the United States. For decades, politicians in the two major parties had intentionally worked to keep slavery out of federal legislation and public debate. The proviso and the support it received brought the issue to the fore. It created a deep fissure within the Democratic Party, whose Northern members had previously been bound by organizational discipline to march in lockstep with its proslavery Southern wing. The willingness of Northern legislators to cross party lines and coalesce around their shared antipathy for slavery's expansion marked a sea change within the Second Party System—one that alarmed Southern Democrats.[36]

As white Americans fretted about what shape the settlement of new territories would take in the future, they began to grow incrementally less concerned with battles of the past. Issues such as banking, tariffs, and internal improvements that once defined the differences between the Whig and Democratic Parties, and around which both white Northerners and Southerners coalesced, began to fade in importance. Many Northern Democrats (such as Wilmot) and Whigs found that they could no longer countenance the proslavery expansionist ambitions of their Southern brethren. Denouncements of the Slave Power—by which they meant a relatively small group of slave-owning Southerners who maintained a disproportionate amount of power in the halls of government and used it to protect their own interests at the expense of average white Americans—grew louder.

The impending presidential election of 1848 provided the impetus for a new antislavery party to form. In May, the Democrats nominated Michigan's Lewis Cass, who was decidedly sympathetic to Southern interests, and adopted a platform that denounced abolitionists. For their part, Whigs planned to paper over policy differences within their party by running war hero and Louisiana sugar planter Zachary Taylor, who, like the entire Whig platform, was notable for his lack of a political position of any sort. Many opponents of slavery were dissatisfied with both two major parties, and in August 1848, thousands of representatives from every free state, as well as Delaware, Maryland, and Virginia, converged in Buffalo, New York, to form the Free-Soil Party. These conventioneers represented an assortment of so-called Conscience Whigs, who opposed both slavery and the late war, Liberty Party members, and Northern Democrats.

At the convention, Chase framed a party platform he hoped would be acceptable to the array of assembled representatives. The Free-Soil platform included pledges to halt the extension of slavery, to end the institution in Washington, and to prevent the federal government from supporting or protecting slavery. It also promoted cheaper postal rates, tariff reform, and, importantly, free homesteads. The platform secure, they adopted as their slogan: "Free Soil, Free Speech, Free Labor, Free Men."[37]

As their motto suggested, the Free-Soil Party ethos rested as much on a vision of who should be able to attain new American land as on one of who should work it. The concept of government-supported westward migration had been developing for decades and, by 1848, had broadened into a broader call for democratic land reform that would reduce the effects of land monopolies and speculation and would include a government-sponsored homestead act to distribute public lands in the West. It sought to mitigate farmers' frustration with the high prices that kept western land out of their reach and presented a panacea for oversaturated urban labor markets. As such, it appealed to urbanites who had never touched a plow. The principle of land support went hand in hand with the idea of slavery as an unrepublican contagion. As the *New York Weekly Evening Post* put it in 1848, "One slaveholder with his gang of negroes elbows out thousands of free settlers who bring only the implements of their toil and their own hardy families."[38]

The Free-Soil Party drew even greater attention by choosing former president Martin Van Buren as their presidential candidate. Van Buren, who was instrumental in developing the Second Party System and instilling into it the concept of party discipline, seemed an unlikely choice. He and his fellow New York supporters had defected from the Democratic Party largely because Polk denied them patronage within his administration. Many abolitionists remained highly suspicious of the man who had consistently opposed antislavery efforts during both his vice presidency and his stint in the Oval Office. Nonetheless he won enough votes to climb atop the ticket, with Charles Francis Adams, son of John Quincy Adams, as his vice presidential candidate.[39]

Not all antislavery partisans were happy with the newly formed party. Free-Soilers worked deliberately to envelop disaffected Whigs and Democrats who prioritized white opportunity and often held blatantly racist attitudes. Liberty Party expats, many of whom called for slavery's immediate end and supported African American social and political rights, were reticent to back a party with a more moderate outlook. Indeed, they complained (and fairly) that the platform adopted in Buffalo diluted their old antislavery principles by neglecting to include any commitment to racial equality or specific formula for ending slavery. Nonetheless, by making opposition to slavery the only basic criterion for support, Free-Soilers were able to form a broad political coalition.[40]

Yet many white antislavery men, among them Cassius Clay, who continued to resist Chase's appeals to abandon the Whigs, found it difficult to abandon their old allegiances. Since returning from Mexico, Clay had continued to rebuff Chase's requests to join the Liberty Party. "I shall not *leave* the Whigs," he said, but promised to "be more *moderate* towards the Democrats who in our state are the labourers in great part." Hoping that the Free-Soil Party would be more viable than the Liberty Party had been, Chase continued to push Clay toward it. But Clay told Chase a month before the convention in Buffalo that although he was pleased by the prospect of the new party, he could not enlist. Explaining that he still depended on Kentucky Whigs for even what little public support he could attract, he informed Chase: "I am much obliged to you for your suggestion of my name as connected with Northern movements," yet his "pledges from the present arising from the circumstances which surrounded me compel me to stand for Old Zack—but still I wish you all success as it will not prevent his election and advance our cause." He hinted, however, that he might eventually capitulate. "I hope by another presidential year that *we* will come together," he wrote. "I want the excitement North to go on. Taylor will be elected which will drive more of the democracy into antislavery formation—also many Whigs—all of which is propitious whilst there will be just punishment to the administration for its proslavery war."[41]

Clay was correct in predicting Taylor's resounding victory. Free-Soilers could, however, also be happy with their showing. Van Buren garnered nearly 300,000 votes, representing 10 percent of the popular vote. Voters sent twelve Free-Soilers to Congress, and in early 1849, Ohioans elected Salmon Chase to the US Senate bearing the party label. The election had been just the start of a burgeoning project. After 1848, Free-Soilers in various states worked to forge alliances within the regular parties. In return for support for antislavery measures, Free-Soilers in Ohio, New York, Massachusetts, and Vermont formed coalitions with Democrats, while in Michigan they allied with Whigs. In 1849, Chase began to refer to the fledgling movement as the Free Democracy. Though Free-Soil alliances would shift in shape and name in the following years, political antislavery was on the American landscape to stay. The election of 1848 showed, as historian Eric Foner has put it, that antislavery politics "was not merely a negative doctrine, an attack on southern slavery and the society built upon it," but rather "an affirmation of the superiority of the social system of the North—a dynamic, expanding, capitalist society, whose achievements were almost wholly the result of the dignity and opportunities which it offered the average laboring man."[42]

In this sense, the presidential election of 1848 was a validation of the principles Cassius Clay had long advocated. Rather than training his attention on national party building in the aftermath, however, Clay resumed his focus on ending slavery within Kentucky, where the prospects for revising the state constitution looked brighter than they had in years. The impetus for most Kentuckians was not the issue of slavery but rather a growing sense that the current constitution, written in 1799, did not reflect the rise in democracy over the intervening half-century. Kentucky voters resented the centralized power held by county courts to appoint local officials, as well as the general assembly's power to gerrymander political districts and raid the state's common school fund to finance what many saw as extravagant appropriation bills. In August 1848, voters went to the polls and voted to convene a constitutional convention the following August.[43]

Clay and other antislavery partisans quickly seized on the opportunity to modify the state constitution in such a way as to make emancipation possible. Clay had been anticipating such an opportunity for years. In 1845, he had described this patient strategy of patience to Salmon Chase, explaining: "We are willing to see the dissatisfaction with the present constitution on other grounds increase" until "we [can] *array* our strength in favour of liberty." Emancipationists, he believed, could take over any constitutional convention and "carry it at once." But their task would not be so easy. They were met with equal pressure from slavery proponents who sought to increase safeguards for the peculiar institution in the new constitution. Proslavery partisans, too, had reason for optimism. In February 1849, they secured the repeal of the much-debated Non-Importation Act of 1833; for the first time in fifteen years, Kentuckians could now purchase enslaved persons imported from out of state. Those who supported the repeal saw it as a way of both increasing the availability and decreasing the price of enslaved labor, thereby shoring up the strength of the institution in Kentucky. Galvanized by the repeal, a proslavery group calling themselves Friends of Constitutional Reform organized around a platform designed to appeal to rank-and-file white Kentuckians, promising to secure both democratic reforms and the protection of slavery. Soon the question of whether the state should end slavery at some near or future point subsumed the discussion of other issues and promised to dominate the agenda at the convention.[44]

Meanwhile, antislavery forces worked to formulate a rationale and vision for the gradual phasing out of slavery that might appeal to voters. This was a challenge, though, since reformers varied in their opinions as to how and when emancipation might occur. Their ranks included a few abolitionists, a substantial number of colonizationists, and others who, like Cassius Clay, favored plans that would allow for postnati manumission and owner compensation. Along with their opposition to slavery, most shared a realistic outlook regarding the potential magnitude of reform. They were under no illusion that a new constitution would bring an end to slavery. Rather, their goals were much more modest. They sought to add a provision for the future ending of slavery through referendum or other popular procedural mechanism that would allow them to bypass a wholesale constitutional revision.[45]

Bridging differences in scope and approach, antislavery forces formed a statewide network of committees to work county by county convincing ordinary voters to elect sympathetic delegates to the constitutional convention. Speaking at an emancipation meeting in Frankfort in May 1848, Clay explained both the strategy and the spirit of the proponents of emancipation and the need to convince the "real people," particularly nonslaveholders, of the importance of emancipation through "agitation." "We must seek them out—at the cross-roads and places of public resorts in their neighborhoods. . . . We want men on the stump. We want to get the ear of the people. The resolutions of the Committee display a magnanimous moderation. Let us pass them, and do battle for them. Let every good friend of the cause buckle on his armor and 'never say die!'" As both pro- and antislavery contingents mobilized, they set in motion what historian Harrold Tallant has called "the most extensive and wide-ranging debate on slavery in Kentucky's history" and one that was, indeed, unique in the nineteenth-century South. Throughout the spring and summer, courthouse lawns, churches, and public squares became sites of rallies, debates, and speeches. One visitor from Pennsylvania described the ubiquity of the slavery issue, noting that it was "the principal topic in [every] stage coach and tavern throughout the state."[46]

Following his own prescription, Clay "buckled on his armor," traveling around central Kentucky to advocate the antislavery platform, often at the peril of his safety. When opponents warned him not to speak, he invoked his constitutional rights to free speech. He later remembered: "I had all the moral and legal forces on my side; and so much physical power as good arms and a brave heart could give men." He spoke not, of course, of his biceps but rather of the carpetbag containing two revolvers and the Bowie knife that he carried with him at all times. Throughout the campaign Clay maintained the same case against slavery he had shared for years. In Anderson County, where he spoke in May 1849, he repeated his familiar tale of Southern privation; that in "in railroads, canals, colleges, schoolhouses, churches, asylums for the deaf and dumb, the blind, the insane, hospitals for the sick and poor, in agricultural productions and agricultural implements, in manufactures, in common schools, in general and diffused education, in benevolent and charitable enterprises—in a word, in every thing which constitutes national prosperity, the slave States are far, very far behind the free States of the Union." He was, by some assessments, very effective. One admiring listener claimed: "So convincing were his arguments that I heard strong pro-slavery men declare that they believed the truth of them could no longer be denied," and declared Cassius's tone so moving that "stoat and stalwart men who have not wept for a quarter of a century, were melted into tears by his pathos and eloquence in vindication of the right of the poor man to his home in his native Kentucky, and higher inalienable right of every man of every color to himself and his own labor."[47]

Yet the proslavery forces were just as formidable. One local paper warned that though "Mr. Clay made an able effort" and was motivated by the "purest motives," his plan, if enacted, "would be productive of the worst consequences—that it would destroy the peace and happiness of our community, and make Kentucky the land of recreancy, dishonor, and shame." Proslavery partisans outside the state also observed the convention process with apprehension, understanding that enfeebling slavery in Kentucky would weaken the security and economy of the slave system throughout the region. "If emancipation is adopted in Kentucky, the immediate consequences will be disastrous," wrote one Huntsville, Alabama, newspaper columnist, predicting that it would prompt slaves farther south to "fly thither as an asylum." The same writer also predicted that the declining value of slaves in Kentucky would prompt their owners to sell them, flooding the market and decreasing the value of slaves throughout the South.[48]

Despite his robust canvassing, Clay realized that he was too controversial to be elected as a delegate to the convention. In June, Clay turned his efforts toward making sure the voters of Madison County elected emancipationist Thomas Burnam as one of two candidates to represent them. In addition to Burnam, three proslavery men vied for a seat, including local attorney Squire Turner. At a debate on June 14, Turner tried to deny Clay the right to speak on the grounds that he was not a candidate. When Cassius managed a turn at the podium anyway, he refuted Turner's remarks more directly and harshly than those of the other candidates. The following day, the candidates held another debate in little hamlet of Foxtown only a mile from White Hall. Clay again showed up to support Burnam. Turner once again monopolized the podium, and after he had spoken for over an hour, Cassius pleaded with him to cede the stage to Burnam. Angered, Turner refused and then proceeded to read incendiary passages from the infamous August 12 issue of *True American*, supporting Black emancipation and civil rights. Clay quickly responded by reminding the crowd that those were not his words and that he regretted printing them.[49]

Sensing the crowd's anger, Clay mounted the stage at the close of Turner's speech and apologized for the interruptions he had caused. As he was leaving the platform, a man in the crowd began to attack Clay's views on school funding. Frustrated by this off-topic criticism, Clay accused the man of being a "tool" of Squire Turner. At this, Turner's son, Cyrus, approached him and shouted that Clay's statement was "a damned lie," before punching him in the face. Clay reached for his Bowie knife, its handle and seven-inch blade concealed beneath his jacket, but Cyrus was quicker, grabbing Clay's arm while a bystander quickly snatched the unsheathed knife from his hand. With his free hand, Clay managed to hit Turner so hard that he fell backward into the crowd.[50]

At this point, several enraged men descended on Clay, and one of them stabbed him in the side, his knife entering between ribs. The hits continued. Alfred Turner, a cousin of Squire, rained blows upon Clay's his head with a stick, and yet another family member, Thomas Turner, took out his pistol, aimed it at Cassius, and tried unsuccessfully to fire it four times. Clay lay dumbfounded and seemingly incapacitated. As he later recalled, he finally noticed the "blood spouting from his side" and managed to rouse himself and break free. He spotted the man who had stolen his knife and managed to wrest it away from him by grabbing it by the blade. In the process he severely lacerated several fingers. His fourteen-year-old son, Elisha, ran to him and, sobbing, proffered him a small pistol. But Cassius was determined to rely on his preferred weapon. Meanwhile, Cyrus Turner, having been clubbed over the head by one of Clay's supporters, stumbled around insensible. Spying him, Cassius ran toward him with his knife out, ready to strike. Turner fell back into a throng of people, which gave way beneath him, leaving him to tumble to the ground. As he lay sprawled on the grass, Cassius plunged the knife into his adversary's abdomen, slicing away until Turner's bowels lay in a bloody heap, exposed to the open air.[51]

The crowd stood stunned. Several men picked up both Clay, who was bleeding profusely from his torso and hand wounds, and the mangled Turner and carried them to a house adjacent to the debate grounds. Convinced he was dying, and dramatic to the end, Clay shouted to the crowd that he had fallen "in defence of the liberties of the people" as he left the scene. Someone rode the short distance to White Hall to break the devastating news to Mary Jane, while another sent a message to Sally Clay Dudley in Frankfort, exhorting her: "If you would like to see [your son] alive, come quickly."[52]

The two men lay in agony in adjoining rooms. Within several hours, Cyrus Turner succumbed to his grievous wounds, denying to the end that it was he who stabbed Clay. Cassius's injuries were so severe that onlookers presumed he would share Turner's fate. Rumors of his demise traveled quickly throughout the state. The *Louisville Daily Courier* reported that in the commonwealth's largest city, "Men gathered in the streets and asked each other, with fearful foreboding whether the disastrous news could be true." Deciding it was, the editor, Walter Haldeman, wrote an obituary in which he proved to be far more generous to Clay in death than he had been in life. Haldeman pronounced that Clay had "offered himself a martyr to what he earnestly believed was the cause of TRUTH" and that "in the cause of Emancipation, he was what Martin Luther was in the Reformation." Word spread beyond Kentucky, as well. On hearing Clay was dead, William Lloyd Garrison reflected on his work for the antislavery cause and lauded his bravery but lamented that "his courage was more of the animal than the moral kind." "Alas! that he should have equipped himself with such weapons to carry on a moral agitation!" Just as quickly, however, came the improbable news that Clay was alive and would recover. One Ohio newspaper remarked: "The Kentuckians say that it's no use to attempt to kill Cash Clay, unless some one gets him down and cuts his head off, as you would kill a turtle."[53]

As Clay convalesced at home, the national press recounted and evaluated the extraordinary Foxtown affray. Contradictory accounts circulated in newspapers, parsing the particulars and assigning blame. Many writers found the incident appalling but could not seem to look away. Reporters fixated on the visceral brutality of the incident and on Clay's choice of weapon. They also questioned whether Clay was justified in stabbing Cyrus Turner, who was, by all accounts, prone and defenseless at the time. Just as after Cassius's confrontation with Samuel Brown in 1843, Americans took him to task for his reliance on uncivilized weaponry, and he found himself, once again, caught in a debate over the role of violence in political debate.[54]

Pacifist abolitionist editors hurled some of the harshest criticism. The *Anti-Slavery Bugle* denounced Clay and the entire honor culture he represented. The editor declared that by arming himself with a knife, Clay had gone looking for a fight, adding that if he had acted with "meekness and Christian dignity, refusing to make himself a brute," bloodshed would have been avoided. Meanwhile, William Lloyd Garrison accused him of "glorying in his shame." A particularly damning assessment of Clay came from the pen of abolitionist Henry C. Wright, who in a letter to the *Liberator* described him as "a queer chap . . . reckless as a hyena; destitute of moral principle as a shark; absurd and ridiculous as a monkey; a bundle of contradictions."[55]

Looking back on this juncture of his career, Clay remarked years later that he had "been between two fires—the Slave-power on one side, and the Abolitionist cranks on the other." He begrudged the latter group for criticizing him, noting that "when John Brown went down in Virginia and foolishly lost his life, he became a hero with the long-haired abolitionists; but when I fell in the defense of the freedom of speech and the liberties of all men, these fellows shed tears, not because I triumphed, but because I used arms and was not killed!"[56]

When he was well enough, Clay dictated a defense of his actions from his sickbed and submitted them for publication in the *National Era*. He insisted that in the moment, he had every reason to believe that Cyrus Turner had stabbed him and was therefore justified in killing him. Although he regretted Turner's death, he did not feel responsible for it. Connecting his behavior with the cause of antislavery, he insisted that he would have met his demise long ago had he not relied on armed self-defense. "How then can you ask me to go unarmed and yet manfully vindicate those doctrines which every where here have been denounced with death," he asked. "What good would it do the cause which I advocate to add myself to the long list of *tame* victims in the South who have been murdered for exercising the liberty of free speech?" He had, he contended, only two options: "either to lie down and die like a dog, or stand up and fight like a man!" In essence, Clay was telling the Northerners inspired by his antislavery convictions that they would have to accept his methods along with the message, for antislavery reform had turned into a deadly business in the Bluegrass State. Indeed, Cyrus Turner was not the only Kentuckian to lose his life during the fraught constitutional convention campaigning in 1849. In Paducah, one candidate killed another at a debate just days before the election.[57]

When balloting for constitutional delegates finally took place in August, the Emancipation Party garnered nearly 10 percent of the statewide vote. Although this was not an insignificant showing in a slave state, it accorded the party only a few delegates. When the convention assembled in October, the majority of attendants, Squire Turner among them, proved to be at least nominally, if not decisively, proslavery. Instead of creating a constitutional mechanism for future gradual emancipation, delegates strengthened the institution through new language that reiterated the status of enslaved persons as property and reaffirmed the property rights of their owners. As one observer later explained, emancipation sentiment in the state had so alarmed many white Kentuckians that they became determined to create a constitution that would forever "render the possession of slave property absolutely and utterly impregnable." Delegates also added provisions that prohibited free African Americans to settle in Kentucky and mandated that manumitted individuals leave the state. The desire for a new constitution had inadvertently led Kentuckians to engage in a highly improbable debate over the fate of slavery—one matched only by Virginia a decade earlier. Yet rather than cracking the door open for future emancipation measures, as Cassius Clay and his antislavery cohort had hoped it would, the constitution of 1850 seemed to permanently close and lock it.[58]

Chapter 6
The Name of Republican

Days after the Foxtown melee, as Cassius Clay lay recovering from his grievous wounds, he received a letter from his mother. Viewing her son's tumultuous life through her faith in divine providence, Sally Dudley pondered: "When I think how often your life according to [appearance] was almost taken, I wonder for what purpose it is sustained." Her son, too, likely wondered. Clay had lived to fight another day, but it was by no means clear what the battle might be. In defense of not just his life but also the antislavery cause, he had now killed a man—a threshold that, for all of his extreme behavior, he had never before crossed. His strategy of eradicating slavery in Kentucky through the state's constitution had also failed miserably. To achieve his goals, Clay now saw that he would need a broader approach. National events would soon speed things along.[1]

In January 1850, as delegates to Kentucky's third constitutional convention finished up their work of making slavery untouchable by political action, Southern politicians in Washington struggled to do the same. That month President Zachary Taylor, whose credentials as a Louisiana sugar planter once led white Southerners to imagine him a kindred spirit on issues of slavery, called for California's immediate admission to the Union as a free state. Realizing the dangerous consequences of any limit placed on the extension of slavery in new territories, Southern legislators mounted fiery opposition. Sensing that the future of free labor in the United States was at stake, many Northern Democrats and Free-Soilers increased the ferocity of their counterdemands that slavery be prohibited in new states. Henry Clay, now weakened by tuberculosis, once again adopted the role of compromiser, proposing measures to appease both Northern and Southern interests. These included the admission of California and the territories of New Mexico and Arizona as free states, outlawing the slave trade in Washington (a symbolic slap to proslavery ideologues), and a stronger fugitive slave law.

Clay's proposals contained something to offend everyone, roiling the Senate. In March, the ailing Southern firebrand John C. Calhoun, who was too weak to speak himself, tasked his fellow senator James Mason to read his words of warning to his Northern counterparts. Slavery, he insisted, must be allowed in new territories to preserve the sectional balance of power, or else Southern states would be permanently disempowered and would have no choice but to leave the Union. This was no idle threat. By 1850, several states had formed Southern Rights Associations, and the governors of South Carolina and Mississippi began to prepare for armed resistance.

In response, the equally elderly but more robust Daniel Webster took to the floor of the Senate to urge colleagues on both sides of the slavery issue to empathize with each other's position. A compromise, he enjoined, was necessary to save the Union.[2] Days after Webster's address, in his first-ever speech before his new colleagues, freshman senator William Seward presented a new approach. He argued that California should be admitted as a free state with no compromises attached. In support of this position, he posited a familiar vision of slavery's legality. The Constitution protected slavery where it existed, he allowed, but any new unincorporated territory was to be unsullied by America's evil inheritance. Into this traditional argument of constitutional antislavery, he added a powerful new contention: that Americans were bound to a "higher law than the Constitution, which regulates our authority over the domain, and devotes it to the same noble purposes." This "higher law," asserted Seward, dictated that human bondage was deemed immoral by God. The country's founders, he argued, had tolerated slavery "only because they could not remove it," and no modern Christian nation would choose to extend it. While Seward's legal reasoning hewed to the strict constitutional formulation that Salmon Chase had posited years before, his invocation of a Christian conscience interjected a moral dimension to political antislavery, thrilling abolitionists and establishing Seward as their chief political spokesman.[3]

In Kentucky, Clay stayed apprised of the congressional strife through newspapers. Seward's words delighted him, and he penned his congratulations, proclaiming: "It was just *the* speech for the occasion." Webster's equivocating stance, however, had left Clay cold, and he wrote to the eminent statesman to tell him so. "As much as a Union is to be loved, it is not to be loved more than a national conscience," he excoriated Webster, telling him that he would prefer national dissolution to the prospect of "slavery and freedom be equally extended forever." Ultimately, Democratic Illinois senator Stephen A. Douglas took over the compromise process, broke up Henry Clay's omnibus bill into separate components, and shepherded them through congressional passage, one by one. White Americans breathed a sigh of relief. It was clear to many, however, that so long as the United States continued to incorporate new territory, the issue of slavery's role in the country's Manifest Destiny would reemerge. As Salmon Chase remarked in the aftermath of the compromise, "The question of slavery in the territories has been avoided. It has not been settled."[4]

Having recovered from his injuries and spoiling for a place in the new battle to end slavery, in early 1851, Cassius Clay made the dubious decision to reenter Kentucky politics, declaring himself a candidate for governor on what he dubbed the Emancipation Party ticket. He entered the race understanding that he had not the remotest chances of winning or even of garnering a significant percentage of the votes. The failures of the election of 1849 and the constitution of 1850 had decimated the ranks of the antislavery forces in Kentucky, and observers inside and outside the state were quick to note the futility of Clay's campaign; as the *New Orleans Times Picayune* mocked, "Cassius reminds us of the man who hung himself just to see how it felt." Clay, however, had two motives. The first was to continue to argue afresh to Kentucky's white laborers that slavery was detrimental to their well-being. To this he added a new mission: to destabilize the Whig Party in the state.[5]

This was a significant shift for Clay. For years he had maintained his devotion to the Whigs, whose economic and social values so closely matched his own. In recent years, however, his loyalty had been tried. During his *True American* trauma, the mob that shuttered his printing office had been largely composed of Whig partisans, and he had not forgiven the insult. But the dominance of proslavery partisans over the Kentucky Whigs became clear during the state constitutional debate in 1849. During the convention, Whig delegates had largely capitulated to the demands of conservatives to ensure slavery's perpetual status. As Clay wrote to William Seward (himself still a Whig) in April 1849, the party had "become the guardians of slavery." In the spirit of revenge, he vowed to diminish Whig strength by peeling away votes with his Emancipation Party.[6]

The combination of his antislavery message and his political vendetta worried Clay's family. "I candidly believe, should Cassius be a candidate for either [governor or lieutenant governor], the probability to be great that he would be killed before the election," warned his brother-in-law J. Speed Smith in a letter of February 1850 to Brutus. "This opinion has been expressed here by several persons from different parts of the state," and there was more "hatred felt towards him than he is aware of." Smith urged his brother-in-law to come to home and persuade Cassius to change his mind. Whether such a visit occurred is unclear, but a letter from Smith to Brutus in March made it clear that the effort was futile: "It is the duty of his friends however to make an effort. . . . My thorough conviction is if he continues the canvas he will not live to see it ended."[7]

Unbowed, Clay wrote Seward in April, "The feeling is very bitter against me but by coolness and adroitness I trust I shall be able to weather it and establish the freedom of debate . . . and organize a party of true progress." He optimistically predicted winning between 5,000 and 10,000 votes, which he considered "a very good nucleus for future action." Canvassing the state tirelessly throughout the summer of 1851, he visited nearly eighty of Kentucky's then 100 counties, facing mostly hostile locals and largely empty venues but sometimes an appreciative crowd. His stump speeches contained familiar material, including statistics and arguments pointing to slavery's detriment to the common white worker. To these he added a critique of the newly strengthened fugitive slave law. This particular criticism, he admitted to Seward, was his "weak point," given his faithful hewing to a constitutional opposition to slavery. After all, article 4 of the Constitution contained a provision mandating the return of fugitives. Furthermore, he realized that this argument was more likely to enrage than to convince white voters. Kentucky shared hundreds of miles of border with free states, making its enslaved laborers more likely to escape and its enslavers supportive of the strengthened provision for their return.[8]

But to many Americans, including Clay, the strengthened fugitive slave clause was the most offensive aspect of the Compromise of 1850. Requiring Northern law enforcement officials to apprehend accused runaways on the thinnest of evidence, the law also mandated a system of federal commissioners who would adjudicate a presumed fugitive's status without the aid of a jury, testimony from the accused (which was prohibited by the law), or substantive evidence. Commissioners received ten dollars for remanding persons to their alleged owner but only five dollars if they did not. All of these stipulations stacked the deck in favor of white claimants, no matter how weak their case. It also spawned images of avaricious slave bounty hunters trolling Northern cities, indiscriminately apprehending African Americans no matter if they were legally free. "How can any lover of liberty or manliness go for *that*!" Clay remarked to Seward.[9]

In accordance with his legal and economic critique of slavery, Clay developed a more constitutionally anchored basis on which to condemn the law, arguing that it imposed an undue burden on the free states to apprehend and return fugitives. In his public writings he criticized the law not because of the tragic and inhumane reenslavement of individuals but as a violation of states' rights. The Constitution placed "no power in congress to compel the seizure and return of slaves at government expense," he wrote in a public letter, contending that the law was "null and void" on these grounds. "To compel Northern men to catch and bring back slaves, and pay the expenses," he continued, "makes them morally and politically responsible, for every slave held in these states!" Kentucky voters did not share Clay's qualms. In the election of August 1851, only 3,621 voters cast their ballots for him. When the Democratic candidate won by only 850 votes, however, Clay claimed vindication in denying the flagging Whig Party a victory. "Though my vote is small," he bragged to Salmon Chase, "I have overthrown the fictions of party."[10]

Satisfied that his work in Kentucky was finished for the time being, Clay pivoted more fully to the national debate. After years of eschewing third parties, he accepted Chase's invitation to join him at a meeting of the self-described Friends of Freedom, in Cleveland, Ohio, in September 1851. Led by Ohio congressman Joshua Giddings, Indiana politician George Julian, and abolitionist Lewis Tappan, the meeting functioned as a reconsolidation of Conscience Whigs, Free Democrats, and Free-Soilers. Free-Soil membership declined after the election of 1848, when many supporters retreated to their regular party homes. White moderates believed that the Compromise of 1850 had staved off the imminent threat of disunion, and their anger at the Slave Power had been offset by a relieved complacency, which meant that even vociferous critics of slavery such as Horace Greeley and William H. Seward continued to cling to the Whig Party.[11]

This was not true of the Friends of Freedom, who made up for what they lacked in numbers with their strident conviction that both Whigs and Democrats were fatally flawed in their willingness to capitulate to the Slave Power. The meeting of fall 1851 was to be a forum to denounce both the Democrats' and the Whigs' unsatisfactory positions on slavery ahead of the presidential election in 1852. Clay was elated to attend. "I'll be with you on the 24th in Cleveland, since you will have it so," he wrote to Chase enthusiastically. Meeting organizers, in turn, delighted in Clay's political conversion and eagerly anticipated his presence at the meeting. Clay's long battle against slavery gave him instant clout, and he was a featured speaker before the large crowd of attendees from ten states. Before them, he announced his regret "in acting so long with a party that has proved recreant to every principle of Liberty and Republicanism." "The time has come," he announced, "when I must separate myself from that party."[12]

Clay's speech also embraced the land policy of the Free-Soil movement, which adhered to Democratic principles in promoting land distribution for white Americans. For years, Clay had emphasized the unfair competition that white laborers endured in a slave economy. But on the question of landholding, Clay had retained a less democratic view that territorial land should be priced at its full value and distributed judiciously to those who paid for it. With his move to the Free-Soil Party came an evolution in his thinking or, at the least, his political strategy. Like other Free-Soilers, he began to talk about the increased availability of land and free labor as two sides of the same antislavery coin. As Clay wrote to Joshua Giddings ahead of the convention, "I differ with your friends on many subordinate matters, but I am willing to merge them in the great question."[13]

More than merging, Clay was broadening his position and increasing his potential political allies. "We must look for strength from the ranks of the Democratic working men of the country," he told his audience in Cleveland. "It should be the policy of the government to make every man a land holder. This will be our standing army." Castigating the position of his old party, he told them, "The Whig party embrace the landed property holders of the country; they are and always have been the conservatives of the country; and it is they who will in the final struggle, join the slave interests of the South." As a Vermont newspaper remarked with satisfaction after the close of the convention, "He now sees, what others have long seen, that the [W]hig party is no place for an antislavery man, and that its instincts are with all who would fatten on the unrequited toils of the masses, whether in the cotton mills of the North or the cotton plantations of the South."[14]

Attending the convention in Cleveland buoyed Clay's spirits and offered him a new sense of purpose. After enduring years of derision and threats at home in Kentucky and mistrust and skepticism from abolitionist circles, he found himself a valued and vaunted member of a viable political movement, leading him to imagine and articulate a role for himself in national politics. To Chase, he wrote: "I regard the liberation of my own state as the main object of my life, and would not willingly do anything to jeopardize that end. At the same time I feel that aid of public sentiment in the North is necessary to success here, and would make any personal sacrifice to forward the great cause of liberty to all North and South for it is at last one cause."[15]

Anticipating that they would not be able to stomach either of the two regular party presidential candidates, the Free-Soilers, who alternately referred to themselves as the Free Democrats, planned to run their own slate in the election of 1852. Sure enough, they found both nominees—Whig Winfield Scott and Democrat Franklin Pierce—unacceptable. New Hampshire native Pierce was a dough-face Northerner ever ready to capitulate to Southern demands, while Scott refused to denounce the Compromise of 1850. Though Free-Soilers understood that they had no hope of electoral victory, like birds of prey patiently circling a mortally wounded animal, they knew it would only be a matter of time before the Second Party System collapsed upon itself.[16]

A number of state Free-Soil organizations, including the Massachusetts State Central Committee and a delegation from Baltimore, mentioned Clay as a possible candidate for vice president. In advance of the convention, however, Clay made clear that he had no wish to run on the ticket in 1852. He wrote a letter to Gamaliel Bailey for publication in the *National Era*, in which he explained that while he was honored, he wished to wait and run at some future time when the chance of "victory and power" might be greater. Eventually New Hampshire's John P. Hale and Hoosier George Julian agreed to stand for president and vice president, respectively.[17]

Clay's plans to attend the Free Democratic nominating convention in Pittsburgh were thwarted when tragedy again struck his household in August. Two of his children died of fever. The first casualty was his eldest son, Elisha Warfield, and next to succumb was his infant daughter, Flora. Their grieving father also fell ill, though less gravely. The loss of sixteen-year-old Elisha, who had been by his father's side three years before during the melee at Foxtown, was particularly crushing for the Clays. Cassius felt a close bond with his firstborn son, whom he had raised to follow in his antislavery footsteps. Noting that Elisha had been "warmly sympathizing" with his cause, he told Seward: "It is a hard blow, and weakens much from all earth's promises of good!"[18]

As Clay remained in Kentucky, ill and sorrowful, the convention went on without him. With Black political leaders in attendance and Frederick Douglass serving as the gathering's secretary, the Free Democrats hammered out a platform that harnessed Free-Soil politics and the abolitionists' rising moral opposition to slavery anywhere. Reprising the Free-Soil Party's position of 1848 against the extension of slavery in new territories and for free federal distribution of territorial land to settlers, the new party condemned the Compromise of 1850 as "inconsistent with all the principles and maxims of Democracy." As for slavery itself, it was "a sin against God, and a crime against man, which no human enactment or usage can make right, and that Christianity, humanity, and patriotism alike demand its abolition."[19]

When Clay recovered from his illness and sought to escape his grief, he swiftly turned back to politics. Joining the Free Democrats' vice presidential candidate George Julian on the stump, Clay's strategy was to focus on Whig-leaning areas of northern Kentucky and condemn Whig nominee Winfield Scott for his commitment to enforcing the fugitive slave law. It proved a dangerous errand. While Clay and Julian found an orderly and attentive crowd in Maysville, it was a different story in Brooksville, a small hamlet in Bracken County, where they were greeted by a "brutalized rabble element." When Julian's entourage entered the courthouse where he was to speak, they discovered that the locals had spread their own excrement around the courtroom. Undeterred, Julian quipped: "Well, we should not complain of the Slave-Power; for this is the *strongest* argument they could have presented!" For all his mirth, however, Julian knew the danger was real. He would later write that "the most remarkable and praiseworthy thing about this congregation of Yahoos was that they did not mob us." Julian had only risked such danger because Clay, with his "right hand in the neighborhood of his revolver and ready for any emergency which the exercise of free speech might produce," could physically protect them both.[20]

In the end, the ticket featuring John P. Hale as president and Julian as vice president fared poorly in November, garnering only 156,667 popular votes (less than 5 percent of the total and a little over half the ballots they won in 1848) and not a single electoral vote. American voters, it seemed, were acting on the conviction that the Compromise of 1850, while not perfect, had settled the issue of slavery extension. Though partisans of Free Democracy were disappointed that Democrat Franklin Pierce, the decisively proslavery candidate, won the election soundly with 254 electoral votes to Scott's 52, they could at least take some consolation in the utter failure of the Whig Party in both the presidential and congressional elections.[21]

As Clay's politics evolved, so did the antislavery environment in which he operated. In May 1853, he traveled north to Boston to attend and speak at a dinner to honor Hale. Among the 1,500 attendees were many of the country's preeminent political abolitionists: Charles Sumner, Horace Mann, Charles Francis Adams, Joshua Leavitt, and Henry Wilson. Dinner guests toasted him as "The Kentucky Pioneer . . . who himself was so free he dared to speak for the slave." In tribute, the band played the War of 1812 tune "The Hunters of Kentucky," whose description of the state's men as being "half horse, half alligator," seemed to aptly capture Clay's muscular antislavery. The appreciative audience listened as he revisited his recent conversion from the Whig Party and encouraged all opponents of slavery to unite, buckle on their armor, and continue the fight. The time for gradualism was over, he insisted, commanding that "there is no other course left for us but to make open and avowed war upon the institution."[22]

His prominent role in the event, as well as the warm reception from his fellow Free-Soil advocates, confirmed Clay's place in an expanding and diverse national antislavery political force. Increasingly, radical and moderate activists who held a range of opinions on the constitutionality of slavery and the proper role of the federal government in ending it banded together. Another notable presence at the Hale dinner was William Lloyd Garrison, who had for decades eschewed political trappings. In his speech he declared that even though those present might quibble over the "best measure to be adopted, or the precise position to be occupied," they could all work together through politics to achieve slavery's end. While Garrison had disparaged Clay for his moderation in the past, he was generous in his praise for his "lion-hearted friend from Kentucky" at the Boston dinner, declaring: "If every man in the Southern States were like this man, we should be here, celebrating the jubilee," instead of making slow progress against slavery.[23]

While in Boston, a group of prominent African American reformers convened a meeting in Clay's honor at Belknap Street Church. The event's organizer was none other than Lewis Hayden, whose flight from slavery in Kentucky had caused such a scandal eight years earlier. In the intervening years, Hayden had made good use of his freedom. He worked for a time as a traveling speaker for the American Anti-Slavery Society, touring Northern cities and regaling audiences with tales of his oppression under slavery as well as his notorious and improbable escape. After settling with his family in Boston in 1849, Hayden became a leader of the Black antislavery community, and his boardinghouse became a "temple of refuge" for fugitives. His profile and activities grew in the years following passage of the Fugitive Slave Act of 1850. Boston was home to hundreds of escaped enslaved people, all of whom were vulnerable to recapture as slave catchers began to comb the city in the early 1850s, attempting to remand the human property of Southern slave owners. Hayden became a central figure in a network of activists who tried to thwart such activity, and he took part in a series of dramatic "rescues" of fugitives captured by authorities.[24]

In this atmosphere the difference between freedom and slavery was no mere abstraction or matter of moral debate. Freedom required action and, when necessary, even violence. Black antislavery reformers in Boston no doubt felt some kinship with Clay's readiness to rely on physical self-defense. At the Belknap Street Church celebration, William Lloyd Garrison offered another glowing tribute to Clay. Repeating old inaccuracies about the manumission of Clay's enslaved laborers, Garrison told the audience that "in spite of his educational training and a murderous pro-slavery sentiment, he gave unconditional freedom to all his slaves, and from that hour proclaimed eternal hostility to the slave system." "You know what he has sacrificed and what he has periled," he added. Then Hayden himself introduced Clay, as the Black audience cheered loudly and waved their handkerchiefs in appreciation. From the podium, Clay addressed his attentive listeners, praising them for "the redemption of their brethren" as well as their "progress on the scale of humanity."[25]

Yet Clay's remarks also laid bare his own complicated racial thinking. The next day, the *Liberator* reported that he offered his African American audience "many useful suggestions on the means of improving their mental, moral, and civil condition," explaining how they might accrue wealth and achieve social advancement. Though Clay's tone was paternalistic, he clearly had come to believe that African Americans, while perhaps not yet prepared for full equality and citizenship, were, in the right circumstance, quite capable of becoming so.[26]

This environmentalist understanding of race was at other times tempered by Clay's reading of contemporary American ethnological thought, which relied on specious theories of skull size and polygenesis to posit African inferiority. Clay's public addresses often bore the marks of such thinking. In 1846, he had summarized this philosophy before a Philadelphia audience: "I am of the opinion that the Caucasian or white is the superior race; they have the larger and better formed brain; much more developed form and exquisite structure. Modern discovery proved that the builders of the pyramids and the Egyptian founders of signs and letters were white. And this long-disputed problem is now settled. Historians now unite in making the Caucasian race the first in civilization through all past time."[27]

Yet he did not think that white superiority was necessarily permanent. His advice to his audience in Boston echoed that which he gave a group of Ohio African Americans who had solicited a letter of support from him a year earlier. In that missive, which organizers of a Cincinnati convention of the "Colored Freeman," read aloud, Clay offered encouraging words about the future, explaining: "I have no faith in the permanent inferiority of nations! I think history proves the opposite. Virtue, patience, energy, self-denial and an eternal purpose to improve, may place the African where the Saxon now is! Whilst the opposite vices may degrade the Saxon below the African!" Clay laid out a prescription for advancement. "The blacks should 'get money,'" he told them. "Let them go into the trades—become farmers—manufacturers—where capital and employment are wanting—let them combine, and thus diminish the expense of living, and increase their productive power. Action—action—action—must be the panacea for your present woes, and the 'Sessame' of future regeneration." He also insisted that they be patient in demanding complete equality with white Americans. "With regard to 'political' rights," he told them, "you must abide your time! I think nothing can be done at present by public resolves . . . the best road to political elevation lies through the road of INDUSTRY and SELF-RESPECT, which will at last wear us into a generous magnanimity. . . . After a while, if your oppressors do not knock off your chains, you will outgrow them!"[28]

Clay was not alone in his insistence that Black men would have to wait for political rights until after they had proved their capability. All but the most liberal-minded white antislavery partisans tended to bear some level of racial prejudice against African Americans. Some viewed Black Americans as biologically inferior, while others believed that societal degradation—caused by subservience or lack of education—was responsible for their reduced condition. Whatever they believed, many white and even some Black abolitionists saw African Americans, as one historian has put it, as "social problems that needed to be fixed." William Lloyd Garrison himself insisted that free African Americans must strive to adopt the habits and values of middle-class white society, including educational, financial, and moral improvement, before they could realistically expect to earn the respect of whites. Thus, while Black freedom was an immediate goal for many white antislavery reformers, Black equality often was not.[29]

Cassius Clay's broadened scope of antislavery action was not limited to his expanding relationships with Northern abolitionists. At home in Kentucky, he began to collaborate with antislavery Christians, a group he had previously largely ignored. Although Clay sought Christian baptism during his college days in Connecticut, he was an infrequent churchgoer and not particularly pious. He did admire the precepts of what he called "true Christianity" but was consistently quick to point out that Christian tenets had just as often served as a justification for the peculiar institution as a rationale for its end. Resenting the tendency of many Kentucky clergy members to view slavery as a practice ordained by God, he believed that they had done "more for infidelity than the infidels." Furthermore, Clay's dedication to constitutional logic had also caused him to eschew abolitionist "higher law" doctrine. For him, there was no "law superior to that of the federal Constitution." But in the early 1850s, for reasons that had little to do with their religious convictions, he began to see antislavery missionaries as useful partners in his work in Kentucky.[30]

Clay's work in his home state to this point had focused on a broad political appeal to Kentucky's white working class. The scant votes he garnered in the election of 1851, however, revealed that instead of simply appealing to white antislavery voters, he would have to cultivate them. The ideal place to attempt this, he decided, was the mountainous eastern portion of the state, in which large-scale agriculture and slave ownership, and thus proslavery principles, were not as prevalent. Clay began to dream of a political base near the foothills of the Appalachians, believing, as he later wrote, that "if [the Kentucky mountaineers] were once committed to liberation of the slaves, we could have a permanent nucleus of political and physical force." Religion could be the conduit, and evangelical ministers could serve as emissaries for a Christian brand of antislavery that would then extend to the ballot box. He planned, he told Salmon Chase, "to [press] the light into the mountains by papers and priests." In 1853, he enticed several men associated with the American Missionary Association to settle in an area of Madison County known as the Glades by offering them small tracts of the land he owned there.[31]

The most prominent of his recruits was John G. Fee. Like Clay, Fee was a native Kentuckian, born into a slaveholding family from Bracken County. As a young adult, he attended Cincinnati's Lane Theological Seminary, where he became simultaneously a committed Christian and an abolitionist. On graduation he sought Presbyterian ordination but soon left the church, in part because it did not support his antislavery convictions and because he had come to embrace a nonsectarian vision of Christianity. In the late 1840s, he wandered from pulpit to pulpit throughout Lewis, Bracken, and other counties in the northeastern part of the state, sustained by small stipends from the American Missionary Association, preaching in whatever churches or homes were open to him.[32]

The two men had begun corresponding in the mid-1840s, and Clay featured some of Fee's writings in the *True American*. Not until the 1850s, however, did they commence what would become a remarkable, if often contentious, antislavery collaboration. Although they shared a similar background and commitment to remaining in Kentucky, there were distinct differences in both their situations and approaches. Fee's family had disowned him, whereas Cassius still relied on the monetary and social support of his kinship network. Where Clay's antislavery conviction was informed by constitutional logic and a stubborn sense of moral and economic rectitude, Fee's was sustained by a fiery and uncompromising conviction of slavery's moral evil. He published several unsparing tracts including *Sinfulness of Slavery* and *Non-Fellowship with Slaveholders the Duty of Christians* in which he castigated proslavery Christianity and demanded that no true Christian worship alongside slaveholders.[33]

When Cassius invited Fee to settle in Madison County, the minister was initially reluctant to leave northern Kentucky. But the chronically penurious pastor realized that Clay could provide a permanent pulpit, a home for his family, and a base for his missionary activities. Clay soon showed himself useful in other ways when, in August 1853, one of Fee's compatriots landed in jail in a neighboring county for purportedly urging an enslaved man to run away. Clay bailed him out of jail and wrote a public letter denying the charges and defending the man's right to free speech. Fee and his fellow missionaries quickly realized the importance of having brave friends in high places.[34]

In addition to building up his antislavery political base in Kentucky, Clay spent much of 1853 improving his ever-languishing finances. He bolstered his livestock business, continuing to raise sheep and cattle, and expanded his operations to include swine. Pork had played a central role in the diets of Americans since colonial times, but its popularity surged in the mid-nineteenth century. It was cheap and, when salt cured, eminently portable and shelf-stable, making it a vital form of sustenance for everyone from midwestern homesteaders and gold miners in California to urban factory workers in the Northeast and enslaved laborers in the Deep South. Clay was advantageously situated to take advantage of the American pork boom. He had fields full of clover, oats, and corn to fatten his stock, and his estate was only a few days' walk from Cincinnati, the largest pork market in the world. Newspapers reported that Clay drove an estimated 3,000 hogs to the city in 1853. The *Chicago Tribune* called him "one of the most successful Pork dealers" in Cincinnati, claiming that he had earned $20,000 that year and stood to make two or three times that the next. His detractors scoffed at the nature of his newfound success. "How the mighty are fallen!" mocked the *New Orleans Crescent*. "From politics to pork! From humanity to hogs! From philosophy to pigs. . . . Still, he is a demagogue; he loves the swinish multitude, and is a whole-hog man!"[35]

But Free-Soil advocates quickly turned Clay's thriving business into a lesson in how free labor might succeed within a slave economy. In a widely reprinted interview with the *New-York Tribune*, Clay explained that the emancipation of his slaves nearly a decade before had "quite unexpectedly to him proved a profitable operation." "Having been an extensive stock-rearing farmer for many years previously, and being every way surrounded and hedged in by slavery and slave labor," wrote the reporter, "he naturally supposed that the liberation of his slaves would subject him to embarrassment and probably loss in his farming operations." To the contrary, however, "his experience ha[d] dissipated all apprehensions." Without acknowledging the numerous enslaved people still residing and working at White Hall, the *Tribune* insisted that Clay had "no difficulty in hiring white labor according to his needs and at reasonable rates" and that he employed "a portion of his former slaves at wages mutually satisfactory." Moreover, the paper reported that his agricultural operation was "considerably improved . . . in fertility and productiveness." Before, "his farm used to run him in debt, or at least yield him no profit," but he was now making money by it. Horace Greeley's paper trumpeted the success of this "single experiment in emancipation, made under the most discouraging and embarrassing auspices." If it could turn out so well, "with slavery and anti-abolition hemming in on every side, with the least possible diversification of labor among the surrounding community," think of the possibilities elsewhere in the South.³⁶

While passing through central Kentucky en route to Texas that year, journalist Frederick Law Olmsted also observed Clay's robust business activity. Olmsted, who had not yet begun the career in landscape architecture that would make him famous, was journeying through the South on a mission to observe and interpret the customs and habits of the region's inhabitants for a book he would title *A Journey through Texas*. On his way from Cincinnati to Lexington, Olmsted's carriage became tangled in a throng of hogs trotting toward a slaughterhouse in Cincinnati. His fellow carriage mates, a storekeeper and a slaveholding farmer from the Bluegrass region, pointed out that the brand marks on many of the hogs identified them as belonging to "Cash Clay." The men had heard that Clay was set to make a good deal of money off his swine, perhaps as much as $40,000.³⁷

The conversation quickly pivoted from Clay's finances to a broader discussion of his character. Olmsted was surprised to learn that though both men disapproved of Clay's politics, they admired his bravery. "I don't like an abolitionist, but by God I do like a man that ain't afraid to say what he believes," claimed one of the travelers. The other concurred, remarking, "I hate an abolitionist, but I do admire a Kentuckian who dares to stay in Kentucky and say he's an abolitionist if he is one." Olmsted heard numerous other assessments of Clay during his stay in Lexington, some of which held a "similar tone of admiration for his courage and great force of character." The Kentuckians Olmsted met seemed to be able to appraise his personal traits and business acumen separately from his political views. "He was considered an excellent farmer," Olmsted noted, but "of course on the subject of slavery, 'deluded' (with an expression of pity), and as to influence, 'losing rapidly,'" sentiments that reflected Clay's unique ability to leverage his success in ventures (such as farming and military service), which earned the respect of his neighbors, to compensate for the views that angered them.³⁸

Cassius's renewed attention to his business and his sedentary interlude must have been a relief for Mary Jane. The recent years had brought both blessings and sadness: the birth of daughter, Laura, in 1849, followed by the double loss of Elisha and Flora in 1852. Cassius continued to mourn the loss of his son in particular, writing William Seward that "it was indeed the hardest blow I ever received, and has for me stripped life of most of its hopes and joys." The stresses of Cassius's political career and his frequent absences from home, combined with the family's precarious finances and emotional losses, had taken a toll on the couple's relationship. When an acquaintance offered to send Mary Jane a copy of Clay's portrait, he told him not to bother, writing: "Mrs. C is not much in love with my face *now*."[39]

His business and familial concerns could not hold Clay's attention for long, however. He was soon lured back into national affairs by a political cataclysm unleashed in 1854. The sense of complacency regarding slavery's expansion into which many white Americans had been lulled in the aftermath of the Compromise of 1850 ended in January 1854, when Illinois senator Stephen A. Douglas submitted a bill to organize the Nebraska Territory. This move, designed to facilitate a transcontinental rail route originating in Chicago, required significant backing from Southern Democratic senators to pass. To ensure that support, Douglas proposed dividing the area into two territories in which settlers would decide for themselves whether those states would legalize slavery. With a significant number of slaveholders already populating the area demarcated as Kansas, the assumption was that settlers there would vote to allow the institution.[40]

As Americans and their elected representatives tried to make sense of it, the legislation "raised," as Douglas himself had anticipated, "a hell of a storm," as it negated the terms of the Missouri Compromise, which had geographically bounded slave and free territory for nearly a quarter of a century. Within the political tumult, however, antislavery politicians saw the Nebraska legislation as the wake-up call the American public needed to realize the true menace of the Slave Power. Days before the bill went before Congress, Senators Salmon Chase and Charles Sumner, along with congressional representatives Joshua Giddings, Edward Wade, Gerrit Smith, and Alexander De Witt, published their "Address of the Independent Democrats in Congress." "We arraign this bill as a gross violation of a sacred pledge," they fumed, "as a criminal betrayal of precious rights; as part and parcel of an atrocious plot to exclude from a vast unoccupied region, immigrants from the Old World and free laborers from our own states, and convert it into a dreary region of despotism, inhabited by masters and slaves." The Nebraska bill, they argued, would take some of the most fertile new land on the continent, degrade it with slave labor, and render it valueless.[41]

The "Independent Democrats" sought not only to fan the flames of abolitionist and free labor indignation in the North but to untether, once and for all, even the moderate foes of slavery from the Whig and Democratic Parties. In 1852, both regular parties had clung to the Compromise of 1850 precisely to preserve the tenuous bonds that held their Southern and Northern wings together. Those bonds could no longer hold. "We shall go home to our constituents; erect anew the standard of Freedom, and call on the People to come to the rescue of the country from the domination of Slavery," Chase and Sumner promised. In the weeks after Douglas presented his bill, disenchanted citizens convened in Jackson, Michigan, and Ripon, Wisconsin, promising to shed old labels and form a new party based first and foremost on opposition to the Nebraska bill. In May, the Wisconsinites assumed the label "Republican," as did thirty members of the House of Representatives. Like-minded (if not yet like-named) political organizations coalesced in states throughout the Midwest, as well as in Vermont, donning such names as "Fusion" and "Union."[42]

At home in Kentucky, Cassius Clay worked to stir up opposition to the Nebraska bill, denouncing it in speeches in Louisville and Mount Vernon. Salmon Chase urged him to take his admonitions farther afield and to travel to the territory in question. He declined, citing his need to attend his business interests. As he told Chase: "Mrs. Clay is of the opinion that as I went to the war for the good of the cause so as to open up debate in Ky. It now devolves on some one else to go to Nebraska." "Be not impatient," he reassured Chase, "for I think I have labored enough to rest awhile if I choose, but I shall 'keep moving.'"[43]

When it came up for vote in May, the Kansas-Nebraska Act proved just as divisive as its detractors had anticipated. Senators voted along sectional lines to approve its passage, 37 to 14. In the House, with the help of Southern Democrats and Southern Whigs, the bill passed 113 to 100, allowing President Pierce to sign it into law. Many Northern Whigs were now ready to abandon the party, and that month, around thirty congressmen adopted the name "Republican."[44]

In June, Clay made good on his promise to Chase to "keep moving." He penned a letter to Horace Greeley for publication in the *New-York Tribune*, in which he characterized the Kansas-Nebraska Act as an ill-considered compromise of politics and principles. "We committed a national crime in joining hands with the slaveholders to commit a determined wrong against the rights of the African," he wrote, "and now in due season, the poisoned chalice is returned to our own lips." He once again denounced abolition but asserted unequivocally that the nation's "only salvation" was "making the overthrow of slavery our dominant idea." No longer could other issues such as tariffs, free trade, and temperance stand as primary considerations in party politics. All elections, "even for the most inferior offices," he added, must "turn on repeal of the Nebraska bill"—with all other policy issues subordinated.[45]

Clay's letter went beyond a prescription for a new antislavery party. In a full display of the aggression for which he was now famous, he sought to hold those who voted in favor of the legislation accountable. The first step, Clay charged, would be to "punish the *traitors*," by "break[ing] them on the wheel of public opinion." He wanted them ostracized in social, business, and political circles. In an even more radical proposal, however, he acknowledged that Southerners had already predicted the "dissolution of the American Union" and urged the Northern public to make some cold, hard calculations about the ultimate compatibility of the slave and free states. Predicting future events with near-perfect accuracy, Clay mused: "Suppose then a Republican elected President on the [issue of slavery], and that the ultras of the South in their madness overawe the more thoughtful citizens, and secede from Congress, and declare the Union dissolved. Then either we must whip them in, or allow a peaceable separation as circumstances shall warrant." Clay calculated hypothetically that since the Americans loyal to the government would "retain the organization—the treasury, the navy, and the army," they would surely win any conflict and could then "compel emancipation." In closing, he announced: "I am ready to complete the sacrifice and triumph of our fathers of 1776 at all hazards. I am for no Union without Liberty—if need be through dissolution and war."[46]

From the pages of the *Tribune*, Cassius's letter quickly made the rounds in newspapers throughout the country. Southern editors were horrified. While they were accustomed to hearing their own threats of disunion, they found it alarming for an antislavery partisan to float the idea and to do so in such specific terms. In Virginia, the *Richmond Enquirer* found Clay's "precise and formal" description particularly disturbing. "We must confess that this system of antislavery aggression is very different from the vain and aimless agitation of the Greeleys and the Garrisons," the editor wrote, but noted with alarm the "consistency and directness in its aim" in Clay's writing "and a bold out spoken courage in its avowal, which distinguish it from the meaningless demonstrations of crazy fanatics." A writer for the *Huntsville Democrat*, meanwhile, worried that Clay's radical views were gaining widespread acceptance in the North. "The suggestions of Cassius M. Clay are themselves entitled to no consideration, for he is known and distrusted as a crazy enthusiast with as little weight of character as sobriety of judgement," stated the Alabama paper, "but it happens that in this instance that the intemperate counsels of the fanatic are approved by the more cautious and conservative members of the anti-slavery party."[47]

Criticism of Clay's letter was not confined to the South. From the nation's capital, the conservative *Washington Sentinel* pronounced: "The worst abolitionist that can be found—and happily for the country they are scarce—is the southern abolitionist." The *Sentinel* columnist accused Clay of being an insane madman, and especially dangerous as "abolitionists resemble those savage tribes among whom the most crazy are deemed the wisest," regarding them as "seers and prophets." Others did not appreciate Clay's moralizing tone. "We cannot think that the fact that Cassius M. Clay liberated his slaves gives him any title to write gasconading letters to the North, and with a dictatorial air, intrude his advice upon us as to how we shall manage our politics," said a writer from the *Buffalo Commercial*. The author lambasted both the "blistering absurdity" of Clay's letter and his suggestion of forming a "great sectional party powerful enough to carry the next Presidential election," the result of which would be "the death blow of the Union."[48]

There is no doubt that Clay's past record of belligerence as well as his Southern provenance added weight to his bellicose statements. "It has been said that the renegade priest makes the most ferocious heretic—that an anti-slavery Yankee becomes frequently the most inveterate slave driver, and the converted slaveholder is sure to eclipse in his zeal for emancipation the most fiery native born abolitionist," stated the *New York Daily Herald*. "It was so with Birney—it is so with Cassius M. Clay. Late a Kentucky slaveholder, he now throws Garrison, Parker, Phillips, and Greeley into the shade with his schedule of radical, practical, and revolutionary abolition projects." Like the *Richmond Enquirer*, the *Daily Herald* noted the alarming calculus of Clay's plan and his national appeal. His critics understood that the very element of his personality that made him dangerous in their eyes might cast him as prophet of political change to others. Clay and his friends thought so, too.[49]

In the summer of 1854, Clay finally took up Chase's charge to help organize the new Republican Party. He headed to Illinois, where the Whig and Democratic Party organizations remained strong and where he hoped to make new converts as well as boost anti-Nebraska candidates in the fall elections. In July alone, he spoke at over a dozen towns and cities, including Alton, Freeport, and Bloomington. He also stopped in Springfield, where he met Abraham Lincoln, then a Whig candidate for Congress, for the first time. At each stop, Clay spoke for two to three hours to large crowds, including an audience of 20,000 in Chicago, denouncing the Kansas-Nebraska Act as a conspiracy of the Southern Slave Power to close vast amounts of new territory to free labor. The time was right, he told his audiences, for a new party that could boldly "strike at the monster aggressor wherever it could be reached under the constitution—an organization of men of whatever politics, of Free-Soilers, Whigs, and Democrats who should bury past animosities and repent past errors."[50]

Reiterating a point he made in his *Tribune* letter, Clay proclaimed that Northerners must not bow down before secessionist threats from Southerners nor compromise free-soil and antislavery principles. "If you want me to love the union," he told them, "you must make it loveable." Southerners were playing a game of bluff, he added. "What have you to fear if 800,000 slaveholders should dissolve the Union?" he asked his audience. "Let them go off if they will! But they will not go. They expect to play the same game of brag, which they have played with so much success; but when they find out you are in earnest, they will acquiesce." Newspapers made note of the large crowds he drew, with one pronouncing: "Clay is making his mark."[51]

The Republican Party was a hard sell in Illinois, whose native son, Stephen A. Douglas, had proposed the Kansas amendment and where many voters still clung to their Whig identity. Still others were drawn to another independent political group, the Know-Nothing Party, so named because its adherents were meant to feign ignorance of its very existence. This party had materialized in 1852 and 1853 as a nativist reaction to a decade of explosive European immigration to the United States. Irish Catholics constituted the majority of the newcomers, raising fears among some Protestants of the immigrants' papist, antidemocratic influence on politics and society. Still others disdained the Catholic cultural acceptance of alcohol. The Know-Nothings, who also referred to their organization as the American Party, aimed to exclude Catholics from public office and to extend the naturalization period for foreigners. They were poised to take advantage of the destabilized political landscape. By 1854, the Know-Nothings boasted a membership of over 1 million, and in 1855, with the fallout over Nebraska, the Know-Nothings stood ready to capture the votes of people who supported the nonextension of slavery, the prohibition of alcohol, and limits on immigration.[52]

The Know-Nothings established strongholds in the Midwest and Northeast and also did well in the Upper South among voters who were not necessarily antislavery but felt that immigrants posed a greater threat to America's future than did limits on slavery's expansion. Among them was Brutus Clay, who briefly affiliated with the party. Cassius himself had no use for Know-Nothingism, finding its tenets antithetical to his aims of increasing white foreign immigration to the Bluegrass State and the rest of the South. He and other Republican politicians focused single-mindedly on the issue of slavery, hoping that Know-Nothingism's surge was brief. He and other Republicans worried that the Know-Nothings' success in congressional elections in Maryland, Kentucky, and Missouri in 1855 would negatively affect their own advancement. As one Kentucky paper put it: "Mr. Clay thinks with Greeley and Julian and Weed, that the American party must be put down, or else that it will put them down."[53]

After he returned to Kentucky, Clay wrote Chase that his trip through Illinois had "greatly encouraged" him but that its residents had "need of more speeches and a more thorough canvas," especially in the Southern part of the state, where the "ignorant from the slave states" had immigrated and settled. He also weighed in on the name of the new party, a subject about which he claimed to be "indifferent." "The name of Republican adopted in several states is significant," he told Chase, but added: "I think we should be less anxious about [new] names—but rather about dropping old ones."[54]

Clay's aims in party building were not altogether altruistic. As he envisioned the possibilities for the burgeoning antislavery party, he also anticipated the prospects for his own political opportunity within it. For years he had watched as his friends Seward and Chase had navigated successful paths, building political coalitions within their states, piecing together constituencies to propel them into state and national offices where they could both effect reform and forge careers. Cassius, of course, enjoyed very little support and much enmity in his home state. As a founding member of a fledgling party, however, he could help build a viable national organization and earn political capital that might propel him into national office, either by nomination or by appointment, circumventing the need for support in Kentucky.

His Illinois trip proved so successful that Clay alighted again in early 1855 for a three-month tour on the antislavery lecture circuit. He made stops in large cities such as Pittsburgh, New York, and Boston, as well as in smaller towns in Pennsylvania and New York. In each, he gave a similar two-hour-long address about the "despotism of slavery." The Kansas-Nebraska Act, he told his audiences, had merely confirmed that the Slave Power enchained not only the South's enslaved workers but the entire country. Indeed, by the time of Clay's tour, the consequences of the Nebraska bill were no longer theoretical. The illusion that voters could determine slavery's future in Kansas in free and fair elections shattered when thousands of proslavery men from neighboring Missouri descended on the polls to cast fraudulent votes in favor of slavery in the newly organized territory. Sympathetic to Southern interests, Franklin Pierce offered no help to his own appointed territorial governor, Andrew Reeder, as Reeder tried to curtail this activity. Referring to the voter intimidation occurring in Kansas in a speech in Pittsburgh, Clay asked: "What do now the advocates of Popular Sovereignty? They come from Missouri by the thousands with bowie knives and revolvers, take possession of the polls, and drive away free voters. This is pitiable." Clay believed that he was effective in winning voters to the new Republican Party and told William Seward, who had himself finally joined the Republican Party, "In my humble way of nightly lectures . . . I trust I am doing good service in the common cause—my audiences are overflowing and enthusiastic."[55]

But while Clay's political prospects appeared to be on the rise, his finances were not. In 1854 and early 1855, he made a series of risky financial decisions based around speculation in the pork market. To fund these ventures, Clay and several other Kentucky investors established a banking house in Cincinnati that opened in September 1854. Clay took out loans to provide his share of the financing and relied on Brutus to serve as his security on them. As collateral, he offered one of his ferries, as well the half-shares of the livestock he co-owned with his brother. Ever the optimist, Cassius believed he could tend to business while simultaneously developing his political career.[56]

Brutus, however, grew alarmed by his brother's risky behavior as well as his absenteeism. Though Cassius tried to justify his lecturing excursions to his ever-sensible brother by explaining that he earned fifty dollars for each speech, it was clear that his physical absence was detrimental to his financial security. As he was touring the Northeast in early 1855, news trickled out that after only a few months in operation, his bank would be closing. Once home, Cassius scrambled to shore up his finances. He planned sell Brutus some property and use the cash to repay creditors. In March, very quietly, he sold his brother an enslaved man named Daniel for $500. Cassius had inherited Daniel in his father's will, which stipulated that he remain in Sally's service during her lifetime. This transfer of human property from one brother to another occurred on a single piece of paper, out of the sight of both Cassius's antislavery followers and his proslavery enemies. The transaction remained unknown to them and perhaps even to Daniel as he toiled away in Sally Dudley's Frankfort home. The following day, in another bill of sale, Cassius transferred to Brutus the ownership of his bull, Locomotive, for $1,750 and his jackass, Republic, for $3,900. In the Clay brothers' accounting, a bovine and a mule were many times more valuable than a man, and the ownership of one could be transferred as easily as another.[57]

Still, Clay could not pay back all of his lenders, and several took him to court. "My creditors are clamorous and relentless," he wrote to John Fee, "my losses by late failures are great, and my whole property is threatened!" He was on the brink of financial disaster but, with Brutus's help, managed to stave it off. Relieved, he wrote Salmon Chase in May: "I have found my creditors much more indulgent than I had any reason to anticipate." He explained, however, that his situation would keep him home and out of the public sphere for a while. "I shall be compelled to devote my whole time to the recruit of my means," he told him. "This I more regret as there are stirring times ahead when I should be glad to be where I used to work in the port of danger if not in the port of honor." He said much the same to William Seward, writing optimistically that he believed that "with every energy and economy," he would escape his "pecuniary difficulties."[58]

But in his own backyard, the fight against slavery in Kentucky continued to distract Clay. Despite his desperate financial straits, Cassius continued to support of Fee and the other missionaries he had coaxed to southern Madison County. Earlier in the year Fee had started a small school, which he named Berea, on the land Clay had given him. He hoped to grow it into a full-fledged college modeled on Oberlin, an Ohio college that coeducated white and Black students. The cash-strapped Clay had also given Fee $200 to build a house for his family. The prospect of having Fee and his establishment as a permanent neighbor distressed the minister's proslavery neighbors. Their alarm intensified when the minister began traveling to surrounding counties, preaching the antislavery gospel. It was dangerous work he was willing to undertake only because he realized that his brazen benefactor could provide physical protection. Fee, who disdained violence and armed himself only with the Gospel, soon found himself in need of a more vigorous defense when rumors developed that he was distributing religious pamphlets to enslaved people, an act that locals feared would lead to rebellion. In July, when he attempted to preach a sermon in nearby Lincoln County, a group of well-armed local residents ejected him from the church, forced him onto his horse, and rode him out of town. Fee sought legal justice, but a local grand jury dismissed the case. Soon after, he went to preach another service in neighboring Rockcastle County, where another gun-toting mob intimidated him.[59]

Incensed, Clay hastened to Fee's defense. On the grounds, as he later wrote, that denying free speech would be the death of "the whole scheme of emancipation," he announced that he would accompany Fee to Rockcastle County, where they would both speak. In contrast to his previous impulsive reactions to such bullying, Clay carefully orchestrated his response to Fee's evictions. A man of both weapons and words, he penned a letter to the *Cincinnati Enquirer*, in which he declared that Fee had been falsely accused of distributing biblical tracts to enslaved people in an effort to incite insurrection. "I come to the rescue of my friend, the defender of my cause," he pronounced.[60]

While the standoffs between Clay, Fee, and antiabolition forces in southeastern Kentucky were local affairs, Clay tied them to the larger national political forces. Comparing the local forces who shut down Fee to the proslavery ruffians in Kansas, he exclaimed that in both instances, the Slave Power had "taken possession of the press, the pulpit, and the government." Clay's reaction was no mere publicity stunt. He sincerely viewed such provincial situations as part of the larger sectional blood contest between free-soil and proslavery forces. In a letter to Salmon Chase, he described the situation he and Fee faced in Kentucky as "a concerted effort through all the south to crush us," adding that "the subservience of the North *has* and does encourage them to do it!"⁶¹

Clay and Fee's cooperative endeavor illustrated the way in which, by 1855, the boundaries between differing antislavery motivations and strategies had softened and blurred. Clay traveled to Rockcastle County with a small posse to speak in defense of Fee's right to free speech. Once there, he encouraged sympathetic audience members to rise to Fee's aid and "to furnish their rifles, if they had any; if no rifle, their double or single barrel shot guns, their Colt's revolvers—and if they had neither, then their kitchen butcher knife." In another sign of changing times, the editors of the *Anti-Slavery Bugle*, who had denounced Clay in the past for both his inconsistent views and his reliance on armed self-defense, reported on Clay's actions sympathetically. This was in part because they supported Fee's moral abolitionism, but it was more broadly an indicator of how antislavery action had changed since the early 1850s. Whether in the context of slave rescues in the Northeast or in resisting ruffians in Kansas, abolitionists found that armed resistance was increasingly central to their fight against slavery.⁶²

To press his point, Clay accompanied Fee to another venue in Lincoln County, where, though warned away by local slaveholders, he spoke unmolested. Newspapers around the country covered their joint activities, judging them either brave or foolish. George Prentice, editor of the *Louisville Daily Journal*, offered measured approval of Clay's stalwart stand for the First Amendment, stating: "We think that such opinions as those of Mr. Clay and Mr. Fee are wrong and of a mischievous tendency, but we rejoice to see Mr. Clay vindicating fearlessly the freedom of speech." "Emancipationists," he asserted, "have a right to speak their opinions publicly in Kentucky so long as they speak them only to white men. We abhor mob law, and we thank every man, who, like Cassius M. Clay, has the manliness to set it at all defiance." The more conservative *Louisville Courier*, however, viewed the public speaking as a dangerous and self-serving ploy on Clay's part. Editor Walter Haldeman described him as "brimming full of fight, and armed to the teeth," and "very anxious to massacre somebody, or be massacred himself, not being very particular, so that he could thereby obtain additional notoriety." The editor of the *Washington Sentinel* agreed, calling Clay a "brave maniac."⁶³

These speaking engagements in 1855 gave rise to a new and indelible legend about Clay. Originating in the *Northern Christian Advocate*, a Methodist antislavery newspaper from New York, the story explained how he managed his audiences with "moral suasion." According to the account, Clay would enter his venue—usually a country church or a rural courtroom—and walk through the crowd approaching the lectern. Addressing his audience, Clay would remove three items from his carpetbag. The first was a Bible, which he claimed was his "appeal to the religious portion of society." The second was a copy of the US Constitution, which he used to "appeal to gentlemen, to patriots, and all True-hearted Americans." His final accessory was a revolver. According to one Indiana newspaper, Clay brandished the weapon, saying: "Here gentlemen, is a six-shooter every barrel of which is heavily loaded with powder and cold lead. This is my appeal to the mobocrats and I will blow its contents through the heart of the first man who offers to lay his hands on me, to silence me in my native State, or to gag free speech in my presence." "This," claimed the newspaper correspondent, "he lays down upon the stand with his two former appeals, ready for action; then he commences in a perfect storm against the peculiar institution, enough to wring the sweat of old Kentucky through every pore," leaving his audience "awed into submissive silence."[64]

Years later, in his autobiography, Clay dismissed this story as untrue. "Thus related," he argued, "it would seem I had made a prepared and threatened exhibition of my courage and prowess, when in fact, I was exerting all my powers of appeal and argument to avoid a conflict; for such avoidance was victory." More practically, he noted that he had no need to carry a Bible, as every country meetinghouse already contained a copy, and moreover, had he laid his pistol out in the open, "some enemy was likely to seize it." Nevertheless, the story spread. The image of the gun, the Bible, and the Constitution seemed to capture the essence of the "fighting Christian" Cassius had become to Americans by the mid-1850s because of his cooperation with Fee. Fee himself enhanced this sanctified version of his collaborator by attesting in the national press that in addition to running his domestic and agricultural operations with free labor, Clay regularly attended an antislavery church.[65]

Both the nature of Clay's relationship to slavery and his opposition to it remained unchanged, however. He continued to own and rely on the labor of enslaved men and women and, when necessary, sold them without remorse. And despite his new collaboration with Christian abolitionists, he continued to stake his antislavery position squarely on constitutional principles. Behind his blustery defense of Fee's right to free speech, Clay understood that the clergyman was walking a fine line and that, by extension, so was he. Clay warned Fee that he could only defend him as far as the Constitution would allow. "I call your attention once more to the only safe ground of opposition to slavery in my judgement," wrote Clay. "That it is the *creature of law*—and we propose not to violate the law—but to *unmake it by law*. That it is our constitutional right to create slavery—the same right in the very way to *un*make it!" As bold as Clay was, he knew that any discussion of antislavery in Kentucky could safely occur only between whites: "As the slaves have no voice in the matter *we have nothing to do with them in anyway*," he instructed Fee firmly. "Any other communication with the slave except through the master is not to be thought of by us." "I trust your views coincide with mine in this respect," Clay wrote in warning. "I cannot make defense on any other grounds." By the mid-1850s, the increasing dissonance between the facts and fictions of Clay's antislavery persona were partially of his own making but magnified by antislavery thinkers of both the political and moral variety who saw in him a compelling figure who could further their cause. Though Clay was in no haste to unmake such a mythological construction, he likely realized that it could not hold for long.[66]

Chapter 7
Shot and Shell

As Clay fought the peculiar institution and its defenders in his own backyard, *National Era* editor Gamaliel Bailey penned an article that captured the state of national antislavery politics. "There is no *Whig*, no *Democratic*, party," he bellowed from the pages of his paper in early August 1855. "There are but two parties—the *Party of Freedom* . . . and the *Party of Slavery*, with its head in the South, and tail in the North, its chiefs, the Slaveholding Oligarchy . . . which they affect to call 'Democratic.'" There was no longer room for equivocation over slavery in American politics. "The Question," continued Bailey, "has thrust aside all other issues, and men must range themselves on one side or the other, Anti-Slavery or Pro-Slavery, for Freedom or against it."[1]

The Washington-based *National Era* had become a leading voice of the new Republican Party and quickly earned a large national readership. Bailey's essay named those he believed ready to carry the new party's banner forward. Among them were John P. Hale and George Julian, who had led the Free-Soil ticket in 1852; prominent abolitionist politicians, including Salmon Chase, William Seward, and Charles Sumner; and Kentucky's leading voice for freedom, Cassius Clay. In this rising pantheon, Bailey did not just mention Clay. Though Clay held no elected office, Bailey singled him out as an ideal Republican vice presidential candidate for the upcoming election in 1856. "Clay is a man of action and governing power," Bailey remarked. "His coolness, self-possession, courage, and decision of character, with his fine presence and dignified carriage, would make him an admirable incumbent of the President's chair in the Senate."[2]

But many obstacles riddled the Republicans' road to power. Despite an increasing discontent with proslavery forces, many Northern voters remained concerned with issues such as tariffs, internal improvements, banking, and immigration. The anti-immigration faction dubbed the Know-Nothings had boasted strong showings in the Midwest, Upper South, and Northeast, where numerous antislavery politicians had formed coalitions with nativists. In Massachusetts, for example, committed abolitionist Henry Wilson allied himself with the nativist movement in order to win election as governor and, ultimately, US senator. As George Julian later wrote, "While the disruption of the old parties seemed easy and imminent, it was equally clear that the organization of their fragments into a new party on a true basis was a totally different problem."[3]

In February 1856, leaders of several Republican state organizations convened a two-day conference in Pittsburgh in an effort to address that challenge. As attendees strategized the best way to court voters, some, such as Horace Greeley, urged a cautious approach so as not to antagonize groups such as the Know-Nothings, whom he hoped might be persuaded into the Republican fold. Others, including the fiery Reverend Owen Lovejoy, hoped that the Republican Party would take far more dramatic action. Encouraging aid for the antislavery forces in Kansas, he offered his services: "If I use my Sharp's rifle, I will shoot in God's name. I am for war to the knife, and knife to the hilt, if it must be so," he proclaimed.[4]

Ultimately the men at the conference in Pittsburgh were, as Julian put it, "not beating a retreat . . . but marching in the opposite direction." This became clear on the second day when an attendee read a letter from the conspicuously absent Cassius M. Clay. "His words," Julian later remembered, "were shot and shell. As an impassioned and powerful arraignment of slavery by a Southern man his letter reminded one of Jefferson's arraignment of George the Third, and through its extensive publication in the newspapers it must have done excellent service in guiding and inspiring the great party then about to be created." Clay's words embodied the muscular tone the Republican Party would take going forward.[5]

The reason for Clay's absence in Pittsburgh soon emerged. By early 1856, his financial circumstances had gone from difficult to dire. He found himself struggling to pay even the interest on his loans. Once again, he called on his brother. In a minor act of contrition, he promised Brutus that he would not seek to earn more income through politics until he repaid his debts. By this time, however, Cassius owed more than $68,000 to nearly forty creditors, too much for even Brutus's good name and robust financial resources to cover. Moreover, Cassius's recently opened Cincinnati-based bank failed. Some newspapers blamed its collapse on a recent downturn in the pork market, though Clay himself later wrote that its demise came as the result of an unsecured short-term loan for $10,000 on which the borrower defaulted. Whatever the cause, the deluge of debt pushed Clay into bankruptcy. In March, Brutus, along with their brother-in-law Madison Johnson, assumed the role of Cassius's assignees and organized a sale of his goods to aid his debt repayment.[6]

In mid-March, an advertisement for an auction appeared in a Lexington newspaper. There, for sale among Cassius Clay's thoroughbred and stock cattle, mules, horses, and sheep, were "twenty two slaves, men women and children." While the legal trust under which Cassius had inherited these twenty-two enslaved laborers prevented him from manumitting them as he had done for nine others in 1844, they were considered real estate that could be sold to satisfy creditors in case of bankruptcy. This sent shockwaves through an American public that had largely forgotten Clay's continued slaveholding. His supposed status as a *former* slaveholder had become part of his trademark, and in the past several years the press had widely praised his farming operations as proof that wage labor was profitable.[7]

Southern and Democratic newspapers quickly capitalized on this bombshell, fully milking the irony and the hypocrisy of Clay's situation. "A REPUBLICAN LEADER A DEALER IN SLAVES," screamed the *Brooklyn Daily Eagle*. "Cassius M. Clay, the great Kentucky anti-slavery martyr, notwithstanding his perambulations through the Free States, lecturing on the horrors of slavery, turns out to be *the owner and poesessor* [sic] *of twenty two slaves himself!* Fie for shame!" A paper from Rock Island, Illinois, where Cassius had recently lectured, stated things more crassly. Under a headline reading "Cassius M. Clay and His Niggers," its editor exclaimed: "The abolitionists of this city and Moline who stood in our court house yard not long since and swallowed the pernicious doctrines of Cassius M. Clay, and yelled themselves hoarse over the devotion of their great champion of 'human freedom,' may be surprised to learn that they were listening to a slavocrat, a dealer in human bodies, and awful slave driver who now advertises his niggers for sale." "What will the negro worshipping party say now?" queried the editor with satisfaction.[8]

The *National Era* tried to tamp down the controversy by explaining that because the slaves were real estate, it was "beyond the power of Mr. Clay to emancipate the persons in question, or divest himself of that interest which, as the natural guardian of his children, the law has invested him with; at least, until his children arrive at maturity." But William Lloyd Garrison, who as recently as 1854 had lauded Clay for emancipating his slaves, was reticent; his *Liberator* made no mention of Clay's predicament aside from reprinting a defense written in Thurlow Weed's *Albany Evening Journal*, which referred to the enslaved individuals as "technical property" and described their sale as "an act of law, not of Clay."[9]

John Fee, who had been well aware that Clay continued to own and depend on enslaved laborers, had never shied from criticizing his benefactor. Months earlier, Clay had hinted that his precarious finances might imperil his enslaved laborers but had defended his continued ownership to Fee, arguing paternalistically that he was doing his "duty to keep my children's slaves together and contract them rather than by disavowing any authority over them." Fee, however, worried not only about the fate of Clay's enslaved laborers but also about the negative impact the situation would have on the antislavery cause. "Let me urge that if at all possible *avoid the sale of those slaves*," he wrote Cassius in April, explaining: "Many men North as well as south will not have all the facts in the case before them . . . do the cause good—and the slaves also perhaps—if you can do the latter you will certainly do the former."[10]

To Americans reading of it in newspapers, Clay's situation may have reminded them of the predicament of Arthur Shelby, the benevolent but hapless Kentucky slaveholder in *Uncle Tom's Cabin*. Initially serialized in the *National Era* over nine months in 1851, Harriet Beecher Stowe's tale of woe began with Shelby's own financial malfeasance, which forced him to sell two of his enslaved laborers. Refuting the Bluegrass State's reputation for milder treatment of enslaved people than Deep South states, Stowe wrote, "Whoever visits some estates [in Kentucky], and witnesses the good-humored indulgence of some masters and mistresses and the affectionate loyalty of some slaves, might be tempted to dream the oft-fable poetic legend of a patriarchal institution, and all that; but over and above the scene there broods a portentous shadow—the shadow of the *law*." For the book's millions of readers, the fiscally irresponsible Shelbys revealed slavery's unavoidable tragedy: the fact that humans could be categorized as chattel property "could cause [owners] any day to exchange the life of kind protection for hopeless misery and toil." Just three years after the sensational publication of Stowe's novel, it seemed that Cassius Clay provided a real-life example of an Arthur Shelby.[11]

And what of White Hall's enslaved men and women whose fate hung in the balance? They appeared by name in Cassius's list of assets and bill of bankruptcy as: Jim, Will, Frank; Sarah and three children; Hannah, Minerva, and seven children; Zack and Jerry; Minerva and two children; and Old Lucy. Collectively their value was appraised at $2,110.00. If that measure was not dehumanizing enough, they were individually, according to market price listed on Cassius's estate inventory, worth less than many of his thoroughbred cattle. They were spared the fate of Stowe's characters, however, when Cassius's stepfather, Jeptha Dudley, agreed to purchase them and allowed Cassius to retain and make continued use of their labor if he repaid him over time. Clay described the arrangement to Salmon Chase with relief, reporting: "The slaves are all sold back virtually to me again and not separated and gone as our *good laws* would have directed!"[12]

Though he was able to retain his human property, Cassius and Mary Jane lost many other valuables in the estate auction, which took place on April 15. The event proved mortifying for them. "I was sold out," he later remembered, "and turned into a public highway." Members of the Clays' extended family, including Brutus, his brother-in-law Madison C. Johnson, and his nephew Sidney, purchased White Hall and the surrounding estate, as well as farm implements, vases, and fine china, with the idea that Cassius could maintain residence and the use of most of the goods while repaying them over time. But Cassius and Mary Jane watched as friends and neighbors purchased other relics of their fine living—marble statues, paintings and mirrors, fine china, a buggy, a tin bathtub, a mahogany sofa, and a library full of books—all of which were lost forever. They found it particularly galling that, unlike members of Cassius's family, Mary Jane's father, Elisha Warfield, refused to aid them and, to the contrary, joined the throng of creditors who called in Cassius's debts. "My father in law," he vented to Chase, "who is very wealthy, and who has never made me any advances meanly left me as he supposed to ruin and the streets! He never came near on sale day nor will I ever care to see him again!"[13]

Of his own reputation, Cassius asked Chase: "What will my sanctimonious revilers now say? I suppose it is as far up the hill as it is down." Defending his business acumen, he wrote Chase: "It was another lie, got off by the slave party that my troubles were owing to pork speculations." Instead, he blamed his antislavery career. "I have spent my money fighting the slave party," he told his friend. "I have had to sustain my cause and thus save my life and cause! Where else has this been done? But I have no regrets and am not cast down! How could I have better spent my large means with which fortune favored me than in contending for the liberties of men, and establishing the liberty of speech and press in the land to which I owed my birth and allegiance!"[14]

The bankruptcy had revealed once more the hypocrisy of his slave ownership and threatened to derail his cause and his career. Only days after the auction, Clay took his case public, explaining his situation at a local Republican Association meeting, invoking his oft-repeated defense that he had liberated all the slaves he legally could. He painted himself as the victim of the situation, declaring that had he liberated his slaves held in trust, he "would have violated the rights of his heirs—and be denounced as a violator of the law, and a 'negro thief.'" Now he found himself "calumniated by the efficacy of the laws, which he had so much struggled to overthrow and which his accusers had against his will, kept on the statute book!"[15]

Meanwhile, across the country in the spring of 1856, battles over slavery grew less rhetorical and more physical by the day. In late May came an attack on Lawrence, the site of Kansas's antislavery opposition government, which had rivaled the illegally elected proslavery legislature in Lecompton. The next day South Carolina congressman Preston Brooks savagely caned Charles Sumner on the Senate floor in retaliation for slandering his proslavery cousin Andrew Butler. Antislavery partisans increasingly turned to force as well. In Kansas, John Brown and his band of followers took broadswords to several proslavery residents at Pottawatomie Creek, resulting in a bloody massacre. Indeed, the situation in Kansas caused pacifistic and moderate men such as Congregationalist minster Henry Ward Beecher to send boxes of Sharps rifles to the state in wooden crates labeled "Bibles" to arm antislavery settlers. Everywhere, it seemed, the lines between nonviolent moralism and armed action were being obliterated. Most Americans believed in enacting change informed by moral and ideological values through the democratic process. As the machinations of the Slave Power began to impede that strategy, citizens committed to limiting slavery's spread began to subscribe to the precept that Cassius Clay had long embodied: that the fraudulent and unconstitutional stifling of antislavery thought and action must, when necessary, be met with force.[16]

The reliance on armed violence that had long defined Clay and had made him seem such an outlier throughout his public career now appeared increasingly to characterize the national fight over slavery, whether in the wilds of Kansas or in the halls of Congress. Thanks to the events of the spring, the spirit of "shot and shell" for which Gamaliel Bailey had praised Clay pervaded the Republican rhetoric, and there was a confluence of Clay's tactics and spirit with those of the new party. For all his complexities, Clay, who had always borne an uncompromising spirit, seemed to embody the path forward during a time when the failures of past compromise were all too clear. This was one reason why his name continued to cross the lips of many in discussions about the Republican ticket in the looming presidential election of 1856. Clay was gratified by the suggestion that he would make an ideal vice presidential nominee.[17]

At the nominating convention in Philadelphia in June 1856, Republicans adopted a platform that was unyielding on slavery. Delegates demanded that Kansas be admitted immediately as a free state and that the federal government prohibit the expansion of slavery into any new territories and end existing slavery in territories under its jurisdiction. Convention-goers nominated John C. Frémont, the dashing, energetic young adventurer who seemed just the sort of man to represent the new party. The vice presidential spot went not to Clay but rather to New Jersey's William L. Dayton. For their party manifesto, the Republicans modified the old Free-Soil slogan to read: "Free Speech, Free Press, Free Men, Free Labor, Free Territory, and Fremont."[18]

The platform embodied the antislavery thinking developed by moderate reformers over the past decades. It acknowledged that the federal government had no right to foster the expansion of slavery but was duty bound to bar it from new territories and to promote, as Salmon Chase phrased it, its "denationalization." Though Republican leaders believed that the Constitution forbade the federal government from supporting the institution, the party's very viability hung on the continued recognition that the founding document protected individuals' rights to hold slave property in slave states. With its forthright treatment of the issue of slavery, the platform marked a significant departure from past party agendas that had sought to avoid it. The platform was far from radical, however, in hewing to a traditional free labor argument for halting the expansion of slavery and in not making any statements regarding racial equality. Despite the smearing label of "Black Republicans" that Democrats soon bestowed on them, concern for the enslaved was secondary to party leaders' concern for the labor prospects of white men. Very few party members believed that free African Americans could or should obtain the full rights of citizenship. Committed abolitionists were quick to point out these shortcomings, but many also saw the Republican Party as the first truly viable antislavery political organization and chose to support it.[19]

The distinction and friction between humanitarian and political antislavery positions emerged in bold relief in a falling out between Cassius Clay and John Fee just weeks after the Republican nominating convention in 1856. Both men appeared as featured orators at a Fourth of July celebration held by the Republican Association of Madison and Rockcastle Counties. Speaking first, Fee waved a copy of the Declaration of Independence in his hand, enumerated the promises it contained, and declared that God-given inalienable rights were for all humans. "That which outrages natural right and Divine teaching is mere usurpation, and correctly speaking, is incapable of legalization," he asserted. Focusing on the Fugitive Slave Law, he proclaimed that "a law confessedly contrary to the law of God ought not by human courts to be enforced." When it was his turn to speak, Clay professed his "high personal regard" for Fee and admitted that the Fugitive Slave Law was inhumane and reprehensible. But, alarmed by Fee's anarchist tone, he cautioned the crowd about the danger of the minister's rationale. "As my political friends," he told them, "I warn you; Mr. Fee's position is revolutionary, insurrectionary. As long as a law is on the statute book, it is to be respected and obeyed until repealed by the republican majority."[20]

The disagreement over principles on the podium that day merely made public the private disagreement over the nature of slavery's constitutionalism and legality that Clay and Fee had held for years, and it cast a pall over the festivities. The picnic food was "eaten without celebration," Fee recalled. "The friends of slavery were not pleased, and the friends of freedom were divided. Some went away saying: 'Fee is religiously right; Clay is politically right.'" The state Republican organization, however, sided with politics and voted to remove Fee from his position as the corresponding secretary. Of more consequence for the minister, Clay turned his back on him, refusing to see him and also withdrew his protective services, leaving Fee exposed to local harassers.[21]

Some of Fee's supporters claimed that Clay had callously abandoned Fee, to which he countered: "I did not withdraw my influence from him, but he his from me." In a letter to a disappointed Fee supporter, Clay asserted that before July 4, 1856, he and Fee had "acted together ... upon the basis of Constitutional opposition to slavery." Once Fee publicly endorsed the tenets of "Radical Abolitionists" in his capacity not only as a "minister of the Gospel" but "as a politician," however, Clay could no longer support him. This kind of thinking, he stressed, had no place in Republican politics. "The Radicals propose a fundamental change in our Government, and in a way not proscribed by the Constitution, but in violation of it," Clay asserted. This would abrogate property rights and promote possible insurrection.[22]

Capturing the Republican Party ethos, Clay instead urged a slow and legalistic approach to ending slavery. "I am in favor of a peaceable and fraternal solution to the slave question," he wrote to Fee's friends. "History teaches me that political institutions grow, and are not made; and sudden changes have always been the cause of retrocession, and not progress." Clay also flipped the script on abolitionists, insisting that he promoted temperate action *because* of, rather than in spite of, his "regard for the black race." Humanitarian extremism would alarm white Americans and "drive [African Americans] to the wall," ending in their annihilation. He restated that his own priorities remained focused on the social and economic ills of slavery and that "if such an issue as extermination should ever threaten either race, I am for my own, the white race, against all other races on earth." In the end, Clay told Fee's supporters that he did not bear ill feelings toward the minister and considered him "honest and godly" but could not "follow the lead" of people who "however conscientious, may jeopard[ize] a good cause by fanaticism and folly."[23]

Clay's denouncement of Fee echoed the defensive moderation Republicans assumed during their inaugural presidential campaign. Democrats sought to equate the new party's demand for the nonextension of slavery with immediate abolition and African American political and social equality, two things that most white Northerners did not support. Republican newspapers such as the *New York Times* denied such fallacious thinking, declaring that their "movement has nothing to do with the negro. It aims solely to release white men, at the South and at the North, from the abject, servile, degraded subserviency in which they are now held." The Republican press found it particularly important to draw this line as party leaders sought to make inroads in midwestern states such as Indiana and Illinois, where nativist Know-Nothings were running Millard Fillmore on the American Party ticket.[24]

That summer and fall, Clay traveled tirelessly throughout the Midwest, stumping for Frémont. He went as far north as Milwaukee and as far east as New York City, where he gave a high-profile address to the Young Men's Republican Central Committee. Most of his appearances, though, came in Ohio, Indiana, and Illinois, states with a strong Democratic and nativist presence. The campaign of 1856 featured energetic, impassioned electioneering, and Clay was thrilled to be part of it. His days were filled with barbeques, brass bands, and torchlight parades. He spoke to huge, adoring crowds (one estimate put the attendance of his Dayton, Ohio, speech at somewhere between 70,000 and 100,000 people and claimed it was the largest midwestern rally of the year). As an Indiana correspondent to the *National Era* put it: "In this latitude, where so many of the people are of Southern origin, Mr. Clay, from his personal knowledge and experience of 'the peculiar institution,' is pre-eminently the man to wield an influence at a crisis like the present. . . . Strange to say, our conservatives have 'thawed out,' that Mr. Clay is here one of the most popular men that ever came into 'these parts!'" In his speeches, he told Northern voters that Southerners would continue to trample on Northern rights and assault their senators with canes because "they believed the North lacked courage" until they showed a backbone and voted Republican.[25]

Clay's bombastic personality was on display, both on stage and off. While traveling from Dayton to Indianapolis, he shared a train with a company of Virginians who were headed to Kansas to take up arms with proslavery forces. When the drunken ruffians repeatedly pulled the bell rope of the train, causing it to make unscheduled stops along the route, Clay strode into their train car, revealed his identity, and announced that if they did not stop, he would kick them off the train. He added that they must know "very well that he never failed to accomplish anything he undertook." According to a reporter, "The speech had the desired effect upon these chivalric Virginians," and they gave no more trouble.[26]

When election day arrived, however, Democratic candidate James Buchanan handily defeated his opponent, garnering 174 electoral votes to Frémont's 114. Nevertheless, Republicans counted the election of 1856 as a remarkable success. They won 1.3 million popular votes and the electoral tally of eleven out of sixteen free states, with Buchanan carrying Indiana and Pennsylvania by a sliver. Also significant for their long-term success, they trounced their Know-Nothing competition and the American Party nominee, Millard Fillmore.

Republican optimism soared in the election's aftermath. Clay, who served as both a standard bearer and a faithful foot soldier for the party, looked with the same sense of promise at his own prospects within it. Anticipating a win in the next presidential election, he wrote Salmon Chase from the campaign trail: "I desire to be sec. of war—when you are *pres.*— help me!" His political opponents, too, understood these aspirations and derided them as crass and opportunistic. "Mr. Clay is ambitious," snarled the *Louisville Daily Courier*. "But his is not the ambition which spurs great men on to great achievements. It is rather that morbid thirst for notoriety, which is the inseparable companion of conscious weakness joined to uneasy vanity of self-consequence." Disparaging both Clay and antislavery reform, the reporter pronounced: "The advocacy of that incendiary cause is the most available and certain means by which a man of mediocre talents may make himself widely known."[27]

Despite his bankruptcy and his political detractors, it seemed that by the end of 1856, Clay had, through a combination of stubborn self-assurance and ambition, survived a very difficult year. Home from the campaign trail, Clay worked dutifully to shore up his finances. In addition to his livestock business, he rented out nearly 2,000 acres of farm and pastureland, at times to as many as eighteen different neighbors, bringing in thousands of dollars. Life, however, dealt the Clay family another brutal blow in spring 1857, when the Clays' thirteen-year-old son, Cassius (the child whom they had accused Emily of poisoning), died on April 15. Clay wrote sorrowfully to William Seward that young Cassius had been a child of "every virtue— the promise truly of our house" and anticipated that his and Mary Jane's grief would be "life-long."[28]

Once again, Clay turned to political action as a salve for familial loss, working to build a Republican Party organization in Kentucky. Whereas his past efforts to build an antislavery voting bloc in the state had been independent, small-scale, and ad hoc, this time his work dovetailed with a larger party strategy. From its inception, the Republican Party had been sectional, appealing to white voters in free states and expecting few in the slave South. Though Republican leaders understood that there was no immediate prospect of gaining a widespread voting constituency below the Ohio River, a significant number of them were coming around to Clay's decades-old understanding that the region was home to millions of poor whites oppressed by the slaveholding oligarchy. Party leaders such as Seward and Greeley began to echo his assessment that these people suffered from lack of education, underemployment, and low wages and that they remained ignorant of the nature of their own oppression because of the lack of free speech and free press in the South. Once enlightened, however, they would become the both the backbone of the free labor economy and the Republican Party in the region.[29]

To initiate this process, party leaders focused on areas of Upper South states where slave ownership was more diffuse and less central to the local economy and where homegrown operatives such as Clay had long been working to establish antislavery beachheads. They enjoyed some notable successes. In Missouri, for instance, Congressman Francis Blair Jr. and his compatriot Benjamin Gratz Brown, editor of the St. Louis *Missouri Democrat*, worked to attract voters to the Republican Party by arguing that gradual emancipation would encourage industrial development and increase land values in their state. Their efforts were explicitly anti-Black, incorporating colonization efforts designed to remove free African Americans from the state. In a speech to the Missouri legislature in 1857, Brown attested that he was concerned with not "the mere emancipation of the black race" but rather "THE EMANCIPATION OF THE WHITE RACE." "I seek to emancipate the white man from the yoke of competition with the negro," he proclaimed. Such rhetoric helped a number of Missouri Republican candidates win significant votes, including Clay's old friend (and dueling second) James S. Rollins, who narrowly lost election for governor.[30]

Some Republicans resorted to more inventive tactics to establish a Republican foothold in the South. In 1857, Massachusetts congressman Eli Thayer, who had organized the settlement of northeastern antislavery partisans to Kansas, launched yet another emigration scheme, this time to entice white Northerners to western Virginia. Collaborating with Republican John C. Underwood of Wheeling, he founded a community called Ceredo, which would model the superiority of free labor and industry. Though Thayer's project suffered from the national economic downturn that year, it did enable the founding and funding of a number of Republican newspapers and led to the establishment of nearby Wheeling as a Republican outpost.[31]

No one, however, reflected Cassius Clay's appreciation for the working whites of the South more than Hinton Rowan Helper, the North Carolinian who, in 1857, published *The Impending Crisis of the South: How to Meet It*. Helper drew his inspiration from Clay's strategy of resting his antislavery argument on cold, hard numbers. In *The Impending Crisis*, Helper marshaled data from the census of 1850 into a 420-page comparison of Southern and Northern productivity. As Clay appraised Kentucky, Helper evaluated an entire region. The end result, as Horace Greeley put it, was a book that combined the "heavy artillery of statistics" with "rolling volleys and dashing charges of rhetoric." Helper urged the nonslaveholders of the South to rise up against their slaveholding oppressors, "in our earnest and timely efforts to rescue the generous soil of the South usurped from the desolating control of these political vampires." Future scholars would point out that Helper wielded his census data selectively and imprecisely, but none of that seemed to matter to the Northern reading public, who eagerly consumed 100,000 copies of the book in its first printing.[32]

Proslavery white Southerners, in turn, found Helper's book particularly alarming not only because of its popularity and the fact that its author was one of their own, but because of its aggression. Helper aimed to incite a sense of grievance among white Southern yeomanry, telling them that by his calculation, slaveholders owed each nonslaveholder $22.73 per each acre of land they farmed—the average difference, he claimed, between the value of a free state and a slave state acre. Helper was no racial egalitarian, however, and like most other Southern advocates of emancipation thought freed African Americans ought to be colonized in Africa or Central America. Despite his overt racism and brash tone, Helper drew the excited support of antislavery reformers, North and South. Horace Greeley, in particular, was quick to celebrate Helper's massive tome, promoting it in the *Daily Tribune*. Newspapers throughout the North and Midwest carried advertisements for the *Impending Crisis*, bearing endorsements from both William Seward and Cassius Clay, who pronounced it: "the best compendium against . . . Slavery—ever published." Determined to make the book even more accessible, a number of reformers including Clay and Frank Blair solicited subscriptions to raise $16,000 in order to produce a shorter version of the book in pamphlet form.[33]

Despite Republican interest in the border South states, Clay was realistic about the party's slim chances in the region. Though party operatives pushed him to actively organize in Kentucky, he kept his head low, concentrating on his business and living with "rigid economy," as he told Seward. With a sense of pragmatism, he wrote William Seward in 1858 that with antislavery as their first and foremost principle, the Republicans could "hardly hope for an electoral vote in the South." "The battle is to be fought by the free states: and their views should be kept always foremost," he told him. Clay held out particular hope for success in Indiana and Illinois, where he believed Republicans could "win and win with our principles."[34]

Indeed, Clay had reason to worry about the young party straying from its priorities; by mid-1858, it appeared that some Republicans might compromise their antislavery standards in the name of political expediency. As the party tried to capitalize on the discontent and anger Northern voters felt over the corrupt political machinations in Kansas, and the Democratic president James Buchanan who supported them, some seemed willing to build coalitions both with Know-Nothings and anti-Buchanan Democrats. In the spring of 1858, Kentucky senator John J. Crittenden suggested a bisectional party that sought to unite breakaway Democrats, American Party adherents, and Republicans. If successful, such an effort would displace slavery as the primary basis of opposition to the Democratic Party. Clay told Seward firmly that the Republicans "had better even have another defeat than abandon our programme . . . we are all the stronger for standing to our name and principles." Even if compromise were to lead to success in 1860, it "might give us a barren victory without the establishment of our principles," he feared. "Suppose all the South lead [sic] coalition or the American delegates and the 'Conservatives' of the cities of the North and some localities where they have power," he posited. "Our principles would be ignored, and all 'compromise' fogies [would] go into office."[35]

In the fall of 1858, in an environment filled with both risk and opportunity, Clay once again left his home and farm. He headed to Illinois to stump for Republican candidates in the upcoming elections for the state legislature, contests that were pivotal because the winners would choose the occupant of the US Senate seat, for which Republican Abraham Lincoln was challenging incumbent Stephen A. Douglas. Many Americans had turned against Douglas for the bloodletting his scheme of popular sovereignty had triggered in Kansas, and he had become appalled himself by President James Buchanan's antidemocratic push to admit Kansas as a slave state. In 1857, he publicly denounced the president and the Southern wing of his party. This redeemed him in the eyes of some Democrats. Even Horace Greeley, who sat the helm of what was then the most important Republican newspaper in the country, expressed elation at Douglas's political turn and the success it might signal for the antislavery cause. From the pages of the *New-York Tribune*, he urged the voters of Illinois to return Douglas to the Senate. But Illinois Republicans were not ready to concede their party's principles to a man so fickle. Attracting national attention, Clay, along with other party leaders such as Thomas Corwin and Salmon Chase, headed to the state to engage in the "hand to hand fight." "All eyes are upon Illinois, and no State election has ever excited deeper interest than the one now about to take place," declared one Vermont newspaper.[36]

The Illinois US Senate race became legendary for spawning a series of debates between Lincoln and Douglas, held over three months and in seven locations across the state. In their face-to-face sparring, the two men clearly laid out the differing philosophies on slavery held not only by their two parties but by white Americans more broadly. In his charges and rebuttals to Douglas, Lincoln developed his viewpoint that slavery was indeed a moral evil. But like most antislavery Americans, Lincoln also believed in innate racial differences between Black and white Americans and could not imagine them peacefully coexisting. In the same speech, he touted colonization as a solution, though admitting its impracticality. He also noted the seeming impossibility of making African Americans politically and socially equal to whites. "My own feelings would not admit of this; and if mine would, we well know that those of the great mass of white people will not."[37]

Although the content of his speeches was not as novel or noteworthy as that of his lanky, plainspoken fellow Kentuckian, Clay drew large crowds in the half-dozen towns that he visited. While Lincoln made a very good showing, the legislature retained a Democratic majority and promptly returned Douglas to the Senate. Despite the disappointing outcome, the campaign had been good for both Clay and the man for whom he stumped. Though disappointed, Lincoln could console himself with the thought that the contest had given him "a hearing on the great and durable question of the age." In this, he was right; the widely published debates with Douglas brought him out of relative obscurity and into public view as voters began to look toward the next presidential election only two years away.[38]

Clay benefited as well. His careful hewing to the Republican agenda was calculated as much to promote his own political success as it was to back Lincoln and preserve the purity of party principles. As ever, Clay understood that his future political success lay in an antislavery party. Within such a political vehicle he would not need to temper his principles. Envisioning a place for himself in a future Republican cabinet, or perhaps even on the second rung of a presidential ticket, he sought to curry favor with his old friends Seward and Chase, both of whom planned presidential bids in 1860. He was not coy about his ambitions. "I felt somewhat disappointed that old pioneers were overlooked last canvass," he told Seward, referring to the election of 1856, and stated that he hoped that the contest of 1860 would not involve "so much *self-sacrifice*!" Clay knew well that Seward had as good a chance at the nomination as any member of the new party. He positioned himself as an ideal running mate, implying that as a Southerner, he would be an asset to any potential ticket and would show the Republicans to be a national, rather than a sectional, party. "We must have one candidate of the two, this next canvass, from *South* of the line," he told his New York friend. "The failure to do so last time was a capital error, and . . . cost us the election."[39]

Clay corresponded similarly with Salmon Chase, not so subtly hinting that his Southern provenance would be advantageous in 1860. "There was a great error in having both men North of Mason's and Dixon's line," as it "gave our enemies the advantage ground just where we were weakest!" Clay told him. "I don't say this on my own account," he demurred, "because I did not desire a nomination, when success was doubtful." Looking ahead, though, he clearly saw a place for himself: "Another time I think we will win with a [clan] banner of religious and political liberty and 'constitutional' opposition to slavery everywhere."[40]

Given the futility of Republican organizing in the region, Clay's argument for a Southern candidate on the presidential ticket seemed to be more a symbolic gesture than a useful strategy. Indeed, any real hope that Republicans might gain a toehold in the region disintegrated in the wake of John Brown's raid on the federal arsenal at Harpers Ferry, Virginia, in October 1859. Just as Brown intended, the specter of a white abolitionist and his followers, filled with Christian zeal and armed with pikes and Sharp's rifles, inciting slave revolt induced terror within Southern whites. What outraged them, however, was the Northern press's transformation of Brown from a fanatic into a hero. Many Southerners viewed Brown's raid as the natural consequence of Republican antislavery policy and rhetoric and were quick to blame any reformer with an alleged association to Brown.

Such accusations quickly fell on Cassius Clay. In a speech in Covington, Kentucky, just a month after the failed raid, Clay addressed the allegations by turning around the blame. "I am going to speak plainly and above board, and without reserve," he told his audience. "In my humble judgement, [Brown's raid] has no connection whatever, with party assignation in these United States, as such." Instead, he reprimanded proslavery partisans, calling the events at Harpers Ferry "nothing else but a sequence and a fruit foreseen by all sensible men, of that invasion of Kansas by the Southern pro-slavery party, united to their Northern allies." "If you don't like that," he told his audience, "you must come home to your bosoms and ask there whether it be true; it is a realization of the scripture truth, that 'they who sow the wind shall reap the whirl-wind.'" Strangely enough, the *Louisville Daily Courier*, the city's proslavery newspaper, exonerated Clay from complicity with Brown and his movement, the editorial staff writing that although they suspected the involvement of Northern abolitionists such as Gerrit Smith and Joshua Giddings, they did "not believe that Cassius M. Clay has that sin to answer for. He is bold and brave, but not a bad man" and "would scorn an association with such robbers and cutthroats as Ossawatomie Brown and his crew."[41]

By contrast, John Brown's raid could not have come at a worse time for John Fee. During the last several years, Clay's erstwhile compatriot built his school at Berea into an institution to educate the mountain poor. Fee recruited a number of antislavery settlers to colonize, build, and teach at the school. The coinciding of this influx of abolitionists with John Brown's planned uprising was enough to spark fear in the breasts of many Madison County whites. What sent them over the edge, however, were newspaper reports of a sermon that John Fee preached to Henry Ward Beecher's Plymouth Congregational Church in Brooklyn, New York, less than a month after Harpers Ferry. Fee told Beecher's congregation: "We need more John Browns—*not in the manner of his action, but in his spirit of consecration* . . . men who would go out, not with carnal weapons but with the 'Sword of the Spirit,' the Bible: and who in love, would appeal to slaveholders and non-slaveholders, if needs be, to give up property and life." Newspapers in Kentucky and around the country divested Fee's message of its Christian pacifism, distorting and misquoting Fee's sermon, and transforming it into a call for violent uprising against slavery and slaveholders. Fee dared not return to Kentucky for fear of his life. Rumors swirled around the state that the Yankee transplants at Berea were receiving shipments of arms and ammunition from Northern abolitionists. Two days before Christmas 1859, a band of sixty-three armed men on horseback confronted the Bereans with an order to leave the state within ten days.[42]

This time Clay did not intercede. With his political future at stake, he could not afford a connection with an immediate abolitionist, and the danger of such association offset his trademark commitment to free speech. Fee was profoundly disappointed in his old friend. Ever a temperate and forgiving man, he gently admonished Clay: "You had the power to protect me . . . if I violate no law I ought to be protected." But Clay did not see it this way. As always for him, the project of ending slavery involved balancing the objective with the proper constitutional, legal, and orderly means.[43]

This was the message he projected when, after two years of little public political activity in Kentucky, he reemerged in a very public fashion, giving a speech at the state capitol on January 10, 1861. Hoping for access to the statehouse chambers, Clay found himself locked out of the building and had to speak outside instead. His address was first and foremost a robust defense of the Republican Party, which Kentucky governor Beriah Magoffin and Vice President (and Kentuckian) John C. Breckinridge had both denounced in recent months. As always, however, Clay had more to say. For three hours, atop the capitol steps, he condemned the Slave Power, Stephen A. Douglas, and the Democratic Party. He listed a litany of their abuses, including the Fugitive Slave Act, the Kansas-Nebraska trouble, and the Dred Scott decision, all of which violated American democratic and constitutional principles.[44]

Clay also offered a spirited defense of the exiled Berea community. While making the reasons for his split with Fee clear, he decried the manner in which Fee's followers were run out of the state for doing nothing illegal. Combining his signature issues of moderate emancipation and its connection between free labor and educational improvement, he argued that the Bereans had turned an area once known for drunken, idle inhabitants into a moral, productive community with appreciating land values. "Why, sir, have they invaded the great state of Kentucky. How? With Sharpe's rifles, pistols, and Bowie knives? No! But with the New Testament, the church, the school house, and the saw mill." Clay particularly lamented that the community's disbandment would come at the expense of the mountain children whom the Bereans were educating.[45]

As the rain started to fall from the skies, Clay moved under the portico of the capitol and revealed the larger purpose of his speech when he pivoted to the topic of his political ally William Seward. Seward had long been a target of Democratic criticism, which had increased in recent years after a speech in 1858 in which he anticipated an "irrepressible conflict" between slave and free states. Now, in January 1860, to the alarm of Southerners, Seward appeared to be the front-runner for the Republican presidential nomination. Clay pointed out, however, that far from being an immediate abolitionist, Seward held views consistent with Republican principles that slavery could be abolished only by individual states or by constitutional amendment. Although Cassius understood that this defense was unlikely to sway many Kentucky voters, he hoped it would put him in good stead with his old friend and might win him a cabinet position should Seward win.[46]

Indeed, Clay's entire speech was designed to earn him a national showing in this key election year, and it worked. Newspapers across the country reprinted large portions of his text, and the *Cincinnati Gazette* distributed several hundred copies in pamphlet form, as did a publisher in Cleveland. Beyond his message, Clay's context spoke volumes. Here was an antislavery man brave enough to stand at the capitol of a slave state, in a town where recently one of John Brown's pikes (given to Governor Magoffin by Virginia governor Henry Wise) was making the rounds as physical evidence of abolitionist malevolence. Clay, true to his old habits, was not afraid to court danger to stand up for the principles of antislavery and free speech.[47]

The *New York Times*, which was fast becoming the voice of the more conservative wing of the Republican Party, was baffled by Cassius's ability to survive such a feat. "Here is a man who speaks out against Slavery with as much frankness as any Northern Free-Soiler," wrote a *Times* reporter. "He condemns it morally, and economically, and politically—declares it to be a curse and a crime, and avows his desire to see it abolished. In short, he talks in the very strain which renders it dangerous for most Northern statesmen to show themselves at this moment in Virginia or South Carolina, and which leaves the whole North hourly exposed to an armed invasion by Governor Wise and ten men." When trying to assess why Clay pulled off such a stunt when others would be tarred, feathered, and run out of town, the *Times* surmised that it was because he had "twice defended his right to free speech, pistol in hand," and had "killed and wounded those who sought to put him down." Urging others to be as brave, encouraging "those who think with him not to hold their tongues, but to follow his example."[48]

The Frankfort speech was merely the first step in Clay's endeavor to take center stage in what most Americans understood might be the most consequential presidential election in a generation. Next, he spoke before the New York chapter of the Young Men's Republican Union at the Cooper Union. There, before an enthusiastic crowd of men and women, Clay repeated a moderate but muscular approach to ending slavery. With characteristic bluster, he claimed that Republicans and antislavery men in national politics had been "too easily frightened" to stand by their principles, "too much accustomed to being whipped." "Put me at the head of the United States and I will whip them," he demanded, as the crowd roared in appreciation. National support continued to build throughout the spring. One Ohio correspondent for the *New-York Tribune* explained that both his bravery and moderation made Clay an ideal presidential candidate. "He is a man of talent. He is a man of nerve. He is a constant man. He is honest. He is conservative. He is more acceptable to the radical Republicans *than any other Conservative man we can choose*. And, finally, is *from a Slave State*," asserted the writer. "By nominating him we will do what the Democracy will not dare to do — *choose a candidate from the South*."[49]

At home in Kentucky, however, Clay's public and vocal political reemergence alarmed his proslavery neighbors. In March, the Madison County "Revolutionary Committee," which had earlier expelled the Bereans, alleged that Clay posed a danger to the community. Citing his defense of the missionaries as well as the antislavery content of his campaign speeches, they threatened to drive the Clay family from the county. In a defiant letter, which gained print in the *New-York Tribune* and other newspapers throughout the nation, Clay pledged to stand his ground. "I lie upon my arms awaiting an attack; my family absolutely refuse to retire saying they will run bullets and aid as in 1776," he wrote. "If driven into the woods, I shall attempt to hold my position as long as possible standing on the Constitution, the laws, and my right, I will defend them or die." He added that he had sent to Cincinnati for the cannon that had once guarded his

True American office, and as if to diminish the manhood of those who felt threatened by him, he ended the letter: "P.S. my *daughters* are as firm as I and Mrs. C." Clay's willingness to stand up for free speech so boldly and bravely earned him praise and respect from party members in the North. The Republicans of the Twenty-First Ward of New York City, for example, passed resolutions "that the heroic bearing and manly courage of Cassius M. Clay, in his efforts in the cause of constitutional emancipation entitle him to the admiration and sympathy of the Republican party, always, and especially in the hour of danger."[50]

As Clay campaigned on the familiar principles and outsized persona he had built over the past twenty years in public life, he could take encouragement from the fact that various Republican newspapers around the country put forth his name on their tickets. Although he believed he had a real chance of winning a vice presidential spot, he also knew that even if he did not, his vigorous campaigning might be rewarded with a cabinet position. His personal brand of fight seemed to match the combative nature of politics in 1860. Clay realized, however, that he needed more than popular backing based on his personality. He also required the support of influential politicians and party operatives on the basis of his policies. In February 1860, he traveled to Washington to seek the support of party members, even hobnobbing with lawmakers on the floor of the House of Representatives. Other Republican operatives gathered there to broker alliances and line up their chosen candidates. Francis Blair invited Clay to visit his estate in Silver Spring, Maryland, where, according to Clay, he promised that if Clay were to support his chosen nominee, Missouri's Edward Bates, then Bates would appoint him secretary of war should he win. Although Clay had no compunction about trading favors, he distrusted Bates's antislavery commitment and so declined the offer.[51]

He had higher hopes for collaboration with William Seward, but these were quickly dashed. While dining together in Washington, Seward showed him a draft of the speech he planned to deliver on the floor of the Senate on February 29. In conciliatory tones, Seward declared that his highest priority as a senator (and presumable presidential nominee) was to the preservation of the Union, whether slave or free. The Republican Party, he promised in the speech, did not seek to tamper with slavery where it existed or "to introduce negro equality." Seward's primary intent was to distance himself from the erroneous idea that he was a radical and uncompromising abolitionist in order to reassure conservative Republicans that he would make a viable candidate in November. This strategy backfired when it came to earning the support of his Kentucky visitor, however. Although Clay did not disagree with Seward's characterization of the party, he found his conciliatory language repulsive. As Clay later wrote in his autobiography: "I read his speech very carefully, and said nothing. The truth was, it *killed Seward with me forever!*" As ever, Clay believed that the Republican Party should prioritize ending slavery over preserving the Union. "I did not see the necessity of making a great party, and a great to-do about slavery," he later recalled, "if we were to end where we began."[52]

Oblivious to Clay's displeasure, Seward dispatched him to New York to see Thurlow Weed, presumably so that he might receive directives on campaigning for him. But Clay decided he would instead try to convince Weed that he, himself, was the most qualified aspirant to the presidency, explaining that his running as a Southern man would silence accusations that the Republican Party was sectional. He told Weed that he could straddle the line between immigrants and the erstwhile xenophobic Know-Nothings who detested them: "I am popular with the Germans everywhere, and not offensive to the Americans." Furthermore, he argued, the many colorful events of his antislavery career would win voters. "There are elements in my history which will arouse popular enthusiasm and *insure without fail success*," he boasted to Weed. Because of all these things, Clay judged himself to be "the second choice of all the 'old line' candidates' friends." But Weed never replied to his missive, so Clay pressed on, turning next to Charles Sumner, who also demurred. In March, Sumner told Clay in a letter: "No person would rejoice to see you President more than I should," but he would not "depart from the rule which I have thus far followed of expressing no preferences."[53]

Despite his lack of success in securing support for his candidacy, it was no small measure of his potential when the May 12, 1860, issue of *Harper's Magazine* included his picture in a composite illustration titled *Prominent Candidates for the Republican Presidential Nomination at Chicago*. William Seward, at this point still considered the heavy favorite, dominated the centerfold. Surrounding him were ten eminent men: Edward Bates, Nathaniel Banks, House Speaker William Pennington, Salmon Chase, John McLean, Simon Cameron, John Frémont, Abraham Lincoln, John Bell, and, in the bottom right-hand corner, Cassius Clay. Aside from Seward, within the crowded field, only Bates and Chase were considered by most political insiders as true contenders.[54]

Days later, thousands of delegates packed into the cavernous Chicago convention hall nicknamed the Wigwam and adopted a platform that was the distillation of twenty years of Free-Soil thinking. To their key contention that the "normal condition of all territory in the United States is freedom," delegates added language denouncing the events in Kansas and the Dred Scott decision. They maintained the pledge to prohibit slavery in US

Clay's inclusion (bottom right) in this Harper's Weekly *composite of possible candidates for the 1860 Republican presidential nomination in May 12, 1860, reflected the peak of his national political career. (Courtesy of Mississippi State University)*

territories and denounced the rationale within the Dred Scott decision that the Constitution protected slave property in any US state or territory. In keeping with Free-Soil ideology, delegates also added a plank proposing homestead legislation, which would sell western federal lands to settlers at affordable prices. Although the platform reflected the antislavery basis out of which the Republican Party was born, several planks focused on protecting immigrant rights, promoting the development of a transcontinental railroad and comprehensive mail service, and guaranteeing fair wages for working men.[55]

The inclusion of these additional planks reflected the fact that even though slavery was the headline issue of the election, it was bound up in a larger collection of concerns held by American voters. By addressing these subsidiary concerns and bundling them together, antislavery Republicans hoped to gain the support of a broad swath of voters. The pragmatic Horace Greeley said as much in a private letter to a friend in 1860. "I know the country is not Anti-Slavery," he wrote with clear realism. "It will only swallow a little Anti-Slavery in a great deal of sweetening. An Anti-Slavery man *per se* cannot be elected; but a Tariff, River-and-Harbor, Pacific Railroad, Free-Homestead man, *may* succeed *although* he is Anti-Slavery."[56]

For all of the Republicans' careful strategy, however, the nomination process at the Chicago convention proved more divisive than the platform and yielded an unexpected result when, on the third ballot, the delegates nominated the homely, plainspoken, and brilliant Abraham Lincoln as their presidential candidate. Lincoln's surprise victory, and the raucous celebration that followed, exhausted the physical and emotional energy of the delegates. The vice presidential nomination, which took place on the evening of the last day of the convention, became an unexciting postscript. For Cassius Clay, however, it was a moment of great consequence, in which all of his life's political ambitions for national political office hung in the balance. Indiana politician Caleb Smith nominated him for the office, where his name sat alongside several others, including Hannibal Hamlin of Maine, Nathanial Banks of Massachusetts, Andrew Reeder of Pennsylvania, Sam Houston of Texas, and Henry Davis of Maryland. Clay came in second on the first ballot, with 101½ votes to front-runner Hamlin's 194. On the second ballot, however, Hamlin soundly beat Clay, 364 votes to 86, securing the nomination.[57]

Had Seward or Chase won the presidential candidacy, Clay would have enjoyed a strong chance of capturing the second spot on the ticket. But because Lincoln was also a westerner and a former Whig like Clay, he rendered moot Cassius's appeal as a Southerner. It would take someone from the Northeast to balance the presidential ticket. In addition to his geographical provenance, Hamlin's status as a former Democrat promised to add further political dimension to the ticket. The *Cincinnati Gazette* explained: "Had all voted for [Clay] at the start whose first impulse was strongly in his favor, he would undoubtedly have been nominated." Delegates, however, felt obliged to vote for someone from the East who would appeal to supporters of the slighted William Seward.[58]

Immediately after Hamlin's victory, convention members sent up three cheers for Clay, and Caleb Smith paid tribute to him, noting, "It is a very easy matter for us who live upon soil unstained by slavery; who breathe the free air of States where the manacles of slavery are never seen, and their wailing never heard, to advocate the principles of the Republican Party." Men such as Clay who did so in slave states, Smith added, "require[d] a degree of moral heroism of which but a few of us can boast." He pronounced that "[the antislavery] cause shall be born in triumph, and its glorious folds shall be expanded to the wings of heaven," where "inscribed upon its brightest folds in characters of living light [would be] the name of Cassius

M. Clay," at which the hall erupted in applause. When Clay later wrote of his defeat, he claimed: "I was well content with the result; and entered heartily into the contest." Whether the first part of that statement was true, the second surely was, for Clay knew that more than ever, the end of slavery as well as the fate of his own political future rested on a Republican win in November. There was no denying, however, that the failure of both Seward and Chase to secure the nomination posed a serious blow to Cassius's political fortunes and meant that he would have to work all the harder to secure them.[59]

Chapter 8
Unrewarded Sacrifice

Two weeks after his own presidential hopes had died, a still devastated Salmon Chase wrote to console his friend of nearly two decades. "I confess I cared little to see you named for [the vice presidency]," he told Clay, dismissing the office as "a post of little influence and responsibility." Optimistically, he told him that a better position lay in store for him should the Republicans win in November. "I doubt not you will be called to take part in the [administration] as a member of the cabinet," Chase told him.[1]

Clay wasted little time trying the realize Chase's prophecy. Immediately after his second-place showing in Chicago, he dashed off a letter to the new presidential nominee. "Well," he wrote Lincoln with forced joviality, "you have 'cleared us all out'! The gods favor you, and we must with good grace submit." Alluding to Lincoln's status as a westerner, Clay made clear that he believed that the Illinoisan's success in Chicago had come at the expense of his own. "After your nomination for the first post," he told him, "my chances were of course ruined of becoming heir to your old clothes!" He also told Lincoln that his own absence on the ticket would be detrimental. "The mistake of putting no Southern man on the ticket will weaken our cause [in the border South] immensely—but we must remedy the evil as far as possible by increased energy!" Pledging himself "truly devoted" to a Republican victory, he asked Lincoln to "command [his] poor services if needed." "It is with sincere gratification that I received the early indication of your unwavering purpose to stand for the right," Lincoln replied days later.[2]

Heartened by Lincoln's recognition, Clay threw himself into the campaign, making his first appearance on July 7 in Louisville. Clay was under no real illusion that he would secure many votes for Lincoln in that city or elsewhere in Kentucky. Political fracturing over issues of slavery meant that Bluegrass State voters had three other candidates from whom to choose. The Democrats had splintered during their rancorous nominating convention in Charleston, South Carolina, the previous April when Northern delegates refused to include a provision in the party platform that would protect the right to hold slave property in any US state or territory. When Southern extremists walked out in protest, the remaining delegates voted to gather again the following month in Baltimore, where they nominated

Stephen A. Douglas. Proslavery Democrats convened in a separate convention and selected Kentuckian (and current vice president of the United States) John C. Breckinridge as their candidate.[3]

Many Kentucky voters looked in yet another direction, toward an upstart faction calling itself the Constitutional Union Party. Composed of former Whigs and Know-Nothings, as well as Democrats disaffected by Buchanan's antidemocratic administration, Constitutional Unionists sought to deescalate sectional and political tensions. "Two great political armies are contending for mastery," as veteran Kentucky politician and party organizer John Crittenden put it. "Both are infuriated with a rage that threatens fearful extremes." Their party may have been new, but their solution was old. Constitutional Unionists sought to bridge the growing national divide through a law-and-order appeal to the idea of states' rights. Many Americans believed that the Constitutional Unionists were burying their heads in the sand, pretending that they could return to a time when political parties were divided over such issues as tariffs, banking, and internal improvements rather than by the future of slavery. Their platform, however, appealed to many, especially to border Southerners who felt that preserving the Union was of paramount importance.[4]

Into this crowded political arena, Clay set off to campaign for Lincoln north of the Ohio River. To win the election, Republicans knew that in addition to the eleven states they carried in 1856, they needed to capture the electoral votes of Illinois, Indiana, and Pennsylvania. Party operatives believed that Clay, whose moderate free-soil, antiabolition message had long resonated in the Midwest, would be an ideal spokesman in such places. Clay's job was to dispel fears of radicalism by emphasizing the cautious, constitutional nature of the Republican antislavery position as spelled out in the party platform. The Kentuckian understood his mission well. The *Louisville Courier Journal* called his speech in that city "temperate" and "more notable for what it left out than what it set forth." This message of moderation set the tone for Clay's campaigining.[5]

Shifting his attention to the conservative Hoosier State, Clay undertook a grueling schedule in Indiana, appearing in eight towns over three weeks. Though the stakes were never higher, a festive atmosphere pervaded his appearances. A rally in Terre Haute attracted wagons filled with families of the "hard-fisted yeomanry" and "sturdy farmers," who "came pouring in on every street." Clay spoke out across an ocean of bonneted and straw-hatted heads, who admired the way he "handled the slave power without gloves." Clay's Terre Haute appearance also added innovations meant to draw a broader audience, featuring a lantern show with a slide showing images of Lincoln's rise from humble circumstances and a "slaveocrat" leading a donkey, symbolizing the Democratic Party, with a "barefooted human chattel" thrown over his shoulder who quipped that he was "going to Kansas with my property." The scene was similar in Vincennes, where wagons drawn by teams of sixteen oxen towed platforms holding men splitting rails in homage to their candidate. Also present was a contingent of local Wide-Awakes, a group of young men who marched in paramilitary fashion in support of the Republican Party.[6]

The Wide-Awake clubs, which became a unique and ubiquitous fixture of the campaign in 1860, traced their origins to a campaign visit Cassius Clay had made to Hartford, Connecticut, the previous February. His speech in the heavily Democratic city occurred against the backdrop of a contentious gubernatorial contest and frequent partisan skirmishing in the streets. After Clay finished speaking, a group of enthusiastic young men bearing flaming torches and marching in step escorted him safely back to his lodgings. Several of them had donned black capes and caps made out of cambric fabric borrowed from the fire department in order to protect their clothing from the oil dripping from their torches. "Their novel half military appearance attracted considerable attention and drew forth the plaudits of the assembled multitude," reported one newspaper. Proving that their appearance was no bluff, after one of the black-clad marchers was attacked, he struck back at the "sturdy Democrat" with his torch.[7]

Accounts of the Hartford group circulated in the following months, prompting other young Republican men to adopt the costume, the fiery torches, and the marching. The Wide-Awakes became a regular feature at campaign events "from Maine to Missouri" and were especially prevalent in heavily Democratic areas of the Northeast and Midwest—"wherever the fight is hottest," as one member put it. As an outgrowth of a new generation of young Republicans coming of age in time to vote in the election of 1860, in their physical prowess and boldness the Wide-Awakes seemed to embody the same pugnacious spirit as Cassius Clay and demonstrated a sort of convergence between his long-standing combative demeanor and mass antislavery politics. Local contingents of Wide-Awakes made appearances at many of Clay's campaign stops, including Indianapolis, where they met him at the train station and, with great fanfare, marched him through the city.[8]

Clay's stumping in Indiana had just the effect Republican organizers had desired. The antislavery message he had honed over the past two decades was now the basis of the Republican Party and everything it stood for, and he relayed it clearly and effectively as he traveled from town to town. One Indiana newspaper distilled Clay's argument as: "Trespass not on the rights of Slave States, nor allow them to trespass on ours. This country is the home of free white men—not slaves; this is the Republican platform," while the *Seymour Times* declared that Clay showed slavery as "a curse to poor white men." The combination of his message, his personality, and his life story drew large and enthusiastic crowds. "Come one, come all!" called the *Evansville Daily Journal* ahead of his visit, "and hear the rights of Free Labor sustained by one who has lived his whole life on slave soil."[9]

Lincoln took notice, writing one of his campaign operatives that he had heard news of Clay's "rousing meeting in Vincennes." In mid-July, he wrote to Cassius personally to thank him for all of his hard work in Indiana and asked him to add appearances in Illinois. Clay was happy to oblige, scheduling nine speeches in the northern half of the state in late August and early September. After a brief break, he pressed onward into southern Michigan and northern Ohio in October, wrapping up his efforts just before election day. Exhausted but satisfied, Clay returned home to Kentucky to see whether the Republicans' bid to expand their electorate paid off.[10]

Indeed, it had. Lincoln captured the electoral votes of every Northern state except New Jersey, which split its votes between him and Douglas. The only other state the Little Giant claimed was Missouri. Predictably, the Breckinridge Democrats swept most of the slave states, except for Kentucky, Virginia, and Tennessee, which went for Constitutional Unionist John Bell. Clay believed that his campaigning, particularly in the Hoosier State, where Republicans previously had a weak showing, played no small part in Lincoln's victory. As he later assessed in his autobiography: "We carried Indiana for Lincoln; and thus saved the election." He and other Republicans who had propelled the upstart party from its tenuous origins only six years before to the highest office in the land were elated.[11]

At home at White Hall, Clay waited patiently, confident that news from Springfield, Illinois, about the role he would play in the new administration would be forthcoming. He particularly coveted the position of secretary of war, and by early December newspapers far and wide reported that it would be his. In preparation for his move to Washington, Cassius consulted with his brother Brutus, who was still handling his finances after his bankruptcy in 1856. After years of personal and financial loss, Mary Jane, too, looked forward to a brighter future in the nation's capital, removed from hostile neighbors and haunting memories of lost children. She anticipated assuming a new role as a cabinet wife and being responsible for entertaining administration dignitaries. With this in mind, Cassius wrote to Brutus's daughter, Martha, asking her to return a set of china that Brutus had purchased from his bankruptcy sale four years earlier. "If Mary Jane goes to Washington, she would like to have the dinner set," he told his niece. "Please number the pieces and pack it carefully," he instructed.[12]

In the waning days of 1860, the Clays hoped to recover their plates and their fortunes, but this turned out to be more difficult than they imagined. Once Lincoln claimed electoral victory, he and his supporters grappled with the swift and devastating fallout. Below the Ohio River, Southerners began to make good on their threat to depart the Union. On December 20, South Carolinians convened a state convention where delegates unanimously passed an ordinance of secession. In the following weeks, Mississippi, Florida, Louisiana, Alabama, Texas, and Georgia followed, while Americans waited anxiously to see if the eight other slave states would follow suit. Unable to respond officially to the crisis of Union until he took office on March 4, Lincoln looked to reassure the remaining Southern states that he did not intend to destroy slavery where it existed.

With his notorious antislavery career and bellicose personality, some Americans worried that appointing Clay to the cabinet, especially to the position of secretary of war, would undermine Lincoln's professed moderation. In early December, Ohioan John Hendershott wrote to Lincoln that there was in his estimation "no man perhaps who would be more repugnant to the South." "Mr. Clay is a bold man, and it is upon this status more than upon the elements of civic renown that his reputation reposes. If any attempt shall be made to propitiate the South, and bring her back from her moonstruck fallacies, then the conclusion would follow, that Mr. Clay would not be a fitting instrument to effectuate this object," assessed Hendershott.[13]

More significant was the opposition to Clay's appointment coming from within Kentucky, a state Lincoln desperately wished to prevent from seceding. Shortly after Lincoln's election, Daniel Breck, a distant relation of his wife, Mary, traveled to Springfield. Speaking as a former Whig and current supporter of the Constitutional Union Party, Breck urged Lincoln to appoint non-Republican Southerners within his cabinet as a way to reassure slave states of his goodwill and prevent them from seceding, warning him that if he were to appoint "obnoxious men" like William Seward and Cassius M. Clay, Kentuckians would feel compelled to follow South Carolina out of the Union. The president-elect pushed back, telling Breck that if leading Republicans seemed hostile to the South, it was only because they were misrepresented by Southern politicians. Lincoln also informed his visitor that he had no intention of offering a place in his cabinet to anyone who "had always fought in and who would still continue to fight and oppose" Republican principles. He promised, however, to think about Breck's assertions.[14]

Clay was furious when he learned of the Kentuckian's visit. On January 10, he wrote Lincoln an eight-page letter in which he laid out the rationale for his appointment to the post of secretary of war. Clay told Lincoln that he would have attained that position had the Republicans won the election of 1856 and that his name had been associated with it "in a more formal way" at the Chicago convention. He reminded the president-elect of his long service to the cause of antislavery politics and of his particular efforts during the recent campaign at Lincoln's behest. "In the success of the party, which you represent, I did feel that my long though humble services, did entitle me to a portion of the controlling interest in the administration of its destiny." His frustration emanated from the pages. "I have quietly awaited events," he told Lincoln, "feeling that it would be supererogatory and indelicate to address you upon the subject," but was now "surprised" to learn from reading the newspapers that his "name had been passed over in silence."[15]

After all that he had done for the cause of antislavery and for the Republican Party, Clay simply could not abide this perceived betrayal. "I should be less than a man, if I did not keenly feel the fact that—whereas I had for a great principle cut myself and family off from all honorable ambition of elevation from my own countrymen, in my own commonwealth—throwing myself upon the *magnanimity* of those whom they regarded as natural enemies—I find myself ignored; and thus *censured* and *deserted* by them also!" he told Lincoln. All pretense and subtlety gone, Clay closed his letter by remarking that some newspapers were now mentioning his name in conjunction with a foreign diplomatic post. If that were true, he told Lincoln, there were "but *two* places" he could accept: as ambassador to England or France. "My family is large," he explained, "and my two daughters and one son are just grown—and my only motive to leave home would be to place them in such social entercourse [sic] as their ages make necessary—at either of those courts could take place—*not elsewhere!*"[16]

Not ready to relinquish his primary ambition, Cassius enlisted Brutus to work within Kentucky to help dispel notions that such an appointment as secretary of war would push Kentucky to secede. "I believe that my course in war and peace warrants the belief that I am loyal to the state," he told his brother, "and that in my large relationship here I gain security and fidelity for Kentucky which no Northern man can gain." Cassius prevailed upon his brother to solicit a letter from prominent politician and family friend Garrett Davis attesting to this idea and requested Brutus to sign it as well, believing that having two proslavery Unionists who had openly campaigned for John Bell vouch for his character would counterbalance his critics.[17]

Though Clay blamed his diminishing prospects on enemies such as Daniel Breck, there is no evidence that Lincoln ever seriously considered such a plum appointment for Clay, who had little military experience to qualify him for the position, or that Lincoln had been swayed by the testimony of moderates and conservatives. When it came to doling out positions of power, influence, and money within his administration, Lincoln not only sought the right man for the job but also worked to repay his greatest political debts. Such were the reasons Pennsylvania political boss Simon Cameron attained the secretary of war position so coveted by Cassius. Cameron had been influential in securing the crucial votes from his state for the Republican column, and Lincoln owed patronage to both Pennsylvania and the man. Lincoln owed no such political obligations to Kentucky, where only 2 percent of voters cast ballots for him.

Lincoln also realized that neither Clay's personality nor his policies lent themselves to the task of preserving the Union. In the tense weeks after the election, Clay repeatedly flaunted his hawkish attitude toward secessionists. In a letter to a group of Ohio Republicans, he explained that though the party had won a great victory, its members must gird their loins for the inevitable fight to come. "The threats of rebellion, and necessary civil war which must attend its actuality, warn us to be on our guard," he told them. Southerners, he said, must have "time to accommodate themselves to the new order of things," but never be allowed to secede. "'Peaceable secession' is but *peaceable rebellion*—an utter absurdity—Neither one slave State, four slave States nor *all* the slave States will be allowed peaceably to secede. Every man of sense sees that civil war would be better than that eternal war which would be the result of a divided nation."[18]

Meanwhile in Washington, members of Congress frantically suggested numerous compromise measures designed to prevent the remaining Southern states from seceding. At the forefront of these efforts was Kentucky senator John Crittenden, who with his border state vantage point and years of statecraft under his belt devised the most viable plan. The so-called Crittenden Compromise proposed to resurrect the old Missouri Compromise line and extend it to the California coast. As under the original iteration, slavery would be protected south of the line and prohibited north of it. Crittenden's compromise entailed five other constitutional amendments that would irrevocably protect slavery and prohibit the federal government from interfering with it. While some Republicans, including William Seward, believed preserving the Union to be worth such concessions, Lincoln told Republican lawmakers that accepting the compromise would "lose us everything we gained in the election" and would reinvigorate the expansion of slavery. With Republican opposition and absent seceding senators, the plan was dead by mid-January. In Kentucky, however, among white voters who wished to maintain both slavery and the Union, Crittenden's politics were representative of the popular will.[19]

Indeed, it was this particular Kentucky context along with his own precarious position that led Clay to interject himself into the diplomacy of disunion. Finding that he could no longer bide his time at home while his fate hung in the balance, Clay decided to combat the idea that he was hostile to the feelings of white Kentuckians by acting as a spokesman for their cause. After a visit to Frankfort to consult with Governor Beriah Magoffin and other lawmakers, Cassius set out for Washington to prove his political relevance. Once there, he announced he had come to help the so-called Committee of Thirty-Three, a group of congressmen intent on negotiating with the border states. On January 23, Clay met with Massachusetts's Charles Francis Adams, a leading compromiser, and offered his support to his plan, which entailed admitting the Territory of New Mexico to the Union as a slave state, tightening (yet again) the Fugitive Slave Act, and adding an amendment to the Constitution ensuring the perpetuity of slavery in the United States. These policies ran counter to both the text and the spirit of the Republican Party platform in 1860 (which was committed to the absolute nonextension of slavery) as well as nearly every principle Clay had promoted for decades. Yet as Adams recorded in his diary, Clay told him that his meetings with Magoffin and members of the Kentucky legislature had convinced him that such a plan would keep his home state in the Union. Clay, Adams wrote, "said he regarded the safety of Kentucky as depending upon it, which would otherwise be swept off into the vortex" of secession.[20]

In the following days, Clay met with other Republican compromisers, including Ohioan Thomas Corwin and William Seward, who had by then agreed to serve as Lincoln's secretary of state. On January 26, he appeared as the headline speaker at a huge gathering of Republicans at Washington's Odd Fellows Hall. As he had so many times before, Clay extolled the virtues of a free labor economy and the weaknesses of slave society. But, in a striking about-face, he told his audience that one day the slaveocracy would realize this as well and give up the institution in their own time. Antagonism would fade and new parties would reorganize themselves along economic and intellectual lines. "I am ready now, at all times, in every place," he told his audience, "to do all short of sacrificing principle itself." Indeed, he argued that the allowances outlined in Adams's plan were not a betrayal of principle but merely a reiteration of preexisting Constitutional rights and touted it as crucial to keeping the border states in the Union. When Cassius finished, crowd members jumped to their feet, cheering long and hard.[21]

Clay's mollifying tone impressed James Bennett, the influential Democratic editor of the *New York Daily Herald*, who praised him for standing "manfully" for compromise, noting that not even such a "radical antislavery republican" had "not the reckless hardihood to stand still and let this Union go to pieces." Cassius received quite a different response from his old friend Salmon Chase. Still engaged in his own fraught negotiations with Lincoln for a cabinet post, Chase found Clay's conciliatory turn outrageous. By letter, he begged Clay to return to his principles. "For the sake of our organization, for the sake of our cause, for the sake of your own future, for the sake of the country," he implored Clay, "give no sanction" to concessions that would undermine the nonextension of slavery. "We want no compromise now and no compromises ever." Perhaps to shame him further, Chase told him that he had only petitioned Lincoln for an administrative position on Clay's behalf "based on the belief" that he, "last of all men, would recommend the surrender and compromise of the victory we have won."[22]

Clay's clumsy foray into peace brokering had no real effect on advancing either a sectional compromise or his own chances for a place within the new administration. Just before he left Washington, he wrote to Lincoln, who had not yet embarked on his own trip to the city, describing his course of business in the capital. He reassured Lincoln that he was "ever ready to *conciliate* but never to *compromise*!" Sounding once again like the Cassius Clay of the mid-1850s who so incensed and frightened Southerners with his detailed dismissal of their secessionist threats, he told the president-elect that he was resigned to a broken union: "I rather think we must take at present a divided empire" and "let disunion fever take its course." The loss of the South could be offset with the addition of Canada, which he told Lincoln the North could obtain by negotiation. As Clay penned his missive, he had no real hope of influencing Lincoln's course, and he likely only did so to display both his usefulness and his frustration at his own idleness. "I shall remain [home] till I hear from you," he told Lincoln.[23]

But the restless Clay, growing more desperate by the minute, did not hold to his word and returned to Washington in early March in one final bid to parlay his life's work into political office. His erratic political maneuvering did seem to convince Seward and Lincoln that it was politically advantageous to place Clay where, if he could not be useful to managing the heightening crisis, he might cause the least harm. On March 11, Seward suggested him for the position of minister to Spain. In his recommendation to Lincoln, Seward told the commander-in-chief that he was "prepared to dispose of the question at once."[24]

When Clay heard the news, he certainly felt he had been disposed of and viewed his appointment as nothing more than a consolation prize. The tradition of awarding diplomatic positions in return for political loyalty had begun as part of Andrew Jackson's "spoils system" and usually happened on the basis of political function rather than a candidate's ability or knowledge of the destination, reflecting the relative disinterest the US government showed to diplomacy except in times of crisis or dispute. Historically, the only two positions of diplomatic importance were the ministries of Britain and France, whose significance was in proportion to the frequency and difficulty of negotiations over boundary and trade disputes. Elected politicians held the remaining diplomatic positions in low regard, and during a recent congressional debate over a consular bill, one representative had declared "the whole mission system" to be "one grand humbug," designed to empower sitting presidents through patronage.[25]

Put simply, the grandiose title of Envoy Extraordinary and Minister Plenipotentiary to Spain bestowed on Clay belied the mainly ceremonial function of the job. As a foreign minister, Clay's responsibilities would include passing along any political intelligence that might prove useful to the United States, as well as any commercial or cultural developments. While the impending Civil War made all diplomacy more complicated and heightened its stakes, such an appointment did not begin to approach the importance of the War Department position he so coveted. Furthermore, Spain was not one of the two foreign posts Clay told Lincoln he would be willing to accept. By the mid-nineteenth century the one-time world power had lost most of its colonial possessions and suffered from a perennially unstable monarchy. Incensed, Clay called on Lincoln in person to refuse "the mission to an old, effete government like Spain." Once again, he reminded him of his long service and sacrifice to the Republican cause and repeated that he would accept posts in either England or France. Lincoln, however, had already proffered those to Charles Francis Adams and New Jersey's William L. Dayton, respectively. Clay became convinced of a conspiracy against him and later wrote in his autobiography that he had seen "the hand of Seward in all my defeats."[26]

Realizing, however, that no better offer would be forthcoming, the frustrated and deflated Clay accepted the post. His disappointment was compounded by the fact that the diplomatic post marked a financial as well as a political setback. While in diplomatic service, he and Mary Jane would be responsible for appearing at court and entertaining dignitaries, which would require massive expenditures on clothing, food, and wine. Historically, diplomatic positions had gone to independently wealthy men who could afford to draw on their personal coffers when mingling with high society in their destinations, rather than to those who might depend on the meager stipend for their livelihood. In 1856, Congress passed legislation establishing more substantial, but still parsimonious salaries for US diplomats. Clay, who had hoped to be financially advantaged rather than burdened by a patronage position, was not shy about admitting this, and he secured the promises of several US senators to raise his annual salary to $15,000 before he accepted the Spanish post.[27]

Within days, however, a new diplomatic opportunity emerged when Lincoln offered Clay the position of minister plenipotentiary to Russia. In an effort to convince him to accept it, Montgomery Blair, now serving as postmaster general, alluded to the business opportunities Clay might find in Russia, suggesting that he could likely "make immense capital." On March 27, Clay acquiesced and telegraphed Blair: "For the sake of the cause I accept the Russian mission." While the Russian legation was a higher-profile position than Spain's, it was also a more expensive one. He wrote to Lincoln to insist on a salary increase given that the court of Saint Petersburg was the most expensive in Europe. If Lincoln refused, some portion of his large family "(seven of us!)" might even have to remain in the United States because they would be unable to afford basic necessities.[28]

With the hope that he would eventually receive a raise, Cassius prepared to relocate to Russia. In addition to Mary Jane and their five children (Brutus, Mary Barr, Laura, Sallie, and Annie) the Clays' entourage included the children's nurse, as well as Brutus's son, Green, whom Cassius enlisted to serve as his secretary of legation, and another relative, William Goodloe, who would serve as his private secretary. As they packed their belongings and prepared to travel halfway around the world, Clay relied on his brother Brutus to handle his financial transactions, manage the affairs of his farm, and oversee the hiring out of his enslaved laborers. Clay divested himself of some household belongings and livestock and put out a handbill stating his intent to hire out "for a term of years my colored servants." As of 1860, Cassius and Mary Jane claimed ownership of twenty-three people, and even in their enslavers' absence, they were, with their labor, expected to cover their own subsistence and earn him income.[29]

The Clays' itinerary took them first to Washington, DC, where Cassius was to pick up his diplomatic instructions before heading to Boston to board a ship to Europe. Once in the capital, the Clays checked into the Willard Hotel at the corner of E and Fourteenth Streets, just a block from the White House. The Willard was a Washington institution and functioned as a center of operations for much of the nation's political business. British journalist William Howard Russell, who visited the establishment earlier that year, claimed that its rooms held "more scheming, plotting, planning heads ... than any other building of the same size ever held in the world."[30]

With upward of 2,500 guests a day passing through its doors, the hotel was a chaotic place, even more so than usual when the Clays arrived on April 15, just two days after the federal army had surrendered Fort Sumter. Surrounded on all sides by slave states and riddled with secessionist residents, Washington lay vulnerable to potential invasion. On the day that Clay arrived, Lincoln declared a state of insurrection and issued an emergency proclamation calling on loyal states to supply 75,000 troops to defend the city. Regiments from Minnesota and Pennsylvania hurried to the capital to shore up its defenses, but the news was little comfort at the moment, given that they would take several days to arrive.[31]

Things grew even more dire on April 17, when neighboring Virginia voted to secede from the Union. Lincoln's private secretaries John Hay and John Nicolay later recalled that the city was thrown into a "military fever," which Clay soon caught. He sent Mary Jane and the children to Philadelphia for safety and then called on Secretary of War Simon Cameron to offer his help in raising a regiment. Surprised, Cameron replied: "Sir, this is the first instance I ever heard of where a foreign Minister volunteered in the ranks," to which Clay glibly rejoined: "Then let's make a little history." His eagerness to step up in the moment of peril earned him adulation among guests at the Willard, where, as the *New York Times* reported, he could be found "surrounded by friends ... shaking hands and congratulating him."[32]

On April 18, Winfield Scott, commander of the US Army, commissioned Clay and James H. Lane, senator-elect from Kansas, to organize two small guard forces. They each conscripted a hodge-podge of men who had come to the city seeking patronage appointments—would-be postmasters and federal clerks, along with some men who already enjoyed distinguished careers in public service, including Pennsylvania senator David Wilmot. Lincoln's secretaries, John Hay and John Nicolay, later described them: "These companies, of from thirty to sixty men each, were what might be called irregular volunteers—recruits from East and West, of all ranks in the great army of politics, who came forward to shoulder a musket without enlistment, commission, paymaster, or commissariat." Lane, who had won fame (and the nickname Grim Chieftain) for his robust defense of antislavery towns in Bleeding Kansas, referred to his geographical provenance when he named his men the Frontier Guards. Cassius nodded only to himself, christening his troops the Clay Battalion. Lane's men were tasked with protecting the White House, while Clay's were assigned to patrol the streets around the Willard during the day and to defend the city's Navy Yard at night.[33]

Unrewarded Sacrifice { 155

The following week featured moments of real anxiety, especially when it seemed as if Virginia troops would surely invade the capital city. All danger aside, though, Clay took himself and his motley assortment of soldiers rather too seriously. Hay parodied them privately. "It is amusing," he wrote in his diary on April 22, 1861, "to drop in some evening at Clay's [Willard Hotel] Armory. The raw patriots lounge elegantly on the benches—drink coffee in the anteroom—change the boots of the unconscious sleepers in the hall—scribble busily in editorial notebooks, while the sentries snore at the doors and the grizzled Captain talks politics on the raised platform and dreams of border battle and the hot noons of Monterrey." Hay described Clay's appearance at a visit to the White House that day: "He wore, with a sublimely unconscious air, three pistols and an Arkansas toothpick and looked like an admirable vignette to 25-cents-worth of yellow covered romance."[34]

As Hay's observations suggested, Clay enjoyed his days as a battalion commander. The experience combined all the elements on which he thrived: armed service, potential of danger, authority, and adulation. The experience was immortalized with a photograph of his men standing at parade rest on the White House lawn, with Clay and President Lincoln standing in the foreground, as well as by a musical composition by his friend William Ross Wallace titled "Cassius M. Clay's Regiment's War Song," which was published as sheet music.[35]

The glory was short-lived. The volunteer troops for which Lincoln called arrived within a week. Clay's battalion disbanded, and he set off to join his family in Philadelphia. The Clay family then traveled on to Boston, where they boarded the Cunard Line's *Niagara* to begin their long journey to Saint Petersburg. They shared the ship with Charles Francis Adams and his family, who were headed to England, where Adams faced the crucial and delicate task of winning the support of the British government for the Union and deterring them from recognizing Confederate independence. Clay fully realized that his own appointment was less fundamental to the Union cause. With each nautical mile the *Niagara* plowed through the icy North Atlantic, Clay felt himself slipping further from political relevance. The exhilarating experience of serving, however briefly, in the military defense of his country exacerbated his doubts about accepting a staid diplomatic office half a world away. With Kentucky in a state of declared neutrality, several of Clay's supporters in Northern states, including Indiana and New York, had offered to put his name forward for a military appointment from their states, and he began to think that this might be a better choice than foreign service. He made it only as far as the coast of Ireland before dashing off a letter to Lincoln. "I think my talent is in the military," he told the president. "Make me a general in the regular service . . . and I will return home at once upon notice."[36]

Clay arrived in Liverpool on May 13, the same day that Queen Victoria issued a proclamation of neutrality recognizing the Confederate States of America as having belligerent rights. Seeing this as one step shy of official diplomatic recognition, Secretary of State William Seward threatened eventual war against Britain should it do so.[37]

Though it was Adams's job to negotiate US policy with Britain, Cassius Clay could not keep himself from entering the fray. While in London, he hobnobbed with the American diplomatic corps and their British allies. He met with key members of Parliament and visited with Prime Minister Lord Palmerston at his home. Eschewing the traditionally understated garb of the diplomatic corps, Clay strode around the British capital clad in his gold-buttoned dress uniform, with a warlike attitude to match. He fired off a letter to the *Times* of London, which appeared in print in the May 20 edition. The United States, he argued, was fighting the Confederacy to suppress treason. Furthermore, it was the Northern rather than Southern states that were the most important trading partner to the British. England, he declared, could not "afford to offend" such a great nation as the United States by "mingling the red crosses of the Union Jack with the piratical black flag of the 'Confederate States of America.'" Not surprisingly, English readers found Clay's audacious lecturing offensive. One diplomatic historian described the letter as an "incredible blunder." "Everywhere in England men discussed this latest example of American arrogance and brutality," and its tone "confirmed the feeling that the Americans were unreasonable to the point of insanity and there was no dealing with them on a normal basis." All of this was lost on Clay, who was quite proud of his missive and sent a clipping to Seward back in Washington. "I trust it will meet your approbation," he told him.[38]

With little sense of the disarray he left in his wake, Clay and his family moved on to Paris, where Napoleon III seemed even closer than British officials to officially recognizing the Confederacy. He took stock of the situation with a cadre of other Americans posted there, including Minister to France William L. Dayton and Anson Burlingame, who was on his way to his own diplomatic post in China. Waylaid in Paris, Clay and Burlingame worked themselves into a frenzy over Britain's inability to comprehend the proper course of action in relation to the American war. Reiterating the message laid out in his *Times* letter, Clay gave another widely quoted speech in which he predicted that France would surely unite with the Union and implied that if Britain did not do the same, it risked confrontation with both countries.[39]

Summing up Clay's attempted diplomacy, the Paris correspondent for the *New York Times* wrote that his London letter "was characterized by his usual fire, but was lacking in both power and discretion, and all friends of the cause here are sorry he wrote it." He further lamented that he had "been foolish enough to make a very violent rejoinder in a speech at an American breakfast in [Paris]. All this is, to say the very least, in very bad taste," assessed the reporter. "The United States is not in such straits that her Ministers need go a begging for the sympathy of foreign nations, and still less need to beg it through newspapers." Far from helping matters, Clay's two public screeds had made Charles Francis Adams's job all more difficult and his footing all the more tenuous. While Adams did not leave any record as to his thoughts on Clay's actions, his son, Henry, did. He wrote to his brother in the wake of Clay's Paris speech disparaging "those noisy jackasses Clay and Burlingame, who have done more harm here than their weak heads were worth a thousand times over," and assessing to another correspondent that they had "made a pretty mess" of things, "giving us and our party here a heavier load to carry that Cassius's own lazy, fat, conceited old carcass would have been."[40]

The time finally came for Clay to move from the excitement and comradery of western European diplomacy to a lonelier existence across the cold reaches of the Baltic Sea. His misgivings only heightened as he traveled across eastern Europe, hemorrhaging funds he did not have. From Paris, he had written William Seward requesting him to advance him more money as his unintended stay in Washington and the expensive passage of his retinue of eight had depleted his resources. Again, he asked Seward to raise his annual salary to $17,500 and begged him to call the president's attention to the matter. Seward did alert Lincoln but, unbeknownst to Clay, recommended against it. The months since the election had brought Clay to the heights of optimism and then to the depths of despair. He had spent years accumulating political capital, but as his missteps compounded, the goodwill he had built up with his fellow Republicans diminished rapidly.[41]

Chapter 9
Undiplomatic Diplomatist

Clay arrived on Russian soil ready to leave it. He could not have imagined that except for a brief return to the United States the following year, he would spend the next eight years of his life there. He could also not have imagined the fundamental changes that would occur in his country, and indeed in his own personal life, during that time. But in June 1861, whatever Clay's misgivings about his posting, he was surely impressed with the grandeur of the Russian capital. Situated at the juncture of the Neva River and the Gulf of Finland, Saint Petersburg was a jewel of a city. Barely a century and a half old, it was the result of Peter the Great's search for a seaport that would not freeze and was designed to be the cornerstone of the maritime empire he determined to create at the dawn of the eighteenth century. Built on marshland that needed draining and reinforcement with untold tons of dirt carted in from the countryside, Saint Petersburg was a feat of modern engineering, but one that had been executed with a distinctly premodern labor system. The czar infamously called up tens of thousands of serfs—a designation given to Russia's poorest peasants who were legally bound to the land on which they lived—to carry out this back-breaking work. The extreme conditions and privations they endured meant that many never survived to return home, giving rise to the axiom that Saint Petersburg was a city built on bones.[1]

By the time the capital was complete in 1712, serfdom, a system that had once been a fixture throughout much of Europe, had died out most everywhere on the continent. By contrast, in Russia, the classification had recently been legally codified in 1649. Throughout the eighteenth century, even reformist Russian monarchs such as Peter the Great (1682–1725) and Catherine the Great (1762–96) passed legislation that increased restrictions on the freedom of their poorest inhabitants and the control that landowners held over them.

Russian serfdom bore some important differences from chattel slavery in the United States. Whereas American slavery had evolved throughout the seventeenth and eighteenth centuries into both a racial and a property designation, Russian serfdom relied on the feudal categorization of class. Serfs were not legally considered chattel property. But the unmitigated power that landowners held over them, and their unfettered ability to coerce their labor as they wished, was similar to that of American slaveholders. Serfs endured compulsory six-day workweeks, severely restricted mobility, brutal working conditions, and corporal punishment.[2]

The unfreedom imposed on over 22 million of their fellow nationals by a comparatively few people appeared to much of the western world to be the defining feature of Russian backwardness, but certainly not the only one. Indeed, the country suffered from some of the same deficiencies Clay and other opponents of slavery attributed to the United States South. The absolutist monarchy ruled with an iron fist, and landownership rights were restricted to the state and to the nobility. Primitive agricultural practices and negligible state-sponsored education meant that the bulk of Russia's population had no promise of the upward mobility inherent in the American vision of republicanism. Thus, Russia seemed to be the antithesis of a modern, enlightened nation.[3]

By the time Clay arrived in June 1861, however, the country had begun dismantling the system that had kept millions of Russians in a state of unfree servitude for centuries. Although a subset of Russian nobles had long recognized both the inefficiency and the inhumanity of serfdom, it took Russia's disastrous defeat in the Crimean War (1853–56) to bring its demise. Both the multitude of peasant uprisings that occurred before the conflict and the poor performance of the undernourished and ill-prepared serf armies during the war brought the weaknesses of the labor system into bold relief. Only a year into his reign in 1856, Czar Alexander II informed the Russian nobility that "the existing condition of owning souls cannot remain unchanged. It is better to begin to destroy serfdom from above than to wait until that time when it begins to destroy itself from below." In March 1861—just months before the Clays arrived—Alexander issued a formal manifesto that emancipated the serfs and gave them full citizenship, including the rights to marry at will and to own property. This document marked a profound paradigm shift for the largest country in the world, making the summer of 1861 a particularly interesting time for an American antislavery reformer to arrive in the Russian empire.[4]

The Saint Petersburg the Clays found on arrival was a city of pastel palaces etched with gilt and efficient canals through which the Neva flowed fast and free in the summers and froze, silvery and still, in the frigid winters. The grandeur of its upper echelon defined the mood of the city and gave little hint of the social transformations underway. Russian nobles were still organized into Peter the Great's famous Table of Ranks, their stature determined by the type of service they provided the state and emperor. The rigid hierarchy and lush splendor of Imperial Russia was on full display

Mary Jane dressed in grandeur for her presentation to the Russian court, in Saint Petersburg, early 1862. (Eastern Kentucky University Libraries, Special Collections and Archives, Richmond)

when Cassius and his secretaries of legation appeared at the Peterhof Palace in July for their formal presentation to the czar. After attending a review of the Russian cavalry, Cassius Clay, Green Clay, and William Goodloe moved inside, where they were welcomed by Prince Alexander Gorchakov, the Russian minister of foreign affairs, and His Imperial Majesty Alexander II in a room overlooking the Peterhof's elaborate golden fountains. At his introduction to the czar, Clay told him that the American people "looked with profound sympathy and great admiration for the reforms which he was attempting in his empire, which without considering the philanthropic view of the movement, by building up the middle class, he would add more to the physical power of his country than did Peter the Great," and that he would exceed him in historical estimation. In a dispatch to Secretary of State William Seward, Clay reported that Alexander was very "moved" by the remarks and replied that he hoped that the two nations would enjoy an even closer relationship now that they were "bound together by a common sympathy in the common cause of emancipation." Following the meeting, Clay and his entourage feasted on a sumptuous dinner featuring multiple courses and six varieties of wine, after which they took an open-carriage tour of the vast palace grounds.[5]

Aside from his forays into court life, however, there was little to keep Clay busy. His initial instructions from Seward charged him merely to maintain the status quo and to develop a market for American goods where possible, especially cotton and tobacco. Unlike his counterparts in England and France, however, Clay could not claim a high-stakes errand for his home nation's great crisis. To be sure, Russian loyalty to the Union was not a forgone conclusion. The country's aristocratic, oligarchic structure influenced the way the ruling class understood the Civil War. Many members of Russia's elite had vigorously pushed back against the Revolutions of 1848 and felt, as Eduard de Stoeckl, the Russian chargé d'affaires in the United States did, that the civil strife in America would "serve as an instructive lesson" to would-be European anarchists and revolutionaries who had viewed the country as a model of republican government. Some dignitaries even watched the unraveling of the American union with satisfaction. But by the same token, antirevolutionary sentiment likely made the Russian government less sympathetic to the Confederacy's aims of self-determination. As such, Russian leaders were not inspired enough by either contestant's ideology to ally themselves militarily with them.

This made Clay's diplomatic agenda relatively straightforward. With little else to do, Clay bided his time by writing letters to both Seward and Lincoln regarding the affairs of foreign relations with England and France. To Lincoln, he offered not only insights into diplomatic issues but also advice on military strategy. He mentioned again how much he would like to take to the field. "I may overrate my abilities," he told him, "but I think I could do good service with volunteers . . . even in a high command with good regular officers under me."[6]

The Clays did enjoy the society of Saint Petersburg, with its frequent and lavish entertainments. As he wrote later in his autobiography, "The centralization of all the wealth, of all the learning, of all military achievements, of all the aristocracy of a great nation in one circle, under the most finished school of refinement, [gave] the Russian high-life the precedence over all others in the world." Life at court did not always go smoothly for Clay, who committed a number of gaffes in his early days, including a breach of court etiquette when he spoke to the Empress Marie before she had first spoken to him. His charm seemed to serve him well, however, as he and Mary Jane attended the many house parties and balls at the homes and palaces of Saint Petersburg's elite, at which he claimed proudly he was "affable to all classes alike."[7]

Yet the glittering night life and the extravagantly wealthy company the Clays kept only underscored their own penury. Again, Cassius wrote to Lincoln asking for a raise. "It is not possible on trial for us to live here on 12,000$, without having all my family excluded from court and all entertainments, which we cannot reciprocate," he complained. "If my salary is not raised, I shall be forced to come home: for Russian etiquette requires certain forms and style—which cannot be evaded with out disgrace—which would make my mission worse than useless." In November, he prevailed upon his old friend Salmon Chase, whom he hoped as secretary of the treasury could help him. His assets back in Kentucky, he told Chase, could hardly cover his tax bill. He conceded to Chase that during a war, he understood that the "public mind will be in a bad mood to listen to a raising of salaries," but went on to demand: *Yet mine must be raised!"*

In addition to the high cost of living, the Clays suffered from the weather, which they found to be too cold even in summer. As Cassius wrote to Brutus, "The climate here is hard and living dear." By fall, Cassius reported that Mary Jane was in "feeble health." They decided that she and the children should return home to Kentucky and that Cassius should follow once he had secured a military or government appointment. In November, Green Clay returned to Kentucky with two of the Clays' daughters, while Mary Jane and the remaining children made plans to leave after Christmas.[8]

Before long, however, Clay learned that the Lincoln administration intended to recall him to the United States. Though this was Clay's wish, he was angry at learning of the news through newspaper reports rather than by official correspondence from Lincoln or Seward. In his stead, they planned to send Simon Cameron, whom Lincoln had relieved of his position as secretary of war because of corruption and incompetence. Cameron had a well-known history of corrupt financial dealings in his home state of Pennsylvania, which he continued in his cabinet position. Under his watch, the US War Department paid textile manufacturers for poorly made blankets and uniforms that soon disintegrated and horse dealers for broken-down animals. The department also negotiated exorbitant contracts with arms manufacturers without competitive bidding and allowed railroads to overcharge the government for their services. The fact that he was very generous to Pennsylvania firms, including a number of railroads in which he was invested, led to congressional scrutiny. Lincoln decided to jettison him in Russia and replace him with the more competent and scrupulous Edwin Stanton. Russia was never a long-term solution for Cameron, but rather, as Clay later put it, "a parachute" that would help him save face. The administration understood that the real work of diplomacy in Russia would be handled instead by Bayard Taylor, a co-owner of the *New-York Tribune*, who was to serve as Cameron's secretary of legation.[9]

Newspapers soon reported that Lincoln would appoint Clay a brigadier general, a common political military commission. While he was happy at the prospect of returning home, Clay was concerned about his new position. "I don't know how I should act in regard to the army—as I fear I shall be underrated," he fretted to Mary Jane, "so I feel very much more and more inclined to return home and devote the balance of my life to domestic quiet and the God-like pursuit of agriculture." He was, he told her, "in a painful state of uncertainty." Believing federal forces closer to victory than they actually were, Clay worried to Lincoln that he would not enter into the field before the war was over and that, even if he did, "the foremost and most desirable positions will of course be occupied." "So," he groused to the president, "I should be called probably into a temporary and inert command, soon to retire to private life," a misfortune he believed could have been avoided had Lincoln awarded his requested appointment sooner.[10]

Clay complained to Lincoln that his "sudden and unforeseen" recall and anticipated short military stint would leave him in worse financial position than he had been in 1860. "If the war should soon cease," he told him, "I should be hopelessly I fear involved in debt, with a large family comparatively destitute! My dear Sir, this debt is a great destroyer of pride: and I must therefore appeal to your known nobility of character." He then suggested that the president might appoint him to the Spanish mission, which Carl Schurz had recently vacated, or that he might even "do well in the navy department." One can only imagine the irritation Lincoln felt at

Clay's self-absorbed complaints about his personal financial problems and his expectation that the president would devote precious time and energy dealing with them.[11]

The beleaguered Lincoln would have been even less sympathetic could he see how his minister to Russia was spending this interregnum as he waited for his replacement to arrive. Alone and bored, Clay threw himself into the social whirl of Saint Petersburg. He visited the Grand Duke Nicholas and his wife and dined at the homes of princesses. He paraded on horseback in a royal review and toured the capital in a carriage as part of a May Day celebration. He also decided that it was only proper to reciprocate Russian hospitality by hosting his own entertainments and committed "a very full investment" of what remained of his bank account to the purchase of furniture, Parisian dinnerware, artwork, flowers, fine wine, and decadent food to impress his guests. Knowing he could never outspend them, Clay aimed to impress the Saint Petersburg elite with his taste rather than his wealth. He also purchased a carriage in which to ride around the capital city. Despite his solo existence, he was soon, as he wrote Mary Jane, "behind my salary."[12]

Cameron finally arrived in Russia in mid-June and promptly announced that he did not plan to stay for long. As Clay explained in yet another letter to Lincoln, the deposed secretary of war intended to ask the president for an immediate leave of absence during which he would travel home, never to return. Believing that the war would soon be winding down, giving him little chance to serve in the field, Clay asked Lincoln to restore him to the position after Cameron's departure so that he might recoup some of the money he had spent there.

By this time, Clay had already begun to look beyond his government salary for financial support, entering a business partnership to market a new lighting technology that used naphtha, a flammable substance distilled from Russia's vast oil reserves. Although this venture never panned out, Clay would try again in future years to use his diplomatic post to access lucrative investment opportunities. His bald opportunism rankled Cameron's secretary of legation, poet and novelist Bayard Taylor, who had his own designs on the ministerial job. Taylor wrote to Vice President Hannibal Hamlin explaining that Clay only wanted to return for mercenary reasons and suggested that if Lincoln offered him an equally remunerative appointment at home, he would be happy to take it. As he prepared for what he now believed would be his temporary absence from Russia, Clay reflected on his time there with satisfaction, writing to Mary Jane: "I was sent as was said to Siberian Exile—but Russia has turned up our trump card. I was called the 'undiplomatic diplomatist' yet have eminently succeeded as the President says in my mission," adding that even Czar Alexander—"the great Autocrat"—had praised him "in the most personal manner."[13]

After leaving Russia, Clay meandered through Europe, stopping in Prussia, where he took the baths at Baden-Baden, and then made his way to Paris and London before sailing for the United States. During the previous year his thoughts had been more preoccupied by his own financial welfare than the antislavery cause. Once back in the United States, however, he could not help but be astonished by the way the issue to which he had devoted his entire career had evolved in his absence. At the outset of the war, for all of their animosity toward one another, the governments of the United States and the Confederate States of America had shared the basic understanding that enslaved property was constitutionally protected in states where it was legal. But that principle quickly began to fray under the war's exigencies. In the weeks after the fall of Fort Sumter, African Americans began to take advantage of the proximity of federal military outposts, fleeing from both their enslavers and the claims of white ownership over their bodies. In May 1861, Gen. Benjamin Butler, stationed at Fort Monroe on the Virginia peninsula, famously proclaimed that federal protections of slave property found in the Constitution and the Fugitive Slave Act of 1850 no longer applied in that state, which now considered itself to be part of a foreign country. Members of the Federal Army under his command, he told angry slave owners, would not be returning these "contraband" people but rather using their labor for the Union Army's benefit and depriving the Confederacy of the same. Butler operated out of a spirit of pragmatism rather than humanitarianism, but his policy set a precedent for other Union commanders. In August, Congress codified this policy in the First Confiscation Act, which allowed Union forces to seize any property (including human beings) used to wage war against the United States.[14]

While African American men and women fled bondage on their own initiative and at considerable risk, the US military soon adopted emancipation as a military strategy throughout the war zones of the South. In August 1861, former Republican presidential candidate John C. Frémont, then commanding Union forces in Missouri, declared martial law there and threatened to confiscate and free the enslaved laborers of all Confederate partisans in the state. He did so in both a desperate effort to extinguish the rampant irregular attacks on Union forces and to appeal to antislavery Republicans in the state. From Russia, Clay viewed Frémont's actions with delight. "I hope you will stand by General Fremont's proclamation—the hour has come for that vital blow to secession and the cause of all our woes!" he wrote to Lincoln. From his executive standpoint, however, Lincoln, who was still desperate to keep the border slave states from joining the Confederacy, held a different calculus. Afraid that Frémont's actions would "alarm our Southern Union friends, and turn them against us—perhaps ruin our rather fair prospect for Kentucky," he quickly countermanded both policies and eventually removed Frémont from his command.[15]

Clay was not alone in embracing the war as an opportunity to permit the federal government to do what the Constitution would not allow in peacetime. By late 1861, many Republicans not only urged that fugitive slaves be permanently emancipated but suggested that the Union arm them to fight. Indeed, only a few months after Frémont's dismissal, Simon Cameron, who was no racial radical, proposed this very thing in his annual report of 1861, concluding that "once liberated by the rebellious acts of their masters, [enslaved people] should never again be restored to bondage."[16]

Lincoln, who had not approved this suggestion, ordered Cameron to redact the portion of his report regarding the armed service of former slaves. By this time, however, the document had circulated within the national press. While Cameron's corrupt financial dealings were the primary reason for his dismissal, his radical policy undoubtedly also played a part. As one Cincinnati newspaper put it, Cameron's downfall derived from "divid[ing] his efforts between Pennsylvania contractors and Massachusetts abolitionists." Lincoln continued this pattern of invalidating emancipation edicts issued by commanders in the field in May 1862 when he annulled Gen. David Hunter's declaration of freedom for all rebel-held slaves in South Carolina, Georgia, and Florida. In doing so, the president was not manifesting personal opposition to emancipation but rather acting in accordance with Republican Party policies to respect property rights and state sovereignty.[17]

Meanwhile, Radical Republicans in Congress were trying to pass legislation that would convey freedom to all enslaved individuals in rebellious areas. They proposed a bill with language that invited Lincoln, as commander-in-chief of the army, to treat such an action as a military necessity and to ensure its enforcement in spite of its questionable constitutionality. In the meantime, Lincoln was still trying to temper the effect that such a policy would have on loyal state slave owners. On July 12, 1862, he met with border state emissaries at the White House, where he not only reassured them that he would continue to honor their right to hold enslaved property but also strongly urged them to accept his proposals for compensated emancipation. He explained what they already surely recognized: that slavery was "being extinguished by mere friction and abrasion—by the mere incidents of war." "It will be gone," he told them, "and you will have nothing valuable in lieu of it." "How much better for you, as seller, and the nation as buyer to sell out, and buy out," he reasoned, than to lose all of their human property by slow measure with no remuneration. But Lincoln's guests would have none of it and accused him, as Kentucky governor Charles Wickliffe put it, of "making war" on their "domestic institutions."[18]

Just days later, Congress passed the Second Confiscation Act, which permanently emancipated enslaved people held by rebellious owners in Union-held territory and allowed the US Army to recruit Black soldiers. Meanwhile, behind closed doors, Lincoln secretly made plans to support the act with the war powers granted him by the US Constitution. On July 22, Lincoln gathered his cabinet and announced the preliminary Emancipation Proclamation, which threatened that if the rebellious states did not lay down their guns and rejoin the Union by New Year's Day 1863, all enslaved persons within their borders would be forever free. Though a consensus in favor of emancipation had been building within the Republican-dominated Congress over the previous months, it was practical military strategy, rather than humanitarian impulse, which lay at the heart of both the Confiscation Acts and the Emancipation Proclamation. In tandem, they would deprive the Confederacy of the enslaved labor that had proved so beneficial to its war efforts. Moreover, the policies signaled a turn toward harsher methods of waging war, which Lincoln intended to inaugurate from his executive perch with policy and which his military commanders were to implement in the field. As the president wrote to one correspondent that month, "This government cannot much longer play a game in which it stakes all, and its enemies stake nothing. Those enemies must understand that they cannot experiment for ten years trying to destroy the government and if they fail still come back into the Union unhurt." Realizing that his proclamation would incur strident opposition from Northern Democrats, Lincoln wanted to delay his announcement until the beleaguered Union Army won at least one decisive victory.[19]

With the preliminary proclamation not yet public, Lincoln's moderation and deliberation frustrated both African American and white abolitionists. Even more moderate opponents of slavery were exasperated by the glacial pace at which Lincoln seemed to move against the institution. On August 20, Horace Greeley, who, like the rest of the American public, knew nothing of Lincoln's plans, unleashed invective on the president from the pages of his *New-York Tribune*. In an editorial titled "The Prayer of 20 Millions," he castigated the president for being "strangely and disastrously remiss" in enforcing the emancipation provisions of the Confiscation Acts and accused him of being "unduly influenced by certain fossil politicians hailing from the Border Slave States." Deference to these people and respect for slave ownership, he argued, was simply encouraging treason and prolonging the war. In response, Lincoln reprised his oft-quoted maxim:

that his "paramount object" of the war was to "save the Union," regardless of the fate of slavery. "If I could save the Union without freeing *any* slave I would do it, and if I could save it by freeing *all* the slaves I would do it; and if I could save it by freeing some and leaving others alone I would also do that," he explained to Greeley. This was no mere front of moderation. Like many Republican moderates, Lincoln believed in Black freedom but not necessarily Black equality. Furthermore, he held a real ambivalence about the possibility that whites and free African Americans could peacefully coexist. He articulated his doubt on August 14, when Lincoln met with Black Washington leaders at the White House. In anticipation of emancipation's imminence, he tried to convince them to embrace colonization as the only way in which there could be racial peace. "I think your race suffer very greatly, many of them by living among us, while ours suffers from your presence," he told the leaders. "If this is admitted, it affords a reason at least while we should be separated." While Lincoln's racist reasoning profoundly dismayed and angered African Americans, it was in line with mainstream Northern public opinion and his pragmatic effort to persuade states to abolish slavery on their own accord.[20]

This was the liminal status of federal emancipation policy when Clay returned to American soil in August, and he wasted no time making his own views on the subject known. As army officials worked to place him, Clay took the opportunity to return to the speaker's podium. In Washington, he gave a blustery speech in which he denounced the Lincoln administration's "wishy-washy, milk-and-cider" policy on emancipation. He was happy to don the Union uniform, he told his audience, but "would strike only for Liberty, and would never draw the sword for the protection of Rebels' slaves." The following week he delivered a similar message to a Pittsburgh audience. This turn to rapid abolition might seem antithetical to Clay's earlier commitment to gradual, state-enacted emancipation. But like John Frémont, David Hunter, and antislavery military commanders he so admired, Clay believed that war provided both the necessity and the opportunity for immediate emancipation in places where it was militarily expedient. Furthermore, like other moderates, he felt that the treasonous rebellion committed by Confederates nullified their constitutional property rights.[21]

Clay's orations thrilled Radical Republicans, who had grown angry and impatient with Lincoln's seeming slowness. Kansas senator Simon Pomeroy wrote to Clay, urging him into immediate armed service. "It's not time for *words*," he exclaimed, "so allow at once to say that we want you to take a *Command West of the Mississippi River! And all West of it!*" He promised to lobby Lincoln on Clay's behalf for a military appointment. Abolitionist

Wendell Phillips also had kind words. "Thank you *heartily* for *coming home*," he wrote Clay. "We need you here. Don't *on any account*, go away again. Your birth, a Kentuckian, your military repute, your political importance, make you, more than almost any man, *able to advise* [and] likely to have *your advice* weighed. I consider you worth at least any half dozen northerners just now."[22]

Clay, however, understood that more moderate Republicans did not share in the enthusiasm at the prospect of his appointment as a political general. By this time, the press had been speculating for weeks about his possible military placement. One rumor held that Lincoln would assign him command over a large department in the Ohio River Valley, while other reports claimed that such a scenario was impossible, given the "violent opposition" to him in his home state. Days later came another report that he would be posted to a command west of the Mississippi. Given the trouble Lincoln had galvanizing even experienced military leaders (and Clay was far from one of these) to fight in 1862, it was no wonder that his War Department was reluctant to assign Clay to a post of any importance. But this clearly rankled him, and it was with a thinly shrouded defensiveness that he told his American audiences that he would refuse to go into the field unless he were allowed to "conduct the war according to his own judgement," adding that he "feared his views of the mode of conducting war, so far as slavery is concerned, could not be harmonized with the Administration." Instead, he anticipated that if he should take to the field, he would only be "hampered" or "shelved like Fremont."[23]

Even radical Republican newspapers feared what might happen if Clay were to be given free rein. The *New-York Tribune*, which had traditionally supported him, commented: "It is sincerely to be hoped that if Gen. Clay is to be assigned a command, in the West or anywhere else, it will be one that does not require the slightest modicum of 'discretion.'" "He is a well meaning man no doubt," the newspaper followed up, "but is about as prudent as a mad bull in high fever, especially where the negro is involved[.] We have had quite enough of 'proclaiming generals'; fighting ones are now in order."[24]

Clay's speaking tour ended abruptly when the War Department finally officially commissioned him a brigadier general and dispatched him to Kentucky in late August. There he was to command a brigade under the direction of Gen. Lew Wallace. His appointment coincided with a bold bid by Confederate commanders Braxton Bragg and Edmund Kirby Smith to retake Union-occupied areas of Tennessee and to "liberate" Kentuckians from federal control while simultaneously extending the northern bounds of the Confederacy to the Ohio River. By the end of the month,

Kirby Smith's troops had marched from Knoxville over the Cumberland Mountains and into central Kentucky. Clay, meanwhile, had made his way to Lexington, where he convinced Wallace to dispatch his brigade south to the Kentucky River, where the federal forces hoped to halt the rebels. On August 24, Clay led his infantry along with a small collection of artillery south from Lexington toward Richmond. The unseasoned men had only recently enlisted as a result of Lincoln's call for more troops in July, and Clay marched them just three miles the first day. That night they camped near the farm of his old enemy, Robert Wickliffe. They woke the next morning to continue their slow move to the north bank of the Kentucky River, where Clay believed that its serpentine contour and steep palisades would inhibit the visibility and movement of Smith's army. Near nightfall, however, Union general William "Bull" Nelson rode up on Clay's encampment and unceremoniously relieved him of his duties and neglected to reassign him to another task.[25]

Angered and disappointed, Clay headed to nearby White Hall for a brief reunion with his family. Two days later, with Union and Confederate forces battling nearby, he headed to Frankfort, where he intended to address the Kentucky General Assembly. He would later write in his autobiography that this appearance before the state legislature came at the suggestion of President Lincoln, who, Clay purported, wanted him to sound out its members' position on emancipation and to win them over to the terms of his yet-unreleased preliminary proclamation. This assertion has been repeated by numerous Clay biographers. Yet, other than Clay's own contention, no evidence exists that Lincoln suggested this idea. Given Clay's injudicious tendencies, it is unlikely that Lincoln would have taken him into his confidence regarding the impending proclamation, the existence of which he had revealed only to his cabinet members. Furthermore, it is doubtful that the politically shrewd Lincoln would have dispatched the controversial and intemperate Clay for such a sensitive operation.[26]

More likely, as some historians have also suggested, Clay was setting himself up as a potential presidential candidate for the election of 1864, a contention supported by the wording of Clay's speech to the state legislature on August 30. Reiterating his conservative constitutional understanding of slave property, he told state representatives: "The Federal Government has no power to make war upon slavery, nor upon any other property as an object or right," but argued that "rebels against its authority forfeit all right to life, liberty and property." Assuming the voice of someone who might one day be in a position to dictate emancipation policy, he explained to the legislative body, which was made up of many enslavers: "In the loyal slave States, I would not inure unnecessarily the loyal slave owner. . . . But in the rebel States I would proclaim liberty to the slaves of the disloyal masters, and disorganize their labor, the basis of all their power, and arm them for the forts, employ them there in the camps and in the marches." "In a word," he explained to his fellow Kentuckians, "I would recall the four millions of black allies whom, in a false magnanimity, we have loaned to the enemy, and bring them into an active defense of the Union, the Constitution and the enforcement of the laws."[27]

He added that loyal slave owners should be compensated by the federal government for whatever slave property might be lost collaterally. Should the rebels change course, lay down their weapons, and return to the Union fold, he would advise a repeal of any confiscation acts, support the return of formerly enslaved people, and encourage a policy of general amnesty toward secessionists. Hewing to Republican principles, Clay reassured assembly members that the federal war aim remained the preservation of the Union rather than emancipation. Once the union of states was restored, he told them, so too would be the rights of slaveholders to their property. Clay was quite pleased with his performance, writing Mary Jane that he had enjoyed "a fine audience and a patient hearing" and that his "speech gave universal satisfaction." "Never before did I and the Kentuckians come so near together" on their views of slavery, he reported contentedly.[28]

Back in Richmond, however, Gen. Bull Nelson was enjoying no such success. Rather than forcing the Confederates to ford the Kentucky River, he drove his own troops south over the water. On the same day that Cassius appeared before the general assembly, the two armies clashed in what became known as the Battle of Richmond. The green federal troops proved no match for Smith's more experienced men, who routed them, inflicting 5,353 casualties while suffering only 451 of their own. Their success at Richmond opened the door of the entire Bluegrass Region to the Confederates, who quickly assumed control over Lexington and Frankfort. This defeat compounded Clay's furor at being relieved of his military duties. "I am placed in a most unpleasant position," he complained to Mary Jane, "superceded so unceremoniously in my command, I shall not again offer my services, and yet I feel outraged to see the enemy destroy my state without striking a blow."[29]

Clay was now back home in Kentucky, free to reunite with his family after more than six months apart from them. There he found Mary Jane engaged in the beginnings of a full-scale renovation project of White Hall. In the months after Lincoln's election, believing that their fortunes were on the rise, the Clays had employed Thomas Lewinski and John McMurtry to redesign the home, which had remained largely the same since Green Clay had added a second story in 1810. Lewinski, the architect who had helped

Cassius to reinforce the *True American* building in 1845, was well known in the region for his Greek Revival designs. He frequently collaborated with McMurtry, a noteworthy Lexington builder. But with the expenses of his Russian sojourn mounting, Cassius had written Mary Jane from Saint Petersburg in March 1862 that they would need to "defer building till we see our way more clearly." Mary Jane, however, had already forged ahead as soon as she arrived home. By the time Cassius returned to Kentucky in late August, she was working to gather tradesmen and building materials.[30]

A week after the Battle of Richmond, Clay received the news that Henry Halleck, general-in-chief of the Union armies, had assigned him to the Department of the Gulf to serve under Gen. Benjamin Butler in New Orleans. Nearly as soon as he issued them, however, Halleck revoked the orders. Clay, who now better understood that the army was not the suitable place to realize his ambitions and that he and Lincoln were both biding time before his return to Russia, made his way back to Washington to do what he could to hasten the process.[31]

On September 22, 1862, in the midst of Clay's limbo, Lincoln finally released his preliminary emancipation proclamation. In its essence—as an act of war that applied only to the states in rebellion—it embodied much of the policy for which Clay had so recently advocated. The proclamation was both revolutionary and conservative in its nature. It was radical in that, for the first time in American history, the United States government officially acted as an agent of freedom for enslaved people, rather than a protector of slaveholder rights. Yet it was also primarily a pragmatic measure of war, and the freedom it offered enslaved people applied only to areas of the South under rebellion and outside of Union control. Those slave owners who remained loyal to the federal government (including Clay himself), as well as those living in areas under federal military control, retained their full rights to own human property.

Through an accident of timing, Cassius Clay found himself in Washington as the culmination of his life's work unfolded before him. On the night Lincoln issued the proclamation, Clay gathered at Salmon Chase's stately Washington abode at the corner of Sixth and E Streets with members of the president's innermost circle, including Attorney General Edward Bates and Lincoln's private secretary, John Hay. A group of singing citizens, who had just come from serenading their commander-in-chief at the White House, beckoned the men outside. Chase offered them a few words of tribute. "It is the dawn of a new era," he told them, "and although the act was performed from an imperative sense of duty, qualified by a military emergency which gave him power to perform it, it is, nevertheless, though baptized in blood, an act of humanity and justice. Later generations will celebrate it."

When Chase finished, Clay stepped forth to address the crowd. He declared himself "gratified beyond utterance" at the proclamation, though a *New York Times* correspondent's comment the next day that his remarks were "somewhat prolonged" belied this claim. At last, he celebrated, there was a "proclamation in behalf of a down-trodden humanity," which he anticipated would unfetter "the oppressed of both races." Belligerent even in exultation, he labeled anyone who did not support the measure—a large group that included hundreds of thousands of Northern whites—traitorous. He also asserted that the proclamation would surely hurt the chances of European recognition of the Confederacy, for Britain and France dared not side against the destruction of slavery, and then sounded a note of warning that the effects of the policy could be sustained only by Union military success.[32]

Hay recorded in his diary that after the serenaders disbanded, several "old fogies," including Clay, remained at Chase's, drinking and talking into the night. The evening must have been especially poignant for the host and his Kentucky friend, who had forged a relationship two decades before based on their mutual commitment to the antislavery cause. Aware of the role that contingency had played in the unfolding of Black freedom, Hay remarked that if "the slaveholders had remained in the Union they might have kept the life in their institution for many years to come." It was only because of war "that what no party or public feeling in the North could ever have hoped to touch they had madly placed in the path of destruction." Hay observed that the men in Chase's parlor "all seemed to feel a sort of new and exhilarated life" and "breathed freer," as if Lincoln's proclamation "had freed them as well as the slaves." "They gleefully and merrily called each other and themselves abolitionists, and seemed to enjoy the novel sensation of appropriating that horrible name."[33]

Although jubilant, both Chase and Clay realized that the proclamation put them in a precarious political position. Chase continued to believe that it was he rather than Lincoln who should be living in the White House. He now felt that the more moderate Lincoln had outmaneuvered him by usurping his cause. Even more so than for Chase, ending slavery had been the sole basis of Clay's political program, and the goal now seemed to have been achieved largely without his help. Without a clear political agenda to push, he felt aimless. At the end of September, he wrote to Lincoln, tendering his resignation in the army pursuant to Cameron's abdication of the Russian ministry. "I do this," he wrote, " to avail myself of your kind promise to send me back to my former mission in the Court of St. Petersburg; where I flatter myself that I can better serve my Country than in the field, under Gen[era]l Halleck, who cannot repress his hatred of liberal men into the ordinary courtesies of life." With no directions to return to Saint Petersburg

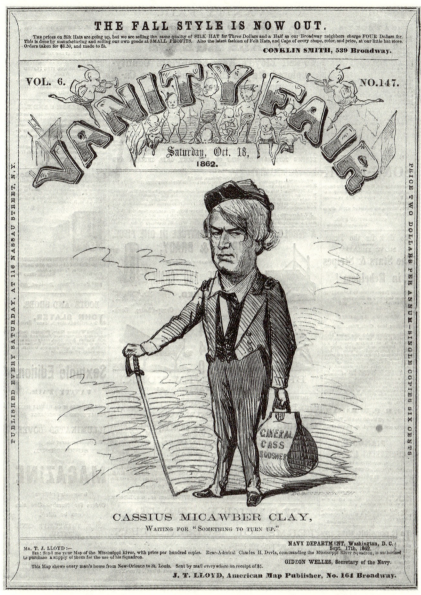

Cartoon from Vanity Fair *magazine, October 28, 1862, lampooning Clay's difficulty in attaining a military placement. The name "Micawber" refers to the Charles Dickens character in* David Copperfield *who optimistically believes that good fortune is imminent. (Eastern Kentucky University Libraries, Special Collections and Archives, Richmond)*

forthcoming, a few weeks later, Clay wrote Lincoln that he was "in receipt of pressing invitations from our friends in the North to make speeches upon the new issues of your proclamation."[34]

As he waited for Cameron to definitively give up the Russian ministry, Clay launched a speaking tour throughout the Midwest. In his speeches, Clay lauded Lincoln's proclamation as a sign of the president's new commitment to wage a harder war while also countering the charge of white Democrats that the proclamation smacked of abolitionist racial radicalism. He sought to assuage the fears of many Northern whites that freed slaves would move North and compete for their jobs. In Cleveland, Clay reassured his audience that African Americans would remain in the South. He instructed them to "educate the slave, give him more capacities and more wants, let him choose where and how he shall work, and as the slave is thus elevated, the white laborer shall also be elevated." As he had been telling his audience for many years, the end of slavery would only increase the esteem for and status of all workers. "Providence has shown His hand in the matter," he told a Chicago crowd. "You of the North have heretofore protected slavery because you have by common consent considered it to be constitutional. Now you can cling to it no longer. Deity has decreed that we must give slavery to all or none."[35]

Clay's speaking engagements provided both the public adulation and the supplementary income that he desperately needed. But they also underscored, once again, the way in which his personal status as a slaveholder was at odds with his public views on slavery. Back in Kentucky, Mary Jane found herself as reliant as ever on enslaved labor. Since her return from Russia earlier in the year, she had been trying to retrieve the family's enslaved laborers hired out before the Clays' departure the year before. She was particularly desperate to reclaim Zack, a young man whose laboring capacity was especially valuable to the family. Even as slavery atrophied by both Black self-emancipation and President Lincoln's pen, it lived on at White Hall much as it had before the war. Slavery in Kentucky, a Union border state, was exempt from the Emancipation Proclamation, and the property rights of the state's slaveholders, including the Clays, remained protected. Cassius's dictum that slavery should be for "all or none" seemed not to apply to himself, and he was content with the legal status of slavery in his own state.[36]

In November, Simon Cameron finally wrote to Clay to tell him that he had returned to American soil and was on his way to Washington to meet with Lincoln, who, for his part, seemed readier than anyone to see Clay safely deposited on another continent. The president said as much to Illinois senator Orville Hickman Browning, telling him that Clay "had a great deal of conceit, but very little sense, and that he did not know what to do with him." Lincoln lamented ever offering a military command to Clay, who, he told Hickman, "was not fit for it" and did not want one "unless he could control every thing—conduct the war on his own plan, and run the entire machine of Government." Now, however, Lincoln realized that Clay was nearly as unfit to resume his duties in Russia, and he told Browning that he regretted promising Clay the opportunity in writing. This sentiment was shared by Bayard Taylor, who remained in Russia and was still hoping to win the ministerial position himself. In a letter to Horace Greeley, Taylor professed: "Between ourselves, [Clay] is much better suited to the meridian of Kentucky than of St. Petersburg." Taylor was more direct and less discrete when he fumed in a letter to a friend that Clay was "a man (*entre nous*) who made the legation a laughing stock, whose incredible vanity and astonishing blunders are still the talk of St. Petersburg, and whose dispatches disgrace the State Department that allows them to be printed." Alleging that Clay's main motivation for returning to Russia was to resume his bachelor lifestyle, Taylor complained that he would "probably be allowed to come back to his ballet girls (his reason for coming) by our softhearted Abraham Lincoln." "Let the government send a man who will not be laughed at," he railed, "—who has a grain of prudence and one drachm of common sense, with a few moral scruples—and I shall gladly give up all my pretensions and go him. From my private correspondence I know that Lincoln says Clay is not fit for my place, but he is an elephant on my hands, and I guess I will give it to him!" But others felt as did one of Simon Cameron's correspondents, who assessed that "Clay should be sent back to Russia where *he can do no harm at least.*"[37]

In the end, Lincoln kept his promise to return Clay to Russia, though the process took longer than either expected. Simon Cameron did not tender his resignation until February 1863, at which point the Senate needed to approve Clay's reappointment. Here things hit a snag. Resistance to his reappointment had grown, thanks to his meddling in British diplomatic affairs, his bombastic refusal to serve in the army lest it be turned into an antislavery machine, and the ire he had drawn from the press for continuing to draw his brigadier general's salary as he traveled around giving speeches and dithered about playing dominoes. Crucially, his opponents included Charles Sumner, who served as the chair of the Senate Committee on Foreign Relations. Incensed by this opposition, Clay fired off a letter to the *New York Times*, in which he alleged he was being calumniated by Henry Halleck, who was "too intensely Pro-Slavery to do justice to any man of my views of the great political issues pending," and William Seward, whom he accused of influencing public opinion against him.[38]

Yet at the same time that Clay publicly complained of repression by anti-emancipation generals, he also increasingly felt outflanked by abolitionist Republicans who felt that *he* was too moderate, Charles Sumner in particular. Referring to Sumner's belief that, by seceding, Confederate states had abrogated their constitutional rights, committing "state suicide," Cassius lamented to Brutus that because he "would not go along with the radical Sumner doctrine of the overthrow of the state organizations to reach slavery, that faction made war upon me in the Senate." Clay complained to Lincoln that he was being "*Calumniated*" and became paranoid enough to request that the president send his nomination to the Senate by one of his personal couriers. "I have reason to believe that there will be *foul play* towards me by delaying it," he told him. He wrote Lincoln again the same day that he had heard that the Foreign Relations Committee would deem him unacceptable, even though, according to him, Russia's emissaries to the United States backed his return. "Don't allow me to be slaughtered by a calumny," he begged the president.[39]

By this time, it was not only members of Congress who had become fed up with Clay's self-absorbed antics. The same day the *New York Times* published Clay's angry letter, the paper issued a response that revealed that the goodwill owed Clay for his long devotion to the antislavery cause had evaporated. "We know and appreciate the zeal and courage with which he became the champion of emancipation in a Slave State, and the services, always gallant if not always prudent, which he rendered for years to the cause of free discussion," the editors conceded, "but, Mr. CLAY must understand that what the country needs now is men and effort suited to the emergency—not reputation based upon something done years ago. We want men who throw their whole souls into the support of the Government—into the defense of the nation against destruction. We want men who think more of the country than of their 'private sentiments,'—who can lay aside all pride of opinion and of past achievement, and wield the sword with heart and zeal against the men who menace the Republic with division and ruin. Mr. CLAY, thus far, has not proved himself such a man."[40]

As the *Times* editorialist pointed out, the time for the grandstanding tactics by which Clay had forged his career was over. A new definition of bravery was called for: one that involved putting personal sacrifice before public righteousness. Over the past two years, thousands of men had died on battlefields in the ultimate commitment of unconditional support to a Union war effort, even as its principles seemed to be changing by the minute. As both his public rantings and his private complaints to Lincoln made clear, Cassius Clay seemed unable to put his own personal interests aside long enough to muster any such selflessness.

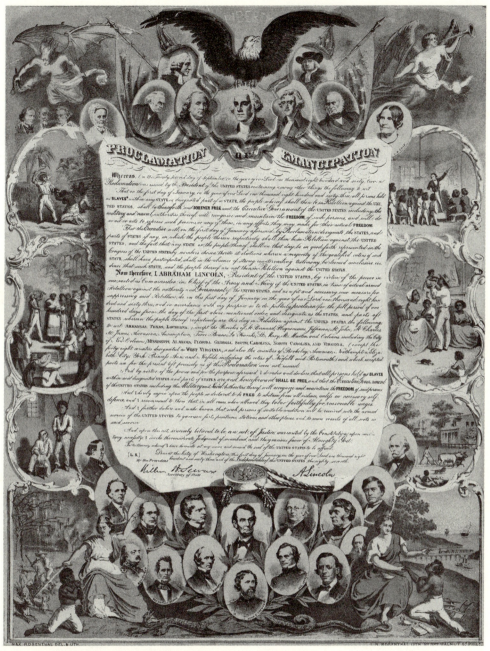

A broadside depicting the Emancipation Proclamation and a legion of antislavery reformers credited with its accomplishment. Clay is pictured at the bottom right of the document. In contrast to the happy scenes of freedom depicted, Cassius and Mary Jane Clay continued to enslave their own laborers until 1865. (Library of Congress)

To his relief, Clay's nomination ultimately prevailed in the Senate. Unfazed that no one but himself believed that he was deserving of reappointment, he prepared to go to Russia once more. He would return alone, leaving his children and Mary Jane in Kentucky to oversee renovations of White Hall as well as all of the duties of child rearing and farm management. Even in the wake of the Emancipation Proclamation, which went into effect in many areas of the South on January 1, 1863, she could depend on the family's enslaved laborers to help her in these tasks. Only days after Lincoln signed the document declaring slavery ended in the seceded states, Mary Jane wrote to Brutus's wife, Ann, to let her know that she had finally repossessed Zack. She could now rely on his labor, safe in the knowledge that as a border state, Kentucky was exempt from Lincoln's policy.

Even as Lincoln's proclamation heralded the promise of freedom for some Black Americans, there was no such pathway. As Cassius returned to Russia after so recently celebrating the national triumph of his life's work, he did so with the knowledge that the institution of slavery lived on in his own household. At no previous point had the contrast between his stated principles and his actions been quite so pronounced. Yet this bald inconsistency in policy and practice contradicted neither his personal ethos nor his constitutional views surrounding slavery, and there is no evidence that he recognized the irony of the situation or even gave it a single thought.[41]

Chapter 10
The Constitution and the Union

Cassius Clay returned to Saint Petersburg unburdened by the hesitation and uncertainty he had carried on his first journey. Having thoroughly investigated (and squandered) his domestic opportunities, he trained his sights on the possibilities that lay before him in Russia. When he arrived at the end of April 1863, he picked up where he left off, reclaiming the belongings and the acquaintances he had abandoned just months before. Clay faced his situation with optimism, complaining to Mary Jane only about the state of his carriage, as Simon Cameron "had sure enough worn it out," in his absence.[1]

Just as during his first stint, Clay found little diplomatic business to keep him busy. The Russian government was preoccupied by an insurrection in Poland, which had erupted in January 1863 in protest over the Russian army's conscription practices there. The governments of England (whom Russians still distrusted in the wake of the Crimean War) and France quickly announced their support for the Poles, and by the time Clay returned in April, Russian officials worried that they might intervene militarily. With tensions still high, the Russian government dispatched its Atlantic fleet to the United States, where it docked in the port of New York in September. Some historians believe that Russia did so to avoid the disastrous situation it faced during the Crimean War when Britain trapped the Russian navy in the Gulf of Finland, while others argue that it was simply a show of naval prowess. Caught up in their own wartime woes, however, Americans overlooked potential Russian self-interest and read the arrival of the naval fleet as a welcome show of support for the Union war effort, as did Clay, who noted to a friend that the "most friendly reception" the New Yorkers gave the fleet added to his own popularity in Saint Petersburg.[2]

Without more pressing matters to occupy him, Clay, like many public servants of the day, turned his attention to lining his own pockets. He found an excellent opportunity in a venture to construct a telegraph line between the United States and Russia. The proposed connection was a project shared by the Russian-American Telegraph Company and Western Union that would cross thousands of miles of territory to connect Saint Petersburg and San Francisco via Siberia and the Aleutian Islands. The project had begun in 1862 during Clay's absence from Saint Petersburg and on his return became the focus of much of his time. In exchange for his assistance in negotiating a favorable profit-sharing agreement with the Russian government, the organizers of the Russian-American Telegraph Company gave Cassius $30,000 worth of stock for himself, as well as hundreds of thousands of dollars more in stock to distribute as a means of gaining backing for the enterprise from the local nobility. The company also gave him extra shares to sell on commission. Clay quickly divested his own shares first and, with the proceeds, was able to send large sums of money home at regular intervals to both Brutus and Mary Jane, enabling him to pay off most of his debts and fund the renovations to White Hall.[3]

Ironically, in August 1863, Brutus, who had never shown political ambition, suddenly attained the sort of success his brother had coveted for three decades. Just a week shy of Kentucky's congressional elections, long-serving politician John J. Crittenden, now a member of the House, died. The state's Union Democratic Party put Brutus Clay on its ticket in his place. With only a few days to campaign, Brutus issued a clear and succinct declaration of his pro-Union, proslavery principles, stating that he had always been "for the preservation of the Constitution and the Union" but also for the war effort necessary protect them. This election fell at a time when the military emancipation applied as a war measure in seceded states inevitably crept into the loyal border states exempt from the Emancipation Proclamation, causing the "friction and abrasion" predicted by Lincoln.[4]

Brutus reassured voters that he would fight the rising tide of emancipation that threatened to engulf them. "At the same time," he added, "I am opposed to the policy of the Administration as to the abolition of slavery, and the enlisting of slaves as soldiers." Lest anyone not understand clearly, he stated unequivocally: "I am not and have never been in favor of emancipation, either gradual, immediate or compensated." But neither would he compromise his loyalty to the Union. "I do not regard Revolution, or Secession, or a submission to the Rebellion, as the remedies for that evil policy, they being evils, incomparably greater," he declared. Such conservative Unionism resonated strongly with the voters of Kentucky's seventh congressional district, and Brutus won handily.[5]

Despite their divergent attitudes toward emancipation, Cassius was genuinely happy for Brutus's success. But along with brotherly loyalty, his joy was tinged with self-interest. Cassius hoped that his brother might help him attain "some office, where the *people* shall decide upon my merits," as he told him. Oblivious to his diminished estimation among the American public, he believed he could exploit divisions within the Republican Party and replace Lincoln as the party's candidate in the next year's presidential election. Should Lincoln not be elected, he hoped that Brutus would compel the "loyal element" in the South, whom Brutus represented, to see him as a favorable alternative to "the faction of unconstitutional radicals and the larger body of Copperhead disloyalists and anarchists." In contrast to the radical faction that seemed to be driving matters in Congress, Cassius believed he embodied the true Republican stance on slavery. "I was for the President's Emancipation Proclamation as a 'war measure,'" he wrote Brutus, but he could not support the blatant "overthrow of the state organizations."[6]

Cassius betrayed his own discomfort with the growing scope of congressional action. Though they had not yet floated the idea of a constitutional amendment to outlaw slavery wholesale, Radicals in Congress were getting bolder in wielding federal authority to end the institution. In the spring of 1862, they had passed a plan for immediate compensated emancipation in Washington, DC, as well as a bill outlawing slavery in current and future US territories. More recently, when they admitted West Virginia to the Union in 1863, they stipulated that it must gradually abolish slavery within its borders as a condition of admission. Though he did not disagree with the results of these policies, Cassius was uncomfortable with the process, steadfastly clinging to his vision of how and under what conditions emancipation should occur. "I hold that slavery is a state and constitutional institution," he wrote to Brutus in September 1863, "and that there is no power in the [federal] government to touch the subject; in times of peace the powers of the states *revive*."[7]

As Clay was writing, both the legal and real status of slavery remained uneven and uncertain, varying across place and space. While the Emancipation Proclamation had declared slaves in disloyal areas forever free, the reality of that liberty often depended on the proximity of the Union Army and the level of federal control over the area. In Kentucky and other areas exempt from the proclamation, slavery remained notionally secured by constitutional property protections. Cassius believed that the Constitution held in check the reaches of this war measure. Imagining a policy he might carry out as president, he proscribed that enslaved people freed under the terms of the Emancipation Proclamation would remain so but that "loyal masters" could maintain their human property. He reasoned that most white Northerners agreed with him on this. "I think upon this ground I could carry almost all of the Republican party, and most of the democrats—all the loyal ones," he told Brutus. "I think my popularity as an earnest anti-slavery man cannot be shaken by the miserable faction of which Sumner is the head; whilst the South could rely upon me as a firm defender of all their Constitutional rights."[8]

Although oblivious to his own dim prospects, Clay rightly characterized the divisions that had emerged over policymaking on the issues of emancipation and reconstruction within the Republican Party. By the fall of 1863, national leaders debated how and under what conditions federally occupied areas of the Upper South and Mississippi Valley might be reintegrated into the Union. In the summer of 1863, Lincoln and congressional Republicans had struggled to come to mutually acceptable terms on their approach. Lincoln's plan showed relative magnanimity to individual rebels—welcoming them back to the Union fold once they pledged loyalty to the federal government. His modest threshold for state readmittance required only 10 percent of 1860's voters to utter loyalty oaths before a seceded state could rejoin the Union. The supposedly loyal residents would be free to reconstitute their state governments, which would, in turn, determine the political and civil rights of their residents.

Radicals, however, were dubious that any real change had occurred in the heads or hearts of secessionist slaveholders and felt that they were not to be trusted. Charles Sumner outlined this view in an article titled "Our Domestic Relations; or, How to Treat the Rebel States," which appeared in the September 1863 issue of the *Atlantic Monthly*. Sumner recapitulated his contention that with the act of secession, Confederate states had committed "state suicide" and could be justly considered territories over which the US government had full dominion. As such, Congress, rather than suspect local governments, could take control of the process of reconstruction, ensuring a drastic restructuring of government and property, with land being redistributed only to the loyal: "patriot soldiers, poor whites, and freedmen." The idea of denying states (even disloyal ones) the right to self-government angered some moderate and conservative Republicans, however. Moderate Republicans worried about what they saw as the potential wholesale usurpation of the federalist system, and many approved of Lincoln's generous 10 percent plan, which, in addition to the low threshold for loyalty, stipulated that rebellious individuals who took an oath of loyalty to the federal government were eligible to reclaim all property except enslaved laborers.[9]

For members of Congress, this debate was no mere procedural dispute but rather a fundamental argument over the very shape of postemancipation America. In the view of Sumner, Thaddeus Stevens, and other Radicals, emancipation was only the first step toward some level of economic and political equality for African Americans. More common, however, were the views of white Americans who opposed slavery but did not wish to accord African Americans social and political rights. They feared that emancipation would lead to job competition and would become, as Montgomery

Blair put it, the "means of infusing [African American] blood into our whole system by blending it with '*amalgamation, equality* and *fraternity.*'"[10]

Although Cassius Clay had never lamented the prospect of an interracial society, he looked with trepidation at the growing threat of federal overreach. He believed Sumner's notion of "state suicide" to be "absurd and revolutionary" and continued to see all loyal states as the rightful authors of policy within their borders. He wrote his friend Salmon Chase: "I still think that *legal* opposition to slavery is, as heretofore, the true and safe plan—that after the rebels are disarmed the states and their rights [should] revive, except so far as individuals may be affected in *legal procedure.*"[11]

Surveying the gradient of views within the Republican Party from half a world away, Clay identified three distinct groups. He described them in a November 1863 letter to his friend Anson Burlingame as the "ultra radicals," spearheaded by Charles Sumner; the "ultra conservatives," led by the Blairs; and the "progressive liberals," represented by Lincoln and Salmon Chase. He described himself as "rather with Chase and Lincoln" in believing that there was "power enough of an unquestionable legal character to throttle the monster, without going into debatable ground—standing by 'the Constitution as it is' and 'the Union as it ought to be' will I avoid the two extremes." "'Without law, there is no liberty!' is my motto," he professed. Clay continued to cling to the constitutional principles that had undergirded his antislavery rationale since the 1830s. By the end of 1863, however, the reality was that everything having to do with the status of slavery was debatable, and rules meant to constrain the extent and terms of liberty were straining under the exigencies of war. Laws were feeble in the face of enslaved people willing to flee and a US Army ready to put them in uniform.[12]

Cassius enjoyed the luxury of assessing the situation from afar, but Brutus did not. He set off for Washington in December 1863 to take his place in the Thirty-Eighth Congress, where he would confront policy over slavery head-on. Bound to represent his prowar, anti-emancipation constituents, Brutus found himself in a tenuous position from the start. Viewing the protection of the property rights of his fellow Kentucky slaveholders as his primary duty, Brutus took to the floor several times to denounce the looming threat of Black enlistment in Kentucky.[13]

Since 1862, the Union Army had enlisted only the enslaved men of disloyal Kentuckians, but by the spring of 1864, in an effort to offset the deficit of white draftees in Kentucky, army recruiters opened the door to all enslaved men. White Kentuckians understood that this would mean permanent freedom for able-bodied Black men who dared to walk away from their homes, as well as for their wives and children, and saw it as a naked violation of their property rights and a gross betrayal of their loyalty. Brutus was no exception. Afraid that federal forces would entice his own enslaved laborers away, he wrote to his wife in March, instructing her to "tell the negroes to run off and get away if [the federal officials] attempt to take any. Tell the negroes what their object is, to put them in the war & have them all killed off under the pretense of giving them their freedom." "They will win no liberty," he declared, "but all be killed off with hard work & exposure & in battle in place of the *cowardly scoundrels* of the North." His male laborers proved readier to believe the promises of the Union Army than the warnings of their enslaver, however, and over the next six months, seventeen of them secured their freedom by joining the US Colored Troops.[14]

From White Hall, Mary Jane also reported an exodus of laborers who left to enlist in the Union Army. "Four of our negro men have gone off & I calculate upon another going which will leave only two old men," she reported matter-of-factly to Brutus in late June. At least one of the men, Franklin Clay, traveled north to Covington, Kentucky, where he enlisted in Company I of the 109th US Colored Infantry. Although Mary Jane anticipated needing to hire laborers for farmwork, she seemed to share little of her brother-in-law's anger and frustration. If the idea of making full use of enslaved labor appeared to little trouble the emancipationist woman, so did its loss. She was gratified, however, when one of her men, Jim, returned home in August "of his own accord."[15]

Her dispassionate response to the loss of her enslaved labor was characteristic of Mary Jane's level-headed resilience during her husband's absence. Despite the disruption and anxiety caused by the near-constant troop movement of armies through their Madison County acreage, she adeptly handled the myriad duties of running her household and farm. She oversaw White Hall's sheep and cattle operations as well as the planting and harvesting of crops and the upkeep of the orchard, and she managed tenant rental contracts with efficiency. She sold meat and produce to Union officers, charging them for the privilege of grazing their horses in the Clays' pastures. This entrepreneurial activity meant there were often dozens of Union soldiers visiting White Hall on any given day. In May 1864, Mary Jane wrote her daughter Laura, who along with son Brutus was away at school in Lexington, that she had "in the last month as many as fifty men here at once in some way or other to be attended to." These accomplishments must have been gratifying to her, given the dependency and constant debt in which she had existed for most of her marriage.[16]

Like many citizens on the Civil War home front, Mary Jane and her children faced their fair share of danger. Her consistent dealings with the Union Army made White Hall a target for Confederate partisans, and in

July 1864, the Clays' carriage house caught fire and burned to the ground. Another outbuilding had suffered a similar fate the previous year, but Mary Jane had thought it an accident. After the second blaze, however, she became convinced both were incidents of Confederate arson. While Mary Jane bemoaned the loss of her best carriage, the greatest loss for future historians would be the incineration of nearly all of her husband's personal correspondence from before the Civil War, which he stored in the building. The Clay family did enjoy moments of pleasure, including a trip to Washington, DC, in early 1864, to visit Brutus. While they were there, they called on Mary Jane's childhood acquaintance Mary Todd Lincoln at the White House and accompanied the president and first lady to Ford's Theatre, where they sat in the same box in which the president would be assassinated little more than a year later.[17]

Mary Jane also pressed on with the renovations to White Hall. By 1864, the functional, if not beautiful, Georgian abode commissioned by Green Clay a half-century before had transformed into a much more imposing and capacious Italianate mansion. The new portion of the house wrapped around two sides of the original dwelling and added a third floor. Construction had doubled the number of bedrooms from five to ten and added a ballroom festooned with decorative friezes and columns. The builders also added indoor plumbing (a rare amenity at the time), as well as a rudimentary system of central heating, a technology that was little known in the United States but which the Clays had first enjoyed in their Saint Petersburg lodgings. White Hall was now a showplace capable of accommodating the prominent guests who were sure to visit when Mary Jane's husband ascended to the political status he so desperately sought.[18]

In Russia, however, Cassius was no closer to achieving this. Lincoln once again headed the Republican ticket in 1864, and Clay resigned himself to remaining in Russia for the foreseeable future. Despite his own frustrations with the Radical faction of the party, Cassius held tight to the belief that his party embodied the true representation of the Union and its constitutional principles. Not so Brutus, who had grown disgusted with his Republican colleagues. "The abolitionist party here are the most unprincipled set of men I have ever met with in my life and I don't suppose there will be such a set of scoundrels ever collected together again in this country," he fumed to his wife. "The Constitution is nothing, law is nothing; their oath is nothing."[19]

Throughout 1864, Cassius and Brutus exchanged increasingly tense letters in which they sparred over the constitutionalism of the war. Cassius refuted Brutus's charges that his party was defying constitutional principles. "If the Republicans pay no regard to the Constitution—neither do the rebels . . . if the Republicans disregard the Constitution, it must be but temporary," he wrote his brother. "Peace will bring a restored country, and the accustomed obedience of people to the *laws*. If the border-state interest is not altogether regarded you must remember that slavery is the cause of all our ills—and by the natural order of things must suffer in its time." Cassius was dismayed when Brutus supported Lincoln's opponent Democrat George McClellan in the presidential election that November. McClellan was openly hostile toward emancipation and ran on a platform that advocated a hasty end to the war through negotiation with the Confederate government. Cassius considered Brutus's vote a betrayal of Union principles, telling him: "I hope that you may not have cause to regret that you were not on the side of the country in this her death-and-life struggle. But after your great tolerance of my opinions, I would not presume to dictate to you your course. Be assured that whoever else may blame you, I will not. For though I think you wrong in going for McClellan, I believe you conscientious—misled however by regard to slavery, which seems to have potent influence over men and nations where it exists." He tried to blunt his patronizing tone by reiterating his fraternal love and respect. "I am under such obligations to you that nothing you could do could put me against you!" he wrote. As further testament of their strong family bonds, in the same letter Cassius reported that he had given Brutus's son Green consent to marry Mary Barr, his daughter. The two cousins had apparently grown fond of each other during their time together in Russia, and though Cassius did not promote the idea of marriage between cousins, he believed that it was "too late to interfere."[20]

Brutus, however, was in no mood for Cassius's moralizing. He returned to his post in the Thirty-Eighth Congress that month to face a group of Republicans who understood both Lincoln's reelection and the congressional supermajority they had won as a mandate to end slavery once and for all. The vehicle for this was the proposed Thirteenth Amendment to the Constitution, which would immediately abolish human bondage everywhere in the United States, putting slavery's fate beyond the reach of individual states where it had existed since the nation's founding. Brutus railed against the bill on the floor of Congress, insisting that it marked a complete undermining of the promises made by Lincoln, Seward, and the legislative branch to citizens in the loyal slave states who had been forever told "that neither the people of the non-slave holding States nor Congress has any power over the subject of slavery." "In this way," he accused, "the State of Kentucky has been led along, step by step, by the pledges you have given her," only to be deceived. Passing the proposed amendment, Brutus argued, would change the entire framework of the American government, which the war was meant to defend. "You go to war to restore the Union and yet change the organic, fundamental laws of the Union. You whip the rebels back in the Union, and yet when they are whipped back into the Union, the old Union has departed." "Is it not a strange anomaly?" he queried. "I want the Constitution and the Union as they were." Three weeks later, the dejected Brutus cast his vote against the Thirteenth Amendment, which passed the House nonetheless.[21]

By the time the Confederacy surrendered two months later, it was clear to all Americans that the Union, while saved, was not the same one that Brutus and Cassius pledged to defend. Four years of war had exacted incalculable human and material cost from many Americans and presented previously unimaginable opportunities for others. It also led to alterations in the Constitution and the inner workings of the American government that were unfathomable four years earlier. As Robert E. Lee's surrender at Appomattox signaled the war's close, Americans on all sides of the struggle wondered what further change lay in store. Their questions and anxiety only intensified when the relief at the war's end turned to shock and despair over President Lincoln's assassination on April 14, 1865.

Many wondered what path the martyred president's successor, Democrat Andrew Johnson, would forge. Placed on the ticket in 1864 in a desperate bid to attract border state conservatives and moderate Democratic voters, Johnson hailed from mountainous East Tennessee, came from humble origins, and in many ways embodied the Southern white yeoman for whom Cassius had been advocating for decades. Like Clay, Johnson disdained the slaveholding class and their stranglehold on Southern society. But Johnson's resentment was also accompanied by a virulently racist attitude toward African Americans, and he shared none of the Radical Republicans' commitment to protecting or extending the rights of freedmen and women in the former Confederate states. Republicans, both Radical and moderate, now looked on anxiously to see how he would approach the difficult task of rebuilding the nation.

They were soon dismayed. With Congress in recess in the summer of 1865, Johnson began generously pardoning hundreds of former Confederate officials, freeing them to run for state elections that fall. Republicans, Cassius Clay included, rightfully feared the character of the state governments that this would produce. "It is not enough to conquer the South, to free the slaves, and restore the Union," he told William Seward in a lengthy dispatch in August 1865. He declared that the South "must be *assimilated*. The seminal ovum determines the future plant and animal: and as the South begins in its reconstruction, so will it end." Comparing the former Confederacy to the dissident provinces of Europe, he continued:

"If the rebel spirit is the nucleus, we will have an Ireland, a Hungary, and a Poland!" Alternately, he predicted that should "liberal men [be] put into power, the rebel spirit will perish and Unionism triumph."[22]

As ever, Clay fixated on the constitutionality of the reconstruction process and the balance between state and federal power. "It is no violation of state-rights to give the initial power in the rebel states to loyal men," he assessed. "It will be not only a 'blunder' but a crime if that is not done. If the leadership is left in slave-holding aristocracy, the masses white and Black will remain disloyal: if the liberal spirit of Republicanism, and equality before the law, gets the ascendancy, the whole mass will be assimilated, and unionism become perpetual." To tamp out the smoldering embers of rebellion, Clay advocated taking a hard line against Confederate leaders. Jefferson Davis should be hanged, he wrote Seward, "to damn forever those fatal heresies."[23]

Clay also pondered the proper next steps in the quest for the freedom and equality of African Americans. He was far more open-minded in his thinking on this matter than some Republicans in his belief at this point that African Americans should have the right to vote. "To deny suffrage to the negro because of his race without regard to his patriotism or fitness, would be a patent error. It is a sequence of our theory of government—the equality of all before the law," he told Seward. Yet he did believe that prospective voters ought to meet some criteria for civic fitness. "We might begin," he suggested, "with requiring a property qualification, or a knowledge of reading and writing; and leave the rest to time and experience." "I know the prejudices of the poor whites against the negro—but those prejudices are the fruits of slavery and should perish with it," he projected optimistically. Distinguishing the political from the social, he asserted: "This is not a question of the equality of the races, fraternization, marriage, and social equality—but of political right. Universal suffrage is the destiny of America. That was decided in 1776, and reaffirmed in 1860–5. Our policy is not to appoint it, but to make it safe. And that can best be done, not by attempted limitation, but by infusing into the masses, without distinction of caste or race, industry, morality, education, distribution and possession of property, and love of country."[24]

The issue of suffrage was still very much on Clay's mind when he wrote Seward again in October, asking him to pass his thoughts along to President Johnson. Despite his firm sense of states' rights, he believed that the federal government, led by Congress, had the right to dictate the parameters of naturalization or citizenship and that legislators should pass "*uniform*" laws by which states would abide. Clay hoped that Congress would confer citizenship on "all male persons (or female as well), about the age of twenty one years, without distinction of colour or nationality, who can read or write." Such an expansive view of suffrage rights put Clay in line with Radical Republicans. Most Northern states denied African Americans the right to vote at this time, and out of their own racial prejudice and with the understanding that it would make reconciling with white Southerners more difficult, few Northern voters embraced this issue. Perhaps Clay's most extreme suggestion was the idea of granting women the right to vote—a proposition he would fully retract in the coming years. The ideas he floated to Seward in the fall of 1865 anticipated the entitlement to birthright citizenship and civil rights, which were granted by the Fourteenth Amendment passed by Congress just a few months later.[25]

Clay's hopes for a forward-thinking "seminal ovum" in the Southern states were in vain, however. By the fall of 1865, nearly all the former Confederate states, save Texas, had reconstituted their governments and reentered the Union. Due to Johnson's leniency, white Southern voters packed their legislatures with elected officials who repudiated the Thirteenth Amendment, refused to nullify their secession ordinances, and sent fifty-eight former Confederates to the House of Representatives. Far from being hanged for their "fatal heresies," high-ranking Confederate officials reemerged in public life, including Alexander Stephens, former vice president of the Confederacy, whom Georgians returned to his US Senate seat. Rather than extending rights to African Americans, Southern state legislatures aimed to constrict them. In 1865, states including Mississippi, South Carolina, and Georgia passed "black codes" designed to reinstate the conditions of slavery as completely as possible. These laws prohibited African Americans from leaving one farm to work on another, owning firearms, serving on juries, and voting, revealing in bold relief the obduracy of white Southerners.[26]

When Congress reconvened in late 1865, Republicans wasted no time in counteracting Johnson's permissive agenda. Even accounting for their prodigal Southern brethren, Republicans outnumbered Democrats three to one in the Thirty-Ninth Congress. Early the next year, they pushed forward two bills. The first was the Civil Rights Act of 1866, which would ensure the right of African Americans to hold property, file lawsuits, and testify in court. The second bill proposed an extension of the Freedmen's Bureau, an agency established the previous year to aid emancipated men and women, as well as some white refugees, in finding food to eat and land to farm. The bureau also established schools and hospitals and helped to negotiate labor contracts. Congress had established the Freedmen's Bureau to provide short-term emergency services during the war; now it sought to expand the bureau's powers and charged it with establishing federal courts to which African Americans could take their grievances against local officials and employers. Because it redistributed confiscated and abandoned Southern lands, and because it served as intercessor for freed African Americans, white Southerners resented the bureau intensely, viewing it as a tool to violate their property rights. Johnson vetoed both bills, earning him the enmity of congressional Republicans.

But, strangely, not of Clay. By February 1866, his hardline attitude toward the Confederate states had softened. He wrote Seward from Saint Petersburg: "While no one would have been more pleased than myself to see the question of negro suffrage finally settled, I am forced to believe that the President is following a legitimate and necessary policy in allowing the return of the Rebel states into the Union so soon as they purge themselves of treason." Clay was calling up his principles of state sovereignty—the very ones in which his constitutional view of emancipation had been couched— to argue that Southern states should have the right to rejoin the Union so long as they confirmed their loyalty. Proper procedure would, he believed, eventually lead to desired results. "The Union once restored, we may leave subordinate issues to time and to the good sense of the American people," he directed the secretary of state.[27]

Two months later, in the wake of Johnson's veto of the Freedmen's Bureau Bill, Clay went even further in his defense of the president. This time, he bypassed Seward and wrote directly to the citizens of the United States, by way of a letter to George Prentice, the editor of the *Louisville Journal*, denouncing "the course of Sumner and Stevens." "I stand by the president's veto of the freedman's bureau bill. Let the states give the freedmen all civil rights, and by degrees extend to them the right of suffrage; or else let an amendment of the constitution make one rule of suffrage for all the states. This attempt of congress to interfere with the rights of the states after the war power ceases, is a usurpation of power unknown to the constitutions and subversive of the whole theory of republicanism, as based upon the old constitution of the United States."[28]

Once back in power, however, former Confederates quickly made it clear that they had no intention of granting freedmen and women rights, either immediately or by degrees. In May 1866, an altercation between white police officers and African Americans in Memphis led to three days of violence during which white residents massacred forty-six freedmen, raped several Black women, and burned Black homes, schools, and churches. Local authorities declined to bring any of the white perpetrators to justice. Just a few weeks later, violence broke out in New Orleans, where rival factions made up of former Confederates and pro-Reconstruction Republicans fought to control the city's government. The local police force, consisting mostly of Confederate veterans, allowed local white residents to attack dozens of white and Black radicals, resulting in thirty-seven deaths and many times more injuries. President Johnson seemed only to encourage such Southern dissidence.[29]

In the following months, a battle royal raged between a Republican Congress (backed by the Northern public) and intransigent white Southerners who refused to accept the new order of things. Paramilitary organizations such as the Ku Klux Klan and the Knights of the White Camellia, bent on maintaining old social, political, and labor relations, inflicted a reign of terror on Southern African Americans and their white allies. By early 1867, Congress realized that only force could make white ex-Confederates submit to the Fourteenth Amendment. Legislators passed the Military Reconstruction Act, dividing the conquered South into five districts supervised by army officials, authorized to dispatch US troops to oversee the fair conduction of local elections. In response, white Southerners raised charges of "bayonet rule." For the next two years, Radical and moderate Republicans locked horns with the obdurate Johnson.

Meanwhile, Clay's relationship with Seward, which had been stable if not warm during his second sojourn in Russia, began to deteriorate. One point of contention was Clay's refusal in 1867 to support the State Department's efforts to collect money owed to a US arms manufacturer named Benjamin Perkins for rifles and ammunition supplied to the Russians during the Crimean War. When Clay examined the claim for $800,000, which had been sold to another party on Perkins's death, he decided that it was inflated and that, whatever its initial veracity, the current case presented by Perkins's widow constituted an abject swindle of the Russian government. He later asserted in his memoirs that Seward pressed the so-called Perkins Claims for his own political and monetary gain and never forgave Clay for refusing to present them to the Russian government.[30]

Seward, however, had soured on Clay long before then, and his antipathy only grew when a scandal involving his injudicious Russian minister surfaced in 1867. The trouble centered around Clay's involvement with the Chautems family, who owned a Saint Petersburg restaurant Clay frequented. He struck up a friendship with the matriarch, an Irish ex-patriot named Eliza, and her two young daughters. In 1866, Chautems found herself unable to pay her bills, and Russian authorities threw her in debtor's prison, at which point her eldest daughter, Leontine (only thirteen or fourteen years of age at the time), appealed to Clay for help. Along with a British embassy official, Clay bailed Eliza out of jail and loaned her enough money to establish a boardinghouse. He became furious when he discovered several months later that she was selling furniture and other goods he had purchased and had no intention of repaying him, and he reported her to Russian authorities. In response, Chautems alleged that Clay had only helped the family in an attempt to seduce Leontine and that he had even attempted to sexually assault Eliza herself. When Russian courts refused to hear her case because of Clay's diplomatic immunity, she turned to the US Congress, where she filed a petition against Clay.[31]

The issue wound its way through the Senate Committee on Foreign Affairs and ultimately made its way to the State Department, where, accompanied by an anonymously written pamphlet titled *A Synopsis of Forty Chapters upon Clay, Not to Be Found in Any Treatise on the Free Soils of the United-States of America Heretofore Published*, it came to Seward's attention. The pamphlet, authored under the pen name Timothy Bombshell, was a sixteen-page satirical, yet comprehensive account of Clay's entire career. Playing with Clay's initials, Bombshell bestowed on him such labels as Colonel Claptrap Makeshift Clay and Brigadier Caricature Marvelous Clay, documenting his lifetime of desperate attempts to attain political office and mocking everything from the hypocrisy of his continued slave ownership to his blustering show of self-sacrifice during the Mexican-American War. Another Bombshell accusation held that Clay, now in his fifties, had begun dying his ever-whitening hair and that a visit to an unskilled barber had turned it green instead. This story resurfaced in a Kentucky newspaper the next year, which reported that Clay "create[d] a sensation periodically in St. Petersburg by appearing one day with very white (natural) hair, and the next day with jet-black (dyed) locks . . . var[ying] in hirsute hue from blue-black to delicate pea-green."[32]

For American readers, however, the pamphlet's most salacious accusations alluded to his relations with women during his time in Saint Petersburg. With "his wife and children in Old Kentuck, the General, as his good lady might have foreseen, goes astray," alleged the author, contending that Clay could often be seen openly walking through the city "with a very pretty but frail piece of humanity hanging on his arm," earning him the characterization Major General Cohabit Misogamy Clay. Yet worse was Bombshell's accusation that Clay was in love with Leontine Chautems and had initiated legal action against Eliza Chautems because she had refused his suggestion that she set up housekeeping with him, thereby "affording the daily society of herself and daughter."[33]

The pamphlet was obviously the slanderous work of some longtime political enemy, but it was damaging nonetheless. William Seward intimated to Clay that the House of Representatives was looking into the scandal and "respectfully invited" him to respond. He then brought charges against Clay before Johnson's cabinet, which included "licentiousness, seduction, refusal to pay his debts," and misuse of his diplomatic immunity. In response, Clay launched a full-throttle campaign to clear himself of such "infamous calumnies," sending Seward affidavits from Russian officials as evidence of his innocence. The British ambassador to Saint Petersburg, Sir Andrew Buchanan, interceded on Clay's behalf, producing documents that largely acquitted him of misuse of any public funds as well as the worst of Eliza Chautems's allegations, while other Russian dignitaries painted her as a prostitute and described her business as a brothel rather than a boardinghouse.[34]

Fortunately for Clay, Congress was apparently too engrossed in domestic issues and battles with President Johnson to consider the matter. In the end, Clay's reputation in Saint Petersburg's sexually permissive society seemed to suffer very little from the incident. Locals had long acknowledged his questionable personal behavior. As early as 1862, Secretary of Legation Bayard Taylor had charged that Clay's main motivation for resuming his diplomatic career had been to return to his "ballerina girls," and over the years, oblique hints of Clay's romantic pursuits surfaced in the press. In 1865, a Cleveland newspaper reported that he "seem[ed] to enjoy his bachelor life" and that his "annual 'jams' [had] become institutions in St. Petersburg." But after years of rumors, the Chautems scandal provided firm proof of Clay's connection with the Saint Petersburg demimonde.[35]

Perhaps it was not surprising, then, that the worst consequence of the affair was the damage it inflicted on his marriage. Mary Jane's patience and goodwill had been tried many times during the Clays' nearly forty-year marriage. She had endured her husband's many foibles, whether they be political, pugilistic, or pecuniary. The hurt and ridicule she suffered with these public revelations became too much, and she wrote to Cassius to tell him she believed the allegations to be true. He in turn, as he later explained in his memoirs, became "indignant, and thus closed our correspondence."[36]

As he faced the Chautems charges, the discovery that William Seward had negotiated the purchase of Alaska from Russia without Cassius's knowledge dealt Clay yet another blow. American officials had been eyeing the Alaska territory and Aleutian Islands for years, believing that ownership would give them a trading foothold in the Pacific. In March 1867, Seward wrapped up the purchase of nearly 600,000 square miles of territory in exchange for $7.2 million in gold. Yet unaware of the untold millions of gallons of crude oil that lay beneath the land's surface, a chorus of American critics regarded the purchase of the remote and frozen land as a fiasco. Clay knew differently and was embarrassed that he played no part in the most significant diplomatic event to occur between Russia and the United States during his tenure. After learning of the treaty, he wrote Seward, rather disingenuously: "I congratulate you on your brilliant achievement, which adds so vast a territory to our Union.... I trust I have aided indirectly in this final cession, which by your address and secrecy took me with most agreeable surprise." Despite the admission of his ignorance in official state correspondence, Clay would forever try to claim responsibility for the deal, telling friends that Seward merely tried to "appropriate all the honor" for the purchase when "all the favors of Russia" were due to his own efforts. Years later, he would also claim that he wished for a one-word inscription on his grave stone: "ALASKA."[37]

By the close of 1867, Seward was fed up with Clay's mishaps. In addition to the Chautems affair, Clay had caused another headache for the State Department by waging an ill-tempered and poorly considered campaign to slander his secretary of legation, Jeremiah Curtin. With little evidence to back his claims, Clay accused Curtin, who had replaced Bayard Taylor in 1864, of being an "abandoned scoundrel" as well as a "habitual drunkard." Most contemporary and later observers, however, felt that the root of Clay's contempt lay in the jealousy he felt toward Curtin, who spoke fluent Russian and proved very popular in Saint Petersburg. With an eye, once again, on lining his own pockets, Clay requested that Seward replace Curtin with a man who was related to a wealthy American developer who was building railroads throughout Russia, a request the secretary of state refused. Shortly thereafter, on December 24, 1867, Clay tendered his resignation, to take effect in April 1868 or as soon as his successor arrived.[38]

Seward all too gratefully accepted it and ordered Curtin to fill Clay's position. Clay, now in a full standoff with Seward, refused to step down until Congress approved an official replacement. The beleaguered body was then in the midst of Andrew Johnson's impeachment trial. The fall presidential election also loomed, and the lame duck Seward made no serious effort to replace Clay, who sat half a world away stewing over his grievances. Still alienated from Mary Jane, he wrote regularly to his eldest daughter, Mary Barr. She had broken off her engagement with her cousin Green, married an Ohio man named Frank Herrick, and given birth to a son. Clay delighted in corresponding with her about his grandchild but grew testy when, in one letter, Mary Barr inquired as to whether the newspaper reports about his unnatural hair color were true. "As to my hair your Editor, of course, lies," he wrote in irritation. "Everyone almost here wears black hair—so I follow the fashion—after a while in America I will return no doubt to the natural state."[39]

As Clay prepared to return home, his thoughts turned once again to political opportunities that might exist for him back in the United States. A month after tendering his resignation, he wrote to Gen. Ulysses S. Grant, the presumed Republican presidential nominee. Clay told Grant that he intended to be home in time to attend the nominating convention, where he would add his vote of support for the illustrious general's nomination to head the "Union" party ticket. His use of the term "Union" was telling, for he had grown even more disillusioned with the faction of the Republican Party that was currently driving Reconstruction policy.[40]

The two men had never met, but Clay saw Grant as a fresh audience for his political ponderings. In the lengthy missive, he offered the general a full overview of the evolution of his political loyalties, as "a dispas[s]ionate looker-on, from out of the sp[h]ere of party heat." "As early as 1862," he explained to Grant, "I took ground against the extinction of state sovereignty by rebellion. . . . I think now the Union party would have been stronger, and wounds of our war would have been healed sooner, if that position had been followed by the Republican policy. I for a long time hoped that President Johnson would have succeeded in carrying over the mass of Republicans to that theory. But having failed, whether through want of the proper temper, or from the inherent difficulties of events, I was not willing to follow him into the camp of the enemies of the union, and of these principles of Enlightened liberty, and Constitutional equality of rights, to which I and devoted, my fortune and life."[41]

Like many moderate Republicans, Clay believed that uncompromising proscriptions on white Southerners would permanently alienate them from the Republican cause. "*I should desire to see all the whites of the South, free to vote*," he told Grant. "The sooner the Union party returns to the *normal conditions of our Constitutional action the better*." For Clay, that meant a hands-off approach; autonomy for the states and the removal of federal presence in the region. "The Freedman's bureau, the army (except as held in aid of the local civil law) should as soon as possible cease to exist in the South. They, the whites and Blacks, once readmitted into the Union should be as soon as possible left to themselves to organize and reorganize the constitutions and all the rights of states to suit themselves." "Otherwise," he posited, repeating the contention he made to Seward, "it seems to me, we make the Southern disaffection by central domination *chronic*—a Poland, and Ireland, and a Hungary! Consistently with the safety of the Union, great magnanimity should be shown to the South—trusting to time to cure the wounds of terrible war."[42]

Halfway across the globe from the complex and often disappointing realities of emancipation, Clay could prioritize his constitutional principles. Grant, who was then the general-in-chief of the armies (and had served briefly as secretary of war), had overseen military Reconstruction in the former Confederacy and understood what would happen if white

Southerners were "left to themselves." Perhaps this is why he never replied to Clay's missive. Clay did not make it home in time for the Republican nominating convention. He would, as he had for the previous six years, watch from afar as political events unfolded without him. As anticipated, Grant won the election of 1868 handily and appointed Hamilton Fish to replace William Seward as secretary of state. The Grant administration's replacement for Clay, former Pennsylvania governor Andrew Curtin, did not arrive until July 1869, at which point Clay finally left Saint Petersburg, headed home to a changed United States and an uncertain future.

Chapter 11
Restoring the Autonomy of the States

In October 1869, a Topeka, Kansas, newspaper editor announced Cassius M. Clay's return to American shores. Noting Clay's lengthy absence, he anticipated that the diplomat would "find his country changed more than himself." Marveling at all that had happened during Clay's foreign tenure, including slavery's demise and the impending ratification of the Fifteenth Amendment, the editor noted that the fulfillment of Clay's career-long goal to end slavery seemed to leave him in need of a new cause. Pondering what Clay's political future might hold, the editor pointed out the obvious: that slavery was "no longer a ground for preferring or condemning a public man." Where, he asked, would Clay fit into the dramatically changed American political landscape? More broadly, where would he, and other antislavery moderates like him, direct the conviction that had once underlain their emancipationist impulses as the process of Reconstruction continued?[1]

This, of course, was the question Clay had been contemplating for years. The Kansas editor was right in assuming that he would reenter American politics. While his Russian sojourn had removed him from the public eye for the better part of eight years, it had done nothing to dampen Cassius's longing for power and fame. But he faced the prospect of operating on a political terrain that was vastly different than the one he had abandoned in 1863. From Russia, he had watched as Republicans disagreed among themselves over questions of Black equality and how far the federal government should go to enforce it. He had defined himself as a man of the middle, a "progressive liberal" who avoided extremes. But what did that mean, practically speaking, in 1869, as Radical Republicans pushing for Black equality sparred with conservative Democrats intent on preserving white supremacy, as well as with politically pragmatic moderates in their own party?[2]

His home state provided one possible point of entry. Emancipation and Reconstruction policy had brought to fruition his vision of a free-labor South, complete with a Republican Party composed of a biracial and often fractious coalition of the white laborers he had championed and the newly enfranchised African Americans. In Kentucky, a small and fledgling group of Republicans had begun to organize after the war. They earned the enmity of many former Unionists and ex-Confederates alike and became the target of violence and intimidation. Although Clay might once have risen to defend their political rights, as he disembarked on American shores in 1869, he showed little concern for their cause and even less interest in returning to Kentucky.

Some of his reticence stemmed from his family life, which seemed broken beyond repair. Clay had not seen his wife or children since 1863. He and Mary Jane remained estranged, and other than sporadic correspondence, he had limited contact with his children. He had missed the weddings of two of his children: Mary Barr to Frank Herrick in 1866 and Sallie to James Bennett in 1867. Perhaps to avoid a possible reunion with her husband, Mary Jane moved out of White Hall, which she had so recently renovated, and relocated to Lexington in December 1869. With his marriage broken and his prospects in Kentucky slim, Clay did not return to White Hall but settled instead in New York City. There, he lived off the proceeds of his Russian business interests and planned to further expand them stateside with the production of a Russian-invented oil-burning "perpetual candle" whose US patent he had obtained.[3]

But Clay's desire for national political fame still burned bright. On his return to the United States, he took up a new high-profile cause: Cuban liberation. In 1868, insurgents on the tiny sugar-producing island began promoting reforms, including an end to the African slave trade and the eventual abolition of slavery altogether, and attempted to overthrow the colonial government. Spanish suppression was swift and brutal. Officials imprisoned hundreds of suspected rebels in internment camps and executed numerous others. President Grant's cabinet members disagreed regarding the appropriate response. Some argued that the United States should recognize the rebels as belligerents and aid the insurgency for both humanitarian and imperialist reasons. They saw intervention as an opportunity for the United States to drive Europe out of the Western Hemisphere and to eventually annex the small but valuable island. Others, including Secretary of State Hamilton Fish, sought to avoid involvement altogether, believing that US interference would lead to armed conflict with Spain and possibly England. Ultimately, Grant's attempt to end the turmoil by negotiating peace and purchasing Cuba failed, and just a month after Clay arrived in New York, the president indicated that the opportunity for American intervention in the island's affairs had passed.[4]

Undeterred, Clay cofounded and assumed the presidency of the Cuban Charitable Aid Society, an organization dedicated to support the Cuban rebels morally and financially. Two other high-profile figures joined the effort: his old friend Horace Greeley, who served as vice president, and

Charles A. Dana, editor of the *New York Sun*. Rather than expanding his political range, however, Clay's involvement with this new issue showcased his inability to relinquish old grievances. He launched the society on January 19, 1870, with a New York speech during which he spent more time castigating William Seward and excoriating the Grant administration than championing the plight of the Cuban rebels. The crowd grew restive and jeered Clay off the stage. The city's Republican press was hardly kinder. The *New York Times* described him as "Rip Van Winkle" returned "to his native place." "Need we say that he began his speech on Cuba by giving the audience a complete retrospective of his entire life?" the writer jibed. Similarly, the *New York Daily Herald* pronounced the meeting "a lamentable fizzle, owing to the desire of Cassius M. Clay, who was the first great gun, to talk more about Clay than Cuba."[5]

Just as American motives for intervention on behalf of the Cuban rebels included both benevolence and self-interest, so did Clay's. Noting that Cassius hoped to use Cuba as an issue around which to build a coalition of moderate Republicans with himself at the head, biographer David Smiley described his venture as "fundamentally the same issue he had always preached—emancipation—and for the same purpose—political office." Whatever Clay's true purpose, the Cuban Charitable Aid Society was a failure. It raised only $2,000, half of which came from a single person: Clay's old antislavery compatriot Gerrit Smith.[6]

The Cuban Charitable Aid Society did provide a platform from which Clay could air his current discontent with the Grant administration and its supporters. The Republican Party that Clay helped found in the 1850s had evolved over the Civil War and early years of Reconstruction. Defined in its infancy by idealistic Free-Soil and antislavery ideologies, by 1870, it had grown into a mature organization replete with party machinery and extensive patronage networks at both the state and national level. Staggering national economic and industrial growth during and after the Civil War accelerated this process. While some Republicans embraced these changes, others viewed the accompanying concentration of wealth into the hands of fewer individuals and corporations as a corruption of Republican principles. They grew particularly concerned about the lobbying influence exerted by rich and powerful entities on state legislatures and individual politicians. They also lamented the nation's wartime adoption of paper money, the proliferation of protective tariffs, and ballooning government patronage, all of which seemed to serve a small number of wealthy capitalists rather than the productive masses.[7]

Republicans also remained divided over Reconstruction policy. The radical faction that had wrested control from Andrew Johnson in 1866 continued to push for active federal enforcement of the Reconstruction amendments. This was no small feat given the commitment of the Ku Klux Klan and similar paramilitary groups to, as Grant himself put it, "deprive colored citizens of the right to bear arms and the right of a free ballot, to suppress schools in which colored children were taught, and to reduce the colored people to a condition closely akin to that of slavery." Throughout the South, the Klan terrorized freed people and their allies, whipping, raping, and murdering Black and white citizens who dared to vote the Republican ticket, seek an education, or demand fair wages. A steady stream of letters from desperate Southern governors and lowly citizens alike landed on the president's desk, describing the dire situations in their states and asking for his help against white terrorists.[8]

Just as it had since 1867, that aid came primarily from the US military. The government continued to maintain army troops in the South who could respond with force to Southern brutality. When white violence persisted, Congress, with Grant's support, passed several "enforcement acts," which allowed federal judges to supervise Southern elections and the president to deploy troops to ensure that they proceeded peacefully. The legislation sanctioned the federal government to bring charges against individuals for impeding civil rights, a license that had heretofore belonged exclusively to states. These measures proved effective in clearing the way for free and fair political contests and in areas of the South with a large Black population, which, in turn, led to the election of African Americans to positions in local, state, and national government.[9]

Yet this shift in the balance of power from states to the federal government disturbed many white Americans. While a large portion of the Northern public did not oppose the new freedom, or even the citizenship and male suffrage, that the Fourteenth and Fifteenth Amendments imparted to African Americans, they grew uncomfortable with the federal government's attendant efforts to enforce them. They found the continued reliance on what amounted to a standing army in a time of supposed peace particularly troublesome. With the amendments in place, more Americans adopted the view that Southern states should be allowed to reconstruct themselves with limited federal influence, just as Clay had been advocating since 1866.[10]

By 1870, a collection of dissident Republicans, Cassius Clay among them, coalesced around their opposition to Grant's economic and Reconstruction policies. Calling themselves Liberal Republicans, they hoped to wrest the party nomination from him before the election of 1872. They struck out against "Grantism"—a term that encompassed a number of the president's purported flaws: his association with corruption, his supposed abuse of patronage, his cozy relationship with big business, and his consistent reliance on the federal government and US military to enforce Reconstruction policies. In contrast, the Liberal Republican movement, as Carl Schurz described it, promised a "reaction against the easy political morals and the spirit of jobbery which have grown and been developed in times of war" and a return to a purer republicanism.[11]

Clay had always thrived within the politics of opposition, and this time was no different. In the spring of 1871, now back in Kentucky and resettled in White Hall, he endorsed the presidential candidacy of Horace Greeley. In letters and speeches, Cassius denounced the corruption in the Grant administration, calling for "universal amnesty," a pet issue for many moderate Republicans who considered the continued deprivation of suffrage to prominent Confederates both antithetical to sectional reconciliation and unconstitutional. In a private letter to *Louisville Courier-Journal* editor and Liberal Republican sympathizer Henry Watterson in April 1871, Clay insisted that Grant and his supporters were for the "centralization, and punishment, [and] subjection of the South [and for] dividing her population and crippling her industry and making her powerless for all time." In another letter, this one widely published, Clay asserted that Greeley was for peaceful reunion, "rather than [Grant] who, refusing amnesty, bares the sword for the eternal subjection of a Saxon people." In blatant racial terms, Clay insisted that the rights of African Americans should not be protected at whites' expense. "The great issue of slavery being settled by constitutional law and [war], and the great mass of the Democratic party having acquiesced in the logic of events," he claimed, "it only remains to reduce the late insurgency and the returned Union forces into peaceful co-operation."[12]

Clay, who had waged a rhetorical war on Southern elites for so much of his career, now called for their exoneration. Yet this was another instance in which he was no outlier among former antislavery reformers. Although nothing less than the very contours of African American freedom was at stake, many of his antebellum compatriots, including such men as Carl Schurz, Charles Francis Adams, Lyman Trumbull, Salmon Chase, and Horace Greeley, shared Clay's antipathy to both military Reconstruction and suffrage restrictions on former Confederates.[13]

Chase, for example, opposed military presence in the South and supported general amnesty for Confederates. He had broken with congressional Republicans years before over these and other issues and drifted back into the Democratic fold. He explained his reasons for doing so in 1868 in a letter to a Democratic Party operative. Congress had been wrong in establishing military governments as well as in denying suffrage to "all classes," Chase wrote, adding that the new Southern constitutions were sufficient to "secure [freedmen] the right of suffrage and thereby the means of self-protection against injustice." Chase believed optimistically that African American voters in the South would be satisfied with the restoration of voting rights to all former Confederates so long as their own were protected. Despite their apparent retreat from policies essential to ensure racial equality, Clay and many of his fellow former antislavery compatriots denied that they had relinquished their concern for the recently enslaved. Rather, they felt that the government's preoccupation with affairs in the former Confederacy was a diversion from other pressing issues, such as tariff reduction and reform of the civil service.[14]

George Julian, the former Free-Soil vice presidential candidate for whom Clay had campaigned in 1848, embodied this outlook. As his biographer later assessed, opposition to slavery was but part of Julian's larger quest for equality. "Devotion to humanity was the basis of the antislavery enterprise, and he regarded the emancipation of the Negro as the prelude to a more comprehensive movement looking to the redemption of all races from all forms of prejudice," whether the oppression be from "slave drivers," large corporations, or the "'legalized robbery of a protective tariff or the power of concentrated capital in alliance with labor saving machinery.'"[15]

The Liberal Republican movement took off as Julian served his final term in the House of Representatives. During his years in Congress, the Hoosier's main concern shifted from opposition to slavery to questions of government land allocation. The federal government's sale of vast tracts of western territory to railroad corporations and the tax exemptions it offered mining companies seemed anathema to the Republican principle that land should be reserved for yeoman farmers. Just as slave labor had posed a detriment to opportunity for the average white farmer before the Civil War, he believed, so did rail corporations in the postbellum era. In apt symmetry, Julian's inaugural congressional speech in 1850 excoriated the Slave Power while he titled his final address, of 1870, "The Railway Power."[16]

Liberal Republicans also fretted over the shifting power balance within the US federalist system. They continued to see states as the proper sites of lawmaking and considered the enormous consolidation of power within the national government during the Civil War a threat. Salmon Chase, whose influential antislavery positive law theory had rested on the idea that only states could determine the legality of slavery within their borders, extended his theory into the postwar era. In 1869, Chase, who was then serving as Chief Justice of the United States, told a South Carolina correspondent that he wished that "the great work consummated by the ratification of the fifteenth amendment could have been accomplished by the States through the amendment of State constitutions and through appropriate State legislation" rather than war.[17]

Even some former abolitionists who had opposed slavery for moral rather than political or economic reasons backed the Liberal Republicans. They included Franklin B. Sanborn (who had once supported John Brown), Elizur Wright, and Anna Dickinson, who argued in a campaign speech for Greeley that the time had come to trust Southern whites with their own governance. If African Americans' right to vote could be enforced only at bayonet point, she insisted, "we might as well confess that the experiment of republican Union is ended."[18]

As he campaigned on behalf of the Liberal Republican movement throughout 1871 and into 1872, Clay repeatedly invoked the idea that state sovereignty had been violated by Reconstruction policy. "The constitution was based upon the vital integrity of the states, and their unhappy overthrow was not necessary to the suppression of the rebellion or to the liberation of the slave," he asserted, insisting that the Grant administration had not only trampled on the prerogative of states to determine their policies but in doing so only extended wartime sectional discord. In a speech he gave in St. Louis, Clay claimed that "the old anti-slavery men" now represented by the Liberal Republicans sought to reunify the country by promoting both rights for freedmen and forgiveness for white Southerners. By denying clemency and self-determination to the latter, Clay argued, mainstream Republicans, whom he identified as those who had gained power during the war, not only prolonged the reconciliation process between North and South but fostered dangerous discontent among the freedmen. "And now they are for a revolution," Clay proclaimed. "They are for setting the blacks against the whites and the whites against the blacks to your ruin and destruction."[19]

In fact, Clay and his fellow Liberal Republicans went even further and blamed supporters of the Grant administration—dubbed "stalwarts"—for the violence in the Reconstruction South, arguing that white Southerners resorted to establishing the Ku Klux Klan only because of the government's "disfranchising of the leading minds of the South, and the fatal attempt to subject the Saxon race," he said in a letter of January 1872 to a group of Missouri Republicans. "I remember no instance in all history where the servile race has been successfully set to rule over the former masters," he continued, "nor do I believe that now such attempt will bear any other fruits than ruin to both parties." Paternalistically, he argued: "No man has made more sacrifices for the liberation of blacks than I," adding that this qualified him "to be considered a faithful adviser with regard to their future."[20]

One person unmoved by Cassius's self-righteous rationale was Frederick Douglass, to whom Clay wrote in July 1871. Realizing that Clay had reached out to him as part of a larger effort to recruit African Americans to the Liberal cause, Douglass's reply was equal parts respectful and incensed. He acknowledged Clay's "glorious efforts in the stormy and perilous past for emancipation" but told him that he was "much astonished" by his current views. Douglass condemned both Clay's narrative and the entire Liberal agenda. "Great Heavens! When, where and what rebels and traitors were ever treated with a levity and liberality equal to that extended to the rebels of the South?" he asked. "When, where and what rebels ever deserved such liberal treatment less?" "The Republican party," he stated, "cannot be broken up at this juncture without putting in peril all that has been gained for freedom by the late terrible war—and without prejudice to the honor and safety of the country." Rejecting Clay's invitation to join the Liberals, Douglass told him that he "might as well ask me to put a pistol to my head and blow my brains out than to ask me to lend myself in anywise to the division and defeat of the Republican party." Douglass closed his letter on a conciliatory note, reassuring Clay that he would never forget his sacrifice for the antislavery cause, but America's preeminent Black abolitionist clearly considered Cassius's current defection from the Republican Party as a betrayal of past principles.[21]

Clay was delighted when Greeley won the Liberal Republican presidential nomination in May 1872, anticipating that a November victory would result in a cabinet position for himself. Not all Liberals were so enthusiastic. They saw Greeley's long history of involvement in fringe social interests, as well as his controversial decision to contribute to Jefferson Davis's bail bond in 1867, as political liability. A larger problem for many in the breakaway party was Greeley's pro-tariff stance. In order to bridge their differences going into the campaign, the Liberals doubled down on the issues that united them, stressing Greeley's commitment to state sovereignty and sectional reconciliation, placing "the southern question" at the center of their platform. As he noted in his acceptance statement, Greeley stood against "federal subversion of the internal polity" of states and local governments and declared that he was ready to see Northerners and Southerners "clasp hands across the bloody chasm which ha[d] too long divided them." So great was the desire of the Democratic National Convention to unseat the Grant administration that delegates endorsed Greeley as their own candidate and adopted the Liberal platform, despite Greeley's long-held and vociferous contempt for the Democratic Party.[22]

Clay campaigned vigorously for Greeley and the fusion ticket throughout the early fall, traversing much of the same midwestern ground he covered in 1860. In speech after speech, he reiterated his trust in white Southerners to abide by the Reconstruction amendments and advocated granting them peace and forgiveness. He also continued efforts to sway African American voters, telling Whitelaw Reid, who was Greeley's campaign manager and editor of the *Chicago Tribune*, that the paper should publish a "campaign document for blacks," which would place his "anti-slavery efforts" in contrast to that of Grant partisans. In a letter published in the Louisville *Courier-Journal*, Clay informed Kentucky's Black voters that they owed nothing to "Grant Republicans." "It was the old 'liberation element'" of the Liberal Republicans, he told them, who secured both their freedom as well as the Reconstruction amendments. Meanwhile, he argued, the Grant administration was full of false promises and "bent on keeping up the strife between blacks and whites that they may keep in office." "When the blacks are ruined in property and character," he warned, Grant partisans would "fly with their ill-gotten gains and leave them to the vengeance of the whites." "Go for Greeley, amnesty and equal rights to all!" he exhorted his readers.[23]

Many African Americans, who understood that the Grant administration's commitment to enforcing Reconstruction legislation was the only hope of maintaining Black rights in the South, were alarmed at Clay's false logic. While Frederick Douglass had previously confined his critique of Clay's flawed reasoning to private correspondence, in June 1872, he offered a blunt and scathing rejoinder in his newspaper, the *New National Era*. Once again, Douglass paid tribute to Clay's antebellum courage but condemned Clay's current departure from his commitment to Black rights. "While we accord Mr. Clay all honor for his old time heroic defense of free speech, when menaced by the revolvers and bowie knives of slave-drivers," he wrote, "we deny his fitness to enlighten or advise colored men as to their political duties in this present crisis. He is a brave man, and that is something, but he has always been more distinguished for physical courage than for political consistency." Douglass's assessment that the situation in the South constituted a "present crisis" could not have been more at odds with the Liberal Republican assertion that the best course of action was to restore the rights of "Home Rule" to white Southerners, who would surely overturn Reconstruction to whatever extent allowable.[24]

It took considerable dissemblance on the part of former antislavery Liberals to believe that white Southerners, if restored to authority, would suddenly change their views and abide by the Reconstruction amendments. In reality, they knew full well that the issues for which they lobbied—civil service reform, state autonomy, and lower taxes—would almost certainly benefit elite whites at the expense of newly empowered African Americans. Greeley himself admitted as much during a visit to the Deep South in 1871. "I am confident that two-thirds of the men, with nine-tenths of the women, who formerly composed the slave-holding caste would this day give half their houses and lands to have their slaves back again," he reported, describing the difficulty with which Southern whites were adjusting to a new reality where African Americans whom they formerly saw as chattel property could demand rights and fair wages. "Their instincts, their training, their habits, are shocked by this," he observed, "just as yours would be if your horse cited you before a court and compelled you to show cause for not paying him ten dollars a month for last year's service."[25]

But while he was willing to acknowledge white Southern intransigence toward the changes emancipation had wrought, Greeley and other Liberal Republicans were equally critical of the Southern Reconstruction state governments, which they viewed as being composed of uneducated men who indiscriminately raised property taxes and increased government spending. For many Liberal Republicans who had once been on the vanguard of political antislavery, Cassius Clay included, political corruption and government overreach, whether at the state or national level, posed a bigger threat to Republican principles than did the abrogation of Black political and civil rights. Although the consequences of their shifting priorities seemed antithetical to their pre–Civil War concerns, the principles themselves were consistent with their longtime belief that issues of freedom, citizenship, and suffrage should be the purview of local and state, rather than the federal, government. They also reflected a long-existing strain of "laissez-faire constitutionalism" within the American public.[26]

In sum, the same adherence to constitutional principle that led Clay and other moderate antislavery reformers to prize white property rights above Black freedom before the Civil War also led to their willingness to undercut Black freedom for the sake of restoring proper constitutionalism during Reconstruction. In the end, though, the Democratic–Liberal Republican fusion was not enough to unseat Grant, who garnered 55 percent of the popular vote and the electoral votes of all but six states—Texas, Georgia, Tennessee, Maryland, Missouri, and Kentucky. Greeley, exhausted and demoralized by the campaign, died before his electors could count the ballots.

Although Greeley's defeat dashed Clay's hopes for a cabinet appointment, he took solace in returning to White Hall, where a new addition to his family awaited him. The previous year he had welcomed a five-year old Russian boy named Leonide Petroff (called Launey) into his family. The legal petition for adoption that Clay completed in the Madison County courthouse listed Launey's parents as Jean and Annie Petroff. Better known in Russia as Anna Petroff, Annie had been a well-known dancer in the Russian Imperial Ballet. Given Clay's well-known penchant for "ballet girls" and the reputation he derived from the Chautems affair, many people believed that when he requested "sole guardianship of said Leonide, for life," he was accepting custody of his own son. Cassius forever remained coy regarding Launey's paternity, never fully claiming nor denying it. He alluded cryptically to his son's provenance in his memoirs, writing that in Saint Petersburg, "that city of isolation, infinite intrigues, and silence—was born in the year 1866, a male child. To the secret of his parentage I am the only living witness—I who have, of all men living, the best reason to know—and that secret will die with me."[27]

Launey's apparition and adoption was a very public embarrassment for Mary Jane Clay and precluded any chance of reconciliation with her husband. She had returned to White Hall from Lexington intermittently since her husband's return, but only in order to keep up the appearance of domestic stability rather than in the interest of an emotional reunion. Cassius later alleged that Mary Jane had "received [me] like a stranger ... my trunk placed in a room where I slept alone." He claimed that she relegated him to a newly renovated part of the house without a working fireplace, where he suffered "cold so intense that icicles froze in my beard."[28]

As the couple's marriage unraveled in the early 1870s, additional points of contention emerged. Cassius complained that Mary Jane had overspent their construction budget while renovating White Hall. Clay later conceded that she had offered to repay him all of the money he had sent home from Russia from an inheritance she had received from her father's estate during the Civil War but that he had refused out of his "instincts as a husband and gentleman." The Clays had been married for forty years, during which time Mary Jane had stood by her husband through the social and monetary hardships brought on by his antislavery career, his near death on several occasions, and the vicious gossip surrounding his purported infidelities. She had raised their children alone for nearly a decade. The twin indignities of Launey's appearance and Cassius's criticism of her handling of the White Hall renovation pushed their discord beyond the point of resolution. He later wrote in his memoirs that one day Mary Jane became "infuriated" and unleashed anger upon her husband "for all the faults and escapades of a life-time ... pour[ing] them on my devoted head like a deluge." Mary Jane left White Hall for good, taking Annie and Laura with her. She lived first with her sister Anne before purchasing her own house in Lexington in 1873. With only his adopted son for company, Clay spent much of 1873 and 1874 at White Hall, where he tended to his livestock and fruit orchards.[29]

In 1875, however, he prepared to relaunch his political career—this time as a Democrat. In the spring of that year, he attended the Kentucky state Democratic convention, where he gave a speech explaining his belief that the party was now "the true defender of the constitutional liberties." For those paying attention, Clay's steady political drift had been evident for some time, but his political conversion caught the notice of the national press. The fact that "the bitterest of bitter Radicals," as one Nebraska paper mischaracterized him, had joined the party of retrenchment was a noteworthy item in newspapers throughout the country. In addition to better reflecting his political principles, this new alliance, Clay realized, offered him a much better chance of political success in Kentucky. Throughout 1875, the man who had once worked so hard to establish a foothold for the Republican Party in the commonwealth canvassed in support of Democratic candidates for state elections. He optimistically anticipated that he might be featured as the vice presidential candidate on the national ticket the following year.[30]

Clay demonstrated just how far from his antislavery past his political permutations had shifted him when, in October 1875, he agreed to take his new political affiliation to Mississippi, where his nephew and former secretary of legation Green Clay was a candidate for the state legislature. After the war, Green settled on the Bolivar County cotton plantation that his father, Brutus, had purchased in the 1850s. The Union war veteran resuscitated the prime Delta land, which had fallen into ruin during the war, and became a prominent member of the community. In 1875, he announced his run for state office as a "reform" candidate who, if elected, would help wrest the state from the clutches of its Reconstruction-minded government.[31]

Following the Civil War, white Mississippians had felt the firm hand of the federal government in their political affairs. In 1869, Mississippi voters only accepted the Fourteenth and Fifteenth Amendments and a new state constitution (the qualifications by which the state gained readmission to the Union) in elections that were supervised by US troops. Under military administration and with a majority Black population, however, Mississippi had seen one of the most dramatic transformations in its government of any state during Reconstruction. The state's biracial state legislature elected two Black men, Hiram Revels and Blanche K. Bruce, to the US Senate. Perhaps more importantly, Mississippi voters elected dozens of African Americans to positions in local government—registrars, tax assessors, and sheriffs—where they oversaw the regulation of people's everyday life. White Mississippians pushed back with brutal determination. Groups calling themselves White Liners began organizing into forces of intimidation and violence intent on disabling Republican activity. By the close of 1874, they could claim success, with Democrats garnering electoral victories whenever the federal government failed to dispatch federal troops on election day.[32]

In this context, the stakes could not have been higher in Mississippi's elections of fall 1875. White voters aimed not only to elect redeemers to local and state offices but also to ensure that their pro-Reconstruction governor, Adelbert Ames, would not be appointed US senator by a sympathetic Republican state legislature. Summer and early fall saw violent clashes between African American voters and their white adversaries. In September, a white paramilitary group in Yazoo County drove the white Republican sheriff from office and murdered several of his Black supporters. In Clinton, a political debate turned deadly when white Democratic partisans jeered a Republican candidate as he took the stage. Tensions escalated, and soon partisans began exchanging shot and shell. A handful of African Americans and whites died at the scene, and casualties mounted when White Liners launched a wider crusade of retaliation, killing several dozen politically influential African Americans in the course of a few days.[33]

When Governor Ames once again requested more federal troops, an exasperated Grant replied: "The whole public are tired out with these annual autumnal outbreaks in the South ... and are ready to condemn any interference on the part of the government." Despite his dismay, however, the president commissioned a proclamation to send troops. Grant's more conservative attorney general, Edwards Pierrepont, undercut the president's order, however, and informed Ames that the federal government would send troops only after the state had committed its own militia to the task. "Let the country see that the citizens of Miss. who are largely favorable to good order, and are largely Republican, have the courage and manhood to *fight* for their rights, and to destroy the bloody ruffians who murder the innocent and unoffending freedmen," Pierrepont told him. Ames met with state Democratic leaders as well as an emissary from the US Attorney General's office to broker an agreement that would avoid election-day confrontation. Although they appeared to have struck a deal, Ames anticipated that the Democratic forces would wait to unleash their terror until after it was too late to summon federal troops. He wrote to his wife, Blanche: "Yes, a revolution has taken place—by force of arms—and a race are disfranchised—they are to be returned to a condition of serfdom—and era of second slavery." "You may think I exaggerate," he added. "Time will show you how accurate my statements are."[34]

This was the high-stakes, highly charged situation into which Clay inserted himself. Along with his avuncular loyalty to Green, he was motivated to work for his nephew's election because he believed that Mississippi's Republican government was incompetent and poorly run. He specifically decried what he considered excessive taxation and government corruption.

As he later wrote in his autobiography, he viewed the state as a place where Black "misrule" had reached its "highest culmination." During his antislavery career, Clay had often castigated white slave owners for their laziness and stunting the progress of the Southern economy, but he now pitied them, noting how heavily they were taxed and the difficulty they had in securing African American laborers. Clay also joined redeemers in exaggerating, then denouncing financial corruption in the state, claiming that the "radicals" were misusing public money and that "general ruin and anarchy prevailed."[35]

Just weeks before the election of November 1875, Clay made appearances and speeches in Vicksburg and Greenville. Green Clay and other Democratic politicians who were hosting him hoped that he would be particularly influential in convincing Black men familiar with his antislavery credentials to vote for the reform ticket. In his Mississippi speeches, Clay reminded Black voters that he had freed his own slaves and attempted to assuage their concerns, asserting that their freedom was secured forever and that no political party could take it from them. Conservatives had their best interests at heart, he told them, while "the carpetbagger [had] no interest here except to fill his pockets and leave." Furthermore, he blamed "white carpet-baggers" for inciting the violence in Vicksburg and Friar's Point, where just days before his arrival whites attacked elected Black officials and then expanded their killing spree into the countryside.[36]

Clay later fondly remembered his trip to Mississippi and the generous reception his largely African American audiences gave him. Of the state's Delta region, he claimed: "The heavy slave counties were peopled mostly from Kentucky, and knew my labors and sacrifices in behalf of freedom. They received me with warm hearts, and were ready to acknowledge me as a leader and friend." Despite visiting shortly after several terrible incidents of violence, including notorious massacres of Black citizens in Vicksburg, Canton, and Friar's Point, he discounted their severity. "That there was some intimidation in Mississippi against the blacks I have every reason to believe," he wrote in his memoirs, but then he dismissed it by equating it with the strong-arm tactics of political machines in Northern cities such as New York and Baltimore. He seemed to thrive on the danger. Where once he had armed himself to the teeth in self-protection while denouncing slavery, now he relished rumors of unrest that his presence sparked as he tried to overturn Reconstruction. "I never felt in more danger in my life," he later remembered of traveling to Friar's Point just two weeks after the massacre there. Referring to the local Black citizens, he assessed: "Not that they would care to kill me particularly, but because in a *melee* they would not care who was killed."[37]

His work done, Clay returned to Kentucky. On election day in Mississippi, armed White Liners, rather than Clay's appeals, determined the outcome. Throughout the state, in small hamlets and in midsized towns, they came out in force, threatening Black voters at gun and cannon point from entering polling places. Knowing that voting would cost them their lives, most African Americans turned back or stayed away. Election results offered stark evidence of the so-called reformers' ruthless efficiency. In many counties where Black Republicans had scored overwhelming electoral victories only two years earlier, their tallies had decreased by thousands of votes. Democrats gained a decisive majority in the state legislature. Once seated, the new class of legislators, Green Clay among them, sent five Democrats to represent Mississippi in Congress. The redeemer legislature also lobbed trumped-up charges of corruption at Governor Ames, compelling him to resign under threat of impeachment. Thus, the election of 1875 in which Clay participated marked the functional end of Reconstruction in Mississippi. The consequences of this election were not limited to a single state, however. Democratic efforts there were so devastatingly effective that the strategy of violent coercion became known as the Mississippi Plan and served as a blueprint that white Southerners in other states would use to formulate their own political terrorism.[38]

The results of the Mississippi elections delighted Clay. Some Mississippians were grateful for his help, including Greenville resident William Alexander Percy, who wrote to offer him "many thanks for myself and my people for the kindly assistance, which you rendered us in our hour of need." In his memoirs Clay boasted of his small role in, as he put it, the "restoration of the autonomy of the states." Viewing the overthrow of Reconstruction as "but another form of the great struggle for the Government of the People, as against the Divine Right of Kings," and an extension of his republican principles, he contended: "These States, ruled by a central power at Washington, by means of patronage and military influence, still bearing the name of Republic, would in fact be a corrupt and tyrannical despotism, without the wholesome check on tyranny."[39]

As he wrote his autobiography in 1885, Clay admitted another reason for his opposition to Reconstruction: his belief in the cultural and racial superiority of whites. "Outside of my being a Southerner, with my knowledge of the two races, I could not have been otherwise than opposed to black rule," he said. Casting the Southern struggle for redemption in universally racialized terms, he asserted: "To throw aside all the facts of superior culture, property, and refinement, which centered in the whites of the South, there remains the sympathy of race." "Till the peace," he concluded, "the right was on the side of the black and the Republican Party, but afterward the right, as well as the sympathy of the white races of all civilization, was on the South against the North, because civilization and the white race were, after their aberration, at odds with the blacks and barbarism."[40]

While Clay remained fully supportive of Black citizenship and suffrage, he continued to believe that African Americans needed to show their "fitness" to exercise those rights. In his estimation, and in that of many moderate Republicans, they had failed to do so, and he had no compunction about returning their erstwhile oppressors to power. In these prejudices and assumptions, Clay was not alone. Nor was he unique in his willingness, by 1875, to prioritize a reading of the Constitution that emphasized state sovereignty and limitations on "special interests" over the more recent rights it accorded to African Americans.

Chapter 12
Lion of Whitehall

Ironically, the end of federal presence in the South—the issue for which Clay campaigned so avidly in Mississippi—was the political trade-off that settled the disputed election of 1876 and ensured that Republican Rutherford B. Hayes won control of the White House. A Democratic presidency might have created a pathway for Clay to reenter national politics. Instead, Clay was consigned to life in Kentucky, with only his son Launey for company. He settled into a lonely bachelorhood inside the rambling, elegant White Hall. In its newly renovated state, the house gained a reputation as one of the finest in Kentucky and had truly become the showplace he and Mary Jane once dreamed it might be. Devoid of human company, Clay filled his home with material treasures: books, fine statuary, and paintings of Russian royalty and dignitaries. Now in his late sixties, he embraced the agricultural pursuits that had bored him in earlier decades. Though still concerned with the current state of politics and race relations in America, Clay began to train his gaze backward, thinking and writing about his role in the country's antislavery past. In doing so, he began constructing a portrait of himself—and a movement—that sometimes obscured more than it revealed and led others to do the same.[1]

Taking stock of the past mitigated the dismal realities of Clay's present. In the waning days of 1877, he filed for divorce from Mary Jane, claiming that they had ceased marital relations in 1869 and had been "living apart without any cohabitation for more than five consecutive years." With the exception of their eldest son, Green, the Clay children's loyalties had followed Mary Jane during their long separation, and the family existed in a state of public estrangement. One newspaper referred to Clay as "a sort of King Lear" and told a pathetic story of him passing his once-beloved daughter Annie in the street without recognizing her. Despite the family's fractured state, Cassius and his children lived in close proximity thanks to the terms of his father's now decades-old will, which stipulated that his Madison County landholdings be divided among his heirs. In 1873, he had partitioned his vast acreage, deeding each of his six living children parcels ranging from 275 to 425 acres, diminishing his own holdings to the house and surrounding 360 acres. In exchange, his children each promised to pay him an annuity.[2]

Yet retiring from public life failed to bring him peace. By the late 1870s, Clay found himself, as he had throughout earlier days, surrounded by enemies, some of whom had once been his enslaved laborers. Even before the ratification of the Thirteenth Amendment in December 1865, the enslaved laborers of White Hall began to claim their freedom. While several of them departed the premises, leaving Mary Jane struggling to find "good and stationary servants," a number of the newly freed men and women, including Sarah White, Frank Clay, and Jerry Clay bought property nearby. By the late 1870s, Sarah was working as Cassius's cook. But the relationship between the former master and enslaved woman was troubled.[3]

His turn away from Reconstruction and the Republican Party, he alleged, earned him the resentment of his Black employees and their children. "The younger set," he claimed, "who knew little or nothing of my history, were my implacable enemies, and ready to injure me in person or property." He soon began to suspect that his employees were stealing silver and other valuables. Worse yet, he discovered that Launey's governess and Sarah White were poisoning the boy's food. Clay then terminated his entire staff, precipitating a conflict with Sarah's son, Perry, who threatened to kill him. In September 1877, an armed altercation between them prompted Clay to shoot White. He turned himself in to local authorities, and when the state of Kentucky tried him for homicide, a jury acquitted him on the grounds that he had acted in self-defense.[4]

Clay's interest in politics continued into his silver years, and he remained involved with the state Democratic Party until, in 1884, he abruptly changed course and once again became a Republican. That fall, he explained his decision while giving a speech in support of James G. Blaine's presidential candidacy in Louisville. He could, he told a large audience at the city's Southern Exposition, no longer abide the corrupt results of the Democratic Party's practices in the South. He lamented that in the years after redemption, white Democrats in nearly every Southern state used violence and intimidation to keep Black and white Republican voters away from the polls, enabling the creation of a one-party "Solid South." Clay's face-to-face encounter with these tactics during his visit to Mississippi in 1875 meant that he could not have been entirely surprised that returning sovereignty to Southern states would result in continued voter suppression.[5]

In a letter he circulated in 1884, however, Clay announced that he was defecting from the Democratic Party for the very same reason he once left the Republican fold: his commitment to "the doctrine of the supreme right of the people by legal majorities to absolute rule." He had abandoned the Republicans in the early 1870s in the interest of "freeing the ballot from Federal and illegal action," but now he realized that white Southern

Democrats were abusing their newfound liberation from federal intervention. Clay personalized the situation, asking, "If I vote for Blaine and Logan am I to be shot down in Kentucky by the Solid South?" Referring to both old and new constitutional protections for voting, he asked: "What becomes of that clause of the old Federal Constitution of 1789 which guarantees a republican form of government to all the States? What becomes of the amendment after the War which places all citizens of the Republic on an equality in civil and political rights?"[6]

Clay seemed not to consider the way in which his dogged devotion to one set of constitutional principles had come at the expense of others. He was unwilling to recognize the role he had played years earlier in Mississippi in helping to usher in a state government run by white politicians who clamored for a return to state sovereignty for the purpose of subverting the very rights promised by the Fourteenth and Fifteenth Amendments. He also disregarded the reality that the same federal legal and military intervention that he and his fellow Liberal Republicans considered "interference" had protected Black and white civil rights. Instead, he blamed the Radical Republican–run federal government for the one-party dominance in the South. "The North had no right to force the people of the South to submit to Negro domination," he told a newspaper reporter in 1884. "If the white southerners had been given a chance to work things out without federal intervention," he asserted, "half the negroes would now be voting the Democratic ticket; the whites would now be divided between the Republican and Democratic parties; there would not now be any Solid South, and the Republican Party would be assured of a much longer lease of power than it now is."[7]

Though he misplaced its genesis, Clay did recognize that the power and prejudice wielded by white Southerners posed seemingly insurmountable barriers to Black citizenship. In a rambling and disjointed essay he penned for the *North American Review* in 1886, he wrote: "The present status shows the supremacy of the whites in social and political rule," despite the fact that, by law, "the blacks have all the legal equality that written constitutions can secure." "Does intimidation, corruption, force, and fraud on the part of the white override all legal enfranchisement?" he asked. "And if so, is there any remedy, if desirable but time?" The article revealed that Clay's views on race remained, as they had for decades, simultaneously liberal and limited. He denounced the efforts of white Southerners to deny African Americans education and declared that all humans ought to stand "EQUAL BEFORE THE LAW." He offered the racialist view, however, that there was an "instinctive repugnance between whites and blacks," which meant that laws against miscegenation and intermarriage were unnecessary because such phenomena were rare, given that people were "happiest where intermarriage [was] confined to the nearest type and closest affinities of rank, education, and sentiment."⁸

Much as he had believed that the most unfortunate consequence of slavery was its negative effect on white workers, he also cast the worst consequence of Black disenfranchisement as its deleterious effect on democracy for white voters. He lamented that Democrats in the postwar Solid South, with the help of sympathetic Northern Democrats, ruled the whole country "by a minority-vote of the whole people," much as they had before the Civil War. As during his antislavery career, it was the antidemocratic consequences of white Democratic supremacy, rather than its racist contours, that Clay viewed as problematic. And as ever, he saw politics as the solution. "The blacks must be divided between the northern and southern parties," he reasoned. "That will break the caste of race. That, and time, will make us one people, and blot out the old Mason's and Dixon's line, and all will be equal before the law." As he had in his antislavery days, he advocated a gradual procedural solution, never minding that it did not comport with the reality that most Southern African Americans were unlikely to vote for a political party dedicated to their oppression.⁹

In the early 1880s, Clay's involvement in party politics waned and he became consumed with a different project: crafting his life story for public consumption. He threw his energy into penning his memoirs and, by 1886, had completed the first of what he hoped would be a two-volume set. Like all autobiographers, Clay believed that his life narrative would be of interest to the reading public; he was also motivated by the desire to render his own account of the antislavery movement and his role within it. At the time he set pen to paper, veterans of the movement—radical abolitionists and moderate emancipationists alike—were busy recounting the decades-long struggle to purge the American nation of its original sin. The weightiest contribution to this literature came from Clay's old confidant Henry Wilson, who wrote the comprehensive three-volume *History of the Rise and Fall of the Slave Power in America*. Published between 1871 and 1877, Wilson's massive tomes comprised nearly 2,000 pages of text, in which he recounted slavery's legal basis, its nefarious embedment within the Constitution, and its corrupting influence on the development of the United States. In laying out a comprehensive context, Wilson hoped to demonstrate the intractability of slavery and to amplify the difficulty of ending it. Before the war, antislavery reformers had carefully self-sorted, according to the varieties of their antislavery commitment, into immediatists and gradualists, moral suasionists and politicians. In his three volumes, however, Wilson interwove the contributions of dozens of antislavery reformers of all motivations and strategies into an overarching narrative of their achievement.[10]

Clay wished to ride the success of Wilson's account but also to correct it. In the seven pages he devoted to Clay, Wilson had profiled the Kentuckian's heroic role in the antebellum antislavery movement, focusing particular attention on his achievement in publishing the *True American* and his subsequent persecution. Clay, however, felt that because he had "taken sides in favor of the autonomy of the South" during Reconstruction, whereas Wilson, who served as Grant's vice president between 1873 and 1875, favored heavy federal enforcement, the author "could not do [him] justice."[11]

In his own 600-page account, Clay made grandiose and groundless assertions to prove his influence in turning the Union war effort into one for emancipation. He claimed responsibility for converting Lincoln to the antislavery cause in the 1850s, as well as for convincing the Kentucky legislature to cooperate with the president's emancipation plans in 1862. Cassius also explained and absolved himself of responsibility for his missteps, including his decision not to defend John Fee and the Bereans in 1859 as well as the Chautems scandal in 1867. The memoirs also became a place for Clay to air his grievances and to heap hostile allegations on political rivals and personal enemies alike. His favorite targets included William Seward, Charles Sumner, and his ex-wife, Mary Jane. Henry Watterson would later say that Clay's autobiography stood "alone in its class" and that "so much conceit, pride, frankness and yet absorbing interest ha[d] seldom been put into one book." "It has been said that Caesar's memoirs made Caesar a hero," he remarked mirthfully, but "Cassius Clay's autobiography makes Cassius Clay a God." Perhaps Clay's greatest show of arrogance was his plan to write a second volume, which he never completed. Like most autobiographers, Clay wrote with posterity in mind. Beyond the particulars, Clay set out to recast his famed career and well-known exploits into a grand synthesis of his antislavery work, his role in building the Republican Party, and his involvement in restoring the Union after the war. Throughout the long account of his own career, Clay insisted on his own pragmatic consistency on issues of slavery, emancipation, and reconstruction. Again and again, he contended that his antislavery position was an avowedly moderate one based on constitutional principles.[12]

Yet he also inadvertently planted the seeds of an alternative narrative, which later biographers and admirers would pluck to generate a different storyline that cast Clay as an abolitionist who opposed slavery for moral reasons. Central to this reading was Clay's four-paragraph description of hearing William Lloyd Garrison speak while at Yale. The abolitionist's ideas were to him "as water to a thirsty wayfarer," he wrote, identifying that moment as the point at which he resolved "to give slavery a death struggle." Though he never endorsed Garrison's approach to antislavery, and though he devoted much more ink to his economic opposition to the peculiar institution within his memoirs, this episode became a canonical tale for Clay's chroniclers, who would insist that an ethical opposition to slavery above other considerations motivated his philosophy.[13]

Whatever personal catharsis Cassius Clay's memoirs brought him, their publication in 1886 did not garner much notice from the press, and what attention they did get was not entirely favorable. The *New York Herald* pronounced them "extremely readable" but assessed Clay's portrayal of his own life with the headline: "Strange Mixture of Bravery, Bravado and Childishness." Furthermore, the admissions made and grievances aired came at great personal cost. His already estranged daughters were livid at his personal revelations and attacks on their mother. Family lore held that that they gathered up every copy of the book they could obtain and piled them into a bonfire. Whether or not this tale was true, the Clay women did work in the ensuing years to counter their father's negative portrayal of Mary Jane. In 1889, Mary Barr published a profile of her in the *Woman's Magazine* that cast her as a strong and accomplished woman who had stood steadfastly by her husband, enduring the danger and strife his political activity had brought on their family.[14]

By the 1880s, Clay's daughters had developed a public reputation of their own through their commitment to woman suffrage. Mary Barr was the first to embrace the issue, striking up a friendship with Susan B. Anthony in the late 1880s. Soon the Clay daughters (with occasional assistance from Mary Jane) took up the cause, working within county- and state-level organizations. In 1883, Mary Barr assumed the presidency of one of the nation's two preeminent women's rights organizations, the American Woman Suffrage Association.[15]

There is no doubt that their own domestic experiences provided the impetus for the Clay women to push for expanded rights for their sex. Though it was Cassius who sued for divorce, Kentucky law deprived Mary Jane of all rights to the home she had spent so much time and effort renovating, as well as the farm she ran so capably for many years. Furthermore, had he demanded to do so, Cassius would have been able to claim sole custody of Annie, their only minor child at the time of the suit. Still, Mary Jane was in better position than most divorced women in the late nineteenth century. During her separation, she and her children resided with her sister in Lexington, and she was able to live out her days in relative comfort, thanks to the trust fund her parents left her. Mary Barr, too, endured marital problems and filed for divorce during the period of her parents' separation, leaving her an unmarried mother of three boys. Experiencing firsthand the disadvantage at which Kentucky's laws held women convinced Clay's former wife and daughters to fight for expanded property and suffrage rights and may have influenced Laura's decision never to marry. Through the cause of woman suffrage, Clay's daughters carried on the family tradition of socioeconomic reform and stirring public oration.[16]

By the close of the 1880s, Clay lived a nearly solitary existence. He tended to his garden and his beloved flock of Southdown sheep and otherwise filled his days reading books and traveling to the odd speaking engagement. He occasionally dipped his toes into current political issues, writing articles in favor of bimetallism and addressing the Kentucky General Assembly in opposition to the proposed Separate Coach Law, which called for segregated train travel within the state. There was no denying his isolation, however. Green, his only child with Mary Jane to remain loyal to him during his divorce, had died in 1883, and Launey had moved away from White Hall after attending college. His only companions were the tenant farmers to whom he rented land and the bodyguards he employed to protect him from enemies, both real and imagined.[17]

Clay did, on occasion, enjoy the rare guest. In 1891, journalist Frank G. Carpenter paid a visit to White Hall, where he found the eighty-two-year-old Clay a bit frayed around the edges but otherwise robust. Carpenter interviewed Clay about his farming operation, his political career, and his lifetime of duels and Bowie knife fights. He pronounced him to be "strong intellectually and physically" and apprised: "His fourscore years have not diminished his courage, and his arm is as ready to strike in his own defense today as it has been in the many deadly encounters of the past."[18]

His days of quiet retreat ended just a few years later in 1894, however, when, at the age of eighty-four, his engagement to his teenaged housekeeper once again landed him in the national news. A headline in the Lexington newspaper announced, "C. M. Clay—The Old War Horse of Antebellum Days—Embarks upon Another Matrimonial Voyage—He Is Eighty-Four and His Bride but Fifteen." Clay's betrothed, Dora Richardson, was an orphan who worked at White Hall. According to newspaper reports, Clay had first developed an affection for her older sister, who also worked as a domestic in his household, but when she married another man, his attention settled on young Dora.[19]

Clay's children rushed to halt the nuptials. His son Brutus persuaded first one and then a second local official to rescind their agreements to perform the ceremony. He failed to prevail upon the third, whom Cassius had flanked with two well-armed guards for the trip to White Hall, where he united the mismatched couple in matrimony. Journalists from around the area descended on the home, where they discovered no shortage of fodder for their stories. There was Clay's characteristic reaction to the mob that showed up to prevent the ceremony by pointing a cannon that had once guarded his *True American* office in their direction. "The house, as you can see, is more like a fortress than a residence, and with four men I could defend it against a hundred," he bragged to a reporter. Also riveting was the determination of the old patriarch to outwit his children's attempts to halt the nuptials. "They thought they had me here like a rat in a cage, and that I was unable to help myself from their machinations," he said of his ungrateful children.[20]

In the days after the marriage, journalists flocked to White Hall to see for themselves what one correspondent called "one of the most remarkable marriages that ever took place in the United States." Clay tried to convince reporters that his motives were altruistic. Channeling the mythical story of Pygmalion, Clay claimed that he married Dora in order to transform her from a rude, unschooled girl into an educated and proper gentlewoman. Clay himself seemed rather embarrassed by her shabby state and would not allow a photographer to take a picture of her, saying that she was not properly dressed or coiffed.[21]

Several of Clay's scandalized Madison County neighbors were less convinced that his intentions were innocent and threatened to rescue Dora from her captivity. Just as in his antislavery days, the specter of opposition made him defensive. He purchased more firearms with which to defend his well-fortified house and employed several local men to serve as his "sentries." The Bowie knives, dueling pistols, and cannons that had defined his antislavery fight decades before now became associated with Clay's outlandish personal behavior.[22]

The public interest in Clay's remarkable domestic affairs did not abate after the marriage. Two years later, William Randolph Hearst's *New York Journal* dispatched a reporter to Kentucky to report on "the love story of [Clay's] old age." There a disheveled Clay, clad in only a bathrobe, greeted him at the door. White Hall looked no better than its owner, overgrown on the outside and shabby within. "No one comes here," Clay told him, "for fear of being killed. I am in a virtual state of siege." Pointing to the weapons that were everlastingly at hand, he told the reporter, "When men have sought my life I have defended it at any cost. I shall do so until the end." He was, he told him, financially insolvent as a consequence of the continuing "vendetta" waged against him.[23]

Clay's marriage to Dora had also revived his reputation as a womanizer. "From his youth up," he had been a "lion among women," wrote the *New York Journal* reporter, recalling "all sorts of gay rumors about the things he did in St. Petersburg," which had resulted in "a child he had left behind in Russia." It also seemed that whatever romance once existed had faded. "I needed a housekeeper," he told the reporter, who asked why he married Dora. "It would have been very foolish to have wedded a woman of quality. We would have turned our backs on each other within a week." Instead, he had settled on someone "who would not be hampered with social aspirations, whose tastes were plain, and who would be content to look after me."[24]

As she grew older, Dora began to chafe at the limited scope of life at White Hall and, one would suspect, her elderly husband. In July 1897, just a few months after the *New York Journal* reporter's visit, she abandoned White Hall and its master. The *Journal* printed an update on the "old, old pitiful story of December and May," replete with an account from Clay himself, in which he blamed Dora's departure on his "political and personal enemies and plunderers." The story also featured a cutaway illustration of White Hall, portraying its elaborate defenses and pitiful inhabitant. Despondent but resigned, Clay filed for divorce a year later. He apparently bore Dora no ill will, however, and continued to support her financially even after she remarried. She, in turn, named her firstborn son, the child of her second husband, Riley Brock, Cassius Marcellus Clay Brock.[25]

With Dora gone, Clay's "stirring life," as his friend Henry Watterson would later explain, "began to tell on him," and he started to manifest signs of what modern medical professionals describe as dementia. His paranoia worsened and made it all but impossible for anyone to help him. He had begun to reconcile with his daughters, but the process was stymied by his obsessive distrust of people. In 1900, Clay invited Mary Barr and her son Green to live with him at White Hall but then inexplicably ordered them off the premises. When young Green tried to return, as a newspaper story recounted, he had "to take refuge behind a tree to escape the murderous bullets of the irate old General who, entrenched in his castle and supported by two armed helpers, seemed determined to defy any and all who came." A local sheriff who tried to intervene met with the same fate.[26]

In the ensuing years, Clay developed kidney and prostate problems that went untreated for months because he would not allow anyone into his home. Rumors abounded that he kept his trusty Bowie knife under his pillow because he believed his children wanted to kill him. He eventually admitted a trained nurse into his home, only to fire her because he believed she was trying to remove his weapons. In early July 1903, Mary Barr and Sallie persuaded a Madison County judge to declare their father legally insane in order that they might access White Hall and care for him. It was too late for efficacious treatment, however, and in his final days, his

William Randolph Hearst's New York Journal *was only in its second year of publication when it dispatched a reporter to cover Clay's armed standoff with locals who were scandalized by his marriage to Dora Richardson.* (New York Journal and Advertiser, *November 28, 1897, Library of Congress*)

children gathered around him, much the way he had kept vigil over his own father seventy-five years earlier. On the night of July 22, 1903, he took his last breath. Despite his weakened and undignified state, "even to the last he burned at a white heat," Henry Watterson wrote in Clay's obituary the next day.[27]

No sooner had Cassius Clay's life ended than the remembrances (and misremembrances) began. Tributes filled the nation's newspapers, their authors smoothing their subject's rough edges and offering generous appraisals of his professional accomplishments. Many of Clay's obituarists painted him in broad strokes, focusing on his antagonistic and forceful personality and the highlights of his long career. Typical was a *Chicago Tribune* author who described him with efficiency as a "warrior, statesman, abolitionist, author, and noted duelist" before concentrating on the better-known aspects of Clay's career, including his service in the Mexican-American War and his diplomatic appointment in Russia. He expended little ink on Clay's antislavery career, with only passing mention of his "abolition paper," and instead focused on his armed conflicts and "sensational matrimonial experiments." Like the *Chicago Tribune*, many newspapers gave short shrift to Clay's antislavery career and misrepresented his brand of antislavery. Dozens of them referred to him as an abolitionist, including the *Detroit Free Press*, which called him "an advocate of abolition," and the Louisville *Courier-Journal*, in which Henry Watterson dubbed him "one of the first to set in motion the abolition movement."[28]

Misrepresentations of Clay's antislavery beliefs were not limited to white newspapers. In St. Louis, a national meeting of the United Brothers of Friendship, an African American fraternal organization, adopted a resolution honoring Clay, "who, in days when the negro was recognized as only fit for chattel, although a Southerner, liberated his slaves and hurled his lance into the arena of public debate, asking no quarter, fearing no foe, suffering ostracism and calumny, and even encountering personal dishonor in the pursuit of what he believed to be just and right for the negro and freedom." The organization praised him for having "the moral courage to light the fires of abolition prior to the sixties." Only slightly more accurate was the Kentucky Grand Lodge of Negro Masons' description of Clay as an "early emancipator" in their tribute to "a man who in his time stood almost single and alone for a defenseless race during the eventful period that tried men's souls." "It was Cassius M. Clay, a giant in intellect and a lion in courage who contended for the emancipation and civilization of our people when it cost more than mere words to do so," members claimed, lauding him for his willingness to be "maimed and scarred for the God-given rights of all mankind."[29]

If Clay's obituarists proved inattentive to the nuances of his antislavery career, they might be forgiven, given the context in which they were living and writing. By the beginning of the twentieth century, key differences in the motivations and strategies of various categories of antislavery reformers had collapsed within the public understanding. Even academic historians did not often take care to differentiate between those antebellum actors who wanted to end slavery for moral reasons and those who were more economically and politically motivated to contain it. As historian Stanley Harrold has asserted, "This made it difficult to understand who the abolitionists were and what they stood for." Furthermore, public appreciation for the importance of antislavery reform of all kinds was blunted by the Lost Cause interpretation of the Civil War and slavery, which portrayed both the institution and the people who engaged in it as benign. By the time of Clay's death, Lost Cause ideology had saturated society in the form of Confederate monuments, popular culture, and all manner of historical and fictional writing.[30]

For his part, Clay had no patience for such veneration of traitors. As he penned his memoirs, he lamented that his own state, which had remained in the Union, was awash in Confederate monuments, "whilst Union soldiers lie in obscure turf-covered graves." "To honor those who have signally failed in the admitted duties of civilized society, for the defense of national life, with posthumous fame is to ignore the existence of good and evil. That should have been the work of private grief," he wrote with conviction. "But to the attempt to overthrow the American Republic, to conserve the meanest of all despotisms—Slavery—should leave but little sympathy or honor for the 'Lost Cause!'"[31]

In an era in which sectional reunion and reconciliation was a national goal, however, many white Northerners were happy to allow their former foes to honor their dead and tell their own war story in whatever way they saw fit. Moreover, they were very likely to buy into the Lost Cause narrative themselves, hungrily consuming literature by such authors as Joel Chandler Harris, Thomas Nelson Page, and Annie Fellows Johnston who depicted the Old South and its social and racial relations as a romantic ideal. Historian David Blight has explained that "the age of machines, rapid industrialization, and labor unrest produced a huge audience for a literature of escape" into a past of plantations and slavery. Once disdained for its antirepublican tendencies, by the early twentieth century the American South had become "the object of enormous nostalgia." Accordingly, as Americans looked back over past decades to remember and assign meaning to the Civil War era, they focused on "shaking hands across the bloody chasm," as Clay's antislavery collaborator Horace Greeley had phrased it. "The memory of slavery, emancipation, and the Fourteenth and Fifteenth Amendments," wrote Blight, "never fit well into a developing narrative in which the Old South and New South were romanticized and welcomed back into a new nationalism, and in which devotion alone made everyone right, and no one truly wrong, in the remembered Civil War."[32]

The Lost Cause interpretation of history, which only intensified in the decades after Clay's death, profoundly influenced the manner in which academic historians wrote about both slavery and antislavery. Beginning with Columbia University historian U. B. Phillips, author of *American Negro Slavery* (1918) and *Life and Labor in the Old South* (1929), scholars contended that slavery would have eventually died on its own had abolitionists not turned their convictions into an incendiary crusade. Phillips set the tone for a generation of professional historians who wrote reams of scholarship in which they cast white Southern slaveholders as benevolent and slaves as both intellectually inferior and content in their bondage. By extension, historians produced a corpus of scholarship that portrayed abolitionists as superfluous, self-righteous busybodies at best and, at worst, as grossly irresponsible zealots who prodded white Southerners into a self-defensive frenzy, provoking an avoidable four-year bloodbath. The interpretation of slavery and antislavery laid out by these academics seeped into the textbooks that educated several generations of American schoolchildren. Not surprisingly, through the mid-twentieth century, when Americans did think about abolitionists, they did not view them in very favorable terms.[33]

In the decades after his death, few Americans thought much about Cassius Clay. His name emerged sporadically in newspapers, often in relation to the abandoned and decaying White Hall, which his grandson Warfield Clay Bennett had purchased at auction following Clay's death. Sporadically, articles bearing such titles as "He Fought for Freedom with His Bowie Knife" appeared in Kentucky newspapers, recapitulating his famous imbroglios and speculating about the whereabouts of his legendary firearms.[34]

A more comprehensive profile of Clay appeared in the *Chicago Tribune* in 1947 courtesy of Roscoe Conkling Simmons, a prominent Black Republican and protégé of Booker T. Washington. Simmons's accommodationist tendencies led him to write a regular column for the *Tribune* titled "The Untold Story," in which he wrote of "the great work done by white men and Negroes in cooperation." The two columns he devoted to Cassius Clay would have greatly pleased his subject. "The story of Cassius M. Clay of Kentucky, one of the bloods of the Blue Grass," Simmons wrote, "is a record of tireless, unceasing combat, of violence of speech and acts, of a man as close to Lincoln as any man thus far revealed as in any manner or shape a comrade of the Emancipator." Simmons cast Clay as a valiant hero to enslaved Kentuckians, who believed he was the Moses of Emancipation. He portrayed Clay as Lincoln's close confidant and credited him with converting the future president to an antislavery position and, later, as among the first people who moved him toward emancipation. Simmons emphasized his bravery and hyperbolized the dangers he faced, declaring that "a hundred attempts were made against Clay's life." He compared him to abolitionists William Lloyd Garrison, Wendell Phillips, and Charles Sumner. "Cassius M. Clay engaged all comers, moral, political, literary, and physical," Simmons declared before repeating the oft-told tale of Clay's public speaking accoutrements: the Constitution, the Bible, and the pistols.[35]

Much of what he wrote seemed to come straight from Clay's autobiography, but it is possible that Simmons learned of Clay through the writings of Kentuckian William Townsend. A lawyer by trade, Townsend wrote several books on the martyred president, including *Lincoln and His Wife's Home Town* (1929), in which he devoted a chapter to Cassius Clay and the *True American*. "I jumped him up like a rabbit, and he almost ran away with the book," Townsend remembered. The author painted Clay in bold relief, describing him as a tall and virile physical specimen, "possessed of a restless energy that never flagged, and iron will that ran rough-shod over all obstacles, utterly fearless, and combative when aroused."[36]

Townsend's depiction of Clay achieved truly legendary status because of a presentation he made to the Chicago Civil War Roundtable in 1952. There the Southern lawyer spoke before an audience of midwestern Civil War buffs, holding them at rapt attention for one-and-a-half hours as he spun the tale of "The Lion of Whitehall." With his estimable oratorical abilities honed before dozens of juries during his years before the bar, Townsend played the role of folksy-yet-erudite Kentuckian to perfection.[37]

Townsend recalled that as a young boy he heard people speak of Clay in mostly negative terms: "I heard that he was a damned rascal, that he was a damned cradle snatcher, and that he was a damned nigger stealer, and worse than any of these or all of them put together, in the opinion of the community, he was a damned Republican," joked Townsend, eliciting peals of laughter. Over the next hour, Townsend painted an inspirational, if highly inaccurate picture of Clay. He elided the emancipationist's gradual transformation into an antislavery politician, insisting that his instantaneous conversion happened after he "fell under the influence of William Lloyd Garrison." Townsend also grossly exaggerated the extent of Clay's slave manumission, claiming vociferously that Clay had "freed them all—a hundred in one batch worth a thousand dollars a piece."[38]

Townsend devoted most of his lengthy talk to the most colorful and violent episodes of Clay's career: his fight with Samuel Brown, his well-fortified

William Townsend in front of a dilapidated White Hall (ca. 1959). Townsend was largely responsible for developing and disseminating the highly exaggerated version of Clay's life story that circulated in mid-twentieth-century popular culture. (Eastern Kentucky University Libraries, Special Collections and Archives, Richmond)

newspaper office, and the fatal encounter with Cyrus Turner. Indeed, details of Clay's sidearms—the Mexican lances, the Bowie knives, the four-pounder cannons—dominated Townsend's tale. The weaponry and its usage was overshadowed only by his titillating accounts of Clay's personal foibles. "For some reason or another, the women [in Russia] seemed to like him," he told the appreciative Roundtable audience. "In fact they stormed the embassy and brought their trunks, and he being a Kentucky gentleman could not say them nay."[39]

"The speech went off to perfection," Townsend's friend J. Winston Coleman Jr., who had accompanied him to the Windy City, later remembered. He noted with fondness that his friend was prone to "'tall tales'" and "was sometimes said to embellish his stories beyond their limits." "Some have even said that his motto was: 'Don't let the truth stand in the way of a good story,'" Coleman remarked. Despite, and perhaps even because of, his outlandish claims Townsend's talk was so entertaining that Ralph Newman, a cofounder of the Chicago Civil War Roundtable and the owner of the city's well-known Abraham Lincoln Bookshop, pressed the recording onto vinyl. He sold the two-record set for ten dollars, distributing it all over the country.[40]

Americans far and wide purchased the LP, and by 1960, Louisville *Courier-Journal* columnist Sue McClelland Thierman asserted that it enjoyed "a growing, irresistible appeal." Politician Adlai Stevenson, she claimed, had "'raved'" about it, while actor Melvyn Douglas had deemed it "'fantastic.'" "President Eisenhower and Winston Churchill both have copies, as do all the Governors of the Southern States," Thierman wrote before inquiring whether Clay might be on the cusp of becoming the nation's "Next Folk Hero."[41]

Later that year, Townsend published an abbreviated version of his talk in *American Heritage*, the widely circulated monthly history magazine aimed at a public readership. His article, titled "The Rage of the Aged Lion," repeated many of the sensationalized and unsubstantiated details from his Chicago address. Townsend thus reintroduced Cassius M. Clay to American readers but made sure they were much more likely to know about his handiness with sidearms and young women than about the issue that made him famous in the first place. When popular accounts did pay attention to his antislavery past, they continued to cast him as an abolitionist. A case in point was the treatment of Clay by best-selling author (and *American Heritage* editor) Bruce Catton in 1961. In the first installment in his Civil War trilogy, *The Coming Fury*, Catton referred to Clay as "an out-and-out radical on the slavery issue," a quality that had, in the author's estimation, cost him the vice presidential nomination in 1860. Ironically, these dueling interpretations of Clay as either robust but politically vacuous or, alternately, principled and fanatical seemed to work in his favor even during a time in which abolitionists were not always accorded much popular respect. More interesting than the bland William Lloyd Garrison but less deranged than John Brown, Clay did seem to be prime folk-hero material.[42]

In 1962, historian David Smiley published the first (and, until now, only) academic history of Clay's life. A professor of history at Wake Forest University, Smiley labored for years, plumbing the depths of the less glamorous episodes of Clay's life, including his inauspicious work campaigning for his cousin Henry in the election of 1844 and his trip to Mississippi in

1875. Unlike other Clay chroniclers, Smiley avoided the inaccuracies within Townsend's talk. He may have recycled the title, but not its hagiographic treatment or grandiose exaggerations. Furthermore, he attributed Clay's motivations to personal political ambition more than pure antislavery principle. "Complex and paradoxical though he was, his career revealed a singleness of purpose," claimed Smiley. "His objective was to attain political power and public office, and his every act was calculated to accomplish it." His assessment was much less complimentary than those of previous (or future) chroniclers. Writing against the backdrop of the Civil Rights Movement, Smiley seemed frustrated by his subject's retreat from Black rights and his consistent realpolitik. "His career is a study in political failure," he wrote of Clay, and "illustrative of the extremes to which an ambitious man would go in his efforts to gratify his ambitions."[43]

J. Winston Coleman read Smiley's manuscript before its publication and advised him to rewrite it, telling him it was "alright for a Ph.D." but "needed livening up a lot before it would sell." When Smiley neglected to heed his advice, Coleman "shook his head dubiously at its chances of popular success." Coleman was right. Indeed, Smiley's interpretation of Clay, with its dogged research and his more critical thesis, remained overwhelmed by myth and legend.[44]

Evidence to this effect emerged in March 1964 when veteran Georgia senator Richard Russell treated his colleagues to a summary of Cassius Clay's career. The battle-hardened and formidable leader of the Southern Democrats was gearing up to fight the Civil Rights Act, which the House of Representatives had passed the previous month. The wide-ranging provisions of the act outlawed discrimination based on race, sex, and national origin in voter registration requirements, public accommodations, and employment practices. Just days before launching a filibuster intended to, as Russell put it, "wear" pro–civil rights colleagues "to a frazzle" and stall the Senate from voting, Russell took to the Senate floor to discuss the Lion of White Hall.[45]

"There has never been a more heroic character, or a more romantic one," than Cassius Clay, he told his colleagues. "As I understand," interjected Michigan Democrat and civil rights proponent Phil Hart, "he was a strong Abolitionist." "Indeed he was," conceded the Georgian, who also described Clay as "the only millionaire in Kentucky," as standing about "six feet, six inches tall," and as having "freed about forty slaves." He then launched into a florid description of Clay's career: a faithful recapitulation of William Townsend's version, with all its details about Bowie knives, cannons, and child brides. "In many ways," pronounced Russell, "Cassius Clay was one of the most remarkable men ever to live in the United States."

As Hart's incredulous question suggested, there was a certain incongruity in the segregationist's high praise of an antislavery reformer. Only days earlier, Russell had proposed a federally sponsored "humanitarian" mass relocation program in order to make the percentage of Black Americans in each state consistent. "If the people of the Southern states are to be forced to accept and conform to some federally dictated social order which is wholly alien to them," insisted Russell, it was "only fair and right that the Negro population be spread more evenly over all sections of the nation." Should the Civil Rights Act pass, a measure such as this was the only "hope of solving the problem of the two races living side by side without the eventual amalgamation and mongrelization of both." A polite racist he was not.[46]

On the day that Richard Russell, who had dedicated his career to maintaining a system of segregation, stood on the Senate floor lauding an antislavery reformer whose life's work had necessitated it, "abolitionist" was still a loaded term in American political culture. Indeed, proponents of expanded civil rights often referred to themselves as New Abolitionists, as did Southern massive resisters who used the term derisively. But by 1964, the legend of Cassius Clay had stripped away the reformer's political substance and enhanced his reputation as a man of action, making it possible to admire him no matter how you felt about his cause.[47]

Legends have a way of perpetuating themselves, and Cassius Clay's was no exception. The revived interest in the Lion raised public concern for his dilapidated lair. After Clay's death, his grandson Warfield Clay Bennett purchased the home and surrounding acreage. During much of the mid-twentieth century, he rented it to tenant farmers, who shared the dwelling with pigs and chickens and used the ballroom to store hay. A newspaper reporter who had poked around the old house in 1951 informed readers that the once-grand mansion had become "a haven for mud-daubers, a sanctuary for field mice and a feeding place for termites; it is a rotting, broken hulk of masonry, a scarred and depleted playground for souvenir hunters." In the mid-1960s, members of the Richmond, Kentucky, Garden Cub waged a campaign to save White Hall and convinced the Commonwealth of Kentucky to purchase the property in 1967.[48]

In 1968, newly elected Kentucky governor Louie B. Nunn and his wife, Beula, launched an effort to restore White Hall. Nunn had developed an interest in Cassius Clay years earlier after purchasing the recording of William Townsend's talk, which he would regularly listen to at home in his library. Despite the home's utter decrepitude, the keen appreciation he developed for Clay convinced the Nunns to make White Hall's restoration a priority of his administration. Beula Nunn dedicated enormous time, effort, and state funds toward renovating the house and outbuildings and searching for furniture, art, and other Clay belongings sold at auction after his death. At a ceremony in the fall of 1971, Governor Nunn declared the renovated house a "state shrine." As the designation connoted, White Hall was now a place Kentuckians should visit to venerate the person who had lived there. On the day of White Hall's dedication on September 16, 1971, in front of a crowd of 500 people, Nunn praised Clay for exhibiting "an abiding commitment to our convictions, willingness to take a position and readiness, if necessary, to weather popular opinion to defend it." "Cassius Marcellus Clay," he declared, "was a man not for a day but for all time."[49]

Yet it was unclear whether the precise outlines of those convictions were impressed on visitors to White Hall. Louisville newspaper reporter Joe Ward, who was invited to tour the house before it opened, told readers what he gleaned from his visit. He referred to Clay as an abolitionist as well as a "Mexican War hero and a Civil War General" before relaying the tale of Clay's unseemly second marriage. Noting the sharp lines of the Italianate house and the pair of "brooding black lions" made of stone that guarded the entry, he insisted that there was "an air about the place that is distinctly cranky." Ward mentioned the telescope through which Clay would keep watch for unwelcome visitors, as well as the cache of weapons he kept on hand to deter them, all on display. He was fascinated by a tunnel connected to the house's basement, through which "runaway slaves were shuttled under the kitchen and out in the woods behind on trips north," implying that White Hall had been a stop on the Underground Railroad. Ward was certainly wrong in this assertion. The tunnel had been part of the first iteration of the house and was used to access a warming kitchen. Laborers would have traversed it daily as a function of their enslavement rather than as a pathway to freedom.[50]

A few days later, Edward Murphy, a Richmond, Kentucky, man familiar with Clay's true convictions, wrote a letter to the *Courier-Journal* complaining about inaccuracies in the article. Murphy alleged that Ward showed a "lack of knowledge" of Clay, noting that Clay was a gradual emancipationist who, unlike the "flaming abolitionists" John Fee and William Lloyd Garrison, did not oppose the institution on moral grounds. A more accurate sense of Clay's true politics, he wrote, "would have disclosed to him that Clay wouldn't have any part of other people's valuable chattels running away." Yet by the second half of the twentieth century, most Americans understood the issue of antislavery only in ethical rather than political, economic, or constitutional terms. Ward was simply recapitulating the version of Cassius Clay with which most Americans were familiar—the version of Clay that had inspired the very rebuilding of his house, the one that most visitors hoped to find at White Hall and without which the house might still lie in ruins. The misconceptions about the nature of Clay's antislavery, which he had himself both purposefully and inadvertently helped to create, contributed to this narrow understanding of both the man and his movement.[51]

⊰ Coda ⊱
The Legend of Cassius Clay

In the early 1960s, just as Cassius Marcellus Clay's reputation was enjoying a certain renaissance, another Cassius Clay eclipsed him. Louisville native Cassius Marcellus Clay Jr. captured America's attention after winning the Olympic gold medal for light heavyweight boxing in 1960. After the boxer turned pro later that year and began to rule the ring, the American public was not quite sure what to make of the loud-mouthed, charismatic braggadocio who proclaimed himself "The Greatest," in a manner reminiscent of his eponym. Clay seemed to dispense with any of the deference and humility expected of young athletes, especially Black ones.

National media could not help but draw comparisons between the young fighter and the man who first bore his name. "He is well named," wrote Atlanta-based syndicated columnist Ralph McGill. "It is fitting that a fighter should be named for him, because he, himself, spent much of his time in personal combat." Influenced by the twentieth-century understandings of both Clay and antislavery, McGill misidentified the first Clay as an "abolitionist" and labeled him an "able, violent man" and "a mover and shaker." "We are indebted to the young fighter," he wrote, "for reminding us of his namesake. No man seeking fame with his fists could be better named." Only six months later, McGill again connected the two men in another column in which he claimed that the original Cassius was "perhaps the most remarkable 'lesser figure' in American history."[1]

Cassius Marcellus Clay Jr. was actually named after his father, Cassius Clay Sr., who, in turn, was named after his uncle Cassius, who was, as census records and newspaper death notices reveal, one of many African American children in mid- and late nineteenth-century Kentucky named in honor of the antislavery reformer. Kentucky was full of white Clays whose ancestors had come to Kentucky from Virginia and had, like Green Clay, purchased enslaved people and stamped them with their surname. Not a few of these Black Kentucky Clays, in turn, named their sons after the white Cassius, whom they admired for taking a bold stand in the name of their freedom.[2]

Cassius Clay's white descendants also continued to recycle the name, which occasionally led to some confusion. A newspaper story titled "Right

Name—Wrong Cassius M. Clay" told of a humorous mix-up that occurred in 1963, when a Cassius Clay and his wife checked into a hotel in London. The staff, who had been expecting the parents of the boxer, had rolled out the red carpet in wait and were surprised when a white couple arrived claiming the identity. When the manager suggested that they might be the boxer's adoptive parents, the white Cassius (who was descended from Brutus Clay) assured him that they were "no kin at all." "It's that old abolitionist ancestor of mine," he told the manager. "He freed all his slaves way back. Most of them took his name. Half Kentucky seems to be called Cassius Marcellus Clay and four or five of them are prize fighters." He may have been exaggerating, but the first name Cassius was bestowed on hundreds of white and Black children with the last name Clay both inside and outside of Kentucky in the nineteenth and early twentieth centuries.[3]

Indeed, boxer Cassius Clay's branch of the family, which had been based in Kentucky for over a century, gained their surname from Henry Clay, who had enslaved them, rather than his distant cousin. Ali's great-grandfather John Henry Clay had served as a manservant to Henry Clay Jr. during the Mexican-American War. Family members believe that their ancestor was the offspring of a sexual union between Henry Clay Jr. or Sr. and an enslaved woman residing at Ashland.[4]

Even without a blood relation, and with a different skin color, there were obvious parallels between the Cassius Clays. In addition to their common Bluegrass State provenance, both men had a way with words and personalities that begged to be unleashed through physical confrontation. Like the antislavery reformer, young Cassius Clay, too, had tales of his fighting prowess set to vinyl, in a spoken-word record he made in 1963. In his characteristically playful timbre, the boxer rhapsodized:

> This is the legend of Cassius Clay,
> the most beautiful fighter in the world today.
> He talks a great deal, and brags indeed-y,
> of a muscular punch that is incredibly speedy.[5]

Yet, despite the boxer's obvious talent, many Americans wondered whether this boastfulness was just a lot of sound and fury. Clay did his best to answer them in February 1964, when he defeated Sonny Liston to win the world heavyweight title. The sporting world was still grappling with this major upset when Clay threw another punch, admitting to reporters that, as rumored, he had joined the Nation of Islam and was discarding his "slave name" in favor of a new one: Muhammad Ali.

The public backlash was immediate. With the civil rights movement in full swing, white Americans were familiar with African American demands for desegregation and equality, whether they agreed with them or not. The Nation of Islam, however, taught that the Black race was superior and that white Americans were hardwired to not only hate but annihilate African Americans. Such radical beliefs caused most white Americans to view the Nation of Islam as a dangerous fringe group and many Black Americans to see its core tenet of Black separatism as being at odds with the project of desegregation.[6]

Converts to the Nation of Islam traditionally changed their names to divest themselves both legally and symbolically of the remnants of the white ownership of their ancestors. This made it all the more frustrating for Ali when reporters refused to acknowledge it. "Don't call me Cassius Clay," he reprimanded reporters at a press conference just after his announcement in March 1964. "That is a slave name. I'm Muhammad Ali, heavyweight champion of the world. That is a beautiful Arabic name." Some of his African American opponents, including Floyd Patterson and Ernie Terrell, also refused to call him Ali. After Terrell repeatedly referred to him as Cassius Clay during a prefight television interview in 1967, an irritated Ali called Terrell an Uncle Tom and demanded that he refer to him by his new name. In the ensuing fight, Ali repeatedly asked Terrell, "What's my name? What's my name?" as he danced around the ring, landing blow after bloodying blow.[7]

Later that year, Ali further outraged the American public when he refused induction into the US Army, which was then drafting men by the thousands to fight in Vietnam. The World Boxing Association immediately revoked his world title and his license to fight. Ali's opposition to the war was based on his religious convictions as well as a worldview defined by the specter of slavery. Explaining his decision to conscientiously object, Ali stood before a crowd in Louisville and proclaimed that he viewed the war as an effort to "continue the domination of white slave masters of the darker people the world over."[8]

In their angry and indignant responses to Clay's intransigence, newspaper columnists sometimes cited the antislavery work of his progenitor. One editorial in a Paducah, Kentucky, newspaper declared, "Cassius Marcellus Clay Jr. is an expert with his fists. But that is his only similarity to his namesake, the great patriot and pre–Civil War abolitionist who despite his prowess in physical combat, nevertheless preferred to rely on his Bowie knife or horse pistol when challenged." Before diminishing the boxer's intelligence, the editor proclaimed that Ali had "been used by the extremists who have got hold of a bloody-minded sector of the civil rights movement. He is a tragic figure, but even if he now goes to jail as a result, he will cut a very uninspiring figure as a martyr." The *St. Louis American* declared that Ali's "casting aside of his given name at birth" demanded "a bit of historic appraisal." After the editor synopsized reformer Cassius M. Clay's career for readers (neglecting his free-labor rationale in the process), the editorialist asserted: "It does seem that if the Black Muslims have any exceptions for eradicating the slavery names of American Negro citizens, they would make such illustrious names as John Brown, Wendell Phillips, Charles Sumner, Thaddeus Stevens and Cassius Marcellus Clay amenable to their ulterior purpose."[9]

Rejecting the boxer's declaration of self-determination, the white press continually refused to honor his new name. It was another seven years before the media consistently referred to him as Muhammad Ali. Ali remembered that as late as 1970, "a barrage of letters from good white friends kept coming at me, urging me to reconsider." That year, a Philadelphia magazine printed an "Open Letter to Cassius Clay." "Why not salute your big-hearted, two fisted Kentucky namesake for his great battling for civil rights, by reclaiming the Clay name, thus conceding that what the world needs is more—not fewer—Cassius Marcellus Clays?" the writer asked.[10]

According to Ali, however, he had long recognized that his forebear's views on antislavery and race were more complicated than most twentieth-century Americans understood. In his autobiography, Clay recalled a teacher who regularly reminded him of the great feats of the original Cassius. "One of my teachers at Central High, proud that I had the name, would constantly say to me 'Cassius Marcellus Clay, if you could just follow in the footsteps of that great friend of Abraham Lincoln, that fighting abolitionist whose name you carry. . . .'" Wanting to instill an appreciation for the reformer, the teacher "directed" Ali to *The Writings of Cassius M. Clay*, the collection of speeches and writings that Horace Greeley had helped Clay publish in 1848.

Remarkably, given that Ali was known as a lackluster student and suffered from dyslexia, his curiosity was piqued and he headed to the public library. When he read Clay's words, he had no trouble understanding the reformer's thoughts on slavery and African Americans. Returning to his teacher, Ali quoted from the speech delivered in Philadelphia in 1846 in which Clay had laid out the basis of his pseudoscientifically based racialist thinking, stating: "I am of the opinion that the Caucasian or white is the superior race. . . . Historians now unite in making the Caucasian race the first in civilization through all past time." After hearing Clay's baldly stated scientific racism, the teacher was, Ali claimed, "embarrassed" and "took the book, [and] read it himself. That was the last time I was called on in school to follow white Clay's footsteps."[11]

In his speech in 1846, Cassius M. Clay did follow up his pronunciation of white superiority by stating that he "utterly deni[ed]" that Black inferiority was "a good basis of enslavement." Nonetheless, by the mid-twentieth century, the shortcomings of Clay's racial theories were all too clear. As Ali put it: "He had gotten rid of his slaves, but held on to White Supremacy." Ali did not need to read a book to understand this. He grew up in Louisville, a Southern city defined by segregation, lived in the all-Black West End neighborhood, and attended a high school that in the wake of the *Brown v. Board of Education* decision remained segregated. His father, a gifted sign painter with frustrated artistic ambitions, felt the oppression of Jim Crow at every turn and shared his anger with his son. Slavery had ended, but Ali understood himself to be a product of the segregationist system that white Americans erected in its place. His exposure to the racial pride instilled by the Nation of Islam prompted him to ask: "Why should I keep a name handed down to me by a slave master, liberal or not? Why should I keep my white slave master's name visible and my black ancestors invisible, unknown, unhonored?" By the time Ali's life story was in print in 1975, African Americans were likely to consider Cassius M. Clay an insufficient hero. Just a few years after the legend of Cassius Clay motivated a Kentucky governor to restore his home and dub him "a man for all time," it was plain that Clay's own words marked him as a man of a particular time.[12]

By the time Muhammad Ali died of Parkinson's disease in 2016, America's opinion of the fighter had softened. In the final twenty years of his life, his boxing license was restored, he served as an international humanitarian ambassador for multiple presidents, enjoyed an audience with the pope, and lit the Olympic flame in Atlanta in 1996. When people called him "The Greatest," it was not with cynicism but with reverence.

Yet, even during the national mourning period, people second-guessed Ali's decision to change his name. One of the most revealing examples of misunderstanding the original Cassius Clay came in a televised remembrance from NBC sports commentator Bob Costas. "When [Ali] said that Cassius Clay was a slave name that was ironic," the journalist told viewers, "because the original Cassius Clay was a white abolitionist who was shot by a pro-slavery guy in Kentucky in the 1840s. Now that doesn't mean that Ali didn't have the right to do what he did and didn't do it for good reasons. But just to correct the historical record, Cassius Clay was an abolitionist."[13]

Writer Ta-Nehisi Coates, in turn, came to Ali's posthumous defense in the *Atlantic* and corrected Costas's self-righteous and errant "well, actually...". After efficiently describing Clay's Free-Soil critique of slavery as well as his gradualist approach to ending it, Coates noted that Clay had owned and sold slaves and revealed him to be anything but an abolitionist. "When you are black and your namesake is literally a slave-holder, there is nothing ironic about calling it a 'slave name,'" he wrote, admonishing Costas's "smug" insistence that Ali had been the one to misconstrue Clay's politics and for posthumously denying him the authority to discern and interpret history. Nevertheless, Coates admitted that he did find Clay "heroic" and brave for remaining in Kentucky, where he was "constantly courting danger." "He did not ask to be a slave-holder. He was born into slave-holding and, at great financial loss to himself, freed those in bondage," he assessed. The problem came when people such as Costas tried to flatten him and make him "the wholly innocent, wholly righteous white guy."[14]

Beyond Costas's comments, Ali's death brought on a whole new round of mislabeling the original Cassius M. Clay, a phenomenon not confined to the popular press. Even a news release from Yale University, which has a postdoctoral fellowship named after their antislavery alumnus, referred to Clay as an "ardent abolitionist." Authors of these news articles were more interested in showing the connection between Clay and his namesake than in painting him as a humanitarian hero. Yet because of contemporary Americans' narrow understanding of the antislavery movement, that is what they did when they casually used the term "abolitionist" to describe him.[15]

In an era in which the connections between current racial inequity and historical remembrance have been illuminated as never before, the tendency to want to oversimplify white men such as Clay is greater than ever. In 2021, conservative radio show host Michael Medved wrote a column in the *Wall Street Journal* titled "Americans Should Know the Story of Abolitionist Cassius Clay." Medved noted that amid the public "racial 'reckoning,'" that year, Americans were "determined to obliterate statues and other public honors for those, such as Confederate generals, who fought to preserve slavery and racism." He lamented, however, that there was "no countervailing effort to remember or honor those who risked everything—career, wealth, prominence and personal safety—to promote emancipation."[16]

Cassius Marcellus Clay, he believed, was a perfect candidate for such reverence. Medved offered readers a brisk and enthusiastic summary of Clay's career, replete with the standard mentions of Clay's Garrisonian inspiration, his "abolitionist" *True American,* his Bowie knives and cannons, and his personal scandals. Reflecting on the reformer's connection to Muhummad Ali, Medved asserted that the boxer had "disparaged" his birth name "without any acknowledgement of the daring, dangerous commitment to emancipation that characterized the life of his namesake." "It's easy enough to sympathize with Ali's sentiments," Medved admitted, but he countered that it made "little sense" for contemporary Americans to "devote so much energy to dismantling the memory of pro-slavery notables while colorful and important antislavery figures like the original Cassius Clay remain, for the most part, invisible, unknown and unhonored."[17]

Medved's column appeared in the *Wall Street Journal* on June 19, 2021, the first Juneteenth designated as a federal holiday. He seemed to channel the sense of unease many Americans felt about efforts to reappraise and think more critically about historical figures. In an era in which the beliefs and actions of past figures were being scrutinized and their stone incarnations literally toppled from their pedestals, many white Americans seemed to long for historical figures to assure them that, in the age of American slavery, not all white people were bad and that there might be someone they could remember, and perhaps even celebrate, without feeling guilty. But to do so requires overlooking the fact that, like many other antislavery partisans, Clay was motivated to end slavery in order to better life for white Americans. It demands acknowledgment that a commitment to racial freedom and equality could be undercut before and after the war by seemingly benign and essentially American protections of state sovereignty and property. It requires acknowledging that people could be on the so-called right side of history for reasons that seem not particularly admirable to us today.[18]

Clay makes an especially attractive candidate for Americans looking back into history for a white man who made the right choices and did the honorable thing. But there is danger in not adequately understanding the specifics of his life—the important nuances and seeming inconsistencies in his motives, rationale, actions, and methods—even if it tarnishes his luster. Only by acknowledging the myriad and, to our eyes, less laudable purposes held by Clay and his compatriots can we understand the enormity of the challenge they faced in ending slavery and how truly remarkable their collective efforts were. And only by recognizing the limits inherent in their motivations and methods can we understand why the end of slavery did not translate to the end of racism and inequality.

Acknowledgments

Writing this account of Cassius Clay's life has been a long process, but not a lonely one. I have benefited from the encouragement and assistance of many people along the way.

Numerous archivists have aided my research, but I am especially grateful to those at the University of Kentucky's Special Collections and the Filson Historical Society, as well as Lance Hale and Walter Bowman at the Kentucky Department of Archives and History; Jackie Couture at Eastern Kentucky University Special Collections; and Sharyn Mitchell at the Berea College Special Collections and Archives.

I also owe a great debt of gratitude to colleagues and administrators in the Mississippi State University College of Arts & Sciences and in the Department of History. The college has twice supported my research, most recently with the tremendously helpful Institute for Humanities Faculty Fellowship. I want especially to thank my fellow fellows, Sol Palaez and Ted Atkinson, and our fearless leader, Julia Osman, for their camaraderie.

I am fortunate to work with wonderfully talented and supportive historians at MSU, including Kathryn Barbier, Mark Hersey, Alix Hui, Andy Lang, Joey Thompson, and erstwhile colleagues and faithful friends Alison Greene and Jason Ward. Thanks also to onetime graduate research assistants Cameron Zinszou and John Burrow for their work. My own graduate advisees, including Kelli Nelson, Christy Davenport, Will Critchfield, and Nathan Smith, have patiently endured my diverted attention. They have also provided a continuous and inspiring reminder of why it is that we make history in the first place. My department head, Alan Marcus, has been, by turns, both patient and badgering and has kept my shoulder to the wheel. Pam Wasson and Brenda Harris have provided much kindness, humor, and clerical support.

I am also grateful for the boundless generosity of my fellow Civil War–era historians. The countless conversations and correspondence I've had with scholars including Steve Berry, Jim Downs, Bob Elder, Sarah Gardner, Matt Hulbert, Carrie Janney, Aaron Sheehan-Dean, Jonathan White, and the late Pete Carmichael have helped shape and hone my thinking on Cassius Clay, slavery, and antislavery. Input from fellow border state and Kentucky historians, including Aaron Astor, Emily Bingham, Luke Harlow, Jim Klotter, Stuart Sanders, and Matt Stanley, has been particularly helpful.

Special thanks go to members of the Delta Women Writers, who offered great feedback on this project in its infancy. I am also grateful to my coparticipants at the Society of Civil War Historians second-book workshop, Paul Quigley and Michael Bernath. Sharing our work (and research and writing frustrations) was a silver lining of a terrible pandemic. Thanks also to our second-book mentors Lesley Gordon and Amy Taylor for a great experience.

Some of my greatest professional and personal inspiration has come from my fellow "Civil War Sisters": Carole Emberton, Judy Giesberg, Lesley Gordon, Megan Kate Nelson, Anne Sarah Rubin, Diane Somerville, Yael Sternhell, Amy Taylor, and Susannah Ural. Your encouragement, humor, incisive criticism, and reality checks have made this creative process and the end result so much better.

Two of my longtime mentors and friends, Catherine Clinton and Bryant Simon, have patiently listened to me prattle on about this project for years. Catherine has inspired me by her example and has been generous with insights and suggestions. Bryant has been a sounding board and a steadfast (if virtual) writing companion. I am ever so grateful to have them both in my private and professional life.

Several other people have offered valuable assistance with this project. Berle Clay was generous with his time and his insights into his family history and lore; Brant Rumble offered valuable editorial advice (some of which I actually took); Megan Bean offered wise counsel on copyright issues; Tom Appleton was kind enough to read this entire manuscript cover to cover, rendering helpful feedback and expert line editing.

Working with the University of North Carolina Press a second time has been a rewarding experience. Aaron Sheehan-Dean has been a patient and supportive series editor, and Mark Simpson-Vos's editorial perspective and carful pruning have been invaluable. I would like especially to thank the two anonymous readers whose extensive and substantive comments have made this a much better book.

Several years ago, I took on a second career when I became the executive director of the Ulysses S. Grant Presidential Library. My new role has added a novel and very meaningful dimension to my historical vocation. More than that, it has gifted me with a brilliant mentor in John Marszalek and an entirely new cadre of colleagues who inspire me and make me laugh every day—thank you Louie Gallo, Kate Gregory, Hannah Krapac, David Nolen, Lis Pankl, Eddie Rangel, Ryan Semmes, and Susannah Ural.

I am so fortunate to have wonderful people outside of professional life who help to make my life full and meaningful. Gina Hubbard and Jennie Samoska, friends since grade school, have steadfastly cheered me on for many years. The members of the YTBN bookclub have offered support and nonhistorical reading assignments. And thank you Starkville besties, Susan Ford, Polly Fulford, Michelle Jones, Holly Potts, Meredith Shapley, and Mary Love Tagert. Our lunches, porch cocktails, and tailgates have put a most generous dose of life in my "work-life" balance, and I am so grateful for your friendship.

My extended family is a great source of joy and support in my life. Thank you, Barb Giesen; Betty, Jeff, and Evelyn Scalia; Katie Giesen; Phil Giesen and Virginia Neff; Matt, Jennie, Meg, and Natalie Durham. I owe you all a copy of this book, but I promise not to make you read it.

My mother, Jan Marshall, has devoted hours of her time (and, if I'm being honest, her angst) to this project. She has read every page and corrected many an error. Her special combination of gifts—the research skills of a reference librarian and the love of a mother—are evident in the end product. I count myself so fortunate to have her in my life to care (and worry) about what I am doing personally and professionally. We lost my father, Bill Marshall, in the midst of this project, but even in his absence, I still feel his inspiration and support. A person could not have been blessed with two better parents.

Last, I want to thank my three favorite people on the planet. Walt and Eleanor Giesen have endured some measure of parental neglect as I wrote this book but have been a source of encouragement, regularly inquiring, "How's your book going, Mom?" Thankfully, they are teenagers now, so even if they have suffered in my absence, they are loathe to admit it. They are smart, funny, impertinent, and mostly sweet. I love them so much. My greatest source of constant support in this, and all other endeavors, is my best friend, soul mate, and historian colleague, Jim Giesen. Our marriage has seen two decades, two children, and a collective four books. He is an eternal joy to me, and I love him more each and every day.

Notes

ABBREVIATIONS

BJC	Brutus J. Clay
CMC	Cassius Marcellus Clay
FHS	Filson Historical Society, Louisville, Kentucky
HSP	Historical Society of Pennsylvania, Philadelphia
LMU	Abraham Lincoln Library and Museum, Lincoln Memorial University, Harrogate, Tennessee
LOC	Library of Congress, Washington, DC
MJC	Mary Jane Clay
SC-BC	Special Collections and Archives, Berea College, Berea, Kentucky
SC-EKU	Special Collections and Archives, Eastern Kentucky University, Richmond
SC-UKY	Special Collections Research Center, University of Kentucky, Lexington
SPC	Salmon P. Chase
WHS	William Henry Seward

INTRODUCTION

1. *Courier-Journal* (Louisville), July 23, 1903.
2. *Courier-Journal* (Louisville), July 23, 1903.
3. *Courier-Journal* (Louisville), July 23, 1903.
4. Clay, *Life*, 55–56.
5. Clay, *Life*, 76. Nonscholarly book-length biographical treatments of Clay's life include Carleé, *Last Gladiator*; Richardson, *Clay: Firebrand of Freedom*; Ellison, *Man Seen But Once*; Segal, *Clay: Man Behind the Legend*; and McQueen, *Clay: Freedom's Champion*. As their titles suggest, their authors are admirers and tend to parrot many of the misconceptions Clay put forth himself. Egerton, "Heritage of a Heavyweight"; Clark, *Kentucky*, 298.
6. Smiley, *Lion of White Hall*. Scholarly works that cast Clay primarily as iconoclastic Southern voice of antislavery include Freehling, *Road to Disunion*, 1:462–74; Degler, *Other South*, 55–60; Harrold, *Abolitionists and the South*; and Pease and Pease, *Bound with Them*, 60–89. Scholarly articles centered on Clay include three by Harrold: "Violence and Non-Violence in Kentucky Abolitionism;" "Clay on Slavery and Race"; and "Clay and Garrisonian Abolitionists"; and one by Lee, "Between Two Fires." For a recent labeling of Clay as an abolitionist, see Varon, *Armies of Deliverance*, 43. Recent considerations of the politics of slavery in Kentucky and the border South include Phillips, *Rivers Ran Backward*; Harlow, *Making of Confederate Kentucky*; Astor, *Rebels on the Border*; Epps, *Slavery on the Periphery*;

Salafia, *Slavery's Borderland*; Robinson, *Union Indivisible*; MacKenzie, *Fifth Border State*; and Burke, *Slavery's Border*.

7. Recent scholarship has revealed the extent and nature of abolitionist influence on antislavery politics. Two review essays consider this work: Brooks, "Reconsidering Politics"; and McDaniel, "Bonds and Boundaries."

Notable contributions to this literature include Brooks, *Liberty Power*; Harrold, *Abolitionists*; Oakes, *Scorpion's Sting*; McDaniel, *Problem of Democracy*; Sinha, *Slave's Cause*, 461–99; and Cirillo, *Abolitionist Civil War*.

Most of this recent scholarship has, however, focused on the role of immediatist abolitionist thought in the electoral process rather than the influence of moderate and gradualist thinkers who formed the base of Free-Soil, and then Republican, politics. The historiography of the latter has remained relatively understudied in recent years but is represented in works including Karp, "Mass Politics of Antislavery"; Blue, *No Taint of Compromise* and *Free Soilers*; Mitchell, *Antislavery Politics*; Earle, *Jacksonian Antislavery*; Sewell, *Ballots for Freedom*; Foner, *Free Soil*; and Gienapp, *Origins*.

8. There were important consistencies within Clay's seemingly knotted antislavery logic. Throughout his decades-long career, Clay's calculus about how far he could go in his opposition to slavery at any given time was informed by his own moral and intellectual compass, which persistently prioritized the constitutional protection of individual property rights and state sovereignty. This pattern of thought continued after the Civil War and through Reconstruction. He held these beliefs in common with a large swath of Americans who, like himself, oriented their politics around political stability, social order, and the sanctity of the Union—a nineteenth-century conservative "silent majority" to whom scholars have recently devoted welcome attention.

With his reform-minded ethos, Clay fits imperfectly within this paradigm of conservatism, but he does illustrate the way in which moderate antislavery reformers and, more broadly, middle-of-the-road Americans were often simultaneously committed to both stability and change. A number of scholars have studied what they describe as a Northern conservative political orientation, whose adherents generally opposed slavery but were ambivalent as to how to end it. See Smith, *Stormy Present*; Lynn, *White Man's Republic*; Towers and Wiley, "Introduction;" Smith, "Emergence of Conservatism"; Alexander, "Wisest Counsel"; and Mason, "Evil Hour."

9. On the similar political evolution of Clay's friend Salmon P. Chase, see Benedict, "Salmon P. Chase." This emphasis on the inherent limits in antislavery thought and their bearing on Reconstruction politics fits best within the historiography of the period, which stresses the relatively limited goals many Republicans had when reconstituting the nation. See, e.g., Benedict, *Compromise of Principle* and *Preserving the Constitution*; and Summers, *Ordeal of Reunion*.

CHAPTER 1

1. Mullins and Mullins, *History of White Hall*, 29–30; Berry, *Voices*, 9.
2. Smith, "'Idea in Heaven,'" 77–79.
3. Harrison and Klotter, *New History of Kentucky*, 53–55.

4. Linklater, *Measuring America*, 14–20; Coward, *Kentucky in the Early Republic*, 4; Mullins and Mullins, *History of White Hall*, 19.

5. Aron, *How the West Was Lost*, 84–51, 102–3; Ellis, Everman, and Sears, *Madison County*, 12, 16; Ireland, *County Courts*, 13. Examples of Green Clay's tenant leases can be found in the Sidney Payne Clay Papers, FHS.

6. Ellis, Everman, and Sears, *Madison County*, 24–26.

7. Ellis, Everman, and Sears, *Madison County*, 15–16, 24–26; Aron, *How the West Was Lost*, 124–49.

8. Simpson, *Bluegrass Houses*, 314–17; Berry, *Voices*, family tree in frontispiece; Mullins and Mullins, *History of White Hall*, 21, 29–31.

9. 1810 Census; Harrison, *Antislavery Movement*, 2–3; Friend, *Kentucke's Frontiers*, 216; Sachs, *Home Rule*, 38; Coward, *Kentucky in the New Republic*, 41–42, 133–40; *Journal of the First Constitutional Convention of Kentucky*, 18; *Journal of the Convention, Begun and Held at the Capitol*, 31–32.

10. Coward, *Kentucky in the New Republic*, 131–33; Sachs, *Home Rule*, 134–43.

11. Harrison and Klotter, *New History of Kentucky*, 71–72.

12. Simpson, *Bluegrass Houses*, 316; Staples, *History of Pioneer Lexington*, 280–81; Clay, *Life*, 41–42.

13. Clay, *Life*, 20–22, 29, 35, 45.

14. Clay, *Life*, 22, 31–33; Green Clay to Sidney Payne Clay, April 4, 1822, Sidney Payne Clay Papers, FHS; see BJC's surveying notebooks in Clay Family Papers, SC-UKY.

15. *Kentucky Reporter*, December 23, 1822; Johnson, *History of Kentucky*, 1321; Ellison, *Man Seen But Once*, 31.

16. Clay, *Life*, 20, 22, 24–25, 39.

17. Henry Clay to Sidney Payne Clay, April 4, 1820, Clay Family Papers, SC-UKY; Berry, *Voices*, 7; CMC to BJC, December 18, 1827, Clay Family Papers, SC-UKY.

18. Sally Clay to CMC, December 17, 1827, and CMC to BJC, February 10, 1828, Clay Family Papers, SC-UKY.

19. Clay, *Life*, 21. Green Clay, will, in *Kentucky, U.S., Wills and Probate Records, 1774–1989*.

20. Green Clay, will; Ellis, Everman, and Sears, *Madison County*, 33; CMC to BJC, December 4, 1831, Clay Family Papers, SC-UKY.

21. Green Clay, will. For a discussion of legalities of slavery in married women's inheritance, see Holton, "Equality as Unintended Consequence."

22. Green Clay, will; Clay, *Life*, 26. The Clay brothers' legal entailment to land and slave property was an example of what legal scholar Lawrence M. Friedman calls "the dead hand" of the settlor controlling the fate of an inheritance "from beyond the grave." He argues that this was "especially important for settlors of dynastic trusts." Friedman, *Dead Hands*, 118.

23. Ford, *Deliver Us from Evil*, 26–44; Tallant, *Evil Necessity*, 5–15; Harrison, *Antislavery Movement*, 21–25.

24. Harrison, *Antislavery Movement*, 27–29.

25. Harrison, *Antislavery Movement*, 27–34, Henry Clay quoted on 32; Henry Clay served as president of the American Colonization Society from 1836 to 1852; Remini, *Henry Clay*, 491–92; Ford, *Deliver Us from Evil*, 26–44; Tallant, *Evil Necessity*, 5–15.

26. Green Clay, will.
27. Green Clay, will.
28. Clay, *Life*, 25–26.
29. Green Clay, will; Clay, *Life*, 25–26; Mullins and Mullins, *History of White Hall*, 37; *Acts Passed at the First Session of the Twenty-Ninth General Assembly*, 7–9; Morris, *Southern Slavery*, 220.
30. Ellis, Everman, and Sears, *Madison County*, 63; Clay, *Life*, 26, 27.
31. Clay, *Life*, 38.
32. Clay, *Life*, 18, 46–47.
33. Clay, *Life*, 66–67; Smiley, *Lion of White Hall*, 25.
34. Wall, "'Richer Land,'" 145–52.
35. CMC to BJC, March 27, 1831, BJC Papers, LOC; Clay, *Life*, 47–54.
36. *Liberator* (Boston), January 1, 1831.
37. Clay, *Life*, 56–57.
38. Clay, *Life*, 174–75.
39. Clay, *Life*, 174–75.
40. CMC to BJC, December 4, 1831, BJC Papers, LOC.
41. CMC to BJC, December 4, June 19, 1831, BJC Papers, LOC.
42. CMC to BJC, June 19, 1831.
43. Clay, *Life*, 66–67, 69–71, 73.
44. Smiley, *Lion of White Hall*, 32–34; Thomas Bodley to William Bodley, February 24, 1833, Bodley Family Papers, FHS.
45. Ellison, *Man Seen But Once*, 31; William Mix to Sidney Clay, February 27, 1833, Sidney Payne Clay Papers, FHS; Clay, *Life*, 71–73.

CHAPTER 2

1. Sally Clay Dudley to CMC, May 30, 1831, November 23, 1833, CMC Collection, SC-EKU.
2. Smiley, *Lion of White Hall*, 38; CMC to BJC, October 21, 1836, May 20, 1837, Clay Family Papers, SC-UKY; Rice, "Importations of Cattle," 45–47; on the role of the Clays in the importation of English cattle in Kentucky, see Allen, *History of Shorthorn Cattle*, 163–70; Henlein, *Cattle Kingdom*, 44–47; and Woods, *Herds Shot*, 78–105.
3. Smiley, *Lion of White Hall*, 34.
4. Smiley, *Lion of White Hall*, 36–37.
5. The enslaved population made up 20 percent of Kentucky's total population in 1810 and 22.5 percent in 1820. Harrison, *Antislavery Movement*, 2. For more on Virginia's debate, see Freehling, *Drift toward Dissolution*.
6. Tallant, *Evil Necessity*, 30–32.
7. Tallant, *Evil Necessity*, 91–92.
8. Harrison, *Antislavery Movement*, 46–48.
9. Howe, *What Hath God Wrought*, 425–30, 512–15; Harrold, *American Abolitionism*, 52–73.
10. Harrison, *Antislavery Movement*, 39–45, quotation on 45.
11. Clay, *Writings*, 46; Tallant, *Evil Necessity*, 108–12.
12. Clay, *Writings*, 46; Harlow, *Making of Confederate Kentucky*, 16–17.

13. Harlow, *Making of Confederate Kentucky*, 16–17.

14. Watkins and Ramage, *Kentucky Rising*, 83, 90–95. CMC to BJC, March 21, 1838, December 19, 1837, January 24, 1839. On Cassius's dealings with personal debt, see CMC to BJC, February 27, 1839; Cassius soon requested to borrow the labor of an enslaved man named Harrison from Brutus to work his mills. CMC to BJC, March 12, 1839. All in Clay Family Papers, SC-UKY.

15. Entry for February 2, 1837, CMC Journal, SC-UKY; CMC to BJC, August 27, 1838, February 23, 1840. In December 1840, he asked for Harrison, Billy, Matt, and Albert. CMC to BJC, December 11, 1840. For another instance of Cassius borrowing money and slaves from Brutus, see CMC to BJC, December 11, 1840. For the financial fallout from George Weddle's bankruptcy, see CMC to BJC, March 14, May 16, 1840. All in Clay Family Papers, SC-UKY.

16. Tallant, *Evil Necessity*, 43–44; Ramage, "Love and Honor," 115–33; Smiley, *Lion of White Hall*, 43–47.

17. Smiley, *Lion of White Hall*, 45–46.

18. Tallant, *Evil Necessity*, 108–12.

19. Clay, *Review of Late Canvass*, 14–16; Roediger, *Wages of Whiteness*, 43–60; Foner, *Free Soil*, 46–47.

20. Tocqueville, *Democracy in America*, 405.

21. Tocqueville, *Democracy in America*, 406. For scholarly consideration of slavery's supposed degradation of white labor, see Foner, *Free Soil*, 44–60.

22. Harrison and Klotter, *New History of Kentucky*, 140–41; Starobin, *Industrial Slavery*, 14, 17–18, 23, 139–40. According to Starobin, in 1850, Kentucky boasted 159 hemp factories, which used the labor of 3,000 enslaved workers. By 1860, the number of laborers grew to 5,000. *Industrial Slavery*, 17–18. Starobin reports that a Kentucky hemp manufacturer who replaced his white laborers with enslaved workers reduced his labor costs by 33 percent. *Industrial Slavery*, 159. On competition between poor white and enslaved labor, see Merritt, *Masterless Men*, esp. 62–113. On the interchangeability of free and enslaved wage labor in the early republic, see Rockman, *Scraping By*; and Wright, *Slavery and American Economic Development*, 113–21.

23. Clay, *Review of Late Canvass*, 14.

24. According to the 1840 Federal Census, Ohio had 218,609 enrolled students versus Kentucky's 24,618. Ellis, *History of Education in Kentucky*, 8, 21–22, quotation on 8.

25. Majewski, "Why Did Northerners Oppose Slavery?," 288–92, Ellis quoted on 292. Majewski's regression analysis indicates that in Kentucky, counties with the most slaves tended to charge the highest common school tuitions. Majewski, "Why Did Northerners Oppose Slavery?," 290; Foner, *Free Soil*, 45.

26. Robert Wickliffe Sr. quoted in Smiley, *Lion of White Hall*, 49; Harry Bodley to William Bodley, July 22, 1840, Bodley Family Papers, FHS.

27. CMC to BJC, August 4, 1840, Clay Family Papers, SC-UKY; Sally Dudley to CMC, August 2, 1840, CMC Collection, SC-EKU.

28. Clay, *Review of Late Canvass*, 14.

29. Clay, *Review of Late Canvass*, 8, 15–16.

30. Tallant, *Evil Necessity*, 97–102, quotation on 101.

31. Clay, *Writings*, 72–74.

32. Clay, *Writings*, 60, 66, 75–76.

33. Freehling, *South vs. South*, 18; Tadman, *Speculators and Slaves*, 12; Harrison, *Antislavery Movement*, 2. In 1830, Kentucky's enslaved population numbered 165,213. See census numbers in Klotter and Harrison, *New History of Kentucky*, 99, 167.

34. Clay, *Life*, 80; Clay, *Writings*, 69.

35. CMC to BJC, April 20, 1841, Clay Family Papers, SC-UKY; Smiley, *Lion of White Hall*, 51–52.

36. Elisha Warfield to BJC, April 27, 1841, and J. Speed Smith to BJC, April 29, 1841, Clay Family Papers, SC-UKY.

37. Mary Robertson to John C. Bullitt, May 9, 1841, Bullitt Family Papers, FHS; Louisa Bullitt quoted in Hollingsworth, "Mag Preston," 106; Coleman, *Squire's Sketches*, 35; Klotter and Harrison, *New History of Kentucky*, 159.

38. Hollingsworth, "Mag Preston," 105; Clay, *Life*, 80–81; "Memoranda for the Terms for a Meeting between C. M. Clay Esq. and Robert Wickliffe Jr., Esq.," undated, Wickliffe-Preston Papers, SC-UKY.

39. Robert Wickliffe Jr. to William Preston, May 27, 1841, Wickliffe-Preston Papers, SC-UKY; *New Orleans Times-Picayune*, May 13, 1841; *Richmond (VA) Enquirer*, May 28, 1841.

40. CMC to BJC, April 19, 1841, Clay Family Papers, SC-UKY; CMC to SPC, March 1842, Salmon P. Chase Papers, HSP.

41. Clay, *Life*, 80–81. For more on the connection between Southern honor and slavery, see Ayers, *Vengeance and Justice*; and Wyatt-Brown, *Southern Honor*.

CHAPTER 3

1. Portions of this chapter appeared previously in Marshall, "'Lamentable Inconsistency." CMC to BJC, December 24, 1841, Clay Family Papers, SC-UKY.

2. Fayette County Tax List, 1841, Kentucky Department for Libraries and Archives, Frankfort; Klotter and Harrison, *New History of Kentucky*, 143; CMC to BJC, February 10, 1842, Clay Family Papers, SC-UKY; Fayette County Tax List, 1841; Lee, "Between Two Fires," 58; Clay, *Life*, 27.

3. Blue, *Salmon P. Chase*, 31.

4. Niven, *Salmon P. Chase*, 45–57, quotation on 53. On Chase's reliance on the terms of the Northwest Ordinance for his "positive law" theory, see Oakes, "Making Freedom National," 411; and Stahr, *Salmon P. Chase*, 53, 68.

5. Blue, *Salmon P. Chase*, 37–38, 40.

6. CMC to SPC, March 1842, SPC Papers, HSP.

7. CMC to SPC, March 1842.

8. Snay, *Horace Greeley*, 45–46, 22, 28; Tuchinsky, *Greeley's "New-York Tribune."* See coverage of Clay in the *New-York Tribune*, August 11, 12, 1841.

9. Clay, *Writings*, 119–20.

10. Clay, *Writings*, 123–29, 134, 133. Little information exists on the *Lexington Intelligencer*, but the Library of Congress record for the paper indicates that it changed editorial hands a number of times in its decade of existence and ceased printing in 1843. "About Lexington Intelligencer," Library of Congress, Chronicling

America, accessed March 6, 2020, https://chroniclingamerica.loc.gov/lccn/sn82015452/.

11. The *Liberator* (Boston) published excerpts of Clay's writings on May 8 and July 21, 1843; threats to Clay's life appeared in the *Liberator* (Boston), March 31, 1843; and *Carlisle (PA) Weekly Herald*, March 29, 1843.

12. Smiley, *Lion of White Hall*, 60–61.

13. *New-York Tribune*, October 18, 1843. Samuel Brown's list of injuries appears in the *Green Bay (WI) Democrat*, August 12, 1843; and *Wisconsin Democrat*, September 7, 1843.

14. Smiley, *Lion of White Hall*, 62; Thomas H. Russell to William A. Russell, August 27, 1843, quoted in Smiley, *Lion of White Hall*, 256n8.

15. *Town Talk* (Alexandria, LA), September 17, 1967; *Natchez Free Trader*, June 29, 1837; *Jacksonville (AL) Republican*, August 31, 1837; *Nashville Tennessean*, March 14, 1838; *Montgomery Daily Journal*, reprinted in *Daily Selma Reporter*, August 26, 1837; the letter of Rezin Bowie is republished in *Niles National Register* (Baltimore), September 29, 1838; *London Times*, June 28, 1838.

16. *Lorain (OH) Republican*, August 23, 1843; *Danville (VT) North Star*, August 23, 1843; *Cleveland Herald*, reprinted in *Sandusky (OH) Clarion*, August 19, 1843; *Brooklyn Daily Eagle*, August 11, 1843; for pro-Brown testimony, see *Baltimore Sun*, August 12, 1843; for Clay's letter, see *Detroit Free Press*, August 12, 1843.

17. CMC to SPC, September 27, 1843, SPC Papers, HSP.

18. See, in particular, Franklin, *Militant South*, 36, 40, 66, 70–79. Dueling in the South has often been linked to the institution of slavery. Although the practice was not exclusive to the South, the theory goes that the patriarchal system of mastery it fostered meant that dueling thrived there longer and more readily than in the North. As Franklin wrote, "Accustomed to the use of firearms and the exercise of almost unlimited power over his dependents, 'he could not brook opposition. When one lord ran up against another in controversy, if the feelings were deeply engaged the final argument was the pistol.'" *Militant South*, 44. Clay, *Life*, 81.

19. *Cleveland Herald*, reprinted in *South Port (WI) American*, August 17, 1843; CMC to SPC, March 27, 1843, SPC Papers, HSP; *Liberator* (Boston), October 20, 1843; *Vermont Union Whig* (Brandon), October 12, 1843.

20. Commonwealth v. Cassius M. Clay, September 28, 1843, Kentucky Department for Libraries and Archives, Frankfort; Heidler and Heidler, *Henry Clay*, 365–67.

21. *New-York Tribune*, October 18, 1843; Clay, *Life*, 89.

22. *New-York Tribune*, December 5, 1843. On education, he noted: "The system of Common Schools has not succeeded in a single Slave State. Slavery and Education are natural enemies. In the Free States one in 53 over 21 years is unable to write: in the Slave States one in 13.3 is unable to write and read."

23. *New-York Tribune*, December 5, 1843.

24. *New-York Tribune*, December 5, 1843.

25. *New-York Tribune*, December 5, 1843.

26. *New-York Tribune*, December 5, 1843; CMC to SPC, January 19, 1844, SPC Papers, HSP.

27. *New-York Tribune*, August 11, 12, 1841; *Liberator* (Boston), May 5, 1845; Harrold, *Abolitionists and the South*, 43.

28. Marenda B. Randall to CMC, December 26, 1843, CMC Collection, LMU; *Liberator* (Boston), May 5, 1843, December 15, 29, 1843. For another rebuke of Clay by Garrison, see *Liberator* (Boston), July 21, 1843.

29. *Liberator* (Boston), December 29, 1843.

30. CMC to BJC, December 1, 1843, January 6, 1844, Clay Family Papers, SC-UKY.

31. The only known extant evidence of the purchase or manumission of these slaves is a deed of emancipation for Adam, Joe, Matt, Scott, Riley, "Henry's Dave," Dave Crews, Lotty, and Zilla, written and signed on March 14, 1844. The deed and a bond for $2,400 signed by his brother-in-law, Madison Johnson, is located in the J. Winston Coleman Scrapbook, 4:104–5, Special Collections and Archives, Transylvania University, Lexington, KY.

The thirteen slaves Cassius claimed to buy are included in his description as: "'Dave Crews,' husband of trust-slave Lucy, Daniel and Fanny 'Shearer,' and child Minerva, Lotty and Zilla, 'Martin,' 'Mammy's son,' paid part of the money for Jim's wife, Judy, to keep her in the neighborhood, Laura and child, Daniel 'Parker' and his two daughters and grandchild." Clay, *Life*, 560.

For the claim in 1845 that Clay freed thirteen slaves, see *Carlisle (PA) Weekly Herald*, May 28, 1845.

32. *Whig Standard* (Washington, DC), March 7, 1844; *Vermont Family Gazette* (Bradford), March 19, 1844; *Brooklyn Daily Eagle*, March 6, 1844; *Vicksburg Daily Whig*, March 25, 1844; *Pittsburgh Weekly Gazette*, March 29, 1844; *Summit County (OH) Beacon*, March 20, 1844; "sixty" slaves figure quoted in the *Detroit Free Press*, July 5, 1844; *New-York Tribune*, March 27, 1844.

33. *Lexington Gazette* and *Ohio Statesman* (Columbus) quoted in the *Detroit Free Press*, July 5, 1844; *Detroit Free Press*, July 11, 1844.

34. Sewell, *Ballots for Freedom*, 43, 78; Blue, *Salmon P. Chase*, 43–46, 50–52.

35. Blue, *Salmon P. Chase*, 50–52; CMC to SPC, September 27, 1843.

36. CMC to SPC, January 19, 1844.

37. Letter printed in the *New-York Tribune*, May 16, 1844; Freeman, *Field of Blood*, 52, 102–3.

38. *Louisville Daily Journal*, May 17, 1844; Clay, *Writings*, 97–116, quotation on 113.

39. Smiley, *Lion of White Hall*, 67.

40. Smiley, "'Emissary from Cousin Henry,'" 116–21.

41. Smiley, "'Emissary from Cousin Henry,'" 116–21; *Louisville Daily Journal*, September 28, 1844; *New-York Tribune*, reprinted in *Mississippi Free Trader* (Natchez), September 22, 1844.

42. Smiley, *Lion of White Hall*, 66–67, 77; *New-York Tribune*, March 27, 1844. Despite Henry Clay's general ambivalence about the peculiar institution and his founding role in the American Colonization Society, his political opponents made ready issue of his status as the owner of dozens of slaves. By his third run for the presidency, in 1844, hyperbolic allegations of slave mistreatment and allegations that he was a slave "dealer" and "catcher" abounded. See Remini, *Henry Clay*, 652.

43. Smiley, *Lion of White Hall*, 72–73.

44. The account and contents of the stolen letter appeared in the *New-York Tribune*, October 2, 1844.

45. Quotation reprinted in *Tioga Eagle* (Wellsboro, PA), October 16, 1844.

46. Quoted in Smiley, *Lion of White Hall*, 78.

CHAPTER 4

1. Clay, *Writings*, 173–83, quotation on 181.

2. See, for example, his reference to this group in *True American* (Lexington), July 1, 1845. On constraints on newspaper publishing during this time, see Eaton, *Freedom-of-Thought Struggle*, 162–69. The figure of 600,000 laborers to whom Clay referred was most likely a generalization derived from faulty usage of 1840 US Federal Census data. The total white population of Kentucky (590,253) was less than this figure. Compendium of the Enumeration of the Inhabitants and Statistics of the United States, Kentucky, www2.census.gov/library/publications/decennial/1840/1840v3/1840c-18.pdf. 1840 Federal Census; CMC to SPC, January 19, 1844, SPC Papers, HSP.

3. CMC to SPC, January 19, 1844.

4. The *True American* prospectus appeared in the *Lexington Observer and Reporter*, February 19, 1845, and is reprinted in Clay, *Writings*, 211–12.

5. Runyon, *Delia Webster*, 1–64.

6. Runyon, *Delia Webster*, 1–64; *Lexington Observer and Reporter*, February 19, 1845, reprinted in Kirwan, "Clay's *True American*," 52–53.

7. Clay, *Life*, 106–7.

8. Clay, *Life*, 106–7.

9. Clay explained this in June 1845 in a statement he released as he was busily printing the *True American*: "A trust slave, named Emily, I have reason to believe, in 1843, killed with poison our infant child, and again in 1845 attempted to poison our infant son since born; she is now in the Lexington jail, *subject to the laws* of the country. Her mother and brother and daughter, I sent to New Orleans and sold them there; because I knew them to be abettors of the crime of Emily." *Cadiz (OH) Sentinel*, June 18, 1845. For the instructions on slaves who "behave amiss," see Green Clay, will, 11, in *Kentucky, U.S., Wills and Probate Records, 1774–1989*.

10. Coleman, *Slavery Times*, 266.

11. *Digest of Statute Law of Kentucky*, 2:1161, 1154–55; *Cincinnati Enquirer*, reprinted in *Cadiz (OH) Sentinel*, June 18, 1845; *True American* (Lexington), June 3, 1845.

12. *Cincinnati Enquirer*, reprinted in *Cadiz (OH) Sentinel*, June 18, 1845; *Cincinnati Gazette*, reprinted in *True American* (Lexington), June 3, 1845.

13. *True American* (Lexington), June 3, 1845.

14. *True American* (Lexington), June 3, 1845.

15. *True American* (Lexington), June 3, 1845.

16. *Lexington Observer and Reporter*, June 7, 1845; *True American* (Lexington), June 10, 17, 24, 1845.

17. *New-York Tribune*, reprinted in *Lexington Observer and Reporter*, July 16, 1845; *Liberator* (Boston), August 8, 1845; *Vermont Watchman and State Journal* (Montpelier), July 31, 1845.

18. John Henry Hammond to John C. Calhoun, August 18, 1845, and Calhoun to Hammond, August 30, 1845, quoted in Harlow, *Making of Confederate Kentucky*, 70.

19. Townsend, *Lincoln in the Bluegrass*, 106–7; *Lexington Observer and Reporter*, July 16, 1845.

20. Howard, "Ante-Bellum Career," 64; *True American* (Lexington), June 17, July 1, 1845.

21. J. Speed Smith to BJC, July 12, 1845, Clay Family Papers, SC-UKY.

22. *True American* (Lexington), July 15, 1845.

23. See *True American* (Lexington), August 3, 1845, for an example of an issue largely filled with outside editorial content; Townsend, *Lincoln in the Bluegrass*, 109–10.

24. *Louisville Journal*, reprinted in *Vermont Phoenix* (Brattleboro), September 4, 1845.

25. *True American* (Lexington), August 12, 1845; Smiley, *Lion of White Hall*, 91.

26. Clay, *Writings*, 290–91; Barre, *Writings of Marshall*, 195–96.

27. Clay, *Writings*, 291–92, 303–5; Smiley, *Lion of White Hall*, 92–93.

28. Clay, *Writings*, 305, 307; Clay, *Life*, 109; *Louisville Journal*, reprinted in *Anti-Slavery Bugle* (New Lisbon, OH), August 29, 1845.

29. Handbill of August 16, 1845, reprinted in *Liberator* (Boston), August 29, 1845.

30. Clay, *Writings*, 294–95, 305, 300.

31. Clay, *Writings*, 305, 300; Barre, *Writings of Marshall*, 197, 199, 201–2.

32. Clay, *Writings*, 202, 205–10.

33. Smiley, *Lion of White Hall*, 99; *Lexington Observer and Reporter*, August 20, 1845; *Louisville Journal*, reprinted in *Vermont Phoenix* (Brattleboro), September 4, 1845; *Cadiz (OH) Sentinel*, September 3, 1845; Eaton, *Freedom-of-Thought Struggle*, 192–93. For a reading of the *True American*'s shutdown in the context of antebellum mob behavior, see Grimsted, *American Mobbing*, 128–32, 138–39.

34. *Anti-Slavery Bugle* (New Lisbon, OH), August 29, 1845; *Liberator* (Boston), September 19, 1845; *Green-Mountain Freeman* (Montpelier, VT), September 11, 1845; *Liberator* (Boston), October 10, 1845.

35. *Vermont Watchman and State Journal* (Montpelier), October 23, 1845; *Lexington Observer and Reporter*, October 4, 1845; Tallant, *Evil Necessity*, 124–25; *True American* (Lexington), October 7, 1845.

36. *Lexington Observer and Reporter*, October 11, 1845; *Richmond (VA) Times*, quoted in the *Carolina Watchman* (Salisbury, NC), November 1, 1845; *Livingston (MI) Courier*, quoted in the *Livingston (MI) Democrat*, November 26, 1845.

37. Commonwealth of Kentucky v. Emily, 1; Clay, *Life*, 1, 565.

38. Coleman, *Slavery Times*, 265. This notice of Emily's trial circulated in a number of newspapers throughout the country. See, e.g., *Portage (OH) Sentinel*, November 12, 1845; and *Pittsburgh Daily Post*, November 5, 1845.

39. Smiley, *Lion of Whitehall*, 88.

CHAPTER 5

1. Seward, *William Seward*, 799.

2. Seward, *William Seward*, 799; CMC to SPC, June 30, 1846, SPC Papers, HSP; CMC to Horace Greeley, January 4, 1846, Horace Greeley Collection, Morgan Library and Museum, New York; *New-York Tribune*, January 14, 1846.

3. *Vermont Watchman and State Journal* (Montpelier), January 22, 1846; *New-York Tribune*, January 31, 1846.

4. Seward, *William Seward*, 799; Stahr, *Seward*, 65; Foner, *Free Soil*, 41–42.

5. Smiley, *Lion of White Hall*, 105, 109–11; *True American* (Lexington) quoted in the *Liberator* (Boston), November 21, 1845; *True American* (Lexington), May 27, 1846.

6. *True American* (Lexington), June 17, 1846.

7. *New-York Tribune*, quoted in *Liberator* (Boston), June 19, 1846; *Cincinnati Herald*, quoted in *Green-Mountain Freeman* (Montpelier, VT), June 25, 1846.

8. "[Letter to] My Dear M. W. Chapman & Sisters."

9. *Lexington Observer and Reporter*, January 14, 1846.

10. *Lexington Observer and Reporter*, February 11, 1846.

11. CMC to SPC, June 30, 1846; SPC to Gerrit Smith, September 1, 1846, in Niven, *Chase Papers*, 130.

12. Greenberg, *Wicked War*, 13, 24, 124.

13. CMC to BJC, June 16, 1846, Clay Family Papers, SC-UKY; Smiley, *Lion of White Hall*, 115–16; *Lexington Observer and Reporter*, July 25, 1846. In his own accounts of his service in Mexico, Clay never mentioned Jack's presence or identity. His niece Sally Clay, writing from Frankfort, mentioned him in a letter to Brutus, noting, "The negro man who went as Clay's attendant passed through here yesterday with two of the Madison company returning on account of sickness." Sally Clay to BJC, November 14, 1846, Clay Family Papers, SC-UKY. Confirmation of his named identity can be found in a letter Clay wrote to Kentucky governor John Crittenden in 1848. Jack was among a group of several dozen other slaves who attempted to escape to Ohio but were ultimately captured. In his efforts to clear Jack from wrongdoing and save him from the gallows, Clay appealed to Crittenden, citing Jack's steadfast service in Mexico and calling him "trusty." Prichard, "Priceless Jewel," 90, 96, 105n63.

For more on Black servitude in the Mexican-American War, see Greenberg, *Wicked War*, 139–40; and May, "Invisible Men," 473–85.

14. Mat. Bullock to John Bullitt, June 11, 1846, Bullitt Family Papers, FHS.

15. *Memphis Enquirer*, reprinted in *Lexington Observer and Reporter*, July 25, 1846.

16. Clay, *Life*, 119–20. For Clay's account of his excursion, see *Life*, 119–34; and *Lexington Observer and Reporter*, October 14, 1846.

17. Smiley, *Lion of White Hall*, 119–20; *Lexington Observer and Reporter*, October 14, 1846.

18. Smiley, *Lion of White Hall*, 119–20; CMC to BJC, October 12, 1846, Clay Family Papers, SC-UKY.

19. CMC to BJC, October 12, 1846. On racism and disillusionment among troops, see Greenberg, *Wicked War*, 130–31, 149–50, Henry Clay Jr. quoted on 150.

20. CMC to BJC, October 12, 1846; Paul Seymour to BJC, October 6, 1846, Clay Family Papers, SC-UKY; Tallant, *Evil Necessity*, 125–26.

21. *Hartford Courant*, October 31, 1846; *Milwaukee Daily Sentinel*, October 20, 1846; *Lexington Observer and Reporter*, November 7, 1846.

22. *Louisville Daily Courier*, October 31, 1846, January 15, 1847; Greenberg, *Wicked War*, 143.

23. *Lexington Observer and Reporter*, March 18, 1847; Smiley, *Lion of White Hall*, 125.

24. Smiley, *Lion of White Hall*, 125.

25. *Lexington Observer and Reporter*, April 28, 1847; Salisbury, "Battle of Buena Vista," 34–53; Greenberg, *Wicked War*, 159–60.

26. Clay, *Life*, 154, 157–60.

27. MJC to BJC, October 11, 1846. For other examples of Mary Jane's duties and financial burdens as well as her reliance on Brutus, see MJC to BJC, October 18, November 28, 1846, March 1, 1847. All Clay Family Papers, SC-UKY.

28. *Baltimore Sun*, April 5, 1847; *Louisville Daily Courier*, April 1, 1847; MJC to BJC, May 3, 1847, Clay Family Papers, SC-UKY; *Louisville Daily Courier*, October 21, 1847; Clay, *Life*, 163–64.

29. *Baltimore Sun*, August 17, 1847; *Lexington Observer and Reporter*, October 23, 1847; *Gettysburg (PA) Compiler*, November 8, 1847.

30. Both newspapers reprinted in *Louisville Examiner*, December 11, 1847.

31. *Louisville Daily Courier*, December 9, 1847; Jeptha Dudley to BJC, December 9, 1847, Clay Family Papers, SC-UKY; *Vermont Watchman and State Journal* (Montpelier), January 6, 1848; CMC to SPC, December 27, 1847, SPC Papers, HSP.

32. After Brutus and Mary Jane declined to continue financing the *True American*, associate editor John Vaughn, with the support of several Northern antislavery reformers, including Salmon Chase, Gerrit Smith, and Lewis Tappan, as well as several Kentucky sympathizers, raised enough funding to relaunch the paper. In an effort to distance the new incarnation, which was now based in Louisville, from its controversial past, Vaughn renamed the newspaper the *Louisville Examiner*. Tallant, *Evil Necessity*, 126–29; CMC to SPC, December 27, 1847; Clay, *Writings*.

33. On Chase's efforts at coalition building, see Blue, *Free Soilers*, 41–60; and Foner, *Free Soil*, 78–83.

34. Stahr, *Salmon P. Chase*, 86–123; CMC to SPC, January 28, 1845, SPC Papers, HSP; for another refusal, see CMC to SPC, February [n.d.], 1845, SPC Papers, HSP.

35. Howe, *What Hath God Wrought*, 767–68.

36. On the fluidity of party identity in the nineteenth century, see Shelden and Alexander, "Dismantling the Party System."

37. Sewell, *Ballots for Freedom*, 156–57; Blue, *Free Soilers*, 80.

38. Earle, *Jacksonian Anti-Slavery*, 59–62; *New York Weekly Evening Post* quoted in Sewell, *Ballots for Freedom*, 197.

39. Sewell, *Ballots for Freedom*, 158–59; Blue, *Free Soilers*, 61–64.

40. Sewell, *Ballots for Freedom*, 160.

41. CMC to SPC, December 27, 1847, July 14, 1848, SPC Papers, HSP.

42. Sewell, *Ballots for Freedom*, 168, 202–30; Blue, *Free Soilers*, 191, 169; Foner, *Free Soil*, 11.

43. Tallant, *Evil Necessity*, 135–37; Coward, *Kentucky in the New Republic*, 139–42.

44. Tallant, *Evil Necessity*, 135, 137–39; CMC to SPC, January 28, 1845.

45. Tallant, *Evil Necessity*, 138–45.

46. Clay, *Life*, 178; Tallant, *Evil Necessity*, 145.

47. Clay, *Life*, 179, 182; *Louisville Examiner*, reprinted in *Liberator* (Boston), June 22, 1849; *Louisville Daily Courier*, May 5, 1849.

48. *Louisville Examiner*, reprinted in *Liberator* (Boston), June 22, 1849; *Huntsville Democrat*, May 9, 1849. Other Southern newspapers covering Clay's activities include the *Nashville Tennessean*, May 1, 1849; and *Vicksburg Daily Whig*, May 16, 1849.

49. Smiley, *Lion of White Hall*, 139–40.

50. Smiley, *Lion of White Hall*, 139–40; *Louisville Daily Courier*, June 25, 1849.

51. *Anti-Slavery Bugle* (New Lisbon, OH), July 21, 1849.

52. *Anti-Slavery Bugle* (New Lisbon, OH), July 21, 1849; *Mississippi Free Trader*, June 27, 1849.

53. *Louisville Daily Courier*, June 18, 1849; "[Letter to] Beloved Friend"; *Louisville Daily Courier*, June 17, 1849; *Toledo Republican*, quoted in *Fremont (OH) Weekly Freeman*, June 30, 1849.

54. *Buffalo Weekly Republic*, July 24, 1849; *Vermont Phoenix* (Brattleboro), June 22, 1849; *Cecil (MD) Whig*, June 23, 1849.

55. *Anti-Slavery Bugle* (New Lisbon, OH), July 21, September 14, July 27, 1849.

56. Clay, *Life*, 187, 211.

57. *National Era* (Washington, DC), August 4, 1849; *Anti-Slavery Bugle* (New Lisbon, OH), July 21, 1849; *Liberator* (Boston), September 14, 1849; *Louisville Daily Courier*, September 15, 1849; *Fayetteville (AR) Weekly Observer*, August 7, 1849.

58. Tallant, *Evil Necessity*, 133–34, 155–56; Willis, "Kentucky Constitutions," 321–25, quotation on 325; Harrison and Klotter, *New History of Kentucky*, 117–18.

CHAPTER 6

1. Sally Dudley Clay to CMC, August 6, 1849, CMC Collection, LMU.

2. Varon, *Disunion!*, 223–31.

3. Willentz, *Rise of American Democracy*, 637–41; *Speech of William H. Seward*.

4. CMC to WHS, April 6, 1850, WHS Papers, LOC; CMC to Daniel Webster, March 20, 1850, transcript in Clay Family Papers, SC-UKY; Chase quoted in Wilentz, *Rise of American Democracy*, 644.

5. *New Orleans Times Picayune*, March 18, 1851.

6. CMC to WHS, April 24, 1851, WHS Papers, LOC.

7. J. Speed Smith to BJC, February 9, March 22, 1851, Clay Family Papers, SC-UKY.

8. CMC to WHS, April 24, 1851; Smiley, *Lion of White Hall*, 146; Freehling, *Road to Disunion*, 1:502–3; Freehling, *South vs. South*, 20, 27.

9. CMC to WHS, December 8, 1851, WHS Papers, LOC.

10. Letter to *Progress of the Age*, reprinted in *Green-Mountain Freeman* (Montpelier, VT), April 10, 1851; Smiley, *Lion of White Hall*, 147; *Southern Press* (Washington, DC), August 27, 1851; CMC to SPC, August 12, 1851, Salmon P. Chase Papers, HSP.

11. Sewall, *Ballots for Freedom*, 231–33; CMC to SPC, August 27, 1851, SPC Papers, HSP.

12. *Burlington Courier*, October 9, 1851; CMC to SPC, August 27, 1851, SPC Papers, HSP.

13. "Letter from Clay to Giddings, September 3, 1851," 33.

14. *Burlington Courier*, October 9, 1851.

15. CMC to SPC, August 12, 1851.

16. Sewell, *Ballots for Freedom*, 241–43.

17. *Sumter Banner* (Sumterville, SC), July 20, 1852; *Pittsburgh Daily Post*, July 27, 1852; *National Era* (Washington, DC), July 15, 1852.

18. *Liberator* (Boston), September 10, 1852; this article mistakenly identifies Clay's daughter as being six years of age. CMC to WHS, August 27, 1852, WHS Papers, LOC.

19. Marshall, "Free Democratic Convention of 1852," 154, 159; Sewell, *Ballots for Freedom*, 244–47.

20. CMC to WHS, August 27, 1852; Clay, *Life*, 500; Julian, *Political Recollections*, 126–27; Clarke, *George W. Julian*, 133.

21. Sewell, *Ballots for Freedom*, 250; Holt, *Fate of Their Country*, 89–91.

22. *Brandon (VT) Post*, May 19, 1853; *Green-Mountain Freeman* (Montpelier, VT), May 12, 1853.

23. *Liberator* (Boston), May 18, 1853.

24. *Liberator* (Boston), May 27, 1853; Strangis, *Lewis Hayden*, 87; Carter, *Force and Freedom*, 67–75.

25. Strangis, *Lewis Hayden*, 71; *Liberator* (Boston), May 27, 1853.

26. *Liberator* (Boston), May 27, 1853.

27. Harrold, "Clay on Slavery and Race," 48–50; Clay, *Writings*, 531.

28. *Letter from Clay to Proceedings*, 284–85.

29. Foner, *Free Soil*, 261–69, 294–300; Kendi, *Stamped from the Beginning*, 168–69.

30. Clay, *Life*, 57–58; Smiley, *Lion of White Hall*, 58; Harrold, "Clay on Slavery and Race," 45.

31. Clay, *Life*, 570; CMC to SPC, March 12, 1854, SPC Papers, HSP; Ellis, Everman, and Sears, *Madison County*, 105–7.

32. Fee, *Autobiography*, 14, 24–25, 81–82.

33. Harlow, *Making of Confederate Kentucky*, 97–100.

34. *Anti-Slavery Bugle* (New Lisbon, OH), September 24, 1853.

35. Anderson, *Capitalist Pigs*, 72–74, 110–11. For more details on Clay's swine operation, see his article "All about Hogs," reprinted from *American Stock Journal* in *Illinois Farmer*, 230–31; *Louisville Daily Journal*, November 5, 1853; *Chicago Tribune*, December 26, 1853; *New Orleans Crescent* in *Thibodaux (LA) Minerva*, February 25, 1854.

36. *New-York Tribune*, reprinted in *American Observer* (Morrisville, VT), August 11, 1853; and *Saturday Express* (Lancaster, PA), June 25, 1853.

37. Horowitz, *Spying on the South*, 4–6, 77–79; Olmsted, *Journey through Texas*, 12–13.

38. Horowitz, *Spying on the South*, 4–6, 77–79; Olmsted, *Journey through Texas*, 12–13.

39. CMC to WHS, June 9, 1853, WHS Papers, LOC; Smiley, *Lion of White Hall*, 157.

40. Holt, *Fate of Their Country*, 102–4.

41. Walther, *Shattering*, 40–41; *National Era* (Washington, DC), January 24, 1854.

42. Sewell, *Ballots for Freedom*, 264; Wilentz, *Rise of American Democracy*, 678–79.

43. *Lancaster (PA) Gazette*, March 16, 1854; *Summit County (OH) Beacon*, March 29, 1854; CMC to SPC, March 12, 1854.

44. Walther, *Shattering*, 44–45; Sewell, *Ballots for Freedom*, 264.

45. Letter reprinted in *Anti-Slavery Bugle* (New Lisbon, OH), June 17, 1854.

46. Letter reprinted in *Anti-Slavery Bugle* (New Lisbon, OH), June 17, 1854.

47. *Wilmington (NC) Journal*, June 16, 1854; *Richmond (VA) Enquirer*, June 9, 1854; *Huntsville (AL) Democrat*, June 22, 1854.

48. *Washington Sentinel*, June 8, 1854; *Buffalo Commercial*, June 8, 1854.

49. *New York Daily Herald*, June 6, 1854.

50. Howard, "Clay and Origins," 54.

51. Howard, "Clay and Origins," 51; *Summit County (OH) Beacon*, July 26, 1854.

52. Walther, *Shattering*, 57–58; Holt, *Fate of Their Country*, 113–15.

53. Freehling, *Road to Disunion*, 2:88–89; Sewell, *Ballots for Freedom*, 270–77; Brooks, *Liberty Power*, 196–201; *Kentucky Tribune* (Danville), August 3, 1855; *Louisville Daily Journal*, September 1, 1855; quotation from *Kentucky Tribune* (Danville), September 21, 1855.

54. Holt, *Fate of Their Country*, 112–13; CMC to SPC, August 1, 1854, SPC Papers, HSP.

55. *Anti-Slavery Bugle* (New Lisbon, OH), March 31, 1855; Walther, *Shattering*, 59–65; *Wayne County (PA) Herald*, February 1, 1855; *Poughkeepsie (NY) Journal*, February 3, 1855; *Anti-Slavery Bugle* (New Lisbon, OH), March 10, 1855; CMC to WHS, February 6, 1855, WHS Papers, LOC.

56. *Boston Evening Transcript*, September 14, 1854; *Brooklyn Daily Eagle*, September 16, 1854; *Herald of Freedom* (Bethel, CT), September 29, 1854; entry for September 29, 1854, CMC Journal/Daybook, SC-UKY.

57. CMC to BJC, November 26, 1854, Clay Family Papers, SC-UKY; *Baltimore Sun*, February 16, 1855; deed of sale for "Daniel," March 14, 1855, Clay Family Papers, SC-UKY; bill of sale for "Locomotive" and "Republic," March 15, 1855, Clay Family Papers, SC-UKY.

58. CMC to John G. Fee, April 5, 1855, John G. Fee Papers, SC-BC; CMC to SPC, May 18, 1855, SPC Papers, HSP; CMC to WHS, June 6, 1855, WHS Papers, LOC.

59. Clay, *Life*, 570; Fee, *Autobiography*, 94–100; Wilson, *Berea College*, 12–17.

60. Clay, *Life*, 75; *Anti-Slavery Bugle* (New Lisbon, OH), July 28, 1855.

61. *Anti-Slavery Bugle* (New Lisbon, OH), July 28, 1855; CMC to SPC, June 4, 1855, SPC Papers, HSP.

62. *Anti-Slavery Bugle* (New Lisbon, OH), July 28, 1855. For more on the breakdown between armed and nonviolent opposition to slavery, see essays in McKivigan and Harrold, *Anti-Slavery Violence*; Jackson, *Force and Freedom*; Pease and Pease, "Confrontation and Abolition"; and Demos, "Antislavery Movement," 522–26.

63. Clay, *Life*, 76–77; *Louisville Daily Journal*, July 28, 1855; *Louisville Courier*, reprinted in *Glasgow (KY) Weekly Times*, August 2, 1855; *Washington Sentinel*, September 1, 1855.

64. *Indiana Republican* (Danville), December 7, 1855.

65. Clay, *Life*, 76; *New-York Tribune*, reprinted in *Anti-Slavery Bugle* (New Lisbon, OH), September 24, 1853.

66. CMC to John G. Fee, July 8, 1855, John G. Fee Papers, SC-BC.

CHAPTER 7

1. *National Era* (Washington, DC), August 9, 1855.

2. *National Era* (Washington, DC), August 9, 16, 1855.

3. Sewell, *Ballots for Freedom*, 270–75; Julian, "First Republican National Convention," 317.

4. Sewell, *Ballots for Freedom*, 278–79; Julian, "First Republican National Convention," 316–17.

5. Julian, "First Republican National Convention," 319–20.

6. CMC to BJC, January 5, 1856, and inventory of debt, February 20, 1856, in Clay Family Papers, SC-UKY; Clay, *Life*, 537; *Louisville Daily Courier*, February 28, 1856.

7. *Kinston (NC) American Advocate*, April 24, 1856; CMC to BJC, February 23, 1856, Clay Family Papers, SC-UKY.

8. *Brooklyn Daily Eagle*, April 3, 1856; *Wayne County (PA) Herald*, April 3, 1856; *Rock Island (IL) Argus*, April 8, 1856; *Vicksburg Daily Whig*, April 17, 1856. Other denunciations appear in *Wilmington (NC) Daily Herald*, March 29, 1856; and *Buffalo Morning Express*, March 29, 1856.

9. *National Era* (Washington, DC), April 10, 1856; *Liberator* (Boston), April 11, 1856.

10. CMC to John Fee, December 18, 1855, and Fee to CMC, April [n.d.], 1856, John G. Fee Papers, SC-BC.

11. Stowe, *Uncle Tom's Cabin*, 8–9; Brooks, *Liberty Power*, 169–70.

12. CMC bill of property, April 1856, Clay Family Papers, SC-UKY; CMC to SPC, May 10, 1856, SPC Papers, HSP.

13. Clay, *Life*, 538; Smiley, *Lion of White Hall*, 156; CMC to BJC, February 23, 1856; Clay bill of property, April 1856; CMC to SPC, May 10, 1856.

14. CMC to SPC, May 10, 1856.

15. *Richmond (IN) Palladium*, April 17, 1856; *Lancaster (PA) Saturday Express*, May 31, 1856.

16. Walther, *Shattering*, 89; Smith, *Stormy Present*, 98–99. On the confluence of violence and mainstream politics by the 1850s, see Freeman, *Field of Blood*.

17. *Kansas Tribune* (Kansas City), April 21, 1856.

18. Sewell, *Ballots for Freedom*, 281–89.

19. Sewell, *Ballots for Freedom* 285–89, Chase quoted on 285.

20. Fee, *Autobiography*, 103–5; Ellis, Everman, and Sears, *Madison County*, 124–26.

21. Fee, *Autobiography*, 103–5; Ellis, Everman, and Sears, *Madison County*, 124–26.

22. Clay, *Life*, 234–36.

23. Clay, *Life*, 234–36.

24. *New York Times*, August 21, 1856.

25. *National Era* (Washington, DC), September 11, 1856; crowd estimate from Howard, "Clay and Origins," 64; *Wellsboro (PA) Gazette*, September 18, 1856; *Louisville Daily Courier*, August 4, 1856.

26. *Pomeroy (OH) Weekly Telegraph*, August 5, 1856; *Baltimore Sun*, September 25, 1856; *Louisville Daily Courier*, October 4, 1856; *Elyria (OH) Independent Democrat*, October 15, 1856; Smiley, *Lion of White Hall*, 158.

27. Holt, *Fate of Their Country*, 118; CMC to SPC, October 9, 1856, SPC Papers, HSP; *Louisville Daily Courier*, September 29, 1856.

28. See land rental ledger from 1858, Clay Family Papers, SC-UKY; *Wisconsin State Journal* (Madison), May 11, 1857; CMC to WHS, April 18, 1858, WHS Papers, LOC.

29. Sewell, *Ballots for Freedom*, 314–17; Foner, *Free Soil*, 119–22. For a full explanation of this Republican trope, see Oakes, *Scorpion's Sting*, esp. 33–35.

30. Sewell, *Ballots for Freedom*, 318–19, quotation on 319.

31. Sewell, *Ballots for Freedom*, 315–16.

32. Frederickson, "Antislavery Racist," 28; Helper, *Impending Crisis*, 98–99; Walther, *Shattering*, 128–30. Helper, for instance, erroneously argued, for example, that Northern hay was worth more than the combined total of the South's most important commodities, including cotton, sugar, tobacco, and rice. He also wildly inflated the price of the average acre of land in the North compared to the South.

33. Helper, *Impending Crisis*, 124, 382, 189; Brown, *Southern Outcast*, 118n54; *Chicago Tribune*, September 26, 1857; *New England Farmer* (Boston), December 18, 1858.

34. Smiley, *Lion of White Hall*, 162; CMC to WHS, July 10, August 8, 1858, WHS Papers, LOC.

35. Holt, *Election of 1860*, 16–20; CMC to WHS, July 10, 1858.

36. *Enterprise and Vermonter* (Vergennes), October 29, 1858.

37. *Speeches and Debates of Lincoln and Douglas*, 20–21, 9, 69.

38. *Chicago Tribune*, October 16, 1858; Goodwin, *Team of Rivals*, 210.

39. Holt, *Election of 1860*, 24; CMC to WHS, November 20, 1857, April 18, July 10, 1858, WHS Papers, LOC.

40. CMC to SPC, March 6, 1857, Samuel P. Chase Papers, HSP.

41. *Chardon (OH) Jeffersonian Democrat*, November 25, 1859; *Louisville Daily Courier*, October 28, 1859.

42. Fee, *Autobiography*, 144–56, quotation on 147.

43. John G. Fee to CMC, February 28, 1860, CMC Collection, SC-BC.

44. *Speech, January 10, 1860*, 1–11, 15–16.

45. *Speech, January 10, 1860*, 3–4.

46. *Wisconsin State Journal* (Madison), January 20, 1860.

47. *Wheeling (VA) Daily Intelligencer*, January 24, 1860; *Cleveland Daily Leader*, February 24, 1860.

48. *New York Times*, January 17, 1860.

49. *New York Times*, February 16, 1860; *New-York Tribune*, reprinted in *Steuben Republican* (Angola, IN), March 10, 1860. Adam I. P. Smith argues that "Conservative" was a widely applied label before the war, used by Americans of various political backgrounds to describe persons who valued political stability, devotion to the Union, and a "measured, mature approach to the problems of the world." *Stormy Present*, 5.

50. *New-York Tribune*, reprinted in *St. Joseph (MO) Weekly Free Democrat*, April 7, 1860; *Bangor (ME) Whig and Daily Courier*, April 10, 1860.

51. *Chicago Tribune*, August 18, 1859; *Bucyrus (OH) Weekly Journal*, March 1, 1860; Clay, *Life*, 244–46.

52. Goodwin, *Team of Rivals*, 214; Clay, *Life*, 241–43. Scholars routinely treat Clay's judgment of Seward's speech to show how it lost him support from uncompromising Republicans without acknowledging that this pronouncement appeared in Clay's autobiography (and nowhere else) a full twenty-six years after he had read it. See, e.g., Egerton, *Year of Meteors*, 118; and Goodwin, *Team of Rivals*, 214.

53. Clay, *Life*, 243–47; CMC to Thurlow Weed, March 8, 1860, quoted in Smiley, *Lion of White Hall*, 165; Charles Sumner to CMC, March 13, 1860, CMC Collection, LMU.

54. *Harper's Weekly Magazine*, May 12, 1860.

55. Holt, *Election of 1860*, 202–5.

56. Isley, *Horace Greeley*, 266.

57. *Chicago Tribune*, May 19, 1860; Clay, *Life*, 250.

58. *Cincinnati Gazette* quoted in *Chicago Tribune*, May 31, 1860.

59. *Chicago Tribune*, May 19, 1860.

CHAPTER 8

1. SPC to CMC, May 30, 1860, CMC Collection, LMU.

2. CMC to Abraham Lincoln, May 21, 1860, in Mearns, *Lincoln Papers*, 1:246. Lincoln to CMC, May 26, 1860, in Basler, *Collected Works of Lincoln*, 53–54.

3. *Chicago Tribune*, July 12, 1860.

4. Holt, *Election of 1860*, 75, 202.

5. Indiana letter quoted in Smiley, *Lion of White Hall*, 169; *Chicago Tribune*, July 12, 1860; Holt, *Election of 1860*, 137.

6. Clay spoke in Owensville, New Harmony, Evansville, Newburgh, New Albany, Vincennes, Terre Haute, and Indianapolis. *Evansville (IN) Daily Journal*, July 14, 1860; *Louisville Daily Courier*, July 16, 23, 1860; *Wabash Express* (Terre Haute, IN), July 18, 1860.

7. On the origin story of the Wide-Awakes, see *Bucyrus (OH) Weekly Journal*, June 14, 1860; and *New York Herald*, reprinted in *Muscatine (IA) Weekly Journal*, October 5, 1860. See also Grinspan, *Wide Awake*.

8. Grinspan, "'Young Men for War,'" 360–62; *Evansville (IN) Daily Journal*, July 18, 1860; *Louisville Daily Courier*, July 16, 23, 1860.

9. *Evansville (IN) Daily Journal*, July 26, 1860; *Seymour (IN) Times*, reprinted in *Evansville (IN) Daily Journal*, July 23, 1860; *Evansville (IN) Daily Journal*, July 26, 1860.

10. Lincoln to Caleb Smith, July 28, 1860, and Lincoln to CMC, July 20, 1860, in Basler, *Collected Works of Lincoln*, 85, 87–88; *Chicago Tribune*, August 17, 1860; *Louisville Daily Journal*, October 26, 1860; *Bangor (ME) Daily Whig and Courier*, October 27, 1860; *Salem (IL) Weekly Advocate*, November 1, 1860.

11. Clay, *Life*, 251.

12. BJC and CMC settlement, November 22, 1860, and CMC to Martha Clay Davenport, November 25, 1860, Clay Family Papers, SC-UKY. See rumors of Clay's appointment in *Alexandria (VA) Gazette*, December 1, 1860; *Nebraska Advertiser* (Brownville), December 6, 1860; and *Dawson's Ft. Wayne (IN) Daily Times*, December 4, 1860.

13. John Hendershott to Lincoln, December 8, 1860, Abraham Lincoln Papers, LOC.

14. Daniel Breck visited Lincoln on November 16, 1860. Burlingame, *With Lincoln*, 10–11.

15. CMC to Lincoln, January 10, 1861, Abraham Lincoln Papers, LOC. In his autobiography in 1886, Clay claimed that Lincoln had all but promised him that he would be made secretary of war, but the information he cites in the letter of January 10 makes clear that any intimations of his appointment had come from the national press and other party officials rather than from Lincoln himself. Clay, *Life*, 250.

16. Clay, *Life*, 250.

17. CMC to BJC, January 12, 1861, Clay Family Papers, SC-UKY.

18. *Wisconsin State Journal* (Madison), November 30, 1860; *Burlington Weekly Free Press*, December 14, 1860.

19. Wilentz, *Rise of American Democracy*, 780–81.

20. Sowle, "Cassius Clay," 144–49; Adams, "Diary entry for January 23, 1861."

21. *National Republican* (Washington, DC), January 28, 1861.

22. *New York Daily Herald*, January 28, 1861; SPC to CMC, January 28, 1861, CMC Collection, LMU.

23. CMC to Lincoln, February 6, 1861, Abraham Lincoln Papers, LOC.

24. WHS to Lincoln, March 11, 1861, in Mearns, *Lincoln Papers*, 2:478–79.

25. Barnes, *Foreign Service*, 68; Carman and Luthin, *Lincoln and Patronage*, 79.

26. Clay, *Life*, 253–56; WHS to CMC, letter of appointment, March 20, 1861, CMC Collection, LMU.

27. Barnes, *Foreign Service*, 75, 86–88, 108–10; CMC to Lincoln, March 28, 1861, in Mearns, *Lincoln Papers*, 2:495.

28. Carman and Luthin, *Lincoln and Patronage*, 84; CMC to Montgomery Blair, telegram, March 27, 1861, in Mearns, *Lincoln Papers*, 2:493; CMC to Lincoln, March 28, 1861; Barnes, *Foreign Service*, 113.

29. Berry, *Voices*, 231; R. P. White to BJC, December 11, 1861, Clay Family Papers, SC-UKY; *Anti-Slavery Bugle* (New Lisbon, OH), April 27, 1861; *1860 Census*.

30. Russell, *My Diary*, 33–34; Foreman, *World on Fire*, 4.

31. Lockwood and Lockwood, *Siege of Washington*, 23; Foreman, *World on Fire*, 11.

32. *New York Times*, April 19, 1861.

33. *Buffalo Commercial*, April 20, 1861; Nicolay and Hay, *Abraham Lincoln*, 4:105–6; Lockwood and Lockwood, *Siege of Washington*, 94; Theodore Talbot to CMC, April 24, 1861, CMC Collection, LMU.

34. Dennett, *Lincoln and Civil War*, 7–8.

35. William Ross Wallace to CMC, April 23, 1861, CMC Collection, LMU.

36. J. W. Gordon to CMC, April 21, 1861, and Clarence Eytinge to CMC, April 22, 1861, CMC Collection, LMU; CMC to Lincoln, May 11, 1861, in Mearns, *Lincoln Papers*, 2:605.

37. Monoghan, *Diplomat in Carpet Slippers*, 95–96; Foreman, *World on Fire*, 89–103.

38. CMC to WHS, May 22, 1861, in Mearns, *Lincoln Papers*, 2:612–13; Foreman, *World on Fire*, 95–97; copy of letter to *Times* (London), May 20, 1861, in Clay Family Papers, SC-UKY; Jordan and Pratt, *Europe and the American Civil War*, 14–15.

39. Speech of CMC in Paris, May 29, 1861, CMC Collection, FHS.

40. *New York Times*, June 22, 1861; Henry Adams to Charles Francis Adams Jr., June 10, 1861, and to Horace Gay Jr., June 17, 1861, in *Letters of Henry Adams*, 238, 241–42.

41. CMC to WHS, May 22, 1861, and WHS to Lincoln, June 10, 1861, Abraham Lincoln Collection, LOC.

CHAPTER 9

1. *Guardian*, March 23, 2016.

2. Dixon, *Modernisation of Russia*, 81; Kolchin, *Unfree Labor*, 41.

3. Dixon, *Modernisation of Russia*, 85–86; Freeze, *Russia*, 125.

4. Chubarov, *Fragile Empire*, 73–75; Hingley, *Tsars*, 261.

5. William Cassius Goodloe to David Goodloe, reprinted in Robertson, *Kentuckian*, 44–47; *Message of the President . . . Second Session of the Thirty-Seventh Congress*, June 21, 1861, 303–5.

6. Waldmon, *Lincoln and the Russians*, 124–25; *Message of the President . . . Second Session of the Thirty-Seventh Congress*, May 6, 1861, 293–97, and August 3, 12, 1861, 306–7; CMC to Abraham Lincoln, July 25, 1861, Abraham Lincoln Papers, LOC.

7. Clay, *Life*, 295–96.

8. CMC to Lincoln, July 25, 1861; CMC to SPC, November 22, 1861, SPC Papers, LOC; CMC to BJC, September 25, November 23, 1861, Clay Family Papers, SC-UKY; Ellison, *Man Seen But Once*, 119.

9. CMC to MJC, February 5, 1862, White Hall Historical Collection, SC-EKU; McPherson, *Battle Cry of Freedom*, 323–24; Clay, *Life*, 299.

10. CMC to MJC, February 5, 1862; CMC to Lincoln, March 1, 1862, Abraham Lincoln Papers, LOC; *Chicago Tribune*, January 21, 1862.

11. CMC to Lincoln, March 1, 1862.

12. Clay, *Life*, 299–300; CMC to MJC, May 14, 1862, White Hall Historical Collection, SC-EKU; CMC to MJC, June 26, 1862, Clay Family Papers, SC-UKY.

13. CMC to MJC, July 7, 1862, White Hall Historical Collection, SC-EKU; Clay, *Life*, 539; CMC to Lincoln, June 17, 1862, Abraham Lincoln Papers, LOC; Bayard

Taylor to Hannibal Hamlin, June 20, 1862, Abraham Lincoln Papers, LOC; CMC to MJC, May 14, 1862.

14. Taylor, *Embattled Freedom*, 2–4; Varon, *Armies of Deliverance*, 35.

15. CMC to Lincoln, September 27, 1861, Abraham Lincoln Papers, LOC; McPherson, *Battle Cry of Freedom*, 352–54.

16. *Louisville Daily Courier*, December 13, 1861.

17. McPherson, *Battle Cry of Freedom*, 357–58; Carman, *Lincoln and Patronage*, 131; Varon, *Armies of Deliverance*, 108; Oakes, *Crooked Path to Abolition*, 187–88.

18. Freehling, *South vs. South*, 104–5; Varon, *Armies of Deliverance*, 108–9; Oakes, *Freedom National*, 290.

19. McPherson, *Battle Cry of Freedom*, 503–5; Oakes, *Freedom National*, 226–55.

20. *New-York Tribune*, August 20, 1862; Lincoln quoted in Varon, *Armies of Deliverance*, 113–14; McPherson, *Battle Cry of Freedom*, 508–9. On Lincoln's state abolition strategy, see Oakes, *Crooked Path to Abolition*, 187–204.

21. Smiley, *Lion of White Hall*, 187; *Elyria (OH) Independent Democrat*, August 20, 1862; *New York Times*, August 22, 1862.

22. Simon C. Pomeroy to CMC, August 14, 1862, and Wendell Phillips to CMC, August 19, 1862, CMC Collection, LMU.

23. *New York Times*, August 9, 19, September 6, 1862; *Leavenworth (KS) Times*, August 22, 1862.

24. *New-York Tribune* reprinted in *Pittsburgh Daily Post*, August 23, 1862.

25. *Cleveland Daily Leader*, August 27, 1862; CMC to MJC, August 23, 1862, White Hall Historical Collection, SC-EKU; Clay, *Life*, 311; Hafendorfer, *Battle of Richmond, Kentucky*, 62–66.

26. Clay, *Life*, 310; Smiley, *Lion of White Hall*, 191–92; Ellison, *Man Seen But Once*, 126–27. More evidence that contradicts the idea that Lincoln would have sent Clay on such an errand comes from the memoirs of Jeremiah Curtin, who served as Clay's secretary of legation during his second term in Russia. Curtin recalled Senator Lafayette Foster of Connecticut telling him that Lincoln had explained that he was reappointing Clay to the Russian mission because the president "was afraid he would join the anti-Unionists in Kentucky and do harm in that state." Curtin, *Memoirs of Jeremiah Curtin*, 178.

27. *Huntington (VA) Democrat*, September 11, 1862; *Rutland Weekly Herald*, September 11, 1862.

28. *Rutland Weekly Herald*, September 11, 1862; CMC to MJC, September 2, 1862, in McQueen, *Clay: Freedom's Champion*, 138.

29. Hess, *Civil War in the West*, 96–97; CMC to MJC, September 2, 1862.

30. Mullins and Mullins, *White Hall*, 31, 57–58; CMC to MJC, March 6, 1862, CMC Collection, FHS; MJC to BJC, March 23 and April 1, 1862, Clay Family Papers, SC-UKY.

31. Order of the Headquarters of the Army, September 12, 1862, CMC Collection, LMU; *Cleveland Daily Leader*, September 13, 1862.

32. Goodwin, *Team of Rivals*, 482; *New York Times*, September 25, 1862.

33. Burlingame, *Inside Lincoln's White House*, 41.

34. Goodwin, *Team of Rivals*, 467; CMC to Lincoln, September 29, 1862 and October 21, 1862, Abraham Lincoln Papers, LOC.

35. *Cleveland Daily Leader*, November 7, 1862; *Wisconsin State Journal* (Madison), November 14, 1862; *Chicago Tribune*, November 10, 1862.

36. MJC to Ann Clay, January 4, 1863; CMC to BJC, April 15, 1862; and MJC to BJC, April 8, 12, 1862, all in Clay Family Papers, SC-UKY.

37. Simon Cameron to CMC, November 15, 1862, CMC Collection, LMU; Pease and Randall, *Diary of Browning*, entry for December 12, 1862, 1:595; Carman, *Lincoln and the Patronage*, 84–85; Bayard Taylor to Edmund Stedman, February 25, 1863, *Unpublished Letters of Bayard Taylor*, 63–64; Joseph Casey to Cameron, November 3, 1862 quoted in Norman, *Distant Friends*, 332.

38. *Standard* (London), February 6, 1863; *Wisconsin State Journal* (Madison), March 23, 1863; *New York Times*, February 26, 1863.

39. CMC to BJC, September 2, 1863, Clay Family Papers, SC-UKY; CMC to Lincoln, February 26, 1863, Abraham Lincoln Papers, LOC.

40. *New York Times*, February 26, 1863.

41. MJC to BJC, April 15, March 23, 1862, and MJC to Ann Clay, January 4, 1863, Clay Family Papers, SC-UKY.

CHAPTER 10

1. CMC to MJC, April 30, 1863, CMC Collection, FHS.

2. Golder, "Russian Fleet," 802–3. Historian Norman E. Saul, however, contends that the move was designed to be a "dramatic demonstration of new Russian naval capability in the Atlantic itself." *Distant Friends*, 343. CMC to Anson Burlingame, November 23, 1863, Anson Burlingame and Edward L. Burlingame Papers, LOC. Thanks to Aaron Sheehan-Dean for sharing this letter, which I first became aware of while reading Gregory Downs's *Second Revolution*, 28, 151n61.

3. Saul, *Distant Friends*, 360–70. For correspondence regarding the telegraph, see *Message of the President . . . First Session of the Thirty-Eighth Congress*, 874–87; and Curtin, *Memoirs*, 176–77. For mention of funds sent back to Kentucky, see CMC to MJC, July 1863, October 8, 1864, CMC Collection, FHS; and CMC to BJC, October 9, 1863, BJC Papers, LOC. The telegraph project was never completed. Western Union called an abrupt halt in to the project in early 1867 on the successful installation of the Atlantic cable. This rendered both the extensive corporate investment and the stock shares worthless, but by that time, Clay had reaped the windfall. WHS to CMC, March 28, 1867, in *Executive Documents . . . Second Session of the Fortieth Congress*, 388.

4. Political broadside, July 29, 1863, Clay Family Papers, SC-UKY.

5. Political broadside, July 29, 1863; Berry, *Voices*, 330, 239, 242–45, 264–66.

6. CMC to BJC, September 2, 1863, Clay Family Papers, SC-UKY.

7. CMC to BJC, September 2, 1863; Jenkins and Peck, *Congress and First Civil Rights*, 44–47.

8. CMC to BJC, September 2, 1863.

9. Sumner, "Domestic Relations," 507–29. For an example of moderate opposition to Sumner's plan, see *Speech of the Hon. Montgomery Blair*, 6; Varon, *Armies of Deliverance*, 300–302; and Gallagher and Waugh, *American War*, 102.

10. *Speech of the Hon. Montgomery Blair*, 4.

11. CMC to BJC, October 9, 1863; CMC to SPC, September 6, 1863, SPC Papers, LOC.

12. CMC to Burlingame, November 23, 1863.

13. Berry, *Voices*, 345–46, 357; *Congressional Globe*, 38th Cong., 1st Sess., February 10, 1864, 579.

14. BJC to Ann Clay, March 12, 1864, Clay Family Papers, SC-UKY; Berry, *Voices*, 408–9.

15. MJC to BJC, June 28, August 14, 1864, Clay Family Papers, SC-UKY; Franklin Clay, Memoranda of the Result of Special Examination, January 28, 1875, Louisville, KY, in *U.S. Freedmen's Bureau Records, 1865–1878*. Based on the rolls for Company I of the 109th USCT Infantry, the other men likely included George Clay and Henry Clay. See entries for both men at National Park Service, *Soldiers and Sailors Database*.

16. Author Betty Ellison claims that Mary Jane earned as much as $80,000 from her business enterprises but does not support this figure with specific evidence. *Man Seen But Once*, 141. Kuby, "Mary Jane Warfield Clay," 69; MJC to Laura Clay, May 23, 1864, quoted in Fuller, *Laura Clay*, 5–6.

17. MJC to BJC, July 21, 1864, Clay Family Papers, SC-UKY; Clay, *Life*, 41, 556; Botkin, *Civil War Treasury*, 515–16.

18. Ellison, *Man Seen But Once*, 103–5; Mullins and Mullins, *History of White Hall*, 58–65.

19. BJC to Ann Clay, April 26, 1864, Clay Family Papers, SC-UKY.

20. CMC to BJC, June 4, 1864, BJC Papers, LOC; CMC to BJC, December 9, 1864, Clay Family Papers, SC-UKY. Although consanguineous marriage between cousins had been a common feature of European nobility in centuries past, Americans in the mid-nineteenth century viewed it as undesirable.

21. *Congressional Globe*, 38th Cong., 2d Sess., January 9, 1865, 181–82; Berry, *Voices*, 424; Jenkins and Peck, *Congress and First Civil Rights*, 54–56.

22. CMC to WHS, August 18, 1865, in *Despatches from U.S. Ministers to Russia*, vol. 20.

23. CMC to WHS, August 18, 1865.

24. CMC to WHS, August 18, 1865.

25. CMC to WHS, October 29, 1865, in *Despatches from U.S. Ministers to Russia*, vol. 20; Clay, *Life*, 70.

26. Jenkins and Peck, *Congress and First Civil Rights*, 87; Foner, *Reconstruction*, 198–206; Gallagher and Waugh, *American War*, 201.

27. CMC to WHS, February 7, 1866, in *Executive Documents . . . Second Session of the Thirty-Ninth Congress*, 401–2.

28. Clay's letter reprinted in *Daily Milwaukee News*, April 14, 1866. Brutus Clay experienced the so-called overreach of the Freedmen's Bureau firsthand. After returning home from Congress to Kentucky, Brutus filed suit against the state's military officials for illegally enticing his enslaved laborers away. In response, they filed a countersuit against him through the Freedmen's Bureau, accusing him of "holding blacks to labor without pay" because he continued to enslave women who were due their freedom by virtue of the service of their male partners in the Union Army. Berry, *Voices*, 455; *Detroit Free Press*, November 4, 1865.

29. Foner, *Reconstruction*, 261–63.
30. Clay, *Life*, 363–64; Saul, *Distant Friends*, 254–56.
31. Smiley, *Lion of White Hall*, 205–8.
32. *Synopsis of Forty Chapters*, 7; *Louisville Daily Journal*, January 21, 1868.
33. *Synopsis of Forty Chapters*, 10–11.
34. Pease and Randall, *Diary of Browning*, entry for April 2, 1867, 2:141; Smiley, *Lion of White Hall*, 207–8; Clay, *Life*, 472; CMC to WHS, April 30, May 2, 19, 1867, in *Despatches from U.S. Ministers to Russia*, vol. 21.
35. CMC to WHS, May 10, 1867, in *Despatches from U.S. Ministers to Russia*, vol. 21; Clay, *Life*, 472; Bayard Taylor to Edmund Stedman, February 25, 1863, in Schultz, *Unpublished Letters of Taylor*, 63–64; *Cleveland Daily Leader*, November 16, 1865.
36. Clay, *Life*, 540.
37. Woldman, *Lincoln and the Russians*, 279–81; Saul, *Distant Friends*, 388–96; CMC to WHS, May 10, 1867; Smiley, *Lion of White Hall*, 212.
38. Smiley, *Lion of White Hall*, 210–12; CMC to WHS, December 24, 1867, *Despatches from U.S. Ministers to Russia*, vol. 21.
39. *Louisville Daily Courier*, April 18, 1868; CMC to Mary Barr Clay Herrick, February 28, 1868, CMC Collection, FHS.
40. CMC to Ulysses S. Grant, February 4, 1868, in Simon, *Papers of Grant*, 502–4.
41. CMC to Grant, February 4, 1868.
42. CMC to Grant, February 4, 1868; Benedict, "Politics of Reconstruction," 101–2.

CHAPTER 11

1. *Kansas Weekly Commonwealth* (Topeka), October 14, 1869.
2. CMC to Anson Burlingame, November 23, 1863, Anson Burlingame and Edward L. Burlingame Papers, LOC.
3. Ellison, *Man Seen But Once*, 143; *Greensboro (NC) Patriot*, May 12, 1870.
4. Summers, *Ordeal of the Reunion*, 217–18; Chernow, *Grant*, 665–67.
5. *New York Times*, January 20, 1870; *New York Daily Herald*, January 20, 1870.
6. Smiley, *Lion of Whitehall*, 217–18; *Richmond (VA) Dispatch*, January 21, 1870; Ellison, *Man Seen But Once*, 151.
7. Slap, *Doom of Reconstruction*, 90–107; Benedict, "Politics of Reconstruction," 124–25.
8. Ulysses S. Grant quoted in Chernow, *Grant*, 701; Lemann, *Redemption*, 121.
9. Foner, *Reconstruction*, 454–55.
10. Summers, *Ordeal of the Reunion*, 271. For a discussion of Americans' discomfort with a standing army in peacetime, see Lang, *Wake of War*.
11. Slap, *Doom of Reconstruction*, 107. On this strain of Republican reform, see Benedict, "Reform Republicans."
12. CMC to Henry Watterson, April 19, 1871, Henry Watterson Papers, LOC; CMC to William Larimer, printed in *New Orleans Republican*, August 16, 1871.
13. Summers, *Ordeal of the Reunion*, 268, 305–6; Slap, *Doom of Reconstruction*, 116–18.

14. SPC to August Belmont, May 30, 1868, in Schuckers, *Life and Public Services of Chase*, 585; Benedict, "Chase and Constitutional Politics," 141–43; Foner, *Reconstruction*, 497.

15. Clarke, *George Julian*, 334–36.

16. Clarke, *George Julian*, 334–36.

17. SPC to Peter Clark et al., March 30, 1870, in Schuckers, *Life and Public Services of Chase*, 531–32. For a full examination of Chase's consistency in constitutional thinking, see Benedict, "Chase and Constitutional Politics."

18. McPherson, "Grant or Greeley?" McPherson contends that "in the Liberal lexicon, 'amnesty' meant more than mere removal of political disabilities; it meant total forgiveness of the Union's former enemies, plus a willingness to entrust to their stewardship all the results of northern victory, including the enfranchisement and equal rights of freedmen." "Grant or Greeley?," 58. Though he estimates that three-quarters of antebellum abolitionists supported Grant in the election of 1872, he also considered the support that the other one quarter gave to the Liberal Republicans to be remarkable. "Grant or Greeley?," 54.

19. *Nashville Republican Banner*, January 31, 1872; *St. Louis Republican*, October 5, 1871.

20. *Nashville Republican Banner*, January 31, 1872.

21. Frederick Douglass to CMC, July 26, 1871, CMC Collection, LMU.

22. McPherson, "Grant or Greeley?," 51; Slap, *Doom of Reconstruction*, 188–94.

23. *Chicago Tribune*, September 2, June 27, 1872; *Lancaster (PA) Intelligencer*, July 31, 1872; Whitelaw Reid to CMC, May 16, 1872, CMC Collection, LMU; *Courier-Journal* (Louisville) article, reprinted in *Chicago Tribune*, June 13, 1872.

24. *New National Era* (Washington, DC), June 27, 1872.

25. Greeley, *Letters from Texas*, 38–39.

26. Summers, *Ordeal of the Reunion*, 365–66; Foner, *Reconstruction*, 509–11; Benedict, "Problem of Constitutionalism," 160, 166–67.

27. Clay, *Life*, 555; Richardson, *Clay: Firebrand of Freedom* 117–18; Ellison, *Man Seen But Once*, 94, 146. In 1894, Clay seemed to claim paternity of Launey, telling newspaper reporters that he had not done "as others have done—disown my flesh and blood—but had that child adopted and made the equal of my other children." *Courier-Journal* (Louisville), November 14, 1894.

28. Clay, *Life*, 547–48.

29. Clay, *Life*, 547–48; Ellison, *Man Seen But Once*, 150; Smiley, *Lion of Whitehall*, 225–26.

30. *Carlisle (PA) Valley Sentinel*, June 18, 1875; *Columbus Nebraska Era*, May 15, 1875. For another example of this mischaracterization, see "Southern Champion of Abolitionism," *Dallas Weekly Herald*, May 15, 1875; Marshall, *Confederate Kentucky*, 32–54; and *Chicago Tribune*, May 12, 1875.

31. Marshall, *Confederate Kentucky*, 32–54; *Chicago Tribune*, May 12, 1875; Berry, *Voices*, 498–99.

32. Lemann, *Redemption*, 73–47, 80–81.

33. Foner, *Reconstruction*, 559–60.

34. Foner, *Reconstruction*, 560; Lemann, *Redemption*, 122–23, 125–26, 129–32.

35. Clay, *Life*, 511. On the connection between the Republican laissez-faire ideology and their view of Southern state governments, see Benedict, "Problem of Constitutionalism," 160–67.

36. Smiley, "Clay and Mississippi Election of 1875," 252–62, 259–60; Clay, *Life*, 515.

37. Clay, *Life*, 512, 515–16.

38. Foner, *Reconstruction*, 562.

39. William Alexander Percy to CMC, November 17, 1875, CMC Collection, LMU; Clay, *Life*, iv–v.

40. Clay, *Life*, 504.

CHAPTER 12

1. Smiley, *Lion of Whitehall*, 231; McQueen, *Clay: Freedom's Champion*, 29; Richardson, *Clay: Firebrand of Freedom*, 140–42; Clay, *Life*, 550.

2. Divorce Petition of Cassius Marcellus Clay and Mary Jane Warfield Clay, December 29, 1877; *Washington Capital*, reprinted in *Harrisburg (PA) Telegraph*, November 29, 1886: the newspaper incorrectly referred to her as Anna rather than Anne; Fuller, *Laura Clay and the Woman's Rights Movement*, 17–18; Clay, *Life*, 550.

3. Mary Barr Clay to Laura Clay, February 26, 1866, and BJC to MJC, November 13, 1865, copies and transcripts from unidentified archive housed in the White Hall Collection, EKU. In the 1870 census, Sarah White, Frank Clay, and Jerry Clay appear to live in residences proximate to White Hall: Jerry Clay, 1870 census, www.ancestry.com.

4. Clay, *Life*, 555–56, 563–70; *Courier-Journal* (Louisville), November 18, 1891.

5. *Nashville Journal*, October 10, 1884.

6. Letter quoted in *Chicago Tribune*, August 13, 1884.

7. *Chicago Tribune*, August 13, 1884; *Courier-Journal* (Louisville), May 18, 1884.

8. Clay, "Race and the Solid South," 134–38.

9. Clay, "Race and the Solid South," 134–38.

10. Wilson, *Rise and Fall of Slave Power*, 628–35; Myers, "Writing of 'Rise and Fall,'" 144–62. For more on antislavery autobiography, see Roy, *Abolitionists Remember*; and Stauffer, "Remembering Abolitionists."

11. Clay, *Life*, 159–62, 259, 301.

12. Clay, *Life*, 310, 233, 258, 278, 284, 76–77, 237, 243, 571–72, 467–78; *Courier-Journal* (Louisville), July 23, 1903.

13. Clay, *Life*, 56–57; *Courier-Journal* (Louisville), May 18, 1884.

14. *New York Herald*, reprinted in *Indianapolis Journal*, December 18, 1887; Ellison, *Man Seen But Once*, 165; Clay, "Brave Kentucky Woman," 72; Clay, *Woman's Magazine*, 234–36, quotation on 236.

15. Fuller, *Laura Clay*, 22–27; Goan, *Simple Justice*, 25–38. Correspondence relating to the suffrage work of Mary Barr and Mary Jane Clay may be found in the CMC Collection, FHS. For Laura Clay's activities, see the Laura Clay Papers, SC-UKY.

16. Fuller, *Laura Clay*, 16–18; Kuby, "Mary Jane Warfield Clay," 72–74.

17. Smiley, *Lion of Whitehall*, 239; *Courier-Journal* (Louisville), November 18, 1894; Marshall, "Kentucky's Anti-Separate Coach Law"; Ellison, *Man Seen But Once*, 181.

18. *Boston Globe*, October 4, 1891; *Kentucky Leader* (Lexington), October 13, 1891.

19. *Kentucky Leader* (Lexington), November 10, 1894.

20. *Kentucky Leader* (Lexington), November 10, 1894; *Courier-Journal* (Louisville), November 14, 1894.

21. *Courier-Journal* (Louisville), November 14, 18, 1894.

22. *Owensboro (KY) Messenger*, December 1, 1894; *Courier-Journal* (Louisville), November 18, 1894.

23. *New York Journal*, February 28, 1897.

24. *New York Journal*, February 28, 1897.

25. *New York Journal*, November 28, 1897; McQueen, *Freedom's Champion*, 39–40.

26. *Courier-Journal* (Louisville), July 23, 1903; *Lexington Daily Leader*, April 6, 1900.

27. *Cincinnati Post*, July 22, 1904; *New York Times*, July 8, 1903; *Owensboro (KY) Messenger*, July 9, 1903; *Buffalo Enquirer*, July 7, 1903; *Brooklyn Citizen*, July 22, 1903; *Courier-Journal* (Louisville), July 23, 1903; Smiley, *Lion of Whitehall*, 243–45.

28. *Chicago Tribune*, July 23, 1903; *Detroit Free Press*, July 24, 1903. For other references to Clay as an abolitionist, see *Austin American-Statesman*, *Altoona (PA) Tribune*, and *Grand Island (NE) Independent*, all July 24, 1903; *Courier-Journal* (Louisville), July 23, 1903; and *New-York Tribune*, July 23, 1903. Multiple newspapers repeated the influence of Garrison's influence on Clay. See *Weekly Missoulian* (Missoula, MT) and *Vermont Phoenix* (Brattleboro), both July 24, 1903; and *New-York Tribune*, July 23, 1903.

29. *Birmingham News*, July 24, 1903; *Lexington Herald*, September 25, 1903.

30. Harrold, *American Abolitionism*, 4. For a succinct description of the definition and development of the Lost Cause, see Foster, *Ghosts of the Confederacy*, 4–7.

31. Clay, *Life*, 220–21.

32. Blight, *Race and Reunion*, 211, 4; Silber, *Romance of Reunion*, 105–23.

33. Novick, *That Noble Dream*, 229–30; Harrold, *American Abolitionism*, 5–6; Dillon, "Abolitionists," 500.

34. *Lexington Herald*, October 23, 1903, January 3, 1932; *Courier-Journal* (Louisville), August 9, 1936; *Lexington Leader*, January 20, 1939; *Richmond (KY) Register*, February 15, 1922; *Park City Daily News* (Bowling Green, KY), March 25, 1939; *Courier-Journal* (Louisville), January 1, 1942.

35. *Chicago Tribune*, August 31, September 7, 1947; *New York Times*, April 29, 1951.

36. Townsend, *Lincoln and His Wife's Home Town*, 112–36, 251–54, 283–86, quotation on 112; *Courier-Journal* (Louisville), January 31, 1960.

37. Townsend, "Lion of Whitehall," 7–8.

38. Townsend, "Lion of Whitehall," 7–9.

39. Townsend, "Lion of Whitehall," 9–10, 12–13, 15–17, 23–25.

40. Coleman, "William H. Townsend," 13–14.

41. *Courier-Journal* (Louisville), January 31, 1960.

42. Townsend, "Rage of the Aged Lion"; Catton, *Coming Fury*, 80.

43. Smiley, "'Emissary from Cousin Henry'" and "Clay and Mississippi Election of 1875"; Smiley, *Lion of White Hall*, viii.

44. *Courier-Journal* (Louisville), January 31, 1960.

45. *Courier-Journal* (Louisville), March 6, 1964. The story about Russell's speech by syndicated columnist Jack Anderson appeared in dozens of newspapers around the United States. See, e.g., *Charlotte (NC) News*, March 28, 1964; *Sheboygan (WI) Press*, March 30, 1964; and *Nashville Tennessean*, March 30, 1964.

46. *New York Times*, March 17, 1964.

47. For examples of the "new abolitionist" label, see Zinn, *SNCC*; and *Jackson (MS) Clarion-Ledger*, July 4, 1865.

48. *Lexington Herald-Leader*, May 31, 1951; Ellison, *Man Seen But Once*, 187–88.

49. Ellison, *Man Seen But Once*, 188–94. White Hall was referred to as a shrine until 1986. See Mullins and Mullins, *History of White Hall*, 149n377; and *Courier-Journal* (Louisville), September 17, 1971.

50. McQueen, *Freedom's Champion*, 95; *Courier-Journal* (Louisville), September 11, 1971.

51. *Courier-Journal* (Louisville), September 21, 1971.

CODA

1. *Atlanta Constitution*, March 12, November 24, 1962.

2. For examples of death notices, see *Memphis Daily Appeal*, June 3, 1870; and *Lexington Daily Herald*, June 10, 1939.

3. *Opelousas (LA) Daily World*, July 17, 1963. A sense of the frequency with which children were named Cassius Clay can be gleaned by a cursory search of US census records.

4. Eig, *Ali*, 3–4. For a detailed analysis of Ali's Kentucky genealogy, see Egerton, "Heritage of a Heavyweight."

5. "Remembering Muhammed Ali."

6. Eig, *Ali*, 153.

7. *Washington Post*, December 20, 2014.

8. Townsend, Osmond, and Phillips, "Where Cassius Clay Ends," 1151.

9. *Paducah (KY) Sun*, May 1, 1967; *St. Louis American*, reprinted in *Minneapolis Star Tribune*, April 13, 1967.

10. *New York Daily News*, March 21, 1964; Townsend, Osmond, and Phillips, "Where Cassius Clay Ends," 1155–56; Wagner, "Muhammad Ali"; the magazine was *Philadelphia Sunday Bulletin Magazine*, June 7, 1970, quoted in Ali, *Greatest*, 41.

11. Clay, *Writings*, 531; Ali, *Greatest*, 40–41.

12. Eig, *Ali*, 11–19; Ali, *Greatest*, 41; *Courier-Journal* (Louisville), September 17, 1971.

13. Lipsyte, "Ali"; Coates, "Costas to Ali."

14. Lipsyte, "Ali"; Coates, "Costas to Ali." It is worth noting that Coates did not mention that Clay retained slaves through the end of the Civil War.

15. Lipsyte, "Ali"; Coates, "Costas to Ali"; Coleman, "What's in a Name"; Peters, "Ali's Name Change"; "Ali Originally Named for Ardent Abolitionist."
16. Medved, "Story of Abolitionist Cassius Clay."
17. Medved, "Story of Abolitionist Cassius Clay."
18. Medved, "Story of Abolitionist Cassius Clay."

Bibliography

PRIMARY SOURCES

ARCHIVES
Filson Historical Society, Louisville, Kentucky
    Bodley Family Papers
    Bullitt Family Papers
    Cassius M. Clay Collection
    Sydney Payne Clay Papers
Historical Society of Pennsylvania, Philadelphia
    Salmon P. Chase Papers
Kentucky Department of Libraries and Archives, Frankfort
    Commonwealth v. Cassius M. Clay, 1843
    Commonwealth of Kentucky v. Emily, 1845
    Tax Lists, Fayette County
    Tax Lists, Madison County
Library of Congress, Washington, DC
    Anson Burlingame and Edward L. Burlingame Papers
    Salmon P. Chase Papers
    Brutus J. Clay Papers
    Abraham Lincoln Papers
    William H. Seward Papers
    Henry Watterson Papers
Abraham Lincoln Library and Museum, Lincoln Memorial University, Harrogate, Tennessee
    Cassius Marcellus Clay Collection
Mississippi State University Special Collections, Starkville
    Frank and Virginia Williams Collection of Lincolniana
Morgan Library and Museum, New York, New York
    Horace Greeley Collection
Special Collections and Archives, Berea College, Berea, Kentucky
    Cassius M. Clay Collection
    John G. Fee Papers
Special Collections and Archives, Eastern Kentucky University, Richmond
    Cassius M. Clay Collection
    White Hall Historical Collection
Special Collections and Archives, Transylvania University, Lexington, Kentucky
    J. Winston Coleman Scrapbook

Special Collections Research Center, University of Kentucky, Lexington
  Cassius M. Clay Journal and Papers
  Clay Family Papers
  Laura Clay Papers
  J. Winston Coleman Collection
  Wickliffe-Preston Papers

PERIODICALS

Atlantic Monthly
Congressional Globe
Lexington Observer and Reporter
New York Times
Harper's Weekly Magazine
Guardian (London)
Woman's Journal

  Chronicling America: Historic American Newspapers Database, Library of Congress
Lexington Intelligencer
New York Journal

  Newspapers.com Database, Ancestry
Alexandria (VA) Gazette
Atlanta Constitution
Altoona (PA) Tribune
American Observer (Morrisville, VT)
Anti-Slavery Bugle (New Lisbon, OH)
Austin American-Statesman
Baltimore Sun
Bangor (ME) Whig and Daily Courier
Belmont Chronicle (Saint Clairsville, OH)
Birmingham News
Boston Globe
Brandon (VT) Post
Brooklyn Citizen
Brooklyn Daily Eagle
Bucyrus (OH) Weekly Journal
Buffalo Commercial
Buffalo Enquirer
Buffalo Morning Express
Buffalo Weekly Republic
Burlington (VT) Weekly Free Press
Cadiz (OH) Sentinel
Carlisle (PA) Valley Sentinel
Carlisle (PA) Weekly Herald

Carolina Watchman (Salisbury, NC)
Cecil (MD) Whig
Chardon (OH) Jeffersonian Democrat
Charlotte News
Chicago Tribune
Cincinnati Herald
Cincinnati Enquirer
Cincinnati Post
Cleveland Daily Leader
Cleveland Herald
Columbus Nebraska Era
Courier-Journal (Louisville)
Daily Milwaukee News
Daily Selma Reporter
Dallas Weekly Herald
Danville (VT) North Star
Dawson's Ft. Wayne (IN) Daily Times
Detroit Free Press
Elyria (OH) Independent Democrat
Enterprise and Vermonter (Vergennes)
Evansville (IN) Daily Journal
Fayetteville (AR) Weekly Observer
Fremont (OH) Weekly Freeman
Gettysburg (PA) Compiler
Glasgow (KY) Weekly Times
Grand Island (NE) Independent
Green Bay (WI) Democrat
Green-Mountain Freeman (Montpelier, VT)
Greensboro (NC) Patriot
Harrisburg (PA) Telegraph
Hartford Courant
Herald of Freedom (Bethel, CT)
Huntington (VA) Democrat
Huntsville (AL) Democrat
Indiana American (Brookville)
Indiana Republican (Danville)
Jackson (MS) Clarion-Ledger

Jacksonville (AL) Republican
Kansas Tribune (Kansas City, KS)
Kansas Weekly Commonwealth (Topeka)
Kentucky Leader (Lexington)
Kentucky Tribune (Danville)
Kinston (NC) American Advocate
Lancaster (PA) Gazette
Lancaster (PA) Intelligencer
Leavenworth (KS) Times
Lexington Daily Leader
Lexington Gazette
Lexington Herald
Lexington Observer and Reporter
Liberator (Boston)
Livingston (MI) Courier
Livingston (MI) Democrat
Lorain (OH) Republican
Louisville Daily Courier
Louisville Daily Journal
Louisville Examiner
Memphis Daily Appeal
Memphis Enquirer
Milwaukee Daily Sentinel
Minneapolis Star Tribune
Mississippi Free Trader (Natchez)
Montgomery Daily Journal
Muscatine (IA) Weekly Journal
Nashville Journal
Nashville Republican Banner
Nashville Tennessean
Natchez (MS) Free Trader
National Era (Washington, DC)
National Republican (Washington, DC)
Nebraska Advertiser (Brownville)
New England Farmer (Boston)
New National Era (Washington, DC)
New Orleans Republican
New Orleans Times-Picayune
New York Daily Herald
New York Daily News
New-York Tribune
Niles National Register (Baltimore)
Ohio Statesman (Columbus)
Opelousas (LA) Daily World
Owensboro (KY) Messenger
Paducah (KY) Sun
Park City Daily News (Bowling Green, KY)
Philadelphia Public Ledger
Pittsburgh Daily Post
Pittsburgh Weekly Gazette
Pomeroy (OH) Weekly Telegraph
Portage (OH) Sentinel
Poughkeepsie (NY) Journal
Richmond (VA) Dispatch
Richmond (VA) Enquirer
Richmond (IN) Palladium
Richmond (KY) Register
Richmond (VA) Times
Rock Island (IL) Argus
Rutland (VT) Weekly Herald
Salem (IL) Weekly Advocate
Sandusky (OH) Clarion
Saturday Express (Lancaster, PA)
Seymour (IN) Times
Sheboygan (WI) Press
Southern Press (Washington, DC)
South Port (WI) American
Standard (London)
Steuben Republican (Angola, IN)
St. Joseph (MO) Weekly Free Democrat
St. Louis Republican
Summit County (OH) Beacon
Sumter Banner (Sumterville, SC)
Thibodaux (LA) Minerva
Times (London)
Tioga Eagle (Wellsboro, PA)
Town Talk (Alexandria, LA)
True American (Lexington, KY)
Vermont Family Gazette (Bradford)
Vermont Phoenix (Brattleboro)
Vermont Union Whig (Brandon)
Vermont Watchman and State Journal (Montpelier)
Vicksburg (MS) Daily Whig
Wabash Express (Terre Haute, IN)
Washington Capital
Washington Sentinel
Wayne County (PA) Herald

Weekly Hawkeye and Telegraph (Burlington, IA)
Weekly Missoulian (Missoula, MT)
Wellsboro (PA) Gazette
Wheeling (VA) Daily Intelligencer
Whig Standard (Washington, DC)
Wilmington (NC) Daily Herald
Wilmington (NC) Journal
Wisconsin Democrat (Milwaukee)
Wisconsin State Journal (Madison)

CENSUS DATA

1810 United States Federal Census [database online]. Provo, UT: Ancestry.com Operations, Inc., 2020.

1840 Census: Compendium of the Enumeration of the Inhabitants and Statistics of the United States, Kentucky [database online]. Washington, DC: Census.gov.

1860 Census: Eighth Census of the United States, Kentucky [database online]. Washington, DC: Census.gov.

1870 United States Federal Census [database online]. Provo, UT: Ancestry.com Operations, Inc., 2020.

LEGAL DOCUMENTS

Commonwealth v. Cassius M. Clay. 1843. Frankfort: Kentucky Department for Libraries and Archives.

Commonwealth of Kentucky v. Emily. 1845.

Divorce Petition of Cassius Marcellus Clay and Mary Jane Warfield Clay. December 29, 1877. Frankfort: Kentucky Department for Libraries and Archives.

Kentucky, U.S., Wills and Probate Records, 1774-1989 [database online]. Lehi, UT: Ancestry.com Operations, 2015. Original data: Kentucky County, District and Probate Courts.

PUBLISHED GOVERNMENT DOCUMENTS

Despatches from U.S. Ministers to Russia, 1808-1906. Washington, DC: US Department of State, 1953. Microfilm M-35, 66 rolls.

Executive Documents Printed by Order of the House of Representatives, during the Second Session of the Thirty-Ninth Congress, 1866-'67. Vol. 1, *1866/1867*. Washington, DC: Government Printing Office, 1867. *Foreign Relations of the United States*, 1861-69. University of Wisconsin Digital Collections. https://digital.library.wisc.edu/1711.dl/SHLYATU2CGF4F8K.

Executive Documents Printed by Order of the House of Representatives, during the Second Session of the Fortieth Congress, 1867-'68. Vol. 1, *1867/1868*. Washington, DC: Government Printing Office, 1868. *Foreign Relations of the United States*, 1861-69. University of Wisconsin Digital Collections. https://digital.library.wisc.edu/1711.dl/KRGVI2434GY5F8E.

Message of the President of the United States, and Accompanying Documents, to the Two Houses of Congress, at the Commencement of the First Session of the Thirty-Eighth Congress. Part 2. Washington, DC: Government Printing Office, 1864. *Foreign Relations of the United States*, 1861-69. University of Wisconsin Digital Collections. https://digital.library.wisc.edu/1711.dl/GFVL47G2UEH2R8M.

Message of the President of the United States to the Two Houses of Congress at the Commencement of the Second Session of the Thirty-Seventh Congress. Vol. 1. Washington: Government Printing Office, 1861. *Foreign Relations of the United States, 1861–69*. University of Wisconsin Digital Collections. https://digital.library.wisc.edu/1711.dl/3V6B36KRR37BV87.

National Park Service. *Soldiers and Sailors Database*. www.nps.gov/civilwar/soldiers-and-sailors-database.htm.

U.S. Freedmen's Bureau Records, 1865–1878 [database online]. Lehi, UT: Ancestry.com Operations, 2021.

OTHER PUBLISHED PRIMARY SOURCES

Acts Passed at the First Session of the Twenty-Ninth General Assembly for the Commonwealth of Kentucky. Frankfort, KY: Kendall and Russell, 1821.

Adams, Charles Francis. "Diary Entry for January 23, 1861." In *Charles Francis Adams, Sr.: The Civil War Diaries (Unverified Transcriptions)*. Boston: Massachusetts Historical Society, 2015. www.masshist.org/publications/cfa-civil-war/view?id=DCA61d023.

Adams, Henry. *Letters of Henry Adams*. Vol. 1, *1858–68*. Edited by J. C. Levenson, Ernest Samuels, Charles Vandersee, and Viola Hopkins Winner. Cambridge, MA: Belknap Press of Harvard University Press, 1982.

"All about Hogs." *Illinois Farmer* 4 (March 1859): 230–31.

Allen, Lewis F. *A History of the Short-Horn Cattle: Their Origin, Progress, and Present Condition*. Buffalo, NY: Published by the Author, 1872.

Barre, W. L., ed. *Writings and Speeches of Hon. Thomas F. Marshall*. Cincinnati: Applegate, 1858.

Basler, Roy P., ed. *The Collected Works of Abraham Lincoln*. Vol. 4. New Brunswick, NJ: Rutgers University Press, 1953.

Clay, Cassius Marcellus. *The Life of Cassius Marcellus Clay: Memoirs, Writings, and Speeches, Showing His Conduct in the Overthrow of American Slavery, the Salvation of the Union, and the Restoration of the Autonomy of the States*. Vol. 1. Cincinnati, OH: J. F. Brennan, 1886.

Clay, Cassius M. "Race and the Solid South." *North American Review* 142, no. 351 (1886): 134–38.

Clay, Cassius M. *A Review of the Late Canvass, and R. Wickliffe's Speech on the "Negro Law," by C. M. Clay, September 25, 1840*. Lexington, KY: N. L. Finnell, 1840.

Clay, Cassius Marcellus. *The Writings of Cassius M. Clay, including Speeches and Addresses*. Edited by Horace Greeley. New York: Harper and Brothers, 1848.

Clay, Mary Barr. "A Brave Kentucky Woman." *Woman's Journal*, March 2, 1889, 72.

Clay, Mary Barr. "The Wife of Cassius M. Clay." *Woman's Magazine* 12 (April 1889): 234–36.

Coleman, J. Winston. *William H. Townsend: Scholar, Raconteur, Lawyer*. Pamphlet, 1980. Frank and Virginia Williams Collection of Lincolniana, Mitchell Memorial Library, Mississippi State University, Starkville.

Curtin, Jeremiah. *Memoirs of Jeremiah Curtin*. Madison: State Historical Society of Wisconsin, 1940.

A Digest of the Statute Law of Kentucky: Being a Collection of All the Acts of the General Assembly, of a Permanent Nature, from the Commencement of the May Session 1822. 2 vols. Edited by William Littell and Jacob Swigert. Frankfort, KY: Kendall and Russell, 1822.

Fee, John G. *Autobiography of John G. Fee, Berea Kentucky.* Chicago: National Christian Association, 1891.

Greeley, Horace. *Mr. Greeley's Letters from Texas and the Lower Mississippi.* New York: Tribune Office, 1871.

Helper, Hinton Rowan. *The Impending Crisis of the South: How to Meet It.* New York: A. B. Burdick, 1859.

Journal of the First Constitutional Convention of Kentucky, Held in Danville, Kentucky, April 2–19, 1792. Published in Commemoration of Kentucky's Sesquicentennial Anniversary, State Bar Association of Kentucky, 1942.

Journal of the Convention, Begun and Held at the Capitol in the Town of Frankfort, on Monday the Twenty-Second Day of July, in the Year of Our Lord One Thousand, Seven Hundred and Ninety-Nine. 1799. UKnowledge, University of Kentucky. https://uknowledge.uky.edu/ky_cons_conventions/1.

Julian, George W. "The First Republican National Convention." *American Historical Review* 4, no. 2 (1899): 313–22.

Julian, George W. *Political Recollections, 1840–1872.* Chicago: Jansen, McClurg, 1884.

"[Letter to] Beloved Friend." William Lloyd Garrison to Elizabeth Pease Nichol, June 20, 1849. Manuscript. Accessed at Archive.org. https://archive.org/details/lettertobelovedfoogarr10.

Letter from Cassius M. Clay to Proceedings of the Convention, of the Colored Freemen of Ohio, Held in Cincinnati, January 14, 15, 16, 17, and 19, 1852. Cincinnati: Dumas and Lawyer, 1852. Accessed at Colored Conventions Project: Digital Records. https://omeka.coloredconventions.org/items/show/250.

"Letter from Cassius Marcellus Clay to Joshua Giddings, September 3, 1851." *Ohio Archaeological and Historical Publications* 28 (1919): 33.

"[Letter to] My Dear M. W. Chapman & Sisters." Lucretia Mott to Maria Weston Chapman, July 23, 1846. Manuscript. Accessed at Archive.org. https://archive.org/details/lettertomydearmwoomott.

Nicolay, John G., and John Hay. *Abraham Lincoln: A History.* Vol. 4. New York: Century, 1890.

Olmsted, Frederick Law. *A Journey through Texas; or, A Saddle Trip on the South-Western Frontier: With a Statistical Appendix.* New York: Mason Brothers, 1859.

Pease, Theodore Calvin, and James G. Randall, eds. *The Diary of Orville Hickman Browning.* Vol. 1. Springfield: Illinois State Historical Library, 1925.

Political Speeches and Debates of Abraham Lincoln and Stephen Douglas, 1854–1861. Chicago: Scott, Foresman, 1896.

Russell, William Howard. *My Diary North and South.* Boston: T. O. H. P. Burnham, 1863.

Schultz, John Richie, ed. *Unpublished Letters of Bayard Taylor in the Huntington Library*. San Marino, CA: Huntington Library, 1937.
Seager, Robert, ed. *Papers of Henry Clay*. Vol. 7. Lexington: University Press of Kentucky, 1982.
Seward, Frederick, ed. *William Seward: An Autobiography from 1801 to 1834, with a Memoir of His Life and a Selection from His Letters, 1831–1846*. New York: Derby and Miller, 1891.
Simon, John Y., ed. *Papers of Ulysses S. Grant*. Vol. 18, *October 1, 1867–June 30, 1868*. Carbondale: Southern Illinois University Press, 1991.
Speech of Cassius M. Clay, at Frankfort, Kentucky, from the Capitol Steps, January 10, 1860. Cincinnati, 1860.
Speech of the Hon. Montgomery Blair (Postmaster General), on the Revolutionary Schemes of the Ultra Abolitionists, and in Defence of the Policy of the President: Delivered at the Unconditional Union Meeting, Held at Rockville, Montgomery Co., Maryland, on Saturday, October 3, 1863. New York: D. W. Lee, 1863.
Speech of William H. Seward, on the Admission of California: Delivered in the Senate of the United States, March 11, 1850. Washington, DC: Buell and Blanchard, 1860.
Sumner, Charles. "Our Domestic Relations: Or, How to Treat the Rebel States." *Atlantic Monthly*, October 1863, 507–29.
Timothy Bombshell [pseud.]. *A Synopsis of Forty Chapters upon Clay, Not to Be Found in Any Treatise on the Free Soils of the United-States of America Heretofore Published*. 1867.
Townsend, William H. *The Lion of Whitehall: Cassius Marcellus Clay*. Dunwoody, GA: Norman S. Berg, 1967.
Townsend, William H. "The Lion of Whitehall." Address delivered at the Civil War Round Table, Chicago, October 17, 1952. Rebroadcast on Ipse Dixit (podcast), season 1, ep. 281, June 25, 2019. https://shows.acast.com/ipse-dixit/episodes/from-the-archives-85-william-h-townsend-the-lion-of-whitehal.
United States Freedmen's Bureau Claim Records, 1865–1872. Familysearch.org.
Wilson, Henry. *History of the Rise and Fall of the Slave Power in America*. Vol. 1. Boston: James R. Osgood, 1871.

SECONDARY SOURCES

Alexander, Erik B. "'The Wisest Counsel of Conservatism': Northern Democrats and the Politics of the Center, 1865–1868." *Civil War History* 66, no. 3 (2020): 295–315.
Ali, Muhammad. *The Greatest: My Own Story*. New York: Random House, 1975.
Anderson, J. L. *Capitalist Pigs: Pigs, Pork, and Power in America*. Morgantown: West Virginia University Press, 2019.
Aron, Stephen. *How the West Was Lost: The Transformation of Kentucky from Daniel Boone to Henry Clay*. Baltimore: Johns Hopkins University Press, 1999.
Astor, Aaron. *Rebels on the Border: Civil War, Emancipation, and the Reconstruction of Kentucky and Missouri*. Baton Rouge: Louisiana State University Press, 2012.

Ayers, Edward L. *Vengeance and Justice: Crime and Punishment in the Nineteenth-Century American South*. New York: Oxford University Press, 1984.

Bailey, Hugh C. *Hinton Rowan Helper: Abolitionist Racist*. Tuscaloosa: University of Alabama Press, 1965.

Barnes, William, and John Heath Morgan. *Foreign Service of the United States: Origins, Development, and Functions*. Washington, DC: Historical Office, Bureau of Public Affairs, Department of State, 1961.

Benedict, Michael Les. "The Politics of Reconstruction." In *Preserving the Constitution: Essays on Politics and the Constitution in the Reconstruction Era*, 93–128. New York: Fordham University Press, 2006.

Benedict, Michael Les. "The Problem of Constitutionalism and Constitutional Liberty in the Reconstruction South." In *Preserving the Constitution: Essays on Politics and the Constitution in the Reconstruction Era*, 152–67. New York: Fordham University Press, 2006.

Benedict, Michael Les. "Reform Republicans and the Retreat from Reconstruction." In *Preserving the Constitution: Essays on Politics and the Constitution in the Reconstruction Era*, 168–85. New York: Fordham University Press, 2006.

Benedict, Michael Les. "Salmon P. Chase and Constitutional Politics." In *Preserving the Constitution: Essays on Politics and the Constitution in the Reconstruction Era*, 129–51. New York: Fordham University Press, 2006.

Berry, Mary Clay. *Voices from the Century Before: The Odyssey of a Nineteenth-Century Kentucky Family*. New York: Arcade, 1996.

Berry, Stephen. *House of Abraham: Lincoln and the Todds, a Family Divided by War*. New York: Houghton Mifflin, 2007.

Birchfield, James. "Some Books We Cannot Read: Kentucky's Bibliographical Ghosts." *Kentucky Review* 7, no. 3 (1987): 62–77.

Blight, David. *Race and Reunion: The Civil War in American Memory*. Cambridge, MA: Belknap Press of Harvard University Press, 2001.

Blue, Frederick J. *The Free Soilers: Third Party Politics, 1848–54*. Urbana: University of Illinois Press, 1973.

Blue, Frederick J. *No Taint of Compromise: Crusaders in Antislavery Politics*. Baton Rouge: Louisiana State University Press, 2006.

Blue, Frederick J. *Salmon P. Chase: A Life in Politics*. Kent, OH: Kent State University Press, 1987.

Botkin, B. A. *A Civil War Treasury of Tales, Legends, and Folklore*. New York: Promontor, 1981.

Brooks, Corey M. *Liberty Power: Antislavery Third Parties and the Transformation of American Politics*. Chicago: University of Chicago Press, 2016.

Brooks, Corey M. "Reconsidering Politics in the Study of American Abolitionists." *Journal of the Civil War Era* 8, no. 2 (2018): 291–317.

Brown, David. *Southern Outcast: Hinton Rowan Helper and the Impending Crisis of the South*. Baton Rouge: Louisiana State University Press, 2006.

Burke, Diane Mutti. *On Slavery's Border: Missouri's Small Slaveholding Households, 1815–1865.* Athens: University of Georgia Press, 2010.

Burlingame, Michael. *With Lincoln in the White House: Letters, Memoranda, and Other Writings of John G. Nicolay, 1860–1865.* Carbondale: Southern Illinois University Press, 2006.

Carleé, Roberta Baughman. *The Last Gladiator.* Berea, KY: Kentucke Imprints, 1979.

Carman, Harry J., and Reinhard H. Luthin. *Lincoln and the Patronage.* New York: Columbia University Press, 1943.

Carter, Kellie Jackson. *Force and Freedom: Black Abolitionists and the Politics of Violence.* Philadelphia: University of Pennsylvania Press, 2019.

Catton, Bruce. *The Coming Fury.* Garden City, NY: Doubleday, 1961.

Chernow, Ron. *Grant.* New York: Penguin, 2017.

Chubarov, Alexander. *The Fragile Empire: A History of Imperial Russia.* London: Continuum International, 2001.

Cirillo, Frank J. *The Abolitionist Civil War: Immediatists and the Struggle to Transform the Union.* Baton Rouge: Louisiana State University Press, 2023.

Clark, Thomas D. *The Kentucky.* Lexington: University Press of Kentucky, 2014.

Clarke, Grace Julian. *George W. Julian.* Indiana Biographical Series, vol. 1. Indianapolis: Indiana Historical Commission, 1923.

Coates, Ta-Nehisi. "Bob Costas to Muhammad Ali—'Well, Actually....'" *Atlantic*, June 6, 2016. www.theatlantic.com/culture/archive/2016/06/bob-costas-loud-and-wrong/623830/.

Coleman, Arica L. "What's in a Name: Meet the Original Cassius Clay." *Time*, June 10, 2016. https://time.com/4363225/original-cassius-clay-muhammad-ali/.

Coleman, J. Winston, Jr. *Slavery Times in Kentucky.* Chapel Hill: University of North Carolina Press, 1940.

Coleman, J. Winston, Jr. *The Squire's Sketches of Lexington.* Lexington, KY: Henry Clay Press, 1972.

Coward, Joan Wells. *Kentucky in the New Republic: The Process of Constitution Making.* Lexington: University Press of Kentucky, 1979.

Degler, Carl. *The Other South: Southern Dissenters in the Nineteenth Century.* New York: Harper and Row, 1974.

Demos, John. "The Antislavery Movement and the Problem of Violent 'Means.'" *New England Quarterly* 37, no. 4 (1964): 501–26.

Dennett, Tyler, ed. *Lincoln and the Civil War in the Diaries of John Hay.* New York: Dodd, Mead, 1939.

Dillon, Merton. "The Abolitionists: A Decade of Historiography, 1959–1969." *Journal of Southern History* 35, no. 4 (1969): 500–522.

Dixon, Simon. *The Modernisation of Russia, 1676–1825.* New York: Cambridge University Press, 1999.

Downs, Gregory P. *The Second American Revolution: The Civil War–Era Struggle over Cuba and the Rebirth of the American Republic.* Chapel Hill: University of North Carolina Press, 2019.

Doyle, Don H. *The Cause of All Nations: An International History of the American Civil War.* New York: Basic Books, 2015.

Earle, Jonathan. *Jacksonian Anti-Slavery and the Politics of Free Soil, 1824–1854.* Chapel Hill: University of North Carolina Press, 2004.

Eaton, Clement. *The Freedom-of-Thought Struggle in the Old South.* New York: Harper and Row, 1964.

Eig, Jonathan. *Ali: A Life.* New York: Mariner Books, 2018.

Egerton, Douglas R. *Year of Meteors: Stephen Douglas, Abraham Lincoln, and the Election That Brought on the Civil War.* New York: Bloomsbury, 2010.

Egerton, John. "Heritage of a Heavyweight." *New York Times Magazine,* September 28, 1980.

Ellis, William E. *A History of Education in Kentucky.* Lexington: University Press of Kentucky, 2011.

Ellis, William E., H. E. Everman, and Richard Sears. *Madison County: 200 Years in Retrospect.* Richmond, KY: Madison County Historical Society, 1985.

Ellison, Betty Boles. *A Man Seen But Once: Cassius Marcellus Clay.* Bloomington, IN: Authorhouse, 2005.

Epps, Kristen. *Slavery on the Periphery: The Kansas-Missouri Border in the Antebellum and Civil War Eras.* Athens: University of Georgia Press, 2016.

Foner, Eric. *Free Soil, Free Labor, Free Men: The Ideology of the Republican Party before the Civil War.* New York: Oxford University Press, 1970.

Foner, Eric. *Reconstruction: America's Unfinished Revolution, 1863–1877.* New York: Harper and Row Publishers, 1988.

Ford, Lacy K. *Deliver Us from Evil: The Slavery Question in the Old South.* New York: Oxford University Press, 2009.

Foreman, Amanda. *A World on Fire: Britain's Crucial Role in the American Civil War.* New York: Random House, 2011.

Foster, Gaines. *Ghosts of the Confederacy: Defeat, the Lost Cause, and the Emergence of the New South, 1865–1913.* New York: Oxford University Press, 1987.

Franklin, John Hope. *The Militant South: 1800–1861.* Boston: Beacon, 1956.

Frederickson, George M. "Antislavery Racist: Hinton Rowan Helper." In *The Arrogance of Race: Historical Perspectives on Slavery, Racism, and Social Inequality,* edited by George M. Fredrickson, 28–53. Middletown, CT: Wesleyan University Press, 1988.

Freehling, Alison Goodyear. *Drift toward Dissolution: The Virginia Slavery Debate of 1831–1832.* Baton Rouge: Louisiana State University Press, 1982.

Freehling, William W. *The Road to Disunion.* Vol. 1, *Secessionists at Bay, 1776–1854.* New York: Oxford University Press, 1991.

Freehling, William W. *The Road to Disunion.* Vol. 2, *Secessionists Triumphant, 1854–1861.* New York: Oxford University Press, 2007.

Freehling, William W. *The South vs. the South: How Anti-Confederate Southerners Shaped the Course of the Civil War.* Oxford: Oxford University Press, 2002.

Freeman, Joanne B. *Field of Blood: Violence in Congress and the Road to the Civil War.* New York: Farrar, Straus and Giroux, 2018.

Freeze, Gregory L. *Russia: A History.* New York: Oxford University Press, 1997.

Friedman, Lawrence M. *Dead Hands: A Social History of Wills, Trusts, and Inheritance Law*. Stanford, CA: Stanford University Press, 2000.

Friend, Craig Thompson, *Kentucke's Frontiers*. Bloomington: Indiana University Press, 2010.

Fuller, Paul E. *Laura Clay and the Woman's Rights Movement*. Lexington: University Press of Kentucky, 1975.

Gallagher, Gary W., and Joan Waugh. *The American War: A History of the Civil War Era*. State College, PA: Flip Learning, 2016.

Gienapp, William E. *The Origins of the Republican Party, 1852-1856*. New York: Oxford University Press, 1987.

Goodwin, Doris Kearns. *Team of Rivals: The Political Genius of Abraham Lincoln*. New York: Simon and Schuster, 2006.

Greenberg, Amy. *A Wicked War: Polk, Clay, Lincoln, and the 1846 U.S. Invasion of Mexico*. New York: Knopf, 2012.

Grimsted, David. *American Mobbing, 1828-1861: Toward Civil War*. New York: Oxford University Press, 1998.

Hafendorfer, Kenneth A. *Battle of Richmond, Kentucky: August 30, 1862*. Louisville, KY: KH Press, 2006.

Harlow, Luke. *Religion, Race and the Making of Confederate Kentucky, 1830-1880*. Cambridge: Cambridge University Press, 2014.

Harrison, Lowell. *The Antislavery Movement in Kentucky*. Lexington: University Press of Kentucky, 1978.

Harrold, Stanley. *The Abolitionists and the South, 1831-1861*. Lexington: University Press of Kentucky, 1995.

Harrold, Stanley. *American Abolitionism: Its Direct Political Impact from Colonial Times into Reconstruction*. Charlottesville: University of Virginia Press, 2019.

Harrold, Stanley. "Cassius M. Clay on Slavery and Race: A Reinterpretation." *Slavery and Abolition* 9, no. 1 (1988): 42-56.

Harrold, Stanley. "The Intersectional Relationship between Cassius Marcellus Clay and the Garrisonian Abolitionists." *Civil War History*, 35, no. 2 (1989): 101-19.

Harrold, Stanley. "Violence and Non-Violence in Kentucky Abolitionism." *Journal of Southern History* 57, no. 1 (1991): 15-38.

Goan, Melanie Beals. *A Simple Justice: Kentucky Women Fight of the Right to Vote*. Lexington: University Press of Kentucky, 2020.

Golder, F. A. "The Russian Fleet and the Civil War." *American Historical Review* 20, no. 4 (1915): 801-12.

Grinspan, Jon. *Wide Awake: The Forgotten Force That Elected Lincoln and Spurred the Civil War*. New York: Bloomsbury, 2024.

Grinspan, Jon. "'Young Men for War': The Wide Awakes and Lincoln's 1860 Presidential Campaign." *Journal of American History* 96, no. 2 (2009): 357-78.

Heidler, David Stephen, and Jeanne T. Heidler. *Henry Clay: The Essential American*. New York: Random House, 2010.

Henlein, Paul C. *Cattle Kingdom of the Ohio Valley, 1783-1860*. Lexington: University Press of Kentucky, 2014.

Hess, Earl J. *The Civil War in the West: Victory and Defeat from the Appalachians to the Mississippi*. Chapel Hill: University of North Carolina Press, 2012.

Hingley, Ronald. *The Tsars: Russian Autocrats, 1533–1917*. London: Weidenfeld and Nicolson, 1968.

Hollingsworth, Randolph. "Mag Preston: Personal Honor in Southern Politics." In *The Human Tradition in the Old South*, edited by James C. Klotter, 99–116. Baltimore: Scholarly Resources Books, 2003.

Holt, Michael. *The Election of 1860: A Campaign Fraught with Consequences*. Lawrence: University of Kansas Press, 2017.

Holt, Michael. *The Fate of Their Country: Slavery, Politicians, and the Coming of the Civil War*. New York: Hill and Wang, 2004.

Holton, Woody. "Equality as Unintended Consequence: The Contracts Clause and the Married Women's Property Acts." *Journal of Southern History* 81, no. 2 (2015): 313–40.

Horowitz, Tony. *Spying on the South: An Odyssey across the American Divide*. New York: Penguin Books, 2019.

Howard, Jean Morford. "The Ante-Bellum Career of Cassius Marcellus Clay." MA thesis, University of Kentucky, 1947.

Howard, Victor B. "Cassius M. Clay and the Origins of the Republican Party." *Filson Club Historical Quarterly* 45 (1971): 49–71.

Howe, Daniel Walker. *What Hath God Wrought: The Transformation of America, 1815–1848*. New York: Oxford University Press, 2007.

Ireland, Robert M. *The County Courts in Antebellum Kentucky*. Lexington: University Press of Kentucky, 1972.

Isley, Jeter A. *Horace Greeley and the Republican Party, 1853–1861: A Study of the New York Tribune*. Princeton, NJ: Princeton University Press, 1947.

Jenkins, Jeffrey A., and Justin Peck. *Congress and the First Civil Rights Era, 1861–1918*. Chicago: University of Chicago Press, 2021.

Johnson, E. Polk. *A History of Kentucky and Kentuckians: The Leaders and Representative Men in Commerce, Industry and Modern Activities*, vol. 3. Chicago: Lewis, 1912.

Jordan, Donaldson, and Edwin Pratt. *Europe and the American Civil War*. New York: Octagon Books, 1969.

Karp, Matt. "The Mass Politics of Antislavery." *Catalyst* 3, no. 2 (2019), www.catalyst-journal.com/2019/10/the-mass-politics-of-antislavery.

Kendi, Ibram X. *Stamped from the Beginning: The Definitive History of Racist Ideas in America*. New York: Bold Type Books, 2016.

Kirwan, Albert D. "Cassius Marcellus Clay's *True American*." PhD diss., University of Louisville, 1945.

Klotter, James C., and Lowell H. Harrison. *A New History of Kentucky*. Lexington: University Press of Kentucky, 1997.

Klotter, James C., and Daniel Rowland, eds. *Bluegrass Renaissance: The History and Culture of Central Kentucky, 1792–1852*. Lexington: University Press of Kentucky, 2012.

Kolchin, Peter. *Emancipation: The Abolition and Aftermath of American Slavery and Russian Serfdom*. New Haven, CT: Yale University Press, 2024.

Kolchin, Peter. *Unfree Labor: American Slavery and Russian Serfdom.* Cambridge, MA: Belknap Press of Harvard University Press, 1987.

Kuby, William. "Mary Jane Warfield Clay (1815–1900): Wifely Devotion, Divorce, and Rebirth in Nineteenth-Century Kentucky." In *Kentucky Women: Their Lives and Times*, edited by Melissa McEuen and Thomas Appleton, 59–80. Athens: University of Georgia Press, 2015.

Lang, Andrew. *In the Wake of War: Military Occupation, Emancipation, and Civil War America.* Baton Rouge: Louisiana State University Press, 2017.

Lee, Jacob D. "Between Two Fires: Cassius M. Clay, Slavery, and Antislavery in the Kentucky Borderlands." *Ohio Valley History* 6, no. 3 (2006): 50–70.

Lemann, Nicholas. *Redemption: The Last Battle of the Civil War.* New York: Farrar, Straus and Giroux, 2007.

Linklater, Andro. *Measuring America: How the United States Was Shaped by the Greatest Land Sale in History.* New York: Plume, 2003.

Lipsyte, Robert. "Ali, 1942–2016." *Time*, June 26, 2016. https://time.com/muhammad-ali/.

Lockwood, John, and Charles Lockwood. *The Siege of Washington: The Untold Story of the Twelve Days That Shook the Union.* New York: Oxford University Press, 2011.

Lynn, Joshua. *Preserving the White Man's Republic: Jacksonian Democracy, Race, and the Transformation of American Conservatism.* Charlottesville: University of Virginia Press, 2019.

MacKenzie, Scott A. *The Fifth Border State: Slavery, Emancipation, and the Formation of West Virginia, 1829–1872.* Morgantown: West Virginia University Press, 2023.

Majewski, John. "Why Did Northerners Oppose the Expansion of Slavery? Economic Development and Education in the Limestone South." In *Slavery's Capitalism: A New History of American Economic Development*, edited by Sven Beckert and Seth Rockman, 277–98. Philadelphia: University of Pennsylvania Press, 2016.

Marshall, Anne E. *Creating a Confederate Kentucky: The Lost Cause and Civil War Memory in a Border State.* Chapel Hill: University of North Carolina Press, 2010.

Marshall, Anne E. "Kentucky's Anti-Separate Coach Law and African American Response, 1892–1900." *Register of the Kentucky Historical Society* 98, no. 3 (2000): 241–59.

Marshall, Anne E. "'Lamentable Inconsistency': Cassius Marcellus Clay and the Dilemma of Anti-Slavery Slaveholders." *Slavery and Abolition* 41, no. 2 (2020): 327–48.

Marshall, Schuyler C. "The Free Democratic Convention of 1852." *Pennsylvania History: A Journal of Mid-Atlantic Studies* 22, no. 2 (1955): 146–67.

Mason, Matthew. "'In an Evil Hour This Pandora's Box of Slavery Was Again Opened': Emotional Partisan Divisions in the Late Antebellum Conservative North." *Civil War History* 66, no. 3 (2020): 256–71.

May, Robert E. "Invisible Men: Blacks and the U.S. Army in the Mexican War." *Historian* 49, no. 4 (1987): 463–77.

McDaniel, W. Caleb. "The Bonds and Boundaries of Antislavery." *Journal of the Civil War Era* 4, no. 1 (2014): 84–105.

McDaniel, W. Caleb. *The Problem of Democracy in the Age of Slavery: Garrisonian Abolitionists and Transatlantic Reform.* Baton Rouge: Louisiana State University Press, 2015.

McDaniel, W. Caleb. *Sweet Taste of Liberty: A True Story of Slavery and Restitution in America.* New York: Oxford University Press, 2018.

McKivigan, John R., and Stanley Harrold, eds. *Anti-Slavery Violence: Sectional, Racial, and Cultural Conflict in Antebellum America.* Knoxville: University of Tennessee Press, 1999.

McPherson, James. *Battle Cry of Freedom: The Civil War Era.* New York: Oxford University Press, 1988.

McPherson, James. "Grant or Greeley? The Abolitionist Dilemma in the Election of 1872." *American Historical Review* 71, no. 1 (1965): 43–61.

McQueen, Kevan. *Cassius M. Clay: Freedom's Champion.* Paducah, KY: Turner, 2001.

Mearns, David. *The Lincoln Papers: The Story of the Collection with Selections to July 4, 1861.* Vols. 1 and 2. New York: Doubleday, 1948.

Medved, Michael. "Americans Should Know the Story of Abolitionist Cassius Clay." *Wall Street Journal*, June 19, 2021.

Merritt, Keri Leig. *Masterless Men: Poor Whites and Slavery in the Antebellum South.* Cambridge: Cambridge University Press, 2017.

Mitchell, Thomas G. *Antislavery Politics in Antebellum and Civil War America.* Westport, CT: Prager. 2007.

Monoghan, Jay. *Diplomat in Carpet Slippers.* Indianapolis, IN: Bobbs-Merrill, 1945.

Morris, Thomas D. *Southern Slavery and the Law, 1619–1860.* Chapel Hill: University of North Carolina Press, 1996.

"Muhammad Ali Originally Named for Ardent Abolitionist and Yale Alumnus Cassius Clay." *YaleNews*, June 9, 2016. https://news.yale.edu/2016/06/09/muhammad-ali-originally-named-ardent-abolitionist-and-yale-alumnus-cassius-clay.

Mullins, Lashe D., and Charles K. Mullins. *A History of Whitehall: House of Clay.* Charleston, SC: History Press, 2012.

Myers, John L. "The Writing of 'The Rise and Fall of the Slave Power in America.'" *Civil War History* 31, no. 2 (1985): 144–62.

Niven, John, *Salmon P. Chase: A Biography.* New York: Oxford University Press, 1995.

Niven, John, ed. *The Salmon P. Chase Papers.* Vol. 2, *Correspondence, 1823–1857.* Kent, OH: Kent State University Press, 1995.

Novick, Peter. *That Noble Dream: The "Objectivity Question" and the American Historical Profession.* Cambridge: Cambridge University Press, 1988.

Oakes, James. *The Crooked Path to Abolition: Abraham Lincoln and the Antislavery Constitution.* New York: W. W. Norton, 2021.

Oakes, James. *Freedom National: The Destruction of Slavery in the United States, 1861–1865.* New York: W. W. Norton, 2013.

Oakes, James. "Making Freedom National: Salmon P. Chase and the Abolition of Slavery." *Georgetown Journal of Law and Public Policy* 13, no. 2 (2015): 407–22.

Oakes, James. *The Scorpion's Sting: Anti-Slavery and the Coming of the Civil War*. New York: W. W. Norton, 2014.

Pease, Jane H., and William H. Pease. *Bound with Them in Chains: A Biographical History of the Antislavery Movement*. Westport, CT: Greenwood, 1972.

Pease, Jane H., and William H. Pease. "Confrontation and Abolition in the 1850s." *Journal of American History* 58, no. 4 (1972): 923–37.

Peters, Lucia. "The Story behind Muhammad Ali's Name Change." *Bustle*, June 4, 2016. www.bustle.com/articles/164840-what-was-muhammad-alis-real-name-he-changed-it-for-a-powerful-reason.

Phillips, Christopher. *The Rivers Ran Backward: The Civil War and the Remaking of the American Middle Border*. New York: Oxford University Press, 2016.

Prichard, James, Jr. "'This Priceless Jewell—Liberty': The Doyle Conspiracy of 1848." In *Slavery and Freedom in the Bluegrass State: Revisiting My Old Kentucky Home*, edited by Gerald L. Smith, 79–109. Lexington: University Press of Kentucky, 2023.

Ramage, Andrea S. "Love and Honor: The Robert Wickliffe Family of Antebellum Kentucky." *Register of the Kentucky Historical Society* 94, no. 2 (1996): 115–33.

"Remembering Muhammed Ali through His Poem, 'I Am the Greatest.'" All Things Considered, NPR Accessed February 10, 2025, www.npr.org/2016/06/10/481590365/remembering-muhammad-ali-through-his-poem-i-am-the-greatest.

Remini, Robert V. *Henry Clay: Statesman for the Union*. New York: W. W. Norton, 1991.

Rice, Otis K. "Importations of Cattle into Kentucky, 1785–1860." *Register of the Kentucky Historical Society* 49, no. 166 (1951): 35–47.

Richardson, H. Edward. *Cassius Marcellus Clay: Firebrand of Freedom*. Lexington: University Press of Kentucky, 1976.

Robertson, James Rood. *A Kentuckian at the Court of the Tsars: The Ministry of Cassius Marcellus Clay to Russia*. Berea, KY: Kentucke Imprints, 1976.

Robinson, Michael D. *A Union Indivisible: Secession and the Politics of Slavery in the Border South*. Chapel Hill: University of North Carolina Press, 2021.

Rockman, Seth. *Scraping By: Wage Labor, Slavery, and Survival in Early Baltimore*. Baltimore: Johns Hopkins University Press, 2009.

Roediger, David. *The Wages of Whiteness: Race and the Making of the American Working Class*. New York: Verso, 2007.

Roy, Julie Jeffrey. *Abolitionists Remember: Antislavery Biographies and the Unfinished Work of Emancipation*. Chapel Hill: University of North Carolina Press, 2012.

Runyon, Paul. *Delia Webster and the Underground Railroad*. Lexington: University Press of Kentucky, 1999.

Sachs, Honor. *Home Rule: Households, Manhood, and National Expansion on the Eighteenth-Century Kentucky Frontier.* New Haven, CT: Yale University Press, 2015.

Salafia, Matthew. *Slavery's Borderland: Freedom and Bondage along the Ohio River.* Philadelphia: University of Pennsylvania Press, 2013.

Salisbury, Richard V. "Kentuckians at the Battle of Buena Vista." *Filson Club Historical Quarterly* 61, no. 1 (1987): 34–53.

Saul, Norman E. *Distant Friends: The United States and Russia, 1763–1867.* Lawrence: University Press of Kansas, 1991.

Schuckers, J. W. *The Life and Public Services of Salmon Portland Chase.* New York: D. Appleton, 1874.

Segal, Carolyn L. *Cassius Marcellus Clay: The Man behind the Legend.* Berea, KY: Kentucke Imprints, 1988.

Sewell, Richard. *Ballots for Freedom: Antislavery Politics in the United States, 1837–1860.* New York: Oxford University Press, 1976.

Shelden, Rachel A., and Erik B. Alexander. "Dismantling the Party System: Party Fluidity and the Mechanisms of Nineteenth-Century U.S. Politics." *Journal of American History* 110, no. 3 (2023): 419–48.

Silber, Nina. *The Romance of Reunion: Northerners and the South, 1865–1900.* Chapel Hill: University of North Carolina Press, 1997.

Simpson, Elizabeth. *Bluegrass Houses and Their Traditions.* Lexington, KY: Transylvania Press, 1932.

Sinha, Manisha. *The Slave's Cause: A History of Abolition.* New Haven, CT: Yale University Press, 2016.

Slap, Andrew L. *The Doom of Reconstruction: The Liberal Republicans in the Civil War Era.* New York: Fordham University Press, 2006.

Smiley, David L. "Cassius M. Clay and John G. Fee: A Study in Southern Anti-Slavery Thought." *Journal of Negro History* 42, no. 3 (1957): 201–13.

Smiley, David L. "Cassius M. Clay and the Mississippi Election of 1875." *Journal of Mississippi History* 19, no. 4 (1957): 252–62.

Smiley, David L. "'An Emissary from Cousin Henry': Cassius M. Clay and Henry Clay in the Election of 1844." *Register of the Kentucky Historical Society* 53, no. 183 (1955): 115–23.

Smiley, David L. *Lion of Whitehall.* Madison: University of Wisconsin Press, 1962.

Smith, Adam I. P. "The Emergence of Conservatism as a Political Concept in the United States before the Civil War." *Civil War History* 66, no. 3 (2020): 231–55.

Smith, Adam I. P. *The Stormy Present: Conservatism and the Problem of Slavery in Northern Politics, 1846–1865.* Chapel Hill: University of North Carolina Press, 2020.

Smith, Daniel Blake. "'This Idea in Heaven': Image and Reality on the Kentucky Frontier." In *The Buzzel about Kentuck: Settling the Promised Land*, edited by Craig T. Friend, 77–98. Lexington: University Press of Kentucky, 2014.

Snay, Mitchell. *Horace Greeley and the Politics of Reform in Nineteenth-Century America.* Lanham, MD: Rowman and Littlefield, 2011.

Sowle, Patrick. "Cassius Clay and the Crisis of the Union, 1860–1861." *Register of the Kentucky Historical Society* 65, no. 2 (1967): 144–49.

Stahr, Walter. *Salmon P. Chase: Lincoln's Vital Rival*. New York: Simon and Schuster, 2022.

Stahr, Walter. *William Seward: Lincoln's Indispensable Man*. New York: Simon and Schuster, 2013.

Staples, Charles R. *The History of Pioneer Lexington, 1779–1806*. Lexington: University Press of Kentucky, 1939.

Starobin, Robert S. *Industrial Slavery in the Old South*. New York: Oxford University Press, 1970.

Stauffer, John. "Remembering Abolitionists and the Meanings of Freedom." In *Rethinking Emancipation: Legacies of Slavery and the Quest for Black Freedom*, edited by William A. Link and James J. Broomall, 216–51. Cambridge: Cambridge University Press, 2015.

Stowe, Harriet Beecher. *Uncle Tom's Cabin; or, Life among the Lowly* [1852]. New York: Viking, 1982.

Strangis, Joel. *Lewis Hayden and the War against Slavery*. North Haven, CT: Linnet Books, 1989.

Summers, Mark Wahlgren. *The Ordeal of the Reunion: A New History of Reconstruction*. Chapel Hill: University of North Carolina Press, 2014.

Tadman, Michael. *Speculators and Slaves: Masters, Traders, and Slaves in the Old South*. Madison: University of Wisconsin Press, 1989.

Tallant, Harold D. *Evil Necessity: Slavery and Political Culture in Antebellum Kentucky*. Lexington: University Press of Kentucky, 2003.

Taylor, Amy Murrell. *Embattled Freedom: Journeys through the Civil War's Slave Refugee Camps*. Chapel Hill: University of North Carolina Press, 2018.

Tocqueville, Alexis de. *"Democracy in America" and Two Essays on America*. Trans. Gerald B. Bevan. New York: Penguin Classics, 2003.

Towers, Frank, and Andrew Wiley. "Introduction: Conservatism in the Civil War North." *Civil War History* 66, no. 3 (2020): 223–30.

Townsend, Stephen, Gary Osmond, and Murray G. Phillips. "'Where Cassius Clay Ends, Muhammad Ali Begins': Sportspeople, Political Activism, and Methodology." *International Journal of the History of Sport* 35, no. 11 (2018): 1149–75.

Townsend, William H. *Lincoln and His Wife's Home Town*. Indianapolis, IN: Bobbs-Merrill, 1929.

Townsend, William H. *Lincoln in the Bluegrass: Slavery and the Civil War in Kentucky*. Lexington: University Press of Kentucky, 1955.

Townsend, William H. "Rage of the Aged Lion." *American Heritage* 11, no. 4 (1960): 34–37, 93–94.

Tuchinsky, Adam. *Horace Greeley's "New-York Tribune": Civil War–Era Socialism and the Crisis of Free Labor*. Ithaca, NY: Cornell University Press, 2009.

Varon, Elizabeth R. *Armies of Deliverance: A New History of the Civil War*. New York: Oxford University Press, 2019.

Varon, Elizabeth R. *Disunion! The Coming of the American Civil War, 1789–1859*. Chapel Hill: University of North Carolina Press, 2008.

Wagner, Laura. "Muhammad Ali Changed His Name in 1964: Newspapers Called Him Cassius Clay for Six More Years." *Slate*, July 10, 2016. https://slate.com/culture/2016/06/muhammad-ali-changed-his-name-in-1964-newspapers-called-him-cassius-clay-for-six-more-years.html.

Waldmon, Albert A. *Lincoln and the Russians: The Story of Russian-American Diplomatic Relations during the Civil War*. Cleveland, OH: World, 1952.

Wall, Mary Jean. "'A Richer Land Never Seen Yet': Horse Country and the 'Athens of the West.'" In *Bluegrass Renaissance: The History and Culture of Central Kentucky, 1792–1852*, edited by James C. Klotter and Daniel Rowland, 131–57. Lexington: University Press of Kentucky, 2012.

Walther, Eric. *The Shattering of the Union: America in the 1850s*. Lanham, MD: Rowman and Littlefield, 2003.

Watkins, Andrea S., and James A. Ramage. *Kentucky Rising: Democracy, Slavery, and Culture from the Early Republic to the Civil War*. Lexington: University Press of Kentucky, 2011.

Willentz, Sean. *The Rise of American Democracy: Jefferson to Lincoln*. New York: W. W. Norton, 2005.

Willis, George L. "History of Kentucky Constitutions and Constitutional Conventions." *Register of the Kentucky Historical Society* 28, no. 85 (1930): 305–29.

Wilson, Shannon. *Berea College: An Illustrated History*. Lexington: University Press of Kentucky, 2006.

Woods, Rebecca J. H. *The Herds Shot round the World: Native Breeds and the British Empire, 1800–1900*. Chapel Hill: University of North Carolina Press, 2017.

Wright, Gavin. *Slavery and American Economic Development*. Baton Rouge: Louisiana State University Press, 2006.

Wyatt-Brown, Bertram. *Honor and Violence in the Old South*. New York: Oxford University Press, 1986.

Wyatt-Brown, Bertram. *Southern Honor: Ethics and Behavior in the Old South*. New York: Oxford University Press, 2007.

Zinn, Howard. *SNCC: The New Abolitionists*. Westport, CT: Praeger, 1985.

Index

Abraham Lincoln Bookshop, 230
Adair, John, 17
Adam (enslaved by CMC), 14, 52
Adams, Charles Francis, 88, 103, 151, 153, 156–58, 203
Adams, Henry, 158
Adams, John Quincy, 55, 88
agriculture, 9–13, 21, 22, 25, 32, 36, 66, 106, 162, 164, 251n22, 263n32. *See also* Clay, Cassius Marcellus: and agriculture
Alaska, 195–96
Albert (enslaved by Brutus Clay), 251n15
Aleutian Islands, 181, 195
Ali, Muhammad, 3, 235–40
Alsey (enslaved by Sidney Clay), 14
American Anti-Slavery Society, 27–28, 104
American Colonization Society, 15, 26
American Indians. *See* Native Americans
American Missionary Association, 107
American Party. *See* Know-Nothing Party
American System, 9
American Woman Suffrage Association, 220
Ames, Adelbert, 211
Anthony, Susan B., 220
Anti-Slavery Bugle, 58, 60, 71, 94, 118

Bailey, Gamaliel, 102, 121, 126
Banks, Nathanial, 140, 142
Bates, Edward, 139–40, 173
Bell, John, 140, 147, 149
Bennett, James, 152, 200
Bennett, Warfield Clay, 227, 232

Benning, Thomas, 38
Berea College, 117, 135–38, 219
Billy (enslaved by Brutus Clay), 251n15
Birney, James G., 28, 41–42, 53–59, 113
black codes, 191
"Black Indians," 44
Blaine, James G., 216–17
Blair, Francis, Jr., 131–32, 139
Blair, Frank, 132
Blair, Montgomery, 154, 184–85
Blight, David, 226–27
Bluegrass system. *See* American System
Bombshell, Timothy, 194
Boone, Daniel, 7
Borland, Solon, 82
Bowie, James, 46
Bowie knife, 2, 44–46, 66, 80, 91–92, 115, 137, 207, 221–23, 227–31, 237, 240
Bragg, Braxton, 170
Breck, Daniel, 148–50
Breckinridge, John C., 27, 35, 136, 145–47
British West India, 49
Brock, Cassius Marcellus Clay, 223
Brock, Riley, 223
Brooks, Preston, 125
Brown, Benjamin Gratz, 131
Brown, John, 94, 126, 135–37, 205, 230, 238
Brown, Mason, 80
Brown, Samuel, 45–47, 61, 64, 80, 94, 228
Browning, Orville Hickman, 176, 177
Brown v. Board of Education, 239
Bruce, Blanche K., 210
Buchanan, Andrew, 195

{ 295 }

Buchanan, James, 129, 133
Buena Vista, Battle of, 83–84
Bullitt, Louisa, 38
Burlingame, Anson, 157–58, 185
Burnam, Thomas, 92
Butler, Andrew, 126
Butler, Benjamin, 166, 173

Calhoun, John C., 65, 96
Cameron, Simon, 140, 150, 155, 164–67, 174–77, 181
Caroline (enslaved by CMC), 72
Carpenter, Frank G., 221
Cass, Lewis, 87
"Cassius M. Clay's Regiment's War Song" (song), 156
Catherine the Great, 159
Catton, Bruce, 230
Centre College, 13, 27
Ceredo (WV), 131
Chapman, Maria Weston, 77
Chase, Salmon P., 5, 41–43, 46, 47, 49, 53–54, 59–60, 74, 78–79, 97, 110–16, 127, 140–44, 152, 153, 173–74, 185, 204; and election to Senate, 89; and Liberty Party, 85–89; and positive law theory, 41–42; and Reconstruction, 203
Chautems, Eliza, 193–96, 208, 219
Chautems, Leontine, 193–96, 208, 219
Chicago Civil War Roundtable, 228–30
Churchill, Winston, 230
Civil Rights Act of 1866, 191
Civil Rights Act of 1964, 231
Clark, Thomas D., 3
Clay, Ann (Brutus Clay's wife), 180
Clay, Annie (CMC's daughter), 154, 209, 215, 220
Clay, Brutus (CMC's son), 83, 154
Clay, Brutus Junius (CMC's brother), 7, 12–14, 22–26, 30, 37–40, 51, 66, 81–83, 98, 114, 116, 122, 124–125, 147, 149, 154, 178, 182–89, 210, 221, 257n15; in Congress, 182, 185–89; as financial supporter of CMC, 30, 40, 51, 81, 83, 116, 122, 124–25, 147; and opposition to emancipation, 182, 185–89
Clay, Cassius (CMC son who died as infant), 55
Clay, Cassius (CMC son who survived infancy), 61, 130
Clay, Cassius Marcellus (CMC): African American suffrage, attitude toward, 190–92; and agriculture, 25, 29, 48, 51, 108, 130, 132, 186, 209, 215, 221; antislavery views of, 35–36, 39, 43–44, 48–49, 56, 57, 73, 106, 121, 137, 248n8; business interests and finances of, 29–30, 40, 51, 115, 122–25, 130, 165; campaign for Henry Clay, 55–58; campaign in Mississippi, 210–13; childhood of, 10–14; and defense of violent self-defense, 95; and Democratic Party, relationship to, 209; education of, 17–23; and Free-Soil movement, 100; and Fugitive Slave Act of 1850, 99; and Kentucky Constitutional Convention of 1849, 90; lecture tours of, 115, 138, 145; legend of, 119; and Abraham Lincoln, 144, 149, 169; in Mexico, 79–84; and military commission, 170; and nomination for vice president, 142; opposition to Kansas-Nebraska Act, 111; opposition to Texas annexation, 55, 56; racial views of, 44, 105, 213, 217; and Reconstruction, 189–94, 197, 212 (*see also* Reconstruction); relationship with Mary Jane Warfield Clay, 109, 209; Republican Party and, 113, 115, 126–28, 130, 138–43, 183, 190–92, 197, 201; rumored death of, 93–94; run for governor, 98; in Russia, 159–66, 181–88, 192–98; and Spain, diplomatic relationship to, 153; violence toward, 44–49, 61, 92–94, 137, 221–23
—on emancipation, 49, 166; and constitutional antislavery, 59, 97, 99, 119, 127, 128, 137, 183; and political

approach, 60, 73; and state-based strategy, 49, 59
—enslaved property of, 1–4, 14–17, 21–22, 25, 29–30, 36, 40, 51, 52, 61–63, 73, 123–26; manumission of, 51–53; sells, 63, 73, 116, 122–24 (*see also names of enslaved persons*)
—and Whigs: loyalty to, 86, 88; rejection of, 98, 101
Clay, Cassius Marcellus, Jr. (boxer). *See* Ali, Muhammad
Clay, Cassius Marcellus, Sr. (Ali's father), 235
Clay, Dora Richardson (CMC's second wife), 221–24
Clay, Elisha Warfield (CMC's son), 93, 102
Clay, Eliza (CMC's sister). *See* Smith, Eliza Clay
Clay, Flora (CMC's daughter), 102, 109
Clay, Frank, 216
Clay, Franklin, 186
Clay, Green (Brutus Clay's son), 154, 188, 196, 210–15, 221
Clay, Green (CMC's father), 7–17, 30, 172, 187; death of, 13, 25; enslaved property of, 10, 13–16, 43, 51, 52, 63; military service of, 12; surveying and economic activity of, 8–11
Clay, Green (CMC's son), 30, 37, 162–63
Clay, Green (CMC's grandson), 223
Clay, Henry, 9, 13, 15, 35, 38, 74, 96–97, 230, 236; 1844 presidential campaign of, 55–58; legal defense of Cassius Clay, 48
Clay, Henry, Jr., 81, 83, 236
Clay, James (Henry Clay's son), 68
Clay, Jerry, 124, 216
Clay, John Henry, 236
Clay, Laura (CMC's daughter), 109, 154, 186, 209, 221
Clay, Leonide "Launey" Petroff (CMC's son), 208
Clay, Mary Barr (CMC's daughter), 37, 154, 188, 196, 200, 220, 223

Clay, Mary Jane Warfield (CMC's wife), 25, 30, 37, 39, 55, 61–62, 72, 79, 81–85, 93, 125, 130, 147–48, 153–55, 161–65, 179–87, 215–16, 219; as manager of White Hall, 83–85, 172–73, 176, 180, 186–87, 216, 258n15, 269n16; relationship with CMC, 18–20, 23, 109–10, 195–96, 200, 209, 215; returns to US from Russia, 163; in Russia, 161–63; as supportive of CMC's career, 55, 68–69; suffrage activities of, 220
Clay, Sallie (CMC's daughter), 40, 154
Clay, Sally Anne Lewis (CMC's mother). *See* Dudley, Sally Anne Lewis Clay
Clay, Sidney (CMC's brother), 7, 12–15, 17, 20, 29
Clay, Sidney (CMC's nephew), 125
Clay Battalion, 155
Clermont. *See* White Hall
Coates, Ta-Nehisi, 239–40
Coleman, J. Winston Jr, 229–31
colonization, 15, 26–29, 31, 35, 49, 90, 131–36, 169
Comanche territory, 80
Comfort (enslaved by Green Clay), 16
Committee of Sixty, 69–72, 151
Committee of Thirty-Three, 151
Compromise of 1820, 86
Compromise of 1850, 99–103, 110
Confiscation Acts, 166–68
Constitution. *See* US Constitution
Constitutional Union Party, 145, 148, 197
Cooper Union, 138
Corwin, Thomas, 133, 151
Costas, Bob, 239–40
Crimean War, 160, 181, 193
Crittenden, John J., 133, 145, 150–51, 182, 257n13
Crittenden Compromise, 150
Croghan, John, 38
Cuban Charitable Aid Society, 200
Cuban independence, 200–201
Currier and Ives, 74–75

Curtin, Andrew, 198
Curtin, Jeremiah, 196, 267
Czar Alexander II, 159–60, 162, 166

Dana, Charles A., 201
Daniel (enslaved by CMC), 116
Daniel (enslaved by Green Clay), 16
Dave Crews (enslaved by CMC), 52
David (enslaved by CMC), 14
Davis, Garrett, 44, 64–67, 149
Davis, Henry, 142
Davis, Jefferson, 190, 206
Dayton, William L., 126, 153, 157
Declarey, John, 23–24, 34, 37
Democracy in America (Tocqueville), 32
Democratic Party, 12, 85–87, 96, 123, 156, 192, 213, 216
De Witt, Alexander, 110
Dickinson, Anna, 205
Douglas, Melvyn, 230
Douglas, Stephen A., 97, 110, 114, 133–36, 145, 147
Douglass, Frederick, 71, 102, 205–7
Dred Scott decision, 136, 140–41
Dudley, Jeptha, 22, 124
Dudley, Sally Anne Lewis Clay (CMC's mother), 7, 9, 12, 22, 25, 34, 66, 68–69, 93, 96, 116
duels, 12, 23, 24, 36–39, 46, 55, 81, 83, 131, 221, 225, 253n18

Eisenhower, Dwight D., 230
elections: of 1852, 100–102, 110, 121; of 1856, 121, 126–30, 134, 145, 149; of 1860, 2, 4, 133–34, 137–51; of 1864, 171, 185–89; of 1868, 198; of 1872, 202, 206–7
Ellis, William, 33
emancipationism, 14–16, 20, 27–29, 49, 185; gradual, 15, 27, 34, 35, 60
Emancipation Party, 73, 95, 98
Emancipation Proclamation, 3, 168, 171–83
Emily (enslaved by CMC), 3, 61–64, 72–73, 130

Emily (enslaved by Sidney Clay), 14
Empress Marie, 163
Encarnacíon, 82, 84
Esther (enslaved by CMC), 14
Everett, Edward, 20

Fairbank, Calvin, 60–61
Fanny (enslaved by Green Clay), 16
Fee, John G., 107, 116–23, 127–28, 134–37, 219, 233
Fillmore, Millard, 129–30
First Kentucky Cavalry, 79
Fish, Hamilton, 198, 200
Foner, Eric, 89
Ford's Theater, 187
Fort Meigs, 12
Foster, Lafayette, 267n26
Foxtown melee, 92–96, 102
Frank (enslaved by Sidney Clay and CMC), 14, 124
Free Democrats, 102
Freedmen's Bureau, 191–92, 197
free labor, 4–5, 21, 31–36, 86–88, 108–110, 131–32, 251n22; CMC as a proponent of, 34–35, 48, 59, 100–101, 151
Free-Soil Party, 2, 87–89, 248n7; CMC joins, 100–103
Frémont, John C., 126, 129, 140, 166–70
Friends of Constitutional Reform, 90
Friends of Freedom, 100
Fry, Joshua, 12, 13, 26
Fugitive Slave Act of 1793, 41–42
Fugitive Slave Act of 1850, 99, 102, 127, 136, 151, 166–67

Gaines, John, 82
Garrison, William Lloyd, 20–21, 27–29, 106, 123, 219–20, 228, 230, 233, 240; criticism of CMC, 50–51, 94, 123; support for CMC, 50–51, 65, 71, 94, 103–4
"Geo. Brand's nurse" (enslaved), 72
Giddings, Joshua, 55, 100–101, 135
Goodloe, William, 154, 162

Gorchakov, Alexander, 162
Grand Duke Nicholas, 165
Grant, Ulysses S., 196–211, 219
Greeley, Horace, 5, 58, 77, 100, 113, 114, 130–33, 141, 177, 200, 226, 238; antislavery views of, 43, 122, 168–69; run for president, 203–8; support of CMC, 43, 48, 50, 53, 65, 74, 108; turn against reconstruction, 203–7
Greene, Willis, 58

Haldeman, Walter, 93, 118
Hale, John P., 102–3, 121
Halleck, Henry, 173–74, 177
Hamlin, Hannibal, 142, 165
Hammond, James Henry, 65
Hannah (enslaved by Sidney Clay and CMC), 14, 72, 124
Hannah (enslaved by Green Clay), 16
Harper and Brothers, 85
Harris, Joel Chandler, 226
Harrison (enslaved by Brutus Clay), 251nn14–15
Harrison, William Henry, 12, 53
Harrold, Stanley, 50, 226
Hart, Phil, 231–32
Hay, John, 155, 156, 173–74
Hayden, Harriet, 60
Hayden, Lewis, 60
Hearst, William Randolph, 222, 224
Helper, Hinton Rowan, 131–32
Henry (enslaved by Green Clay), 16
"Henry's Dave" (enslaved by CMC), 52
Herrick, Frank, 196, 200
Herrick, Green, 223
History of the Rise and Fall of the Slave Power in America (Wilson), 218
honor, 22–24, 37–39, 46–48, 68–69. *See also* duels
horse racing, 19, 25
Houston, Sam, 142
Huldy (enslaved by CMC), 14
Hunter, David, 167, 169
"The Hunters of Kentucky" (song), 103

Impending Crisis of the South, The (Helper), 131–32
Irvine, Edmund, 12, 24
Irvine, Sally Ann Clay (CMC's sister), 7, 12, 24

Jack (enslaved by CMC), 79, 257n13
Jackson (enslaved by Sidney Clay), 14
Jackson, Andrew, 20, 153
Jim (enslaved by Sidney Clay and CMC), 14, 124, 186
Joe (enslaved by CMC), 14, 52, 72
John (enslaved by CMC), 14
John Jr. (enslaved by CMC), 14
Johnson, Andrew, 189–97, 201
Johnson, Madison C., 12, 61, 122, 124
Johnson, Richard Mentor, 12
Johnston, Albert Sidney, 38–39
Johnston, Annie Fellows, 226
Julian, George, 100–103, 114, 121–22, 204
Juneteenth, 241

Kansas-Nebraska Act, 110–11, 136
Kendall (soldier with CMC), 80
Kentucky Abolition Society, 15
Kentucky Anti-Slavery Society, 28
Kentucky Association, 19
Kentucky Colonization Society, 26–27, 31
Kentucky constitutional conventions: of 1792, 9–10, 15; of 1799, 10, 15; of 1849, 89–90, 95
Kentucky Grand Lodge of Negro Masons, 225
Kentucky Society for the Gradual Relief of the State from Slavery, 28
Kilmore (Green Clay and Sally Anne Lewis residence), 9
Kitty (enslaved by Green Clay), 16
Know-Nothing Party, 114, 121–22, 129–33, 140, 145
Ku Klux Klan, 193, 202, 205

Lafayette, Marquis de, 74
Lane, James H., 155

Lane Theological Seminary, 41, 107
Leavitt, Joshua, 103
Lee, Robert E., 189
Lewinski, Thomas, 61, 172
Lewis, Thomas, 9
Lexington (race horse), 20
Lexington Intelligencer, 43–44
Liberal Republican Party, 2, 202–8, 217
Liberia, 15, 27
Liberty Party, 53–58, 86–88
Lincoln, Abraham, 2, 65, 219, 227, 228, 230; as president, 151–58, 162–90; as presidential candidate, 140–42, 144–45, 147–50; as Senate candidate, 133–34; and wartime emancipation, 166; as Whig congressional candidate, 113
Lincoln, Mary Todd, 187
Lincoln and His Wife's Home Town (Townsend), 228
"Lion of Whitehall," (CMC nickname and book) 4, 228
Liston, Sonny, 236
Locke, John, 10
Locust Grove, 38
Logan, John A., 217
López de Santa Anna, Antonio, 82
Lost Cause, 226–27
Lotty (enslaved by CMC), 52, 72
Lovejoy, Elijah, 59
Lovejoy, Owen, 122
Lucy (enslaved by Sidney Clay), 14, 124
Luke (enslaved by Sidney Clay and CMC), 29–30

Magoffin, Beriah, 136–37, 151
Mann, Horace, 103
Marshall, Humphrey, 79
Marshall, Thomas, 55, 64–65, 68–70, 80–82
Mary Jr. (enslaved by Green Clay), 16–17
Mason, James, 96
Matilda (plaintiff in fugitive slave case), 41–42
Matt (enslaved by Brutus Clay), 251n15

Matt (enslaved by CMC), 14, 52, 72
McClellan, George, 188
McGill, Ralph, 235
McKee, William, 38, 39, 83
McKinney, W. L., 56
McMurtry, John, 172–73
Medved, Michael, 240–41
Megowan's slave pen, 63
Mexican-American War, 2, 76, 194, 225, 236
Mexico, 54, 76–88, 257n13
Military Reconstruction Act, 193
Milly (enslaved by CMC), 14
Minerva (enslaved by CMC), 124
Mingo (enslaved by CMC), 14
mining, 32, 204
Missouri Compromise, 86, 110, 150
Monterrey, Battle of, 81–82, 156
Morton Place (house), 30, 74
Mott, Lucretia, 77
murder, 3, 16–17, 61–63, 68, 72, 78, 92–94, 211
Murphy, Edward, 233

Nancy (enslaved by CMC), 72
Nancy Jr. (enslaved by Green Clay and CMC), 14, 16, 25
Nation of Islam, 236–37, 239
Native Americans, 8, 10, 80
nativism. *See* Know-Nothing Party
Nat Turner's Rebellion. *See* Turner, Nat
Neale, William L., 61
Ned (enslaved by CMC), 14
Nelson, William "Bull," 171–72
New England Anti-Slavery Society, 27
Newman, Ralph, 230
Nicholas, George, 10
Nicolay, John, 155
Nonimportation Law of 1833, 27, 31, 43
Northwest Ordinance of 1787, 33, 41
Nunn, Beula, 232–33
Nunn, Louie B., 232–33

Oberlin College, 60, 117
Old Lucy (enslaved by CMC), 124

Olmstead, Frederick Law, 109
Owsley, William, 79

Page, Thomas Nelson, 226
Palmerston, Lord, 157
Patterson, Floyd, 237
Payne, John, 16
Percy, William Alexander, 213
Perkins, Benjamin, 193
Peter (enslaved by Green Clay), 16
Peter the Great, 159
Petroff, Annie, 208
Petroff, Jean, 208
Petroff, Leonide. *See* Clay, Leonide "Launey" Petroff
Phillips, U. B., 227
Phillips, Wendell, 170, 228, 238
Pierce, Franklin, 101, 103, 111, 115
Pierrepont, Edwards, 211
Polk, James K., 58, 77, 79, 82, 86, 88
Pomeroy, Simon, 169
pork, 108, 116, 122, 125
Prentice, George, 69–70, 118, 192
Princeton University, 12, 14
Proclamation Line of 1763, 7

Rachel (enslaved by Sidney Clay and CMC), 14, 63
Randall, Marenda B., 50
Reconstruction, 2, 184, 189–203, 211–14
Reeder, Andrew, 115, 142
Reid, Whitelaw, 207
Republican Party, 2, 4, 122, 127–31, 136–42, 167, 182, 199, 201, 206, 210, 213, 216–19; and election of 1860, 140–42, 146, 151; formation of, 111–15, 121; Radical, 183–86
Republic of Texas. *See* Texas
Revels, Hiram, 210
Revolutionary War, 7–8, 14, 27
Richmond, Battle of, 172–73
Richmond (KY) Garden Club, 232
Riley (enslaved by CMC), 14, 52, 72
Rodes, Paulina Clay (CMC's sister), 7, 12, 14, 29

Rodes, William, 12, 14, 29
Rollins, James, 23, 131
Russell, Richard, 231–32
Russell, William Howard, 154
Russell's Cave, 44–47
Russia. *See* Clay, Cassius Marcellus: in Russia
Russian-American Telegraph Company, 181–82
Russian Imperial Ballet, 208

Saint Joseph's College, 13
Sanborn, Franklin B., 205
Sarah (enslaved by CMC), 124, 216
Sarah (enslaved by Green Clay), 16
Schurz, Carl, 164, 203
Scott (enslaved by CMC), 14, 52
Scott, Winfield, 83–84, 101–3, 155
Second Great Awakening, 20
Second Kentucky Infantry, 81
serfdom, 159–60, 211
Seward, William H., 5, 109, 115–16, 130, 132–34, 148, 150, 188–91; antislavery views of, 121, 137, 139–43; and election of 1860, 137; and friendship with CMC, 74, 76, 139, 151–53, 157–58, 177, 193–201, 219; and "higher law" principal, 97–102; as secretary of state, 162–63
Seymour, Paul, 72, 74, 81
Shelby, Isaac, 9
Simmons, Roscoe Conkling, 227–28
slave trade, internal, 18, 33, 36, 40, 63, 73. *See also* Nonimportation Law of 1833
Smiley, David, 4, 201, 230–31
Smith, Caleb, 142
Smith, Edmund Kirby, 170
Smith, Eliza Clay (CMC's sister), 7, 12, 14, 16, 38
Smith, Gerrit, 28, 79, 110, 135, 201
Smith, J. Speed, 12, 14, 38, 66, 98
Solomon (enslaved by Sidney Clay and CMC), 14, 63
South Church (New Haven, CT), 20–21

Southern Rights Associations, 97
Squire (enslaved by Green Clay), 16
Stanton, Edwin, 164
"state suicide," 178, 184–85
Stephens, Alexander, 191
Stevens, Thaddeus, 184, 192
Stevenson, Adlai, 230
Stevenson, T. B., 61
Stoeckl, Eduard de, 162
Stowe, Harriet Beecher, 124
Sumner, Charles, 103, 110, 121, 125, 140, 184–85, 219, 228, 238; antagonism between CMC and, 177–78, 183–85, 192

Tallant, Harrold, 91
Tappan, Lewis, 100, 258
Taylor, Bayard, 164, 165, 177, 195–96
Taylor, Zachary, 82, 87, 89, 96
tenant farmers, 8, 12, 186, 221, 232
Terrell, Ernie, 237
Texas, 38, 76, 78–81; annexation of, 54, 56, 76–77
Thayer, Eli, 131
Thierman, Sue McClelland, 230
tobacco, 8, 9, 11, 162
Tocqueville, Alexis de, 32
Todd, Robert, 65, 67
Townsend, William, 228–32
Transylvania University, 18–20, 23, 38
True American (newspaper), 2, 59–74, 77–78, 81, 85, 92, 98, 107, 139, 173, 219, 222, 240
Trumbull, Lyman, 203
Turner, Alfred, 92–95
Turner, Cyrus, 92–95, 229
Turner, Nat, 22, 26, 28
Turner, Squire, 92–95
Turner, Thomas, 93
Tyler, John, 53–54
typhoid fever, 66–67, 71

Uncle Tom's Cabin (Stowe), 124
Underwood, John C., 131

Underwood, Joseph, 35
Union Democratic Party, 182
United Brothers of Friendship, 225
Ursley (enslaved by CMC), 14
US Colored Troops, 185–86
US Constitution, 3, 5, 43, 49, 76, 106, 187–88; Thirteenth Amendment, 5, 188–89, 216; Fourteenth Amendment, 191, 193, 202, 210, 217, 227; Fifteenth Amendment, 199, 202, 204, 210, 217, 227

Van Buren, Martin, 20, 88–89
Vaughn, John, 72, 74, 81, 258n32
Victoria, Queen, 157
Vietnam War, 237
Virginia controversy, 76

Wade, Edward, 110
Wallace, Lew, 170–71
Wallace, William Ross, 156
Ward, Joe, 233
Warfield, Elisha, 19–20, 37, 72, 125
Warfield, Lloyd, 72
Warfield, Maria Barr, 19, 23
War of 1812, 12, 79, 103
Watterson, Henry, 2–3, 203, 219, 223, 225
Webb, James Watson, 55
Webster, Daniel, 20, 53, 97
Webster, Delia, 60–61, 63
Weddle, George, 30
Weed, Thurlow, 55, 76, 114, 123, 140
Whig Party, 53–54, 64–66, 86–89, 110–14; CMC as member of, 26, 56, 65, 85–86; CMC's turn against, 98–103
whiskey, 9
White Hall (formerly Clermont), 9, 11, 13, 16, 22, 25, 29, 85, 92, 108, 125, 172, 176, 182, 200, 208–9, 215, 222–23, 227–34; CMC defends from attack, 222–24; CMC inherits, 13, 22; CMC and Mary Jane Warfield Clay renovate, 172–73, 180, 187;

Green Clay constructs, 9; as historical site, 232–34
White, Perry, 216
White, Sarah, 124, 216
White Liners, 210–11, 213
Whittier, John Greenleaf, 20
Wickliffe, Charles, 38, 45, 168
Wickliffe, Robert, Jr., 30, 34, 37–39, 44–46, 48, 53
Wickliffe, Robert, Sr., 30, 31, 34, 37–39, 48, 64, 171
Wide-Awakes, 146
Will (enslaved by CMC), 124
Willard Hotel, 154–56
Wilmot, David, 86, 87, 155
Wilmot Proviso, 86

Wilson, Henry, 103, 121, 218–19; *History of the Rise and Fall of the Slave Power in America*, 218
Wool, John Ellis, 80, 82
World Boxing Association, 237
Wright, Elizur, 28, 205
Wright, Henry C., 94

Yale College (and University), 20–23, 25, 28, 219, 240
Young, John C., 27, 35
Young Men's Republican Union, 138

Zack (enslaved by CMC), 89, 124, 176, 180
Zilla (enslaved by CMC), 52, 72